# Study Guide
# and Problems

# Study Guide and Problems

to accompany
## LIPSEY/SPARKS/STEINER
## ECONOMICS, third edition

prepared by
## DOUGLAS A. L. AULD
University of Guelph

## E. KENNETH GRANT
University of Guelph

## DASCOMB R. FORBUSH
Clarkson College of Technology

## DOROTHY F. FORBUSH

**HARPER & ROW, Publishers**
New York, Hagerstown, Philadelphia, San Francisco, London

Study Guide and Problems to accompany Lipsey, Sparks, and Steiner, ECONOMICS, Third Edition

Copyright © 1973, 1976, 1979 by Harper & Row, Publishers, Inc.

ISBN 0-06-040394-2

# contents

iv    Contents

# to the student

This book is intended to do two things: to help you study and review independently the basic material in Lipsey, Sparks, and Steiner, *Economics*, Third Edition, and second, to deepen and extend your understanding of economic analysis through the use of problems, many of which use the case approach. These functions complement the approach to economics used in the text, which stresses the need for testing hypotheses against empirical data. You will find the review questions and exercises useful in your studying. We hope that you will be challenged and intrigued by such problems as "Sale of Imported Wines," "Positive Thinking About a Negative Income Tax," and "Was the 1965 Tax Cut Inflationary?" If you are discouraged at times by graphical analysis and numerical relationships, you should recognize that the graphs are useful visual aids to understanding economic relationships and that quantitative measurement is essential for testing economic theories.

Each chapter in the *Study Guide and Problems* corresponds to a chapter in the text and is divided into five basic sections. The key concepts, definitions, and checklist sections in each chapter are a reminder of the important terms used in the text. You should learn definitions of terms not by memorizing them but by understanding them through reviewing their meaning in the context of the textbook itself.

The second section of each chapter, the review questions, should not be tackled prematurely. You should not use the review questions as a short cut or bypass to learning from the text; if you have to take frequent looks at the answers supplied, you are not ready. The degree of ease with which you travel through this section will indicate to you how well you have comprehended the contents of the chapter. These questions are of two types—choosing the correct answer from among two or three supplied, and filling in blanks. In general, the questions follow a train of reasoning designed to clarify as well as to review the material.

Specific details and facts not covered in the review questions may show up in the section of multiple-choice questions, along with a rephrasing of material already touched upon. When you answer these questions, avoid the temptation to leap at the first answer that seems plausible. For each question there is one best answer, and you should be able to explain why any other answer is not so satisfactory as the one that you have chosen.

Probably the greatest reinforcement to learning this subject is to be found in the exercises, in which you are usually asked to demonstrate numerically or graphically the sense of what has been expressed verbally.

One or more problems conclude each chapter. Usually in case form, they are intended to enhance your understanding of economic analysis by providing empirical data and illustrations of economic behavior. If the problem is to serve as a basis for class discussion, you will find space beneath the questions to jot major points that you might make in class.

Do not be discouraged if you have difficulties with certain problems. Some are quite challenging for a beginning economics student, and full understanding of the points involved is expected only after a subsequent class discussion or lecture; make your questions on them as explicit as possible. The answers to the problems at the end of the *Study Guide* are in no way exhaustive. What we have tried to do is to highlight the main issues surrounding the problem.

## ACKNOWLEDGMENTS

We would like to express our gratitude to our colleagues at the University of Guelph, who assisted with the preparation of the Third Edition through their comments and criticisms on the First Edition.

# 1

# The Economic Problem

## Key Concepts and Definitions

1. Economics is the study of the use of scarce resources to satisfy human wants.
2. Problems in economics arise when it comes to making choices about how to use the scarce resources to satisfy wants.
3. A <u>production-possibility curve</u> depicts what can be produced with given resource endowments. What combination of outputs will occur depends on the economic institutions that prevail in a society. Different combinations of output imply alternative allocation of resources.
4. A point on the production-possibility curve indicates that resources are <u>fully employed</u>; inside the boundary implies unemployment or an inefficient use of resources.
5. An outward shift in the production possibility curve reflects an increase in resources or the introduction of technical innovation.

| CHECKLIST | Make certain that you also understand the following concepts: factors of production; production; consumption; scarcity; opportunity cost; resource allocation. |
|---|---|

## Review Questions

1. The central problem of economics is that resources are ___*scarce*___, but but human wants seem to be ___*unlimited*___.

2. It is therefore (~~possible~~/impossible) to satisfy all wants, and, when faced with several alternative wants to fill or commodities to produce, we have to make a ___*decision*___.

3. If one alternative is chosen, another must be sacrificed; this sacrifice is called the ___*opportunity cost*___ of the alternative chosen.

4. The process of assigning scarce resources to the production of commodities is called ___*resource allocation*___.

5. Scarcity, opportunity cost, and the necessity for choice are illustrated in a diagram called a ___*production - possibility curve*___.

6. On this graph, the *boundary* line shows ___*attainable combination of goods at full employment*___.

7. On the two axes of the production-possibility diagram, we put _amount of two_ _alternate competing kinds of good_ .

8. On this graph, the rate at which the commodity on one axis is sacrificed to obtain more of the other is shown by _the slope of the boundary line_ .

9. If an economy is considered to be operating at a position *inside* the boundary, it indicates one or both of two situations: a. _unemployment of resources_ , b. _miss use of resources_ .

10. The only way an economy can attain a production point *outside* of the boundary is _growth of economic capacity_ .

11. That part of economics dealing with resource allocation and with the question of what, how much of, and how commodities are produced is called _microeconomy_ .

12. A policy of noninterference by government in the economy is often called a policy of _free market (laizzez-faire )_

13. When the government intervenes with an economic policy measure, the economist should ask what the specific _object or goal_ of the measure is.

---

If you have not answered all questions correctly, review the text in order to be sure that you have all of the important concepts clearly in mind before going on to the next chapter.

1. scarce; unlimited  2. impossible; choice  3. opportunity cost  4. resource allocation
5. production-possibility diagram  6. attainable combinations of goods at full employment
7. amounts of two alternate or competing kinds of goods  8. the slope of the boundary line
9. unemployment; inefficiency in the use of resources  10. growth of economic capacity
11. microeconoics  12. laissez-faire  13. objective or goal

---

## MULTIPLE-CHOICE QUESTIONS

1. The fundamental problem of economics is, in short,
   (a) too many poor people
   (b) finding jobs for all
   (c) the scarcity of resources relative to wants
   (d) constantly rising prices

2. Scarcity is a problem that
   (a) proper use of resources could eliminate
   (b) will probably exist as long as man finds new wants to be satisfied
   (c) the twentieth century has solved
   (d) is confined to poor countries

3. Drawing a production-possibility boundary for swords and plowshares will help us to
   (a) estimate how much it is necessary to spend on defense (swords)
   (b) estimate the amount of unemployment that is likely to result from a given federal expenditure on housing (plowshares)
   (c) illustrate the cost of defense (swords) in terms of the expenditure on nondefense commodities (plowshares) that will have to be forgone
   (d) show the relative desires of the public for plowshares and guns

4. Opportunity cost
   (a) is measured by how much of one commodity you have to forgo in order to get some stated amount of another commodity
   (b) measures how many different opportunities you have to spend your money
   (c) measures opportunities in terms of their relative prices
   (d) is the same as money cost

5. If tuition plus other costs of going to college come to $2,500 per year, and you could have earned $4,000 per year working instead, the *opportunity cost* of your college year is
   (a) $2,500
   (b) $4,000
   (c) $6,500
   (d) $1,500

6. If a commodity can be produced without sacrificing the production of anything else,
   (a) its opportunity cost is zero
   (b) the economy is on its production-possibility boundary
   (c) the opportunity-cost concept is irrelevant and meaningless
   (d) its opportunity cost equals its money cost

7. Points to the left of the current production-possibility boundary
   (a) are currently unobtainable and are expected to remain so
   (b) will be obtainable if there is economic growth
   (c) will result if some factors of production are unemployed or used inefficiently
   (d) have lower opportunity costs

8. A country's production-possibility boundary shows
   (a) what percentage of its resources is currently unemployed
   (b) what choices in production and consumption are currently open to it
   (c) what it is actually producing
   (d) the available methods of production

9. A shift outward in the production-possibility boundary
   (a) would result if more of one product and less of another were chosen
   (b) could reflect higher prices for goods
   (c) could reflect increased unemployment
   (d) could result from the increased productivity of resources

10. The question of what goods and services are produced, and how much of them, is covered by the general term
    (a) resource allocation
    (b) macroeconomics
    (c) consumption
    (d) scarcity

11. The causes of general unemployment and inflation are topics studied in
    (a) resource allocation
    (b) macroeconomics
    (c) opportunity costs
    (d) production possibilities

12. Even government policy measures have "opportunity costs," which means
    (a) higher taxes will be necessary
    (b) moving toward one goal may require moving away from another goal
    (c) government action is usually inefficient
    (d) government action provides new opportunities

---

Answers to multiple-choice questions: 1(c)  2(b)  3(c)  4(a)  5(c)  6(a)  7(c)  8(b)  9(d)
10(a)  11(b)  12(b)

# EXERCISES

1. Chapter 1 gives a six-way classification of economic problems. List them here in the order presented, numbering them from 1 to 6. Then, after each of the topics listed below, place the appropriate number indicating in which classification it belongs.

   (1) _____

   (2) _____

   (3) _____

   (4) _____

   (5) _____

   (6) _____

   (a) A blight hits the corn crop; harvest is 15 percent below previous year. (     )
   (b) Farmers are seeking a different kind of corn seed to plant in order to avoid blight, but it is more expensive. (     )
   (c) Unemployment rose in most of the nation in 1972. (     )
   (d) Statistics indicate that the distribution of income has become somewhat less unequal in recent years in Canada. (     )
   (e) The standard of living in Canada, measured by real GNP per capita, has risen steadily over the last century. (     )
   (f) The cost of living rose at about 4 percent per year during the latter part of the 1960s. (     )
   (g) Neither the government nor private business was willing in the mid-1950s to go ahead with building the Avro Arrow jet fighter. (     )
   (h) Whether our future power needs will be met by nuclear energy or by fossil-fuel plants depends not only on technology but also on the relative availability of uranium and petroleum. (     )

2. The following data show what combinations of corn and beef can be produced annually from a given piece of land.

   | Corn (bushels) | Beef (pounds) |
   | --- | --- |
   | 10,000 | 0 |
   | 8,000 | 900 |
   | 6,000 | 1,200 |
   | 4,000 | 1,400 |
   | 2,000 | 1,450 |
   | 0 | 1,500 |

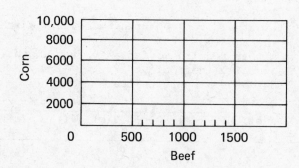

   (a) On the graph above, draw the production-possibility boundary for this piece of land.
   (b) Can this acreage produce 5,000 bushels of corn and 500 pounds of beef?

(c) Can this acreage produce 8,000 bushels of corn and 1,200 pounds of beef?

(d) What is the opportunity cost of expanding beef production from 900 to 1,200 pounds per annum?

(e) What would the production of 5,000 bushels of corn and 500 pounds of beef suggest about the use of this acreage?

(f) What would be required for this community to go beyond the production-possibility boundary?

# PROBLEM

## EXPENDITURE FOR THE ENVIRONMENT

In spite of the widespread feeling that pollution abatement is a priority goal for Canadian society, there are those who argue against spending vast sums of money on improving the quality of the environment. It has been estimated by the federal Department of the Environment that roughly one and one-half billion dollars per annum will have to be spent in Canada to achieve a significant reduction in pollution by 1980.

Those arguing against such expenditure claim that if the government spends the money, other "important" goals such as health and education programs will have to be reduced if taxes are not to rise too high.

### Questions

1. What is the basic concept referred to by the above statement?

2. How is the cost of pollution abatement being measured?

3. Label the production-possibility curve below for the above argument and indicate the move that more pollution abatement would imply.

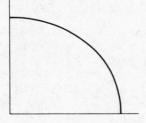

4. If taxes were increased to pay for pollution abatement, there would be less personal income for expenditure on automobiles, vacations, and other private goods. Label the production-possibility curve below to show this, and indicate the move that more pollution abatement would imply.

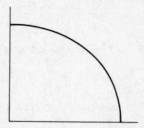

5. Some people argue that by imposing pollution control on firms, the price of products produced by these firms will rise and less will be purchased, resulting in lower production and unemployment. What is the fallacy in this argument?

# 2

# Economics as a Social Science

## KEY CONCEPTS AND DEFINITIONS

1. Statements or questions concerning <u>positive</u> issues may be settled by empirical investigation while those of a <u>normative</u> nature involve a strong element of value judgement.
2. By appealing to evidence related to specific questions, the scientific approach can be used to answer positive questions.
3. The difficulty in predicting individual human behavior does not preclude a scientific approach to economics if groups of individuals are the subject of investigation.
4. Theory is important to the scientific investigation of economic phenomena. An <u>economic theory</u> consists <u>of a set of definitions of the variables to be used in the analysis</u>, <u>consumptions related to the conditions in which the theory is to apply</u> and a set of <u>testable hypotheses</u> emanating from these definitions and assumptions.
5. Theories are used to construct testable hypotheses of a conditional nature; e.g., <u>if one (or more) event occurs, then certain consequences follow</u>. Statistical analysis is then employed to determine the significance of the prediction.
6. There are basically two categories of variables used in theoretical analysis; <u>endogenous variables</u> which are explained within the theory and <u>exogenous</u> variables which influence endogenous variables but whose value/size is determined outside the framework of the theory.
7. It is convenient to measure both endogenous and exogenous variables in terms of <u>flows</u> (which have a time dimension) and <u>stocks</u> (which have no time dimension).

> CHECKLIST   Make certain that you also understand the following concepts: scientific method; a priori; normal curve of error; functional relations; time series; error term.

## REVIEW QUESTIONS

1. After each phrase below, write *P* or *N* to indicate whether a positive or normative statement is being described.
    (a) a statement of fact that is actually wrong      P
    (b) a value judgement      N
    (c) a prediction that an event will happen      P
    (d) a statement about what the author thinks *ought* to be      N
    (e) a statement that can be tested by evidence      P

2. The scientific method involves testing the factual accuracy of (positive/normative) statements.

3. Even though individuals singly may take odd and unlikely actions, human behavior in general can be predicted, thanks to the "law" of ___large numbers___.

4. An attempt to explain the process of a sequence of economic events is called a hypothesis or a ___theory___.

5. A theory that turns out to explain cause and effect well and that is shown by events to fit the observed facts will indicate to us the consequences of a particular event or policy measure, and thus be useful for the purpose of ___prediction___.

6. In order to theorize in economics, it is usually necessary to simplify complex reality by setting certain conditions, or ___assumptions___.

7. A problem in testing economic theories that is not the case with laboratory sciences is that the environment for the experiments cannot be ___controlled___.

8. It is hypothesized that annual consumer spending depends on annual income and the value of personal assets. Consumer spending is thus an (exogenous/endogenous) variable and wealth a (stock/flow) variable.

---

If you have not answered all questions correctly, review the text in order to be sure that you have all of the important concepts clearly in mind before going on to the next chapter.

1. *P; N; P; N; P*  2. positive  3. large numbers  4. theory  5. prediction  6. assumptions
7. controlled  8. endogenous; stock

---

# MULTIPLE-CHOICE QUESTIONS

1. Which of the following statements is most appropriate for economic theories?
   (a) The most reliable test of a theory is the realism of its assumptions.
   (b) The best kind of theory is worded so that it can pass any test to which it could be put.
   (c) The most important thing about the scientific approach is that it uses mathematics heavily.
   (d) We expect our theories to hold only with some margin of error.

2. Positive statements concern what is; normative statements concern
   (a) what was
   (b) what is the normal situation
   (c) what will be
   (d) what ought to be

3. A natural science that has much the same problem as economics in testing theories is
   (a) animal psychology
   (b) astronomy
   (c) microbiology
   (d) organic chemistry

4. In economic theory, an exogenous variable
   (a) is one which can be predicted with accuracy
   (b) has no influence on the theory
   (c) is not determined by other variables in the theoretical framework
   (d) is always constant

5. The law of large numbers asserts that
   (a) physical and social sciences are the same
   (b) experiments must always be based on large numbers of observations
   (c) random changes in a large number of items offset each other to some extent
   (d) accurate individual measurement is not necessary to scientific approach

6. A theory may contain all but one of the following:
   (a) an unorganized collection of facts about the real world
   (b) a set of definitions of the terms used
   (c) a set of assumptions defining the conditions under which the theory will be operative
   (d) one or more hypotheses about how the world behaves

7. The term "empirically testable" means that a theory
   (a) is a priori obvious and therefore needs no testing
   (b) is capable of being shown to be a probable explanation of a given event
   (c) is proved to be true
   (d) is not testable, really

Answers to multiple-choice questions: 1(d)   2(d)   3(b)   4(c)   5(c)   6(a)   7(b)

# EXERCISE

The following information is made available to you.

| Annual Change in Housing Starts in Province X | Annual Change in the Average Mortgage Rate |
|---|---|
| -10,000 | +1.2% |
| -10,000 | +1.5% |
| +8,000 | -1.0% |
| -5,000 | +0.5% |
| +13,000 | -2.0% |
| +10,000 | -1.1% |

(a) What can you say about the relationship, in general, between housing starts and the mortgage interest rate?

*When mortage rate increase, Housing decrease*

(b) Would these data enable you to test the hypothesis that, "For every 1 percent change in the mortgage interest rate there is always an opposite change of 10,000 in building starts?

*Yes.*

# PROBLEM

## THE NORMATIVE VERSUS THE POSITIVE

1. Classify each of the statements below as positive (P) or normative (N).
   (a) "That environmental pollution is the major cause of elevated levels of mercury in fish is shown by the 100-fold increase in mercury in certain species of fish in Lake St. Clair between 1935 and 1970." (*Environment*, May 1971) ___P___
   (b) "While government must assume a major role in economic management, the bulk of productive and distributive activity should be carried on by the private enterprise units. . . ." (*Growth, Employment and Price Stability*, Report of the Standing Senate Committee on National Finance, Information Canada, 1971) ___N___

(c) "In the long-term interests of the economy as a whole, it is essential for us to continue our efforts to maintain reasonable price stability in Canada." (Hon. J. Turner, Minister of Finance, *House of Commons Debates,* Vol. 116, No. 47, May 8, 1972) ___N___

(d) "During the high growth period of the 1960's capital imports amounted to a relatively low percentage of GNP." (Economic Council of Canada, *Performance and Potential: mid 1950's to mid 1970's,* Information Canada, 1970, p. 35) ___N___

(e) "One of the best-established facts about the American economy is the long-run tendency for prices on the average to rise at about the same rate as unit labor costs on the average." (Council of Economic Advisers, *Inflation Alert,* December 1, 1970) ___P___

(f) "If inflation is not beaten, we cannot have lower interest rates without precipitating a flight of capital from Canada." (*Ontario Budget Speech,* 1977, p. 8)    N

2. (a) Indicate how the positive statements above might be tested.

(b) What value judgements and assumptions of fact might have led to each normative statement?

# The Role of Statistical Analysis

## KEY CONCEPTS AND DEFINITIONS

1. Economic theories are tested by checking their predictions against actual evidence. Statistical analysis is central to this testing.
2. It is not always possible to measure or obtain information on each economic agent or fact. Instead, a sample of a finite population is used and if this sample is <u>randomly selected</u>, the chance that the features of the sample do not represent the population can be calculated.
3. The relationship between two economic variables can be graphically depicted on a <u>scatter diagram</u>. For more than two variables, <u>regression analysis</u> allows us to measure the degree of association among two, three, or more variables.
4. Regression analysis is also useful to test whether or not one or more variables offer a significant explanation of some economic phenomena.

| CHECKLIST | Make certain that you also understand the following concepts: function; coefficient of determination; cross-classify; decision rule; slope; time series, cross-section data; non-linear function. |
|---|---|

## REVIEW QUESTIONS

1. The expression $Q = f(P)$ may be read that quantity is a ___*function*___ of price. $Q$ and $P$ in this expression are ___*variables*___.

2. The amount of income earned per year is a (~~stock~~/flow) because it has a ___*time*___ _____ dimension. The size of one's bank account is a ___*stock*___.

3. Economic theories usually treat weather (measured by temperature, rainfall, etc.) as an (~~endogenous~~/exogenous) variable because the theory (~~does~~/does not) attempt to explain weather. Such a variable may be helpful in economic theory to explain the price of wheat, an ___*endogenous*___ variable.

4. The hypothesis that the amount of skis sold (Y) depends upon their prices (P) and the amount of snow (X) that can be expressed ___*as a function*___ $Y = f(P, X)$. In such a theory, X is an ___*exogenous*___ variable.

5. To say that the amount borrowed is a decreasing function of the interest rate paid means that borrowing varies (~~directly~~/inversely) with the interest rate.

6. All theories and measurements (are/are not) subject to error. In functional notation, this can be shown by adding an _____*error*_____ term.

7. In deducing the implications of a theory, three methods—verbal, geometrical, and _____*mathematical*_____—can be used.

8. The purpose of statistical analysis is to _____*test*_____ theories and to _____*measure*_____ quantitative relations between economic variables.

9. In laboratory sciences, experiments (can/cannot) be controlled; in economics, factors (can/cannot) actually be isolated one at a time.

10. If two related economic variables such as beef consumption and income are plotted on a scatter diagram, the points "scatter" rather than form a line for primarily two reasons: _____*error of observation*_____ and _____*omitted causal variables*_____

11. Usually, a hypothesis (can/cannot) be proved wrong or right. But the probability that it is wrong or right (can/cannot) be estimated, if available data meet certain sampling criteria.

---

If you have not answered all questions correctly, review the text in order to be sure that you have all of the important concepts clearly in mind before going on to the next chapter.

1. function; variables  2. flow; time; stock  3. exogenous; does not; endogenous  4.
4. $Y = f(P, X)$; exogenous  5. inversely  6. are; error  7. mathematical  8. test; measure
9. can; cannot  10. errors of observation; omitted causal variables  11. cannot; can

---

# MULTIPLE-CHOICE QUESTIONS

1. If the demand for snowmobiles is higher, the lower the average temperature,
   (a) the demand for snowmobiles is an increasing function of the average temperature
   (b) the demand for snowmobiles is a decreasing function of the average temperature
   (c) the demand for snowmobiles varies directly with the average temperature
   (d) both (a) and (c) are correct

2. We must remember that for every real-world economic function there is
   (a) an exact equation
   (b) demand and supply
   (c) an error term, whether explicit or implicit
   (d) a direct relationship between the variables

3. Which of the following equations is consistent with the hypothesis that beef consumption ($Q$) is an increasing function of income ($Y$), a decreasing function of price ($P$), and an increasing function of the price of pork ($K$)?
   (a) $Q = 25YP/K$
   (b) $Q = 25 - 1.85P + .08Y + .6K$
   (c) $Q = 25 + .08Y + 1.85P + .6K$
   (d) $Q = 25 - .6K - 1.85P + .08Y$

4. Economists use mathematics because
   (a) mathematics is the only good economic tool
   (b) mathematics puts variables in relationships of cause and effect
   (c) mathematics can definitely prove hypotheses for the economist
   (d) mathematics is a relatively short and clear language for expressing complicated relationships

5. As part of the study of campus opinion concerning careers in industry, which sampling method will probably yield the best results?
   (a) interviewing students on the steps of the business administration building
   (b) randomly drawing a sample of students' names from the dormitory residence lists
   (c) throwing darts blindfolded at a complete list of student numbers or names
   (d) obtaining a comprehensive list of officers of student organizations

6. The relationship between two variables on a scatter diagram
   (a) may be obscured by the movement of another variable
   (b) cannot be significant because of errors of observation
   (c) will show a wavelike pattern if the variables are related to time
   (d) will usually be a straight line

7. A single observation will not refute a hypothesis because
   (a) our theory may be wrong
   (b) errors of observation are possible
   (c) economic theories are deterministic
   (d) the observation may not have come from a random sample

8. Many economic data are similar to those relating high death rates to prolonged cigarette smoking in the following respect(s):
   (a) they do not depend primarily on controlled experiments in which all causes except one are held constant during each individual experiment
   (b) more than two variables are likely to be involved
   (c) they represent observations taken over a period of time
   (d) all of the above

9. To study consumer spending behavior, a random sample of consumers is selected for statistical analysis
   (a) because the total population cannot be relied upon
   (b) since it guarantees each household has an equal chance of being in the analysis
   (c) to ensure conformity of the sample

10. A substantial rise in the consumer price index means
    (a) that it is more expensive for everyone to live
    (b) that a weighted average of prices for a particular set of goods and services has risen
    (c) very little; not really significant errors are large
    (d) that all prices of consumer goods and services are necessarily higher

11. A rising straight line on a semilog scale between a variable and time indicates
    (a) growth by a constant percentage rate
    (b) growth by the same numerical amount each year
    (c) no change in the value of the variable
    (d) growth by a constant percentage rate but a decreasing absolute rate

---

Answers to multiple-choice questions: 1(b)  2(c)  3(b)  4(d)  5(c)  6(a)  7(b)  8(d)  9(b)  10(b)  11(a)

---

# EXERCISES

1. On the graph at the top of the next page, plot the following equation, assuming that $X$ and $Y$ are positive numbers: $X = 9 + 1.5Y$.
   (a) What is the slope of this line?

   1.5

   (b) Why is $Y$ the exogenous variable?

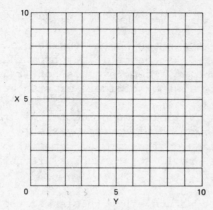

2. Given the following relation between saving (S) and income (Y), $S = -\$100 + .10Y$, what is the amount of S for each of the indicated values of Y? Plot S on the graph.

| Y | S |
|-------|-------|
| 0 | -100 |
| 500 | -50 |
| 1,000 | 0 |
| 1,500 | 50 |
| 2,000 | 100 |

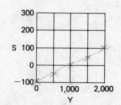

3. Put the following statements in the form of equations (use symbols as suggested).
   (a) The amount of saving (S) out of income (Y) averages 7 percent.    $S = .07Y$
   (b) A certain household will spend $1,000 on consumption (C) at zero income (Y), plus 95 percent of any income it receives.    $C = 1,000 + 0.95Y$
   (c) Cost per unit (c) equals total cost (C) divided by output (Q).    $c = \frac{C}{Q}$
   (d) Total revenue (R) equals price (P) times quantity sold (Q).    $R = PQ$
   (e) Profit ($\Pi$) is the difference between total revenue (R) and total cost (C).    $\Pi = R - C$

4. Indicate whether you would expect the pairs of variables below to vary directly or inversely with each other (other things being equal)
   (a) savings, income    directly
   (b) price, quantity demanded    inversely
   (c) temperature, use of air conditioners    directly
   (d) sales of hot dogs, sales of hot dog rolls    directly
   (e) total income, income tax receipts of government    directly

5. Regardless of the number of visitors to a recreation park, there are certain fixed expenses of $500 that must be met for gate attendants, light, and basic security. The cost of clean-up, however, does depend on the number of visitors and is equal to $0.10 per visitor.
   (a) If TC is the total cost of running the park and N is the number of visitors, write the equation for the total cost of the park operation.
   (b) Graph the two different cost relationships (the one for the fixed costs and the one for the cleanup costs) on the graph below.

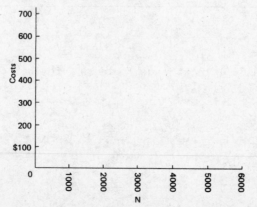

# PROBLEMS

## 1. SCATTERED INCOME AND TIME SERIES PLOTS

Time series data similar to those in the text on real personal disposable income and real consumer expenditure (in per capita terms) are shown below.

| Year | $C$<br>Consumption Expenditure<br>(constant dollars) | $Y_d$<br>Disposable Income<br>(constant dollars) |
|---|---|---|
| 1950 | 1142 | 1217 |
| 1951 | 1127 | 1252 |
| 1952 | 1167 | 1300 |
| 1953 | 1216 | 1253 |
| 1954 | 1224 | 1300 |
| 1955 | 1294 | 1366 |
| 1956 | 1358 | 1450 |
| 1957 | 1364 | 1450 |
| 1958 | 1374 | 1470 |
| 1959 | 1418 | 1485 |
| 1960 | 1435 | 1500 |
| 1961 | 1411 | 1475 |
| 1962 | 1458 | 1560 |
| 1963 | 1501 | 1598 |
| 1964 | 1561 | 1635 |
| 1965 | 1627 | 1719 |
| 1966 | 1679 | 1791 |
| 1967 | 1728 | 1834 |
| 1968 | 1786 | 1883 |
| 1969 | 1841 | 1932 |
| 1970 | 1865 | 1987 |
| 1971 | 1967 | 2124 |
| 1972 | 2069 | 2283 |
| 1973 | 2189 | 2445 |

## Questions

1. Plot this information on a scatter diagram.

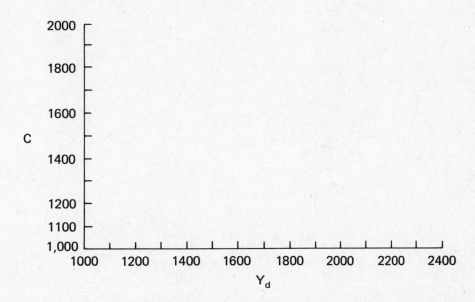

2. Draw a line through these observations to obtain some idea of the relationship between consumption spending and disposable income.

3. What (roughly) is the slope of the line you have drawn?

4. How good does the "fit" of this relationship seem to be?

5. If you had set out, as a hypothesis, that $C = f(Y_d)$, would you accept or reject your hypothesis? Why?

## 2. THE SPENDING VERSUS THE INCOME PLOT

As a contrast to the time series data on consumption and disposable income in the previous question, the table below gives cross-sectional data on family disposable income in a given year—1969—in Canada. These data are obtained by Statistics Canada through a sample survey of Canadian families.

| Family Disposable Income | Family Spending Goods and Services, and Taxes |
|---|---|
| $ 1,834 | $ 2,370 |
| 3,283 | 3,615 |
| 4,133 | 4,475 |
| 4,940 | 5,047 |
| 5,794 | 5,852 |
| 6,586 | 6,450 |
| 7,389 | 7,196 |
| 8,182 | 7,613 |
| 8,966 | 8,352 |
| 9,813 | 8,976 |
| 11,147 | 9,571 |
| 16,237 | 12,801 |

## Questions

1. Plot these data on a scatter diagram.

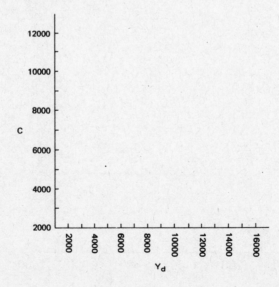

2. Can the relationship between the two variables be explained by a straight (linear) or curved (nonlinear) line drawn through the points on the scatter diagram?

3. If the latter, what is happening to the slope of the line as disposable income and consumption increase?

4. Does the evidence from the data above cause you to reject or to accept the hypothesis that family consumer spending is a function of disposable income?

# An Overview of the Economy

## KEY CONCEPTS AND DEFINITIONS

1. The kind of economic system that exists in Canada is based on specialization in the labor force. Money is a measure of the value of work and is used to exchange labor services for goods and other services.

2. A system where prices and outputs are determined through exchange among agents is called a market economy. Any complex economy is made up of many markets and the functioning of these markets is a subject of economic analysis.

3. Acting through markets, the decisions of buyers and sellers automatically determine where resources will be allocated throughout the economy. This automatic allocation through the market by household and firm decisions may be altered by government decisions.

4. In a market economy, the price system provides signals to firms and households regarding relative scarcity and demand for products. In response to changes in relative prices, resources are reallocated to those sectors where they are needed as households respond to price changes.

5. Payments to factors of production become the money income for households to purchase goods. The payments made for goods provided is available to the firm to hire factors of production.

6. The process whereby money goes from firms to households and back to firms is known as the circular flow.

7. The circular flow can be broken in two ways. If income received by a household is not passed back to domestic firms, there is a withdrawal from the circular flow. Alternatively, if one group receives income that does not arise out of the spending of the other, there is an injection.

* 8. Macroeconomics is concerned with matters relating to the aggregate circular flow of income. Microeconomics focuses attention on the behavior of individual markets.

| CHECKLIST | Make certain that you also understand the following concepts: market mechanisms; price system; free-market economy; command economy; mixed economy; household; firm; central authority; factor market; product market; real flow; money flow; division of labor |
|---|---|

## REVIEW QUESTIONS

1. Three basic types of economic decision makers are ___*consumers (households*___, ___*firms*___, and ___*government*___. The initial assumption is that households seek to maximize ___*wants*___, that firms seek to maximize ___*profit*___, and that central authorities have (~~one~~/more than one) objective.

2. Commodities for the use of households are sold in ___*free*___ markets. The services of households are sold in ___*labour*___ markets.

3. A change in the willingness of the consumer to purchase a particular product because of a change in something other than price is called a change in ___*demand*___.

4. When consumers' tastes were assumed to shift toward brussels sprouts and away from carrots, eventually a ___*reallocation*___ of resources took place through a sequence of events that included the following: a ___*rise*___ in the price of brussels sprouts; a ___*decrease*___ in the price of carrots; the prospects of ___*greater*___ profits in sprout production and ___*smaller*___ profits in carrot production; the movement of additional resources toward ___*brussels sprouts*___ production and away from ___*carrots*___ production.

5. The events in question 4 (include/do not include) an increase in supply because an increase in supply of a product (is/is not) defined as resulting from an increase in price.

6. Prices are determined by both ___*supply*___ and ___*demand*___. A change in either the demand for or supply of a commodity will usually result in ___*price*___ changes, which act as ___*signal*___ for households and firms on how to alter their behavior.

7. The amount of money is a (~~flow~~/stock) and (~~is~~/is not) equal to flow of total income.

8. The fact that households do not spend all of their income and that firms may retain profits leads to ___*withdrawal*___ from the circular flow.

9. When withdrawals from and injections into the circular flow are the same, we predict that income will be ___*unchanged*___.

---

If you have not answered all questions correctly, review the text in order to be sure that you have all of the important concepts clearly in mind before going on to the next chapter.

1. households, firms, central authorities; satisfaction or utility, profits, more than one
2. product; factor  3. demand  4. reallocation (or shift); rise; fall; greater; smaller; sprouts, carrot  5. do not include; is not  6. demand; supply; price, signals or information
7. stock; is not  8. withdrawals  9. unchanged

---

## MULTIPLE-CHOICE QUESTIONS

1. An increase in supply, as the term is used in this chapter, is
   (a) an increase in the efficiency of transporting commodities to market
   (b) an increased willingness of firms to produce a commodity for reasons other than its price
   (c) a glut, or surplus
   (d) an increase in the amount consumers want to buy

2. A change in consumers' preferences toward chicken and away from pork may be predicted to lead to
   (a) a rise in the price of chicken
   (b) a fall in the production of pork
   (c) a fall in the incomes of owners of land particularly well suited for raising pigs but not chickens
   (d) all of the above

3. A fall in the price of peas could result from
   (a) a shift in producers' preferences, with an increased willingness to grow string beans and a decreased willingness to grow peas
   (b) decreases in the amount of land available for growing vegetables through the expansion of suburbs
   (c) a shift in consumers' preferences, with an increased willingness to eat string beans and a decreased willingness to eat peas
   (d) an unusually small crop of peas because of adverse weather conditions

4. The circular flow of real goods and services
   (a) refers to actual dollars exchanged
   (b) refers only to the products sold by firms
   (c) moves in the same directions as monetary flows
   (d) refers to outputs of firms and to the factor services of households

5. An example of an injection into the circular flow of income is
   (a) the purchase of General Motors stock by a household
   (b) an increase in foreign demand for Canadian goods
   (c) increased purchases of hypodermic needles
   (d) the decision of a liberated wife to seek a job

---

Answers to multiple-choice questions: 1(b)   2(d)   3(c)   4(d)   5(b)

---

## EXERCISES

1. Given the circular flow diagram below, indicate where the following should be placed.
   (a) family expenditure on clothing and food = $25 M
   (b) man-hours worked at textile plants and food processors = 10,000 hours
   (c) production of yards of clothing = 5,000 pounds
   (d) production of food = 2,000 pounds
   (e) wages and salaries paid to employees in food and clothing = $40 M

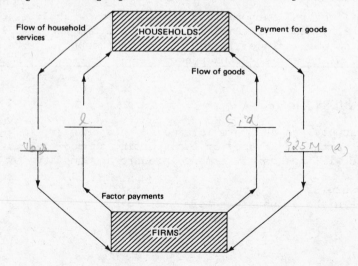

2. Indicate the initial effects on the price of beef, profits in the beef industry, and resources employed in the beef industry as a consequence of the following.

|  | Price | Profit | Employment of Resources |
|---|---|---|---|
| (a) A steady decline in the price of pork and poultry | decrease | decrease | down |
| (b) Increased desire on the part of consumers for steak and roast beef | up | up | up |
| (c) A general decline in household income | down | down | down |
| (d) A substantial rise in the cost of feed for beef cattle | up | down | down |

# Demand, Supply, and Price

## KEY CONCEPTS AND DEFINITIONS

1. The <u>quantity of any commodity demanded</u> is an expression for a <u>desired</u> level of purchase given that the individual is able to purchase that quantity at the given price.
2. For a given good, the amount of quantity demanded depends upon the price of that good, income, preferences, population, the price of other commodities and the distribution of income.
3. A <u>demand curve</u> is a graphical representation of how the quantity demanded varies with the price of the product being demanded, all other influences assumed constant.
4. The demand curve will shift in the event that one or more factors (other than price) that influence the quantity demanded are changed.
5. Movements along the demand curve are <u>changes in the quantity demanded</u> while shifts in the demand curve are changes in demand.
6. The <u>quantity of a good supplied</u> is influenced by technology, the prices of factors of production, the price of the product being supplied and the price of other commodities.
7. If only price is allowed to vary, the amount that producers are willing to supply at varying prices represents the supply schedule and it can be graphed as a <u>supply curve</u>.
8. The supply curve will shift if any factor (other than price) that influences quantity demanded changes.
9. In a free market, any <u>excess demand</u> or <u>excess supply</u> will be removed because buyers/sellers, respectively, will bid-up/reduce prices so an <u>equilibrium price</u> will be reached.

> CHECKLIST  Make certain that you also understand the following concepts: inferior good; equilibrium price; surplus, excess demand; excess supply; comparative statics; substitutes; complements; laws of supply and demand.

## REVIEW QUESTIONS

1. The amount of a commodity that households wish to purchase at various prices is called the _____ *demand* _____ for the commodity.

2. The quantity demanded depends upon consumers' tastes and preferences, population size, _____ *people* _____, the distribution of _____ *income* _____, the commodity's own price, and the _____ *prices* _____ of many other commodities.

3. The demand curve is a representation of the functional relation between ___*price*___ and ___*quantity*___. It differs from the demand function because values of the other determinants of demand are assumed to be ___*constant*___. This assumption is frequently described by the Latin term ___*ceteris paribus*___.

4. A shift in the demand curve may be caused by changes in any determinant of the demand function except the ___*price*___ of the commodity.

5. When an increase in the price of another good causes an increase in the demand for a commodity, the other good is called a ___*substitute*___; if it causes a decrease, the other good is called a ___*compliment*___.

6. A movement along a demand curve is the equivalent of a change in ___*price*___ and therefore in the quantity ___*demanded*___.

7. Neither the quantity demanded nor the quantity supplied is a stock but rather a ___*flow*___, and each is expressed as a quantity per ___*a period*___.

8. The quantity supplied depends upon the goals of the ___*supplier (firm)*___; the initial assumption is that the goal is to ___*maximize*___ profits.

9. The quantity supplied also depends on the state of ___*technology*___, the price of the commodity, the prices of all other ___*commodities*___, and the prices of the factors of ___*production*___.

10. The supply schedule shows the ___*quantity*___ that will be supplied at every ___*price*___.

---

If you have not answered all questions correctly, review the text in order to be sure that you have all of the important concepts clearly in mind before going on to the next chapter.

1. demand  2. income; income; prices  3. price, quantity; constant; *ceteris paribus*  4. price
5. substitute; complement  6. price; demanded  7. flow; time period  8. firm; maximize
9. technology; commodities; production  10. quantity; price

---

## MULTIPLE-CHOICE QUESTIONS

1. An increase in supply, as the term is used in this chapter, is
   (a) an increased willingness of firms to produce a commodity for reasons other than its price
   (b) the creation of glut or surplus
   (c) an increase in the amount consumers want to buy
   (d) a description of the increased quantities supplied at higher prices

2. A decrease in income can be predicted to
   (a) invariably cause leftward shifts in demand curves
   (b) increase the quantity demanded of an "inferior good"
   (c) invariably cause rightward shifts in demand curves
   (d) decrease the quantity demanded of an "inferior good"

3. A simultaneous increase in supply and demand for a given commodity would
   (a) result in less output sold
   (b) unambiguously raise the price of the commodity
   (c) unambiguously lower the price of the commodity
   (d) result in more of the commodity being purchased

4. When we draw a market demand curve, we
   (a) ignore tastes and incomes and all other prices
   (b) assume that tastes, incomes, and all other prices do not matter
   (c) assume that tastes, incomes, and all other prices change in the same way prices change
   (d) assume that tastes, incomes, and all other prices stay constant

5. A leftward shift in the demand curve for Corn Flakes would be predicted from
   (a) an increase in the average number of breakfast eaters
   (b) a change in tastes away from hot cereals
   (c) a rise in the price of Corn Flakes
   (d) a fall in the price of Wheaties

6. Consumer tastes and preferences are
   (a) always treated as exogenous to the economic system
   (b) always treated as endogenous to the economic system
   (c) so unpredictable that demand analysis is virtually impossible
   (d) altered by such economic activities as advertising and demonstration effects

7. The supply curve of houses would probably shift to the left if
   (a) construction workers' wages increased
   (b) cheaper methods of prefabrication were developed
   (c) the demand for houses showed a marked increase
   (d) the cost of building materials declines

8. A rise in the price of washing-machine components would probably lead to
   (a) a fall in the demand for washing machines
   (b) a rise in the supply of washing machines
   (c) a leftward shift in the supply curve of washing machines
   (d) a rightward shift in the demand curve for washing machines

---

Answers to multiple-choice questions:  1(a)   2(b)   3(d)   4(d)   5(d)   6(d)   7(a)   8(c)

---

# EXERCISES

1. The demand and supply schedules for good X are hypothesized to be as follows:

| (1) Price per Unit | (2) Quantity Demanded (units per time period) | (3) Quantity Supplied (units per time period) | (4) Excess Demand (+) Excess Supply (−) (units per time period) |
|---|---|---|---|
| $1.00 | 1 | 25 | − 24 |
| .90 | 3 | 21 | − 18 |
| .80 | 5 | 19 | − 14 |
| .70 | 8 | 15 | − 7 |
| .60 | 12 | 12 | 0 |
| .50 | 18 | 9 | 9 |
| .40 | 26 | 6 | 20 |

(a) Using the grid at the top of the next page, label the axes and plot the demand and supply curves. Indicate the equilibrium level of price and quantity of X.
(b) Fill in column (4) for values of excess demand and excess supply. What is the value of excess demand (supply) at equilibrium?
(c) Indicate and explain the likely direction of change in the price of X if excess demand exists. Do the same for excess supply.

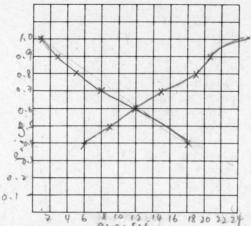

2. *The hypotheses of demand and supply:* Fill in the table below. Draw new curves on the graphs to aid you. Show the *initial* effects predicted by the hypotheses of the indicated events on the markets. For changes in demand and supply (meaning shifts in the curve), equilibrium price, and quantity, use + or - to show increase or decrease; for no change, use 0. If effect cannot be deduced from the information, use U.

| Market | Event | | D | S | P | Q |
|--------|-------|---|---|---|---|---|
| 1. Canadian wine | Early frost destroys a large percentage of the grape crop in British Columbia. | 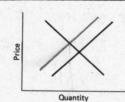 | 0 | − | + | − |
| 2. Copper wire | The Bell Telephone Co. greatly increases orders for wire to satisfy transmission needs. | 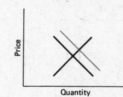 | + | 0 | + | + |
| 3. Pine antique furniture | "Antique hunting" becomes popular and Canadians attempt to furnish their homes with antique pine chairs and tables. | 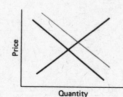 | + | 0 | + | + |
| 4. Auto tires | Incomes and population rise as synthetic rubber, cheaper than natural rubber, is invented. | 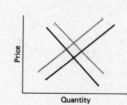 | + | + | U | + |

| Market | Event | | D | S | P | Q |
|--------|-------|---|---|---|---|---|
| 5. Cigarettes | A new law requires this notice on each pack: "Warning: The Department of National Health and Welfare advises that danger to health increases with amount smoked." | | — | O | — | — |
| 6. Automobile fuel | Middle East oil producers restrict the total amount of crude oil going to North America. | | O | — | + | — |

# PROBLEMS

## 1. THE CHANGING APPETITES OF CANADIANS

In this problem, you are asked to formulate hypotheses concerning the most important elements in the demand functions for various types of food that are consistent with the data given and that might be tested against further facts. The data here can be found in the *National Income and Expenditure Accounts* published by Statistics Canada.

TABLE 1   Food and Consumption Expenditures

| | 1950 | 1960 | 1970 | 1970 ÷ 1950 |
|---|------|------|------|-------------|
| Total consumption expenditures (billions of dollars) | 12.5 | 25.5 | 50.0 | 4.0 |
| Total expenditures on food[a] (billions of dollars) | 2.7 | 4.8 | 7.9 | 2.9 |
| Food expenditures as a percentage of total consumption | 21.6 | 18.8 | 15.8 | |

[a]Excluding alcoholic beverages

TABLE 2   Price Indexes, Population, and Income

| | 1950 | 1960 | 1970 | 1970 ÷ 1950 |
|---|------|------|------|-------------|
| Consumer price index—food[a] | 102.6 | 128.3 | 166.8 | 1.63 |
| Consumer price index—all items except food[a] | 101.0 | 128.6 | 166.2 | 1.65 |
| Canadian population (millions) | 13.7 | 17.9 | 21.4 | 1.56 |
| Per capita disposable income (current dollars) | 971.0 | 1486.0 | 2523.0 | 2.60 |
| Per capita disposable income (1958 dollars) | 946.0 | 1158.0 | 1518.0 | 1.60 |

[a]1949 = 100

TABLE 3   Per Capita Canadian Consumption and Average Retail Prices: Selected Foods[a]

|  | 1950 | | 1960 | | 1970 | | 1970 ÷ 1950 | |
|---|---|---|---|---|---|---|---|---|
|  | Q | P | Q | P | Q | P | Q | P |
| 1. Beef (round steak) | 50.5 | 78.6¢ | 69.2 | 89 ¢ | 84.0 | $1.27 | 1.66 | 1.62 |
| 2. Pork (rib chops) | 60.8 | 28.5¢ | 55.2 | 74 ¢ | 55.3 | 98.3¢ | .91 | 3.45 |
| 3. Eggs (dozen) | 19.7 | 56.5¢ | 23 | 52 ¢ | 21.8 | 54.5¢ | 1.11 | .96 |
| 4. Butter | 20.2 | 60.3¢ | 16.9 | 69.8¢ | 15.5 | 71.8¢ | .77 | 1.19 |

[a]1, 2, and 4 are given in pounds.
*Source: Prices and Price Indices* and *Handbook of Agricultural Statistics.*

## Questions

1. (a) From 1950 on, the percentage of disposable income spent on food has declined. This is reflected in the lower percentage of total consumption expenditures represented by food expenditures. What hypothesis might explain this?

   (b) Suggest a modification of this hypothesis that would account for a larger percentage spent on food in 1950 than in the war years 1939-1945.

2. A simple hypothesis is that the consumption of a commodity will vary proportionally with the number of people. This would indicate that over time the per capita figures would be reasonably _____. This hypothesis would be confirmed, accepting 10 percent as a reasonable variation, only for two products: _____ and _____.

3. Dieticians among you will recognize that items 1 and 2 in Table 3 are major sources of protein, and 3 and 4, of fats. Formulate a general hypothesis incorporating the variables of income and price to explain relative consumption of protein and fats. Do the data above support the hypothesis? Explain.

## 2.  EFFECTS OF IMPORTED WINE ON CANADIAN SALES

The Liquor Control Board of Ontario stated in early 1975 that the prices of French wines in the United States would decline dramatically while less spectacular declines would occur in Canada.

The reasons given for these expectations were (1) the growing acceptance in the United States of California wines, and (2) the excellent grape crop in France in 1973 and 1974.

### Question

1. Using basic supply and demand analysis, explain how each of the above factors operates to reduce the expected price of French wines. (Use the simple supply and demand diagram.)

## 3.  ARABS RAISE PRICES

Suppose there were an open world market for crude oil and that the price of Middle East oil and Canadian oil in various parts of Canada were as follows, the differences reflecting transportation costs.

|           | Middle East | Canadian   |
|-----------|-------------|------------|
| Maritimes | $5.00/bbl   | $6.50/bbl  |
| Central   | 5.50/bbl    | 6.00/bbl   |
| Western   | 6.00/bbl    | 5.00/bbl   |

The price of Middle East oil suddenly rises by 100 percent.

### Questions

1. Given that the supply for both sources in the short run is fixed, what will happen to the demand for Canadian oil? To the demand for Middle East oil?


2. What will happen to the price of Canadian oil? To the price of Middle East oil?

# Elasticity of Demand and Supply

## KEY CONCEPTS AND DEFINITIONS

1. <u>Elasticity</u> is a concept which describes the responsiveness of one variable to changes in another.
2. The elasticity of demand is a measure of how the quantity demanded responds to a price change. If the percentage change in quantity demanded exceeds the percentage change price, demand is said to be price <u>elastic</u>; if the reverse is true, demand is price <u>inelastic</u>.
3. The elasticity of demand can also be measured in terms of whether or not a price change increases total revenue, decreases total revenue or leaves it unchanged.
4. Quantity demanded may change if income changes and this responsiveness is known as the <u>income elasticity of demand</u>. The responsiveness of the quantity demanded to income changes determines whether or not the good is a <u>normal good</u> or an <u>inferior good</u>.
5. For a given good, the quantity demanded may change when the price of some other good changes. This responsiveness is the cross elasticity of demand.
6. The elasticity of supply is the <u>analogue</u> of the elasticity of demand and measures the responsiveness of supply to changes in price.

> **CHECKLIST** Make certain that you also understand the following concepts: *Appendix:* arc elasticity; point elasticity.

## REVIEW QUESTIONS

1. *Elasticity* of demand (or supply) measures the degree of response of quantity demanded (or supplied) to changes in ____price____.

2. If for a fall in price, the quantity of a commodity demanded increases, elasticity of demand is greater than ____zero____.

3. If for a fall in price, the percentage increase in quantity demanded is greater than the percentage change in price, elasticity of demand is greater than ____one____.

4. If, when the price of a good falls, the total revenues received by the industry rise, elasticity of demand is greater than ____one____.

5. (a) The term "elastic demand" means one whose elasticity is ___*more than one*___.
   (b) The term "inelastic demand" means one whose elasticity is ___*less than one*___.
   (c) The term "unitary elasticity" of demand means one whose elasticity equals ___*one*___.

6. If elasticity is unitary, a fall in price will cause total revenue to ___*remain the*___ ___*same*___.

7. If, when the price of a commodity is increased, total revenues also increase, *ceteris paribus*, elasticity of demand must be ___*inelastic*___.

8. If there are few available substitutes for a good that is a necessity, elasticity of demand would probably be ___*inelastic*___.

9. (a) If, as an individual seller in a market, you think you can sell all you can produce at the going market price, then for you the elasticity of demand seems ___*infinite*___.
   (b) On the diagram this demand curve would appear ___*horizontal*___.

10. (a) If buyers are totally impervious to price, and continue to buy the same quantity no matter what the price, elasticity of demand is ___*zero*___.
    (b) On the graph this demand curve would be ___*vertical*___.

11. *Income elasticity* measures the response of quantity demanded to ___*income change*___.

12. If a rise of 10 percent in income is associated with a 5 percent increase in the sale of shoes, income elasticity is ___*0.5*___.

13. If a fall in the price of Y results in a decrease in the sale of X, the two goods appear to be (substitutes/~~complements~~) and the cross-elasticity would be (positive/~~negative~~).

14. If a small rise in price of a good results in a large increase in the amount supplied, we should say that the supply is ___*elastic*___.

## APPENDIX

15. Of two parallel, downward-sloping demand curves, the more elastic one would be (~~further from~~/closer to) the origin.

16. Given a straight-line downward-sloping demand curve, the elasticity of demand becomes greater as the price (rises/~~falls~~).

17. When price and quantity changes are small, we can use a simpler formula than that given for arc elasticity in Chapter 6, namely, _____, where $p$ and $q$ are taken as the _____ rather than the average amounts.

18. The slope of a downward-sloping straight-line demand curve can be symbolized as: _____, that of a tangent to a point on a curve can be symbolized as: _____.

---

If you have not answered all questions correctly, review the text in order to be sure that you have all of the important concepts clearly in mind before going on to the next chapter.

1. price  2. zero  3. one  4. one  5. greater than one; between zero and one; one  6. remain unchanged  7. inelastic or less than one  8. inelastic or less than one  9. infinite; horizontal  10. zero; vertical  11. changes in income  12. 0.5  13. substitutes; positive  14. elastic  15. closer to  16. rises  17. $(\Delta q/\Delta p) \times (p/q)$; original  18. $(\Delta p/\Delta q)$; $dp/dq$

---

## MULTIPLE-CHOICE QUESTIONS

1. To say that the demand for a commodity is *elastic* means
   (a) that the demand curve slopes downward to the right
   (b) that more is sold at a lower price
   (c) that a rise in price will increase total revenue
   (d) that the change in quantity sold is proportionally greater than the change in price

2. When the demand is elastic,
   (a) a fall in price is more than offset by an increase in quantity sold, so that total revenue rises
   (b) the good is probably a necessity
   (c) a rise in price will increase total revenue, even though less is sold
   (d) buyers are not much influenced by prices of competing products

Questions 3 through 6 refer to the figure below.

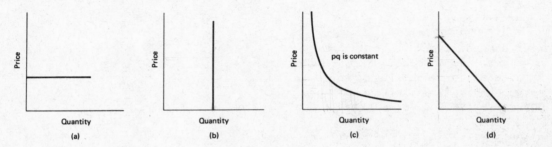

3. The demand curve with an elasticity of 0 is
   (a) a
   (b) b
   (c) c
   (d) d

4. The demand curve with an elasticity of 1 is
   (a) a
   (b) b
   (c) c
   (d) d

5. The demand curve with an elasticity varying from 0 to ∞ depending on price is
   (a) a
   (b) b
   (c) c
   (d) d

6. The demand curve with an elasticity of ∞ is
   (a) a
   (b) b
   (c) c
   (d) d

7. The demand for pork is probably more price elastic than the demand for
   (a) food
   (b) housing
   (c) beer
   (d) Fords

8. A demand curve is completely inelastic if
   (a) a rise in price causes a fall in quantity demanded
   (b) a fall in price causes a rise in sellers' total receipts
   (c) the commodity in question is highly perishable, like fresh strawberries
   (d) a change in price does not change quantity demanded

9. If a 100 percent rise in the membership fee of a club caused the number of members to decline from 600 to 450,
   (a) demand was inelastic
   (b) demand was infinitely elastic
   (c) demand was elastic
   (d) the price rise caused a shift in demand for membership, so it is impossible to say

10. Which of the following would you expect to have the highest income elasticity?
    (a) spaghetti
    (b) bus rides
    (c) skis
    (d) baby carriages

11. Inferior commodities
    (a) have zero income elasticities of demand
    (b) have negative cross-elasticities of demand
    (c) have negative elasticities of supply
    (d) have negative income elasticities of demand

12. Margarine and butter probably have
    (a) the same income elasticities of demand
    (b) very low price elasticities of demand
    (c) negative cross-elasticities of demand with respect to each other
    (d) positive cross-elasticities of demand with respect to each other

13. If price elasticity of demand for a product is 0.5, this means that
    (a) a change in price changes demand by 50 percent
    (b) a 1 percent increase in quantity sold is associated with a 0.5 percent fall in price
    (c) a 1 percent increase in quantity sold is associated with a 2 percent fall in price
    (d) a 0.5 percent change in price will cause a 0.5 percent change in quantity sold

14. If, when incomes rise by 5 percent, the quantity sold of a commodity rises by 10 percent, income elasticity is
    (a) −2
    (b) 2
    (c) −(1/2)
    (d) 1/2

15. In a certain market, when the price of hotdogs rose from 76 cents per pound to 84 cents per pound, the quantity of hotdog buns sold went from 11,000 to 9,000. Indicated cross-elasticity of demand is
    (a) 1/2
    (b) −(1/2)
    (c) 2
    (d) −2

16. Price elasticity of demand for a commodity tends to be greater
    (a) the more of a necessity it is
    (b) the closer substitutes there are for it
    (c) the less important it is in our budget
    (d) the lower the price

# EXERCISES

1. Fill out the following table:

| | Price Elasticity | Change in Price | Change in Total Revenue (up, down, or none) |
|---|---|---|---|
| (a) | 2 | up | down |
| (b) | 1 | down | none |
| (c) | 1 | up | none |
| (d) | 0 | down | down |
| (e) | .6 | up | up |

2. *Demand Elasticities and Total Revenue*

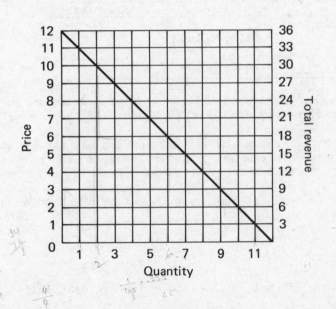

(a) You are given the demand curve in the diagram above, for which several price changes are contained in the table below. Calculate the elasticities for the price changes shown on the table below. Draw in the total revenue curve on the diagram above (note right hand scale).

| Price Change From | To | Percentage Change in Price | Percentage Change in Quantity | Elasticity |
|---|---|---|---|---|
| $10 | $6 | 50% | 100% | 2 |
| 3 | 2 | 40% | 10.5% | 0.26 |
| 11 | 1 | 167% | 167% | 1 |

(b) What is the relationship between total revenue and elasticity for the three changes noted in (a)?

(c) Assume that the demand curve shifts to the right with two more units sold at every price. Calculate the elasticity for the price change in (a) to illustrate the proposition that the new demand curve is less elastic than the old at a given price change.

(d) What is the equation for the demand curve in (a)?

$$P = 12 - p$$

3. *Riders for Nippon's Monorail*. In October 1968, the Tokyo Monorail Company denied that it was facing backruptcy. It stated that its operating results were much improved since it had reduced its fare from 250 yen to 150 yen (70 cents to 42 cents) on its 12-mile run from Tokyo airport to the center of the city.

   Assume that this price cut was completely responsible for its increase in revenues from 460,000,000 yen in 1966 to 640,000,000 yen in 1967. Calculate the indicated elasticity of demand.

|      | P   | Q         | Revenue     | Elasticity |
|------|-----|-----------|-------------|------------|
| 1966 | 250 | 1840000   | 460,000,000 |            |
| 1967 | 150 | 4276666.6 | 640,000,000 | 1.52       |

0.7947
100
200
0.2

4. *Toronto Public Transit*. In 1973 the Transportation Commission in Toronto voted to abolish the "two-fare" system whereby some people, because of where they lived, had to pay the fare twice to reach downtown.

   Those opposed to the change stated that the transit system would lose money because of the lower fare paid by some people. Those in favor argued that the quantity of transit service demanded would increase sharply, thereby offsetting any revenue loss due to lower fares.

(a) What might the advocates of the new proposal be thinking about the elasticity of demand for public transit?

(b) How will they know if their assumption about the elasticity was correct?

(c) If total revenue rises, what might one forecast for the price of automobile parking spaces downtown?

# PROBLEMS

## 1. RAISING THE RATES ON WATER

To pay for the treatment of sewage and thus avoid pollution, it has been suggested that water rates be increased, and in some Canadian cities this has occurred. Suppose water rates in a community are now $2 per 100 gallons and total consumption is 20 million gallons per year. Rates are doubled, and revenue is expected to double, but in actual fact it increases only one and one-half times.

Questions

1. What was the expected elasticity of demand for water in the community?

2. What actually was the elasticity of demand? (Give the numerical value.)

3. If rates were quadrupled, would you expect the elasticity of demand to be the same as it was in question 2 above?

## 2.   RAISING UNIVERSITY TUITION RATES

The Board of Regents at the University of Wisconsin reduced the tuition fees for undergraduate students at two colleges in 1974. At one college, tuition fell from $515 to $180 per annum, and enrollment increased by 23 percent. At the other, tuition was reduced from $476 to $150, and enrollment increased by 47 percent.

Questions

1. What do these statistics say about the price elasticity of demand for university education in these two areas?

2. Who would bear the cost of such a reduction in tuition fees?

# Supply and Demand in Action: Price Controls and Agricultural Problems

## KEY CONCEPTS AND DEFINITIONS

1. Through legislation, government can establish a <u>price ceiling</u> for one or more products/ services. If this price is below the equilibrium market price, a situation of excess demand will result.
2. <u>Rent control</u> is a legislated price ceiling which requires that landlords not charge rent beyond a certain level or not increase the rent by more than a certain percentage.
3. A <u>black market</u> exists when goods, purchased at the controlled price, can be resold (illegally) above that price, due to the excess demand created by the price ceiling.
4. A <u>price floor</u> can be established by government which states the minimum price at which a good can be sold. If the price floor is above the free-market equilibrium, there will be excess supply.
5. The effect on agricultural prices of unplanned changes in output depends to a considerable extent on the elasticity of demand for farm products.
6. Government can maintain the price of a commodity at an equilibrium level by purchasing excess supply and selling its own holdings of the commodity when there is excess demand. Unless the amount bought and sold is in inverse proportion to changes in farmers' output, farm income will not be stabilized.
7. <u>Marketing board quotas</u> are used to limit supply and keep prices higher than would be the case without a quota. For those that are allowed to produce, the marketing board can alter profit levels.

> | CHECKLIST | Make certain that you also understand the following concepts: crop restriction, supply lag; cobweb; minimum wage; Canadian wheat board. |

## REVIEW QUESTIONS

1. If a government sets an enforceable price ceiling on a good below the equilibrium price, a (shortage/~~surplus~~) of the good will result. At the ceiling price, the amount demanded (exceeds/ ~~is less than~~) the amount supplied.

2. If a government sets a price ceiling on a good below the equilibrium price but wishes everyone to be able to obtain some of it, it must be prepared to set up a system of
   ___ _rationing_ ___.

3. If a government sets a legal minimum price on a good or service, a surplus will develop if the price is (~~below~~/above) the equilibrium price because the amount demanded will (~~exceed~~/be less than) the amount supplied.

4. If a minimum wage is set above the equilibrium wage, there will be a (surplus/~~shortage~~) of workers available at that time.

5. The gap between the desire to produce goods and a change in actual production is called the _____(time) supply_____ lag.

6. If the Canadian Wheat Board agrees to buy wheat from farmers at a fixed price, farmers face a perfectly _____elastic_____ demand curve.

7. Farmers' short-run supply curves are very (~~elastic~~/inelastic).

8. Demand curves for many farm products seem to be quite (inelastic/~~elastic~~). This reflects the probable fact that if food prices fell by 10 percent, you probably (~~would~~/would not) increase the amount you eat by 10 percent.

9. Demand inelasticity coupled with fluctuating supply has tended to make farm prices historically (~~stable~~/unstable).

10. Government policy to aid farmers most often has been to put a floor under (prices/~~incomes~~), which has results in (~~shortages~~/surpluses). In order to prevent surpluses from increasing, the government may resort to _____quotas_____ such as acreage restrictions.

11. Technological developments such as pesticides, agricultural machinery, and improved crop varieties have permitted individual farmers to raise more crops, thus shifting supply curves to the _____right_____. At the same time, demand has risen (less than/~~more than~~) proportionally to the rises in income.

12. These developments have led to the problem of reallocating resources (~~into~~/out of) agriculture and have tended to keep agricultural incomes (below/~~above~~) average incomes.

---

If you have not answered all questions correctly, review the text in order to be sure that you have all of the important concepts clearly in mind before going on to the next chapter.

1. shortage; exceeds  2. rationing  3. above; be less than  4. surplus  5. supply  6. elastic  7. inelastic  8. inelastic; would not  9. unstable  10. prices; surpluses; quotas  11. right; less than  12. out of; below

---

## MULTIPLE-CHOICE QUESTIONS

1. Price ceilings below the equilibrium price and price floors above the equilibrium price
   (a) lead to production controls
   (b) lead to rationing
   (c) lead to a drop in quality
   (d) lead to a reduction in quantity bought and sold

2. In a free-market economy, the rationing of scarce goods is done by
   (a) the price mechanism
   (b) the government
   (c) business
   (d) consumers

3. One prediction made about minimum-wage legislation is that
   (a) it will reduce employment in those industries affected by it, given competition in the labor market
   (b) no one benefits in the long run
   (c) it will actually lower wages
   (d) it will raise productivity

Questions 4 through 7 refer to the figure below.

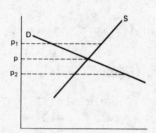

4. If $p_1$ is a minimum price,
   (a) it will have no effect
   (b) it will lead to shortages and probably to black-market activity
   (c) it will lead to surpluses and possibly to undercutting of the minimum price
   (d) it would represent a response to Nader's Raiders

5. If $p_2$ is a minimum price,
   (a) it will have no effect
   (b) it will lead to shortages and probably to black-market activity
   (c) it will lead to surpluses and possibly to undercutting of the minimum price
   (d) it would represent a response to Nader's Raiders

6. If $p_1$ is a maximum price,
   (a) it will have no effect
   (b) it will head to shortages and probably to black-market activity
   (c) it will lead to surpluses and possibly to undercutting of the minimum price
   (d) it would represent a response to Nader's Raiders

7. If $p_2$ is a maximum price,
   (a) it will have no effect
   (b) it will lead to shortages and probably to black-market activity
   (c) it will lead to surpluses and possibly to undercutting of the minimum price
   (d) it would represent a response to Nader's Raiders

8. A cobweb cycle for an agricultural product means
   (a) there will be excess supply
   (b) there will be excess demand
   (c) price will be unstable for a period
   (d) demand never changes

9. The main reason for price supports is to
   (a) stabilize farm incomes
   (b) make certain there are always extra stocks of goods on hand
   (c) give the government control over agriculture
   (d) reduce competition

10. Rent controls which establish a rent below the market equilibrium rent will
    (a) ensure everyone of adequate housing over the long run
    (b) cause rents to decline eventually
    (c) likely reduce the supply of rental units
    (d) stimulate the construction of rental housing units

11. Unplanned fluctuations in the supply of agricultural produce
    (a) cause larger price changes when demand is elastic than when it is inelastic
    (b) cause price variations that are in the same direction as the fluctuations
    (c) make the supply more elastic
    (d) cause price fluctuations that will be larger the more inelastic demand is

12. A price completely stabilized by government's buying surpluses and selling its stocks when there are shortages means that
    (a) poor farmers will benefit the most
    (b) there will be no storage costs
    (c) farmers' revenues will be proportional to output
    (d) all farms will have satisfactory incomes

13. Agricultural output in Canada has increased substantially since World War II mainly because
    (a) many people are going back to farming
    (b) productivity and yields have risen
    (c) rising demand has kept prices steadily increasing
    (d) it has had good growing weather

14. The long-run problem of overproduction in Canadian agriculture is intensified by
    (a) the population explosion
    (b) low income elasticity of demand for agricultural products
    (c) the continued use of cheap hand labor
    (d) increased foreign demand

Answers to multiple-choice questions: 1(d)  2(a)  3(a)  4(c)  5(a)  6(a)  7(b)  8(c)  9(a)
10(c)  11(d)  12(c)  13(b)  14(b)

# EXERCISES

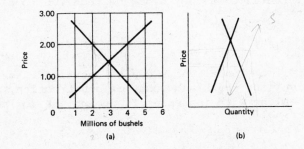

1. On graph (a), illustrate the effects of the government's setting a minimum price of $2.00 per bushel. Label all significant points of interest. (Assume that the government maintains the price by purchasing any surpluses, and that there are no acreage controls.)
    (a) Farmers' total revenue: _____ 8 millions _____
    (b) Consumers will get _____ 2 millions _____ bushels at $2.00 per bushel.
    (c) The government will have to buy _____ 2 millions _____ bushels at a total cost of _____ 4 millions _____ .
    (d) At the equilibrium price, consumers would have bought _____ 3 millions _____ bushels at about what price? _____ 1.5 dollars _____

2. Show by drawing a new curve on graph (b):
    (a) a large shift in agricultural supply due to great technological improvements in agriculture. What has happened to farmers' total revenue, judging from the graph?

    revenue ↓

   (b) a shift in the demand for agricultural products due to rising population. In the long
       run, which shift, (a) or (b), has the more serious implications for the world?

3. As the cost of shelter rose rapidly in the early 1970s, there was considerable pressure
   for governments to introduce rent control. Most provincial governments responded to the
   federal government's plea to do so.
      The figure below represents the market for rental housing units.

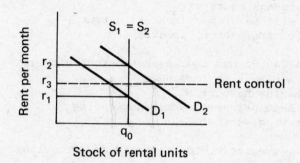

Stock of rental units

From period 1 to period 2, demand shifts from $D_1$ to $D_2$ with no corresponding increase in
supply. Rent rises to $r_2$ per month.
(a) What would you expect to happen to the stock of rental units eventually following the
    rise in rents? Why?

    *Stock of rental units will eventually increase since ↑ prices will encouraged the supplier.*

(b) In period 3, the government responds to the call for rent control and fixes rent at
    $r_3$. What supply of rental units would now be required to clear this market?

(c) Over time, the supply of rental units can be increased. Assume that because of increas-
    ingly more expensive land costs and costs of construction, the supply of rental units
    is as shown below (along with increases in demand due to increases in population).

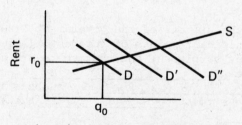

Long run supply of rental units

What might you expect to happen to the quality of housing as landlords attempted to
provide rental units so as to maximize total rental income with rents fixed at $r_0$?

    *↓ quality*

# PROBLEMS

## 1.  CANADIAN WHEAT SUPPLIES

Warm winds will soon be blowing across Canada's Prairies, melting snow and thawing some
of the richest farmland in the world. Already farmers are tinkering with tractors, ready-
ing them for the day when they will move out onto the land to work the soil for this year's
crop.

The crop this year, however, will be far different from any other in recent memory.
While wheat has historically been by far the biggest single crop in the mix of agricultural
products on Canada's Prairies, if the Federal Government's recently announced plan to induce farmers to take up to 22 million acres out of wheat production this year were to have
its maximum impact, practically no wheat would be grown in Western Canada in 1970.

This situation would be a complete reversal of that which existed only a few years ago.
In the mid-sixties, it will be recalled, contracts for the sale of huge quantities of wheat
negotiated with the U.S.S.R. and China caused concern over Canada's ability to meet export
commitments and farmers were urged to increase production. Now, with export sales falling
and world wheat markets glutted, Canadian wheat stocks have been rising sharply. In fact,
the Minister responsible for the Canadian Wheat Board estimates that at the end of the current crop year (July 31, 1970) stocks of wheat on hand will still amount to 950 million
bushels, nearly double estimated annual domestic consumption and expected export sales.*

### Questions

1. Given that the world demand curve for wheat is downward sloping, what would happen to the
   price of wheat if the Wheat Board were to place the stocks of wheat on the market?

2. By inducing farmers to take acreage out of wheat production, what is the government attempting to achieve?

3. If farmers do not grow wheat but instead plant oats and barley, what will happen to the
   price of these crops if (a) their demand does not change; (b) their demand increases
   greatly?

## 2.  THE FEDERAL BEEF SUBSIDY

In March 1974, the federal government introduced a subsidy of $7.00 per hundredweight on pre-
mium beef, when marketed, as a means of supplying more beef to the market at a lower price to
the consumer. The need for this subsidy suggests that beef producers were not willing to market
more cattle because of the effect such action would have on the price and total revenue they
would receive.

### Questions

1. What does the last statement above suggest about the elasticity of the demand schedule for
   beef?

---

*Source: Business Review, Bank of Montreal, March 25, 1970.

2. The effect of a subsidy is to shift the demand schedule up by the amount of the subsidy. Illustrate the effect of the subsidy on beef prices to the consumer and the revenue to the producer if the demand schedule is: (a) inelastic; (b) elastic. (Consider this a short-run situation where the *actual* supply of beef put on the market and the *potential* supply are both completely inelastic.)

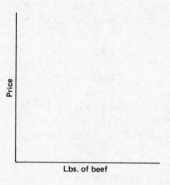

## 3. THE FLUID MILK SUBSIDY

In early 1975, the federal government removed a 6-cent-a-quart subsidy on fluid milk while maintaining its 34-cent-a-pound (or 8.5-cent-a-quart equivalent) subsidy on skim milk powder.

### Questions

1. What would you predict about the demand for fluid milk and milk powder following the removal of the subsidy?

2. If fluid skim milk was retailing for 40 cents a quart before the subsidy was removed, and the elasticity of demand for fluid milk is estimated at 0.62, what would be the percentage decline in fluid milk consumption if the subsidy removal was reflected in a price rise of 6 cents a quart?

3. Does it make any different at all to the dairy farmer whether the subsidy is given to fluid or skim milk production? Justify your answer.

# 8

# International Trade and Exchange Rates

## KEY CONCEPTS AND DEFINITIONS

1. Nations trade goods and services among themselves. When payments for these items are made, the purchaser generally is required to pay the seller in the seller's currency. That is, the purchaser must exchange his domestic currency to obtain a foreign currency or foreign exchange.

2. The price that one currency trades for in terms of another currency is called the foreign exchange rate.

3. In a free-exchange market, the equilibrium foreign exchange rate is determined by the forces of demand and supply for the particular currency. In such a situation, the country is said to be operating on a floating exchange rate system.

4. Foreigners who buy Canadian exports must exchange their currency for Canadian dollars. This transaction constitutes a demand for dollars and a supply of foreign exchange. When Canadians buy imports, they demand foreign exchange and supply dollars.

5. A change in the foreign price of dollars causes a movement along the demand and supply curves of dollars. A lower foreign price of dollars, a depreciation of the dollar, increases the quantity demanded of dollars and decreases the quantity supplied of dollars. A depreciation of the dollar has the effect of increasing the price of imports and decreasing the price of exports.

6. An increase in the foreign price of dollars, an appreciation, has the effect of increasing the quantity supplied of dollars and decreasing the quantity demanded of dollars.

7. The foreign price of dollars will change if the demand and/or the supply curve of dollars shifts.

8. If a government is committed to maintaining the foreign price of its currency at a particular level, this country is operating on a fixed exchange rate system. If the government lowers the foreign price of its currency, this is called a devaluation of the currency. Alternatively, a revaluation occurs when the government takes action to increase the foreign price of its currency.

CHECKLIST — Make certain that you also understand the following concepts: multiple exchange rates; arbitrage; balance of trade; trade surplus; trade deficit; tradables; nontradables; unstable exchange rates.

# REVIEW QUESTIONS

1. The exchange rate is the _____*price*_____ at which purchases and sales of foreign currency (or claims on it) take place. The foreign currency traded (or claims on it) is called ___*foreign exchange*___.

2. When one dollar exchanges for .5 pounds sterling, one pound sterling exchanges for _____*2*_____ dollars.

3. Sales and purchases of foreign exchange to keep several exchange rates at mutually consistent ratios are called _____*arbitrage*_____ operations.

4. If a Canadian purchases a car directly from England which is valued at 3000 pounds sterling and the exchange rate is .5 pounds per dollar, he must exchange _____*6000*_____ dollars to obtain the 3000 pounds.

5. If the dollar value of Canadian exports exceeds the dollar value of imports, a trade _____*surplus*_____ is said to exist.

6. If the dollar price of the British pound falls, the prices of those British goods that were exported to Canada _____*fall*_____ while the pound sterling prices of Canadian goods exported to Britain _____*rise*_____.

7. When Canadians import goods and services, they supply _____*dollars*_____ and demand foreign currencies. When foreigners buy Canadian goods and services, they _____*demand*_____ dollars and _____*supply*_____ their own currency.

8. An increase in the Canadian demand for German-made cars shifts the demand curve for German marks to the _____*right*_____ and the supply curve of dollars to the _____*left*_____; with a floating exchange rate, the dollar price of marks will _____*increase*_____ while the mark price of dollars will _____*fall*_____.

9. If the prices in country A rise relatively to those in other countries, A's imports will probably _____*rise*_____ and its exports will _____*fall*_____. Assuming the foreign price of its currency does not fall initially, a trade (surplus/deficit) will result. However, assuming that this country operates on a floating exchange system, the foreign price of its currency will eventually (depreciate/~~appreciate~~).

10. Suppose the government of a country fixed the foreign price of its currency above the equilibrium price that would have existed in a free market. A trade _____*deficit*_____ would be created, or viewed in another way, an excess _____*supply*_____ would result for its currency. To maintain this high foreign price, the government would have to (buy/~~sell~~) its currency in the international foreign exchange market.

---

If you have not answered all questions correctly, review the text in order to be sure that you have all of the important concepts clearly in mind before going on to the next chapter.

1. price; foreign exchange  2. two  3. arbitrage  4. 6000  5. surplus  6. fall; rise  7. dollars; demand; supply  8. right; left; rise; fall  9. rise; fall; deficit; depreciate  10. deficit; supply; buy

---

# MULTIPLE-CHOICE QUESTIONS

1. In the exchange market between dollars and sterling, a demander of dollars is also
   (a) a supplier of dollars
   (b) a supplier of pounds
   (c) a demander of pounds
   (d) everyone is always all these simultaneously

2. If, in a free market between Canadian and American dollars in which the rate is allowed to fluctuate, Canadians wish to purchase fewer American goods, *ceteris paribus*,
   (a) at the new equilibrium, it will take more Canadian dollars to buy an American dollar than before
   (b) at the new equilibrium, it will take the same number of Canadian dollars to buy an American dollar as before
   (c) at the new equilibrium, it will take fewer American dollars to buy a Canadian dollar than before
   (d) at the new equilibrium, it will take more American dollars to buy a Canadian dollar than before

3. A dollar price of 25 cents for marks can be expressed as a mark price of dollars of
   (a) 4
   (b) 1/4
   (c) an indeterminant amount
   (d) 2.5

4. Suppose that the American demand for Canadian dollars is 5 billion Canadian dollars per year at an exchange rate of $.93 (U.S.) for a Canadian dollar, and 6 billion Canadian dollars a year at an exchange rate of $.90. The elasticity of demand for Canadian dollars can be estimated as
   (a) inelastic
   (b) unit elastic
   (c) greater than one but less than two
   (d) greater than two

5. Suppose that the domestic supply price of Canadian-produced snowmobiles falls, the foreign demand for snowmobiles is elastic, and a floating exchange rate exists. *Ceteris paribus*,
   (a) the supply-of-dollars curve would shift to the left and cause a depreciation in the value of the dollar
   (b) the supply-of-dollars curve would shift to the left and cause an appreciation in the value of the dollar
   (c) the demand-for-dollars curve would shift to the right and cause an appreciation in the value of the dollar
   (d) the demand-for-dollars curve would shift to the right and cause a depreciation in the value of the dollar

Answers to multiple-choice questions:  1(b)   2(d)   3(a)   4(d)   5(c)

# EXERCISES

1. Assume that the Bank of England is trying to maintain a fixed rate of about £1 = $2.40. Given the demand and supply curves in the diagram, will it have to be prepared to buy or to sell pounds to maintain this price? _____ About how much? _____

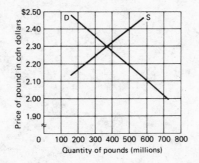

2. Suppose Jane Doe, a member of the foreign-exchange department of a large New York bank, is given the responsibility of checking the cross-rates of American dollars, pounds, and Italian lire each day. If disorderly or inconsistent rates should arise on any day, she is to report this to the manager. Suppose that on February 6 she obtains the following information which is displayed in the table below.

| One unit of this currency | Exchanges for stated number of units of this currency | | |
| | U.S. Dollar | Lira | Pound |
| --- | --- | --- | --- |
| U.S. dollar | 1 | 600 | 0.417 |
| Lira | 0.00167 | 1 | 0.000833 |
| Pound | 2.40 | 1,200 | 1 |

The first row indicates that 1 U.S. dollar trades for 600 lire and .6 pounds sterling.

(a) Is the pound price of dollars (.417) consistent with the dollar price of pounds?

(b) Is the lira price of dollars (600) consistent with the dollar price of lire?

(c) Is the pound price of lire consistent with the lira price of pounds?

(d) Is the cross-rate of pounds to lire in terms of dollars consistent with the pound price of the lire? Hint: Divide .417 by 600 and compare with the pound price of lire in the second row.

(e) Would this bank make profits by using $1000 to buy lire, then purchase pounds with the lire, and then purchase dollars with the pounds? How much?

3. Suppose that the Canadian economy is highly dependent on foreign oil supplies, domestic oil supply is not sufficient to satisfy domestic demand, domestic oil prices are generally kept in line with foreign oil prices, and Canada operates on a floating exchange-rate system. Suppose in the short run that the oil-producing countries raise the price of oil and Canadians cannot reduce their need for oil products because no substitute products exist. To keep the analysis simple, assume that oil products are Canada's only import.

(a) Draw a diagram of the demand and supply curves for the Canadian dollar before the increase in oil prices. Given the information above, what shape will the supply-of-dollars curve have?

(b) Show the effect of the increase in the price of oil on the price of the Canadian dollar.

4. Suppose that Canada has adopted a flexible exchange-rate system and that the current price of a Canadian dollar in terms of American dollars is .98. That is, 98 U.S. cents equal 1 Canadian dollar. The diagram below depicts this situation.

   Various factors that will shift the demand curve or supply curve of Canadian dollars are listed below. Indicate how each factor will affect the appropriate curve by inserting a check mark in the correct column. Then decide how each factor will affect the price of Canadian dollars. (For example, if you anticipate the price to rise about 98 U.S. cents, insert a + sign.)

   (a) an increase in U.S. income
   (b) increased oil imports into the United States from Canada
   (c) more inflation in Canada than in the United States
   (d) increased tariffs on U.S. goods coming into Canada

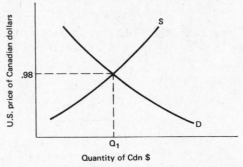

| Factor | Demand Curve | Supply Curve | Increases (+) in Price Decreases (−) in Price |
|--------|--------------|--------------|-----------------------------------------------|
| (a)    |              |              |                                               |
| (b)    |              |              |                                               |
| (c)    |              |              |                                               |
| (d)    |              |              |                                               |

# PROBLEM

## PROF ESCAPES THE CANADIAN WINTER

Suppose that Professor Claude Scholar, an instructor at a Saskatchewan university, is granted a six-month study leave with full pay beginning October 1, 1976. He has never been too keen on the Canadian winter, and so he decides to take his study leave at a state university in North Carolina, U.S.A.

He reckons that $4800 (U.S.) will be sufficient to give his family a comfortable living standard during his six months in the sunny south. Although he is not an expert in financial matters, he is quite concerned about future movements in the price of the Canadian dollar. He therefore considers two options to finance his stay in North Carolina. First, he considers liquidating his savings of $4670 (Canadian) which earn 4 percent on a semi-annual basis. He will then buy U.S. dollars around October 1, 1976. The second option involves buying U.S. dollars at the beginning of each month from his salary which is automatically deposited into the chequing account.

He chooses the second option. He instructs his bank manager to convert his monthly salary into $800 (U.S.) for each of the six months and send the funds to North Carolina.

The following table shows that happened to the price of U.S. dollars in terms of Canadian dollars.

| Month | Monthly Average Price of U.S. Dollars |
|-------|---------------------------------------|
| October 1976 | .9722 |
| November 1976 | 1.0364 |
| December 1976 | 1.0088 |
| January 1977 | 1.0180 |
| February 1977 | 1.0457 |
| March 1977 | 1.0539 |

Questions

1. What was the total cost in Canadian dollars of obtaining $4800 U.S. Dollars on a monthly basis over the six-month period?

2. What would have been the total cost in Canadian dollars to Professor Scholar if he had chosen the option of using his savings and buying U.S. dollars ($4800) in October 1976?

# Household Consumption Behavior

## KEY CONCEPTS AND DEFINITIONS

1. The market demand schedule is simply the horizontal addition of all individual demand schedules.

2. Marginal utility is the additional satisfaction a person receives as a consequence of consuming a little more of some good or service. In choosing between alternative increases in consumption, the concept of marginal utility is important.

3. If, as additional units of a good are consumed by a household, the marginal utility derived from each additional unit becomes smaller and smaller, the household is said to experience diminishing marginal utility.

4. A basic assumption of household consumption behavior is that whatever the activities of the household, it seeks to maximize total utility. For a given dollar outlay, this means that spending will be allocated to ensure that the utility of the last dollar spent on each item is equal.

5. The formal condition for household utility maximization where two goods (X and Y) are being purchased is the following: $MU_X/P_X = MU_Y/P_Y$ which, when rearranged, becomes $MU_X/MU_Y = P_X/P_Y$.

6. The household demand schedule for any commodity will be an inverse relationship between price and quantity demanded given that the household (a) maximizes total utility and (b) there is diminishing marginal utility for each good.

7. The elasticity of demand, which relates changes in quantity demanded to changes in price, depends on the marginal utility of the good in the range of the price change.

8. A budget line indicates the quantities of two goods that a household can purchase with a given income and fixed prices. Parallel shifts in the budget line result from changes in the household's income. Changes in the slope of the budget line result from changes in the relative prices of the goods.

9. An indifference curve shows different combinations of two goods that give the same level of total utility to the household. The slope of an indifference curve at any point on the curve is the marginal rate of substitution, or the rate at which one good can be substituted for another without changing total utility.

10. Household consumption equilibrium occurs at the point where the slope of the indifference curve (marginal rate of substitution) is tangent to the budget line.

| CHECKLIST | Make certain that you also understand the following concepts: isocost; relative price; absolute price; money income; real income; price level; income consumption line; price consumption line; free good; paradox of value; substitution effect; income effect. |

# REVIEW QUESTIONS

1. The budget line shows combinations of two types of commodities obtainable, given household _____*income*_____ and the commodities' _____*prices*_____. It shows a household's purchasing power, or _____*real*_____ income.

2. The budget line's slope reflects the ratio of the _____*prices*_____ of the two types of commodities shown; because it also represents the rate at which one commodity must be given up to gain more of another, it shows the _____*opportunity*_____ cost of a particular combination.

3. To find out where the budget line intersects the vertical, or $Y$, axis, household money income is divided by _____*the price of Y*_____.

4. How would the following events be pictured on the budget-line diagram, *ceteris paribus?*
   (a) household money income rises _____*parallel shift outward*_____
   (b) relative prices of commodities change _____*rotate, slope of the line changes*_____
   (c) income rises, price level rises by equal percent _____*no change*_____
   (d) income rises, price level rises by greater percent _____*shifts to the left*_____

5. The budget line on the accompanying diagram is drawn for an income of $300 per week. Referring to it, determine the following:
   (a) price of product A— _____*15*_____
   (b) price of product B— _____*10*_____
   (c) To buy one more unit of A, if the household is spending all of its income, it must give up how much B? _____*1.5 unit of B*_____
   (d) opportunity cost of A, in terms of B— _____*1.5 unit of B*_____

6. Show on the diagram the effect of the following changes, and tell whether real income has risen or fallen or whether we have insufficient information to know:
   (a) money income becomes $400; real income _____*risen*_____
   (b) money income = $300, $P_A$ = $20, $P_B$ = $12; real income _____*fallen*_____
   (c) money income = $330, $P_A$ = $12, $P_B$ = $15; real income _____*cannot tell*_____

7. An indifference curve shows various combinations of two commodities that give to the buyer _____*same utility (total satisfaction)*_____

8. An indifference curve farther from the origin than another shows points where total satisfaction is _____*greater*_____ than the other.

9. (a) The slope of an indifference curve shows what we call the marginal _____*rate*_____ _____*of substitute*_____.
   (b) If a household is indifferent between 21 units of food, 30 of clothing and 20 of food, 32 of clothing, the rate of substitution of food for clothing is _____*½*_____.

10. (a) Satisfaction is maximized at the point where an indifference curve is tangent to a
    _____*budget line*_____.

    (b) At this point, the marginal rate of substitution must be equal to the ratio of
    _____*prices*_____.

11. A rise in the price of one commodity, *ceteris paribus,* will move the budget line to a
    point of tangency with a (lower/higher) indifference curve.

12. Successive increases in real income will shift the budget line _____*upward*_____,
    and the several points of tangency with (higher/lower) indifference curves will enable us
    to derive a line call an _____*income consumption*_____ line.

13. (a) To construct a demand curve for a certain commodity A from an indifference map, we put
    on the two axes of the map: _____*quality of A*_____ and
    _____*values of all other goods*_____.

    (b) As the price of A falls, the budget line's tangencies with (higher/lower) indifference
    curves produce a line called _____*price - consumption line*_____.

14. Consumers tend to value a commodity less the more of it they have; this is called diminish-
    ing _____*marginal utility*_____. Thus, with constant incomes, consumers are usually un-
    willing to buy more of a product beyond their present rate unless
    _____*price fall*_____.

15. (a) If the marginal utility of a good is zero, a household will be willing to pay a price
    of _____*zero*_____ for it.

    (b) A free good, one so plentiful as to have no price, will be used up to the point where
    its marginal utility is _____*zero*_____.

16. A household maximizing the utility or satisfaction obtained with a given income will allo-
    cate its spending among commodities so that the last dollar spent on each brings equal
    _____*marginal utility*_____.

17. The more rapidly the marginal utility of extra units of a particular good falls, the
    (greater/less) will be the elasticity of demand.

## APPENDIX

18. A fall in the price of a commodity, *ceteris paribus,* will lead to more of it being sold as
    a result of two effects: _____ and _____.

19. The substitution effect of a price fall always leaves the amount demanded either the same
    or _____ than before.

20. The income effect of a price, if positive, will result in a (greater/smaller) quantity de-
    manded.

21. For a good to have an upward-sloping demand curve, the income effect must be both
    _____ and _____ than the substitution effect.

---

If you have not answered all questions correctly, review the text in order to be sure that
you have all of the important concepts clearly in mind before going on to the next chapter.

1. income, price; real  2. prices; opportunity  3. the price of *Y*  4. parallel shift outward;
slope of line changes; no change; line shifts to left  5. $15; $10; 1½B; 1½B  6. has risen;
has fallen; cannot tell  7. the same total satisfaction  8. greater  9. rate of substitution;
½  10. budget line; prices  11. lower  12. outward; higher; income consumption  13. quantity
of A, value of all other goods; higher, price-consumption line  14. marginal utility; the
price falls  15. zero; zero  16 marginal utility  17. less  18. substitution; income
19. greater  20. greater  21. negative; larger

# MULTIPLE-CHOICE QUESTIONS

1. A change in household income will always shift the budget line parallel to itself if
   (a) money prices stay constant
   (b) relative prices stay constant with money prices changing by the same percentage as income
   (c) real income stays constant
   (d) prices change in the same direction

2. Halving all absolute prices, *ceteris paribus,* has the effect of
   (a) halving real income
   (b) halving money income
   (c) changing relative prices
   (d) doubling real income

3. A change in one absolute price, with all other things remaining constant, will
   (a) shift the budget line parallel to itself
   (b) change money income
   (c) cause the budget line to change its slope
   (d) have no effect on real income

4. An indifference curve includes
   (a) constant quantities of one good with varying quantities of another
   (b) the prices and quantities of two goods that can be purchased for a given sum of money
   (c) all combinations of two goods that will give the same level of satisfaction to the household
   (d) combinations of goods whose marginal utilities are equal

5. Households may attain consumption on a higher indifference curve by all but which of the following?
   (a) an increase in money income
   (b) a reduction in absolute prices
   (c) a proportionate increase in money income and in absolute prices
   (d) a change in relative prices caused by a reduction in one price

6. The slope of the budget line with product Y on the vertical axis and product X on the horizontal axis is
   (a) $-(P_Y/P_X)$
   (b) $-(X/Y)$
   (c) $-(Y/X)$
   (d) $-(P_X/P_Y)$

7. Where the budget line is tangent to an indifference curve,
   (a) equal amounts of goods give equal satisfaction
   (b) the ratio of prices of the goods must equal the marginal rate of substitution
   (c) the prices of the goods are equal
   (d) the household has revealed a preference for that combination of goods

8. Indifference curve theory assumes that
   (a) buyers can measure satisfaction
   (b) buyers can identify preferred combinations of goods, without necessarily being able to measure their satisfaction
   (c) buyers always behave consistently
   (d) all buyers have the same preference patterns

9. The hypothesis of diminishing marginal utility states that
   (a) the less of a commodity one is consuming, the less the utility obtained by an increase in its consumption
   (b) the more of a commodity one is consuming, the more the utility obtained by an increase in its consumption
   (c) the more of a commodity one is consuming, the less the utility obtained by an increase in its consumption
   (d) marginal utility cannot be measured, but total utility can

10. According to utility theory, for a consumer who is maximizing total satisfaction, $MU_a/MU_b$
    (a) equals $p_a/p_b$
    (b) equals $p_b/p_a$
    (c) will not necessarily be related to relative prices
    (d) equals $TU_a/TU_b$

$$\frac{MU_a}{MU_b} = \frac{p_a}{p_b}$$

11. Elasticity of demand
    (a) varies inversely with total utility
    (b) varies inversely with marginal utility
    (c) is less, the greater the substitution effect
    (d) is greater when marginal utility declines slowly rather than rapidly

12. The "paradox of value" is that
    (a) people are irrational in consumption choices
    (b) the total utilities yielded by commodities do not necessarily have a relationship to their market values
    (c) value has no relationship to utility schedules
    (d) free goods are goods that are essential to life

---

Answers to multiple-choice questions: 1(a)   2(d)   3(c)   4(c)   5(c)   6(d)   7(b)   8(b)   9(c)
10(a)   11(d)   12(b)

---

# EXERCISES

1. *Budgeting and Price Changes.* From 1920 to 1940, consumer prices were generally declining or stable; from 1940 to 1970, consumer prices were occasionally stable but usually rose. This is shown in the table below for food and for all items but food, where prices are expressed in 1957-1959 dollars (i.e., 1957-1959 index = 100). Representative budgets based on the disposable income for an employed family are also shown.
   (a) Draw budget lines for 1920, 1940, and 1970 on the graph and complete the table below. Each unit of food and of items other than food is the amount that could be purchased in 1957-1959 for $1. For example, for each $100 of income, 100/.70 or 143 units of food could be bought in 1920.

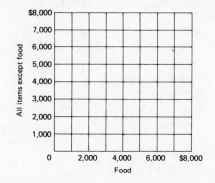

| | Price Indexes | | Family | Food | "Other" |
| | Food | "Other" | Income | Intercepts | Intercepts |
|---|---|---|---|---|---|
| 1920 | 70 | 70 | $ 2,200 | _____ | _____ |
| 1940 | 40 | 52 | 2,000 | _____ | _____ |
| 1970 | 135 | 135 | 10,000 | _____ | _____ |

(b) Does the graph indicate that absolute price declines can be the equivalent of rises in income? Explain briefly.

(c) The budget line for which year is the least steep? _____ Explain.

2. *Deriving Household Demand Curves from Indifference Maps*

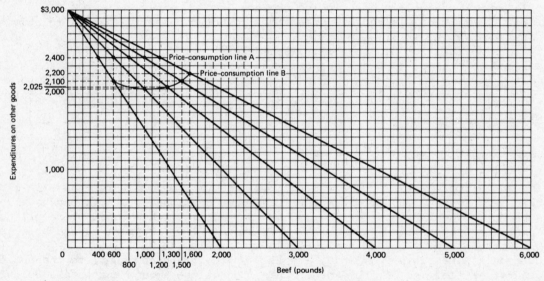

(a) On the graph above, sketch in (using two different colors) indifference maps that could lead to price-consumption lines A and B.

(b) From the price-consumption lines, derive demand curves A and B and enter on the chart at the top of the next page.

(c) What is price elasticity of demand for household A? _____
At what price does elasticity of demand for household B approach 1?

| P | $Q_A$ | $Q_B$ | Total Expenditure on Beef A | B |
|---|---|---|---|---|
| $1.50 | ___ | ___ | ___ | ___ |
| 1.00 | ___ | ___ | ___ | ___ |
| .75 | ___ | ___ | ___ | ___ |
| .60 | ___ | ___ | ___ | ___ |
| .50 | ___ | ___ | ___ | ___ |

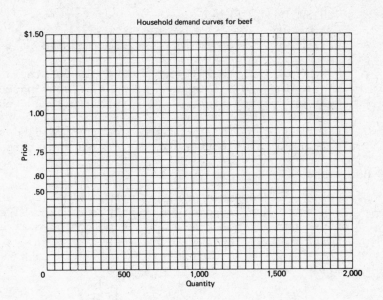

Household demand curves for beef

# PROBLEMS

## 1. CHANGES IN FAMILY CONSUMPTION PATTERNS

The following table shows how a "typical" family in the income range $7000-$8000 spent their income on certain items, for the years 1959 and 1969. (Assume that the family nominal income is $7500.)

| | 1959 | 1969 |
|---|---|---|
| Food | $1575 | $1500 |
| Clothing | 750 | 580 |
| Transportation | 460 | 1005 |
| Alcohol and tobacco | 315 | 290 |

*Source; Family Expenditure Survey,*
1959 and 1969, Statistics Canada.

Over the same period, the percentage increases in the price index for these commodities and services were as follows:

| | |
|---|---|
| Food | 26% |
| Clothing | 28% |
| Transportaion | 22% |
| Alcohol and tobacco | 27% |

## Questions

1. Over this period the general increase in the price level was 28 percent; hence a family with income of $7500 in 1969 was less wealthy than in 1959. How has the real consumption pattern for these goods changed over this period?

2. Can you estimate the price elasticity of demand for these goods with the data that you have? If so, indicate how you would make the estimate. If not, indicate why it cannot be done.

## 2.  THE SWITCH TO BREAD

An April 3, 1975, report in *The Globe and Mail* stated that:

> In the past 15 years, with rising disposable income per capita consumption of bread was decreasing and consumption of meat increasing but the trend has levelled off. . . . With meat prices too high . . . we've all arranged our food budget a little.

The report went on to say that per capita bread consumption had declined over the past 15 years from 90 to 75 pounds but was now on the increase.

## Questions

1. Using indifference-curve analysis, illustrate what has been happening as money income rises and meat becomes relatively more expensive in recent years. (Assume that, for the first two periods, the relative prices of meat and bread do not change and that, in the third period, the change occurs.)

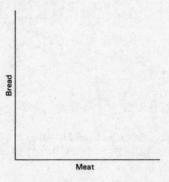

2. With reference to bread, what is the direction of the income effect between the first and second periods?

3. If, because of the recent recession (1974-1975), nominal incomes were to fall, what do you think would happen to the amount of bread consumed per capita, assuming no change in relative prices?

# 10

# Demand Theory in Action

## KEY CONCEPTS AND DEFINITIONS

1. In terms of price changes, goods which are <u>substitutes</u> tend to have an elastic demand, but as a group, demand may well be inelastic.
2. Luxury goods tend to be <u>income elastic</u>; basic goods or "necessities" are income elastic.
3. The measurement of demand schedules requires careful statistical analysis to ensure we are actually measuring the quantity demanded at a given price.
4. Consumer behavior may, from time to time, be irrational on the part of households. Or, there may be some households that behave in an irrational manner all the time. Both of these possibilities are consistent with a downward-sloping demand curve which only requires that most households behave in a rational manner at a given moment.
5. Empirical knowledge of the response of households to income changes is essential to predicting long-term commodity demands.

| CHECKLIST | Make certain that you also understand the following concepts: identification problem; Giffen good; conspicuous consumption good; perfectly inelastic demand. |
|---|---|

## REVIEW QUESTIONS

1. The most common use of the theory of demand is to predict the market behavior of (individual households/the aggregate of all households).

2. The downward slope of the demand curve requires that (all/most/some) households behave according to the theory.

3. (a) An upward-sloping demand curve would mean that, if the price of a good rose, people would buy (more/less) of it.
   (b) This may be true of a few goods called _____Giffen_____ goods, which are (normal/inferior) goods that take a (large/small) part of the household budget.

4. (a) Evidence indicates that income elasticities are (fairly stable/very unstable) over time.
   (b) Income elasticities seem to follow (the same/different) patterns in different countries of the West.

5. Low income elasticity for food seems to be (the rule/the exception) in most advanced industrial countries.

6. In production, machines and their operators are used together, so they are _complimentary_
   _____ goods; a fall in the price of one leads to a ___rise_____
   in the demand for the other.

7. Changes in taste are (measurable/unmeasurable); we (should avoid using/feel free to use)
   them to explain every departure from what the theory of demand would predict.

8. In the attempt to measure and plot actual demand curves, use of pairs of actual price and
   quantity sold will result in an "identification problem" if there has been a shift in
   (the demand curve/the supply curve/both curves).

---

If you have not answered all questions correctly, review the text in order to be sure that
you have all of the important concepts clearly in mind before going on to the next chapter.

1. the aggregate of all households  2. most  3. more; "Giffen," inferior, large  4. fairly
stable; the same  5. the rule  6. complementary; rise  7. unmeasurable; should avoid using
8. both curves

---

# MULTIPLE-CHOICE QUESTIONS

1. Which one of the following variables, which cannot be measured directly, could be easily
   misused as an alibi whenever it appeared that the theory of demand had been refuted?
   (a) income
   (b) supply
   (c) tastes
   (d) price

2. A series of observations in which the lower the price, the lower the quantity sold, could
   represent all but one of the following:
   (a) an unchanged supply with a changing demand
   (b) a conventional demand with a changing supply
   (c) the demand for a "Giffen" good with a changing supply
   (d) a changing supply and a changing demand

3. To demonstrate that elasticities are not stable, it is necessary to
   (a) give at least three or four good reasons why they should not be stable
   (b) show that two elasticities of demand for the same commodity are not exactly the same
   (c) demonstrate their instability by logical, deductive reasoning
   (d) investigate the matter by measuring elasticities over time

4. Demand studies have indicated that the price elasticities of demand for most foodstuffs
   (a) are less than 1
   (b) are greater than 1
   (c) are of unitary elasticity
   (d) have no general tendency that has been noted

5. The category of expenditures classed as meals purchased at restaurants
   (a) has been observed to have low income elasticities
   (b) has been observed to have high income elasticities
   (c) has been observed to have negative income elasticities
   (d) shows no consistent relationship with income

---

Answers to multiple-choice questions: 1(c)   2(b)   3(d)   4(a)   5(b)

## EXERCISES

1. By mid 1977, Canadian lumber prices had risen substantially compared with earlier in the year. It was stated at the time that the price rise was due to increased U.S. demand for housing and a reduction in the inventories on the part of Canadian forest industries which led to reduced supplies in the short run.

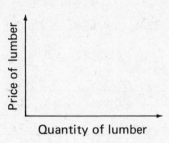

(a) Illustrate graphically what happened to this market between early and mid 1977.
(b) from the lumber producers' point of view, why would it be important to know what the elasticity of lumber is?

(c) If builders thought that the price was going to be even higher in six to eight months time, what action might they take and what effect would this have on the market?

2. Suppose the graph on the left below shows a sample of household gasoline consumption patterns over the 1960 to 1973 period while the graph on the right illustrates a sample pattern for the 1974 to 1977 period.

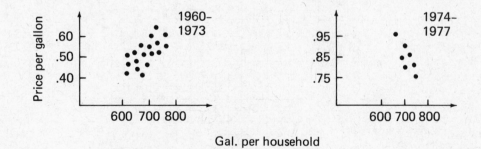

(a) What major factor, not considered in the graph, makes it possible to state that these curves are not accurate reflections of price elasticities?

(b) Given the answer in (a), why is the 1974-1977 curve likely to be more of a reflection of the price elasticity of gasoline?

## Problems

### 1. REAL PER CAPITA CONSUMPTION AND REAL PER CAPITA INCOME

The table below shows per capita real consumption of three commodities or commodity groups. along with data on real per capita income.

| Year | Categories of Spending (per capita) | | | Real Per Capita Disposable Income |
|------|------|------|------|------|
| | Food and Non-alcoholic Beverages | Alcohol | Automobiles | |
| 1960 | 338 | 64 | 71 | 2009 |
| 1961 | 330 | 65 | 73 | 1967 |
| 1962 | 330 | 66 | 84 | 2083 |
| 1963 | 330 | 69 | 94 | 2132 |
| 1964 | 340 | 69 | 107 | 2179 |
| 1965 | 343 | 74 | 122 | 2293 |
| 1966 | 338 | 78 | 126 | 2388 |
| 1967 | 351 | 82 | 126 | 2446 |
| 1968 | 347 | 81 | 134 | 2513 |
| 1969 | 359 | 84 | 137 | 2576 |
| 1970 | 373 | 90 | 114 | 2609 |
| 1971 | 391 | 98 | 132 | 2779 |
| 1972 | 404 | 104 | 149 | 2978 |
| 1973. | 412 | 114 | 174 | 3175 |
| 1974 | 418 | 116 | 170 | 3296 |

*Source:* Statistics Canada, *Natioanl Income and Expenditures Accounts*, Cat. 13-531.

### Questions

1. Graph the relationship between real per capita income and each of the per capita consumption columns.

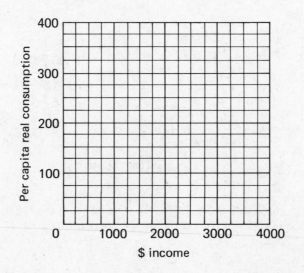

2. If we assume that consumption was equal to demand, calculate the income elasticity of demand for each commodity over the 1960-1974 period.

3. Does the income elasticity confirm the theory suggested in the textbook?

## 2. PER CAPITA CONSUMPTION

In the table below are annual per capita consumption data on pork and eggs along with the price change for each good in the years noted.

Per Capita Consumption and Price Change

| Years | Pork | Price Change | Years | Eggs | Price Change |
|-------|------|--------------|-------|------|--------------|
| 1964 | 51.8 lb. | | 1963 | 32.1 doz. | |
| 1965 | 47.9 lb. | +11.4% | 1964 | 32.0 doz. | -13.7% |
| 1970 | 58.7 lb. | | 1966 | 30.7 doz. | |
| 1971 | 68.3 lb. | -16.9% | 1967 | 31.3 doz. | -15.6% |
| 1974 | 59.4 lb. | | 1972 | 30.8 doz. | |
| 1975 | 50.9 lb. | +28.0% | 1973 | 29.2 doz. | +44.4% |

*Source: Handbook of Food Expenditure, Price and Consumption,* Agriculture Canada, 1977.
*Note:* The years were deliberately selected to ensure a substantial change in the price of the commodity.

### Questions

1. Assume that the change in per capita income from one year to the next has a negligible impact on per capita spending of selected food items and that the short-run response is to price fluctuations. Calculate the price elasticity of demand for the pairs of years above for each commodity.

2. What do these elasticities suggest about the importance of the two products in family consumption patterns.

3. Do these elasticities confirm demand theory?

# 11

# The Firm, Production, and Cost

## KEY CONCEPTS AND DEFINITIONS

1. The firm in Canada can assume one of several legal structures, each one having a particular bearing on the liability of owners/managers for debts incurred, the ability to raise funds for capital expenditure and the dispersion of actual ownership.

2. In a modern corporation, the wider the distribution of ownership, the less influence any one shareholder has on decision making in that firm.

3. The goals of a firm may be many, but of considerable importance is the objective of maximizing profit.

4. The combination of inputs or factors of production in a manner that produces the most output with a minimum of inputs is said to be a technologically efficient method of production.

5. An economically efficient use of inputs refers to one that minimizes factor costs and hence depends on technological efficiency and the price factors.

6. Opportunity cost is a concept used to measure the benefit foregone by not doing something in its best alternative use.

7. Physical assets of a firm such as building and machinery wear out eventually in the process of being used to produce an output. The annual wear and tear on assets is called depreciation and the monetary value of that wear and tear is a depreciation cost chargeable to the firm.

8. The meaning of profits depends on what is included in revenue and costs. It is possible to have a situation where, in an economic sense, a firm has not profit while in an accounting sense, there is profit. This occurs because the accounting definition does not include as a cost, the necessary return to capital for opportunity cost and risk.

| CHECKLIST | Make certain that you also understand the following concepts: firm; single proprietorship; partnership; corporation; limited liability; dividends, factors of production (inputs); capital and capital goods; roundabout production; cost; imputed cost; normal profit; interest; interest rate. |
|---|---|

## REVIEW QUESTIONS

1. In predicting the behavior of firms in the market, it is assumed that large firms have (the same/different) motivation than small ones do.

2. If a person owns his own business, it is called a _single proprietorship_.

62

3. In a general partnership firm of two partners, one of them would be liable for (all/half) of the firm's debts.

4. To collect an unpaid debt from a corporation, one would sue (the owners/the company).

5. (a) The most important aspect of a corporation from the point of view of its owners is that their liability is _____ limited _____.
   (b) This means that the risk of putting your money into shares of a corporation would tend to be (greater/less) than investing in a partnership.

6. It is assumed that firms make decisions so as to make their profits (satisfactory/ a maximum).

7. Basically, all production is made with the services of three kinds of inputs or factors: _____ land _____, _____ labour _____, _____ capital _____.

8. The process of producing machines with which to produce other machines with which to produce consumer goods is called _____ roundabout production _____.

9. If an electric typewriter permits a student to type 10 percent faster than with a mechanical typewriter, it is _____ technological _____ efficient but not necessarily _____ economical _____ efficient.

10. Because economic efficiency is affected by the costs of inputs, the firm must consider not only the technical efficiency of various methods but also the _____ opportunity cost _____ of the inputs.

11. Profits from production consist of the difference between the value of the outputs and the _____ value of inputs _____.

12. If you own a summer cottage which you could rent for July and August to some family for a net gain of $600 after expenses and taxes, the opportunity cost of living in it yourself for the summer is _____ $600 _____.

13. The cost of using owned rather than purchased or hired factors in production is called an _____ imputed _____ cost; it is estimated by the earnings they could have received in _____ their best estimated employment _____.

14. If a firm's machinery has no possible alternative use, its opportunity cost is _____ zero _____.

15. The loss in value of a capital asset over time is called _____ depreciation _____.

16. In making profit-maximizing decisions, a firm should compare present and expected returns or benefits with (past/present and future) costs.

17. The extra return on money put into a venture to compensate for the possibility of not getting it back is considered a return for taking _____ risk _____.

18. (a) If in its present production a firm is earning a lower rate of return than it could earn if its factors were used in their best alternative use, an economist would say that its profits are _____ negative _____.
   (b) If that same firm shows an excess of revenues over money costs, its owners will probably consider that profits are _____ positive _____ but inadequate.

19. To most economists, dividend payments sufficient to keep shareholders from taking their invested money capital out of the business would be included in (cost/profit). Some economists would refer to such dividend payments as _____ normal profit _____.

20. (a) In a free market with profit-maximizing firms, it is predicted that resources will be reallocated into an industry where economic profits are (zero/positive).

(b) A firm that shows profits to an accountant or to the Internal Revenue Service is not necessarily making _____*economic*_____ profits.

## APPENDIX

21. (a) Balance sheets report the assets and liabilities of a firm (over a period/at a moment) of time; they thus measure a (stock/flow).

(b) Income statements show the stream of revenues and expenditures (over a period/at a moment) of time; they thus measure a (stock/flow).

22. Mr. Maykby's company showed a profit on its income statement because he had neglected these imputed costs: (a) _____; (b) _____;
(c) _____.

---

If you have not answered all questions correctly, review the text in order to be sure that you have all of the important concepts clearly in mind before going on to the next chapter.

1. the same  2. single proprietorship  3. all  4. the company  5. limited; less  6. a maximum  7. land; labor; capital  8. roundabout  9. technically; economically  10. prices  11. value of the inputs  12. $600  13. imputed; their best alternative employment  14. zero  15. depreciation  16. present and future  17. risks  18. negative; positive  19. cost; normal profits  20. positive; economic  21. at a moment; stock  over a period; flow  22. his own services; interest on his own money; part of depreciation

---

## MULTIPLE-CHOICE QUESTIONS

1. Economically efficient methods of production have which of the following relationships to technologically efficient methods?
   (a) All technologically efficient methods are economically efficient.
   (b) All economically efficient methods are technologically efficient.
   (c) Some economically efficient methods are not technologically efficient.
   (d) Both (a) and (b) are true because economically efficient and technologically efficient methods must coincide.

2. Which of the following groups of claimants would be the last to have their claims honored in a bankruptcy?
   (a) bondholders
   (b) commercial creditors
   (c) common stockholders
   (d) employees owed back wages

3. Limited liability for the claims against a firm is an advantage for
   (a) single proprietors
   (b) corporate shareholders
   (c) paid employees
   (d) general partners in a partnership

4. Which of the following is *not* an advantage of the corporate form of business organization?
   (a) limited liability
   (b) separate legal existence
   (c) close identification of owners with management
   (d) relative ease of obtaining capital funds

5. The difference between economic profits and normal profits is that
   (a) normal profits are smaller
   (b) normal profits are necessarily larger for all firms
   (c) normal profits are part of opportunity cost, whereas economic profits are returns in excess of opportunity costs
   (d) normal profits take into account monopoly power; economic profits do not

6. If you give up a full-time job to go to college, the major cost is
   (a) tuition and fees
   (b) room and board
   (c) the income you could have received from employment
   (d) social and miscellaneous expenses

7. We can be *certain* of the usefulness of opportunity-cost concepts when our purpose is
   (a) to help a firm make the best decision it can to achieve maximum profits
   (b) to predict the responses of the firm to a change in conditions
   (c) to describe the firm's actual behavior
   (d) to predict the money costs of a firm's activities

8. The major role of economic profits, as seen in this chapter, is
   (a) to provide income for shareholders
   (b) to prodive income for entrepreneurs
   (c) to act as a signal to firms concerning the desirability of devoting resources to a particularly activity
   (d) to encourage labor to reform the system

9. "Profits are necessary for the survival of Canadian business." This chapter
   (a) disagrees with this viewpoint entirely
   (b) accepts this viewpoint but defines the necessary profits as costs
   (c) accepts this viewpoint without qualification or clarification
   (d) does not consider the subject

10. Inputs to productive processes
    (a) can be the outputs of other firms
    (b) are solely land and labor
    (c) can be clearly distinguished from factors of production
    (d) consist primarily of capital equipment in a capitalistic society

11. Economic theory frequently assumes that firms try to maximize profits
    (a) because firms always maximize profits
    (b) because firms ought to maximize profits to be fair to their stockholders
    (c) because use of this simple assumption has frequently led to accurate predictions
    (d) because economists wish thus to criticize the greed of firms

12. Depreciation is defined as the loss of value of an asset associated with its use in production, and thus it
    (a) is clearly a cash cost
    (b) is a function only of wear and tear in use
    (c) is not an economic cost if the asset has no market value or alternative use
    (d) does not apply to used equipment

---

Answers to multiple-choice questions: 1(b)   2(c)   3(b)   4(c)   5(c)   6(c)   7(a)   8(c)   9(b)
10(a)   11(c)   12(c)

# EXERCISES

1. Assume that there are two basic methods of producing vegetables for sale from a garden plot, and that the grower can sell all output at a given price. One method involves hand tools and labour, the other, power tools and labour. The following information gives an idea of the production processes involved. (Output from the garden is proportional to the size of the lot.)

| Garden Size (square feet) | Man-Hours to Produce Output | |
|---|---|---|
| | Hand Tools | Power Tools |
| 200 | 50 | 20 |
| 500 | 125 | 50 |
| 1000 | 250 | 100 |
| 2000 | 500 | 200 |

*Note:* (1) The hand tools are depreciated at $10 per year; (2) the power tools are depreciated at $300 per year; (3) labour cost is $4 per hour.

(a) At what garden size is it economically efficient to use power tools?

(b) If the price of labour declined to $3 per hour, would this affect the answer in (a)? How?

2. (This is a true story: Only the numbers have been changed to protect the business.) In the early 1970s, an enterprising student decided to enter the paper and glass recycling business. He left university, where he had been studying economics, and set about establishing a business, using his meagre savings, to collect and deliver used paper and glass to paper mills and glass using firms. His (hypothetical) monthly costs and revenues were:

| Costs | | Revenue | |
|---|---|---|---|
| Rent of old warehouse | $250 | 12 tons of paper at $50 per ton | $600 |
| Depreciation of truck | 100 | 1000 pounds of glass at $.40 per pound | 400 |
| Labour (other than his own) | 300 | | |
| Miscellaneous | 100 | | |

Shortly after being in business, large provincewide companies in the scrap business entered the recycling business. The buyers of used paper and glass were flooded with material, and the price of used paper plummeted to $30 per ton. Large companies simply intensified the use of capital in the recycling business to cut costs.

Our young entrepreneur sought to increase the capital intensity of his firm and upgrade the quality of his capital but was unable to find anyone who would lend him the money to do so at less than an exhorbitant rate of interest. He closed his business and returned to complete his degree in economics.

(a) Why did this business feel the need to enter truck depreciation as a cost?

(b) What was the level of monthly accounting profits for the business before the price decline? What is inappropriate about using this figure as a profit figure?

(c) Given that the owner of the business worked 40 hours per week, do you think there were any "excess profits" in the firm?

(d) What was the opportunity cost of going back to university?

(e) The owner was unable to borrow funds for renovating his business. What does this say about the financial market's view of such an operation as the kind discussed above?

## PROBLEM

### STOCKS AND BONDS

Listed below are selected stock and bond prices, and other information relating to certain securities listed on the Toronto Stock Exchange.

STOCKS

| 1975 High | 1975 Low | Company | Recent Dividend | Last Price 6/17/75 | Latest Price |
|-----------|----------|---------|-----------------|--------------------|--------------|
| 48 3/8 | 43 3/4 | Bell Telephone | $3.44 | 45 | |
| 44 3/4 | 34 5/8 | Bank of Nova Scotia | 1.60 | 44 3/4 | |
| 29 3/4 | 26 | Steel Co. of Canada | 1.30 | 27 5/8 | |
| 4.10 | 1.75 | Koffler | 0.10 | 3.45 | |

BONDS

| Corporation or Government | Recent Bid Price | Contractual Interest | Latest Bid Price |
|---------------------------|------------------|----------------------|------------------|
| Government of Alberta (1991) | $ 86.00 | 7 7/8% | |
| Seagrams Distillers (1995) | 102.50 | 10 7/8% | |
| Government of Canada (1983) | 80.38 | 4 1/2% | |
| Ontario Hydro (2000) | 102.25 | 10 1/4% | |

Questions

1. For the stocks above, what was the dividend as a percent of price on June 17, 1975? Find
   out the latest stock price and estimate the dividend as a percent of this latest price.

2. What might you infer about Bell Telephone from its dividend and its price fluctuations?
   What about Koffler?

3. Compute the present rate of return on the bonds listed above (contractual interest divided
   by the latest bond price). Why do you think that Government of Canada bonds yield the lowest rate? Compare these returns using the latest bid price on the above bonds.

4. Why do you think it is usually the case that the actual rate of return on stocks, measured
   by dividend divided by price, is less than the rate of return on bonds?

# 12

## Production and Cost in the Short Run

### KEY CONCEPTS AND DEFINITIONS

1. If we consider a time horizon where a firm's fixed factors, such as a building, cannot be varied, the firm is operating in the short run. Those factors of production that can be varied in such a time horizon are called variable factors.

2. For the purpose of analyzing the firm in the short run, it is important that at least one important factor is fixed.

3. A long-run time horizon is said to exist when all factors are variable, but the technology of production is unchanged. If the latter is also allowed to change, the time horizon is said to be the very long run.

4. The relationship between factors of production and outputs is the production function.

5. For a given production process, an important concept is marginal productivity: the change in total product or output that occurs when one more variable factor is used in the production process.

6. The hypothesis of eventually diminishing returns or the law of diminishing returns describes the phenomena that if more and more of a variable factor is applied to fixed factors of production, the addition that this makes to total output starts to fall.

7. A firm must pay for both its fixed and variable factors of production. A fixed cost is one that does not vary with the level of output. Variable costs do change with output levels. A firm that wished to cut production by 10 percent would still have to pay rent for land, but its energy costs would decline.

8. If output is increased, costs will usually increase. The increase in total cost due to producing one more unit of output is called the marginal cost.

9. The law of diminishing returns showed that average product increased and then began to decrease as more labour (variable factor) was used. Each unit of labour, however, added the same amount of cost. Thus, average variable costs fall and then starts to increase.

10. Average total cost is the sum of average variable cost and average fixed cost. It will decline as output is expanded initially, but at some time the rising average variable cost will cause average total cost to rise.

| CHECKLIST | Make certain that you also understand the following concepts: total product; average product; point of diminishing average productivity; point of diminishing marginal productivity; total cost; average total cost; average fixed costs; capacity; excess capacity; diminishing returns; law of variable proportions. |
| --- | --- |

# REVIEW QUESTIONS

1. A production function relates the amount of output to *the factors of production*

2. The period of time over which one or more inputs cannot be varied is called the *short - run* .

3. The period of time over which all inputs may be varied, but technological methods of production are fixed, is called the *long - run* .

4. The period of time long enough for basic production methods to be varied is called the *very long - run* .

5. Factors and costs that do not vary in the short run, regardless of the amount of output produced, are called *fixed cost* factors and *fixed* costs. Factors and costs that change in amount as quantity of output changes are called *(direct) variable* costs.

6. In the short run, total output or product can be increased by adding variable factors to fixed factors. The amount added to total product by adding one more variable factor is called the *marginal product* of that factor. Total product divided by the quantities of variable factors used to produce it is called the *average product* of those factors.

7. The hypothesis of eventually diminishing returns states that, as variable factors are added to fixed factors, there will be at some point a decline in first the *marginal* and then the *average* product. When diminishing returns have set in, the proportions of factors being used are (more/less) efficient and the factors are (more/less) productive than at lower outputs.

8. The average product rises whtn the marginal product is (higher/lower) than the average, and falls when it is (higher/lower) than the average.

9. By applying factor prices paid or imputed to factor quantities used in production, we get *production cost* .

10. (a) To get *average cost* we divide *total cost* by *total output in units*
    (b) "Spreading overhead costs" is demonstrated by dividing increasing amounts of output into *the fixed cost* .
    (c) Average fixed costs plus average variable costs equal *average total cost* .
    (d) Marginal costs are not affected by changes in (variable/fixed) costs.

11. At low levels of output, average costs usually fall because *average fixed* costs are falling rapidly; as output increases, this is often offset by rising *average variable* costs, so that average costs eventually (rise/fall) in the short run.

12. When average product per variable factor is a maximum, average variable cost will be *at a minimum* .

13. The level of output at which short-run average cost is at a minimum is called *plant capacity* .

---

If you have not answered all questions correctly, review the text in order to be sure that you have all of the important concepts clearly in mind before going on to the next chapter.

1. the quantity of inputs used  2. short run  3. long run  4. very long run  5. fixed, fixed; variable or direct  6. marginal product; average product  7. marginal, average; less, less

8. higher; lower  9. production costs  10. (a) total cost, total output in units; (b) fixed costs; (c) average total costs, or average cost; (d) fixed  11. average  fixed, average variable, rise  12. at a minimum  13. plant capacity

## MULTIPLE-CHOICE QUESTIONS

1. The production function relates
   (a) cost to input
   (b) cost to output
   (c) wages to profits
   (d) inputs to outputs

2. Which of the following is an example of a production decision in the short run?
   (a) A contractor buys two additional cement mixers and hires two new drivers for them.
   (b) A contractor decides to work his crew overtime to finish a job.
   (c) A railroad decides to eliminate all passenger service.
   (d) A paper company takes only three weeks to install antipollution equipment.

3. Short-run average costs eventually rise because of
   (a) rising overhead costs
   (b) rising factor prices
   (c) falling marginal and average productivity
   (d) decreasing returns to scale

4. The hypothesis of eventually diminishing returns applies to production function
   (a) having at least one fixed factor
   (b) in the long run only
   (c) in the very long run preferably
   (d) in which inputs are applied in fixed proportions

5. Long-run decisions
   (a) do not affect short-run decisions
   (b) can consider all factors variable
   (c) are not very important because the long run is a succession of short runs
   (d) are taken with fewer alternatives open than in the case of short-run decisions

6. Plant capacity is
   (a) the output at which unit costs are a minimum
   (b) the maximum output possible for a firm
   (c) where unit costs are a maximum
   (d) where marginal cost begins to rise

7. In the short run a firm wishing to maximize profits or minimize losses will
   (a) shut down unless fixed costs are met by revenue
   (b) produce as much as possible
   (c) operate at the plant's capacity whenever possible
   (d) produce as long as revenue exceeds all variable costs

8. Which of the following necessarily declines continuously?
   (a) marginal cost
   (b) average fixed cost
   (c) average variable cost
   (d) total fixed cost

9. When average cost is declining,
   (a) marginal cost must be declining
   (b) marginal cost must be above average cost
   (c) marginal cost must be below average cost
   (d) marginal cost must be rising

10. The "law of diminishing returns" describes
    (a) the fact of inevitable eventual unprofitability
    (b) the reduction in revenue resulting from falling prices
    (c) the declining marginal productivity of productive factors
    (d) the decline in total output from a given production function

Answers to multiple-choice questions: 1(d)  2(b)  3(c)  4(a)  5(b)  6(a)  7(d)  8(b)  9(c)  10(c)

# EXERCISES

1. (a) The relationship between a variable input and output for a firm is shown in the first and second columns in the table below. Calculate the average and marginal productivity.

| Variable Input | Output | Average Product | Marginal Product |
|---|---|---|---|
| 1 | 20 | 20 | 20 |
| 2 | 60 | 30 | 40 |
| 3 | 120 | 40 | 60 |
| 4 | 200 | 50 | 80 |
| 5 | 270 | 54 | 70 |
| 6 | 324 | 54 | 54 |
| 7 | 364 | 52 | 40 |
| 8 | 384 | 48 | 20 |
| 9 | 396 | 44 | 12 |
| 10 | 404 | 40.4 | 8 |

(b) Graph the average and marginal product.

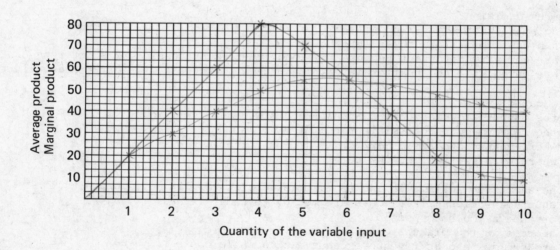

(c) The cost structure for the same firm is shown in the first and second columns at the top of the next page. Complete the columns in the table.

| Output | Fixed Cost | Total Variable Cost | Total Cost | Average Fixed Cost | Average Variable Cost | Average Total Cost | Marginal Cost |
|---|---|---|---|---|---|---|---|
| 20 | 168 | 80 | 248 | 8.40 | 4 | 12.40 | 12.40 |
| 60 _40_ | 168 | 160 | 328 | 2.80 | 2.67 | 5.47 | 2.00 |
| 120 _60_ | 168 | 240 | 408 | 1.40 | 2.00 | 3.40 | 1.33 |
| 200 _80_ | 168 | 320 | 488 | 0.84 | 1.60 | 2.44 | 1.00 |
| 270 _70_ | 168 | 400 | 568 | 0.62 | 1.48 | 2.10 | 1.14 |
| 324 _54_ | 168 | 480 | 648 | 0.52 | 1.48 | 2.00 | 1.48 |
| 364 _40_ | 168 | 560 | 728 | 0.46 | 1.54 | 2.00 | 2.00 |
| 384 _20_ | 168 | 640 | 808 | 0.44 | 1.67 | 2.10 | 4.00 |
| 396 _12_ | 168 | 720 | 888 | 0.42 | 1.82 | 2.24 | 6.67 |
| 404 _8_ | 168 | 800 | 968 | 0.42 | 1.98 | 2.40 | 10.00 |

(d) Graph the average-total-cost curve and the marginal-cost curve.

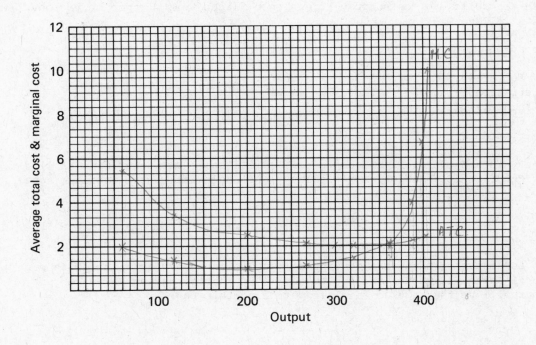

2. The marginal-cost schedule of a firm producing good X is shown in the graph at right.
  (a) Complete the table below (assume that the marginal cost from the graph applies to output level at the next highest whole number (e.g., *MC* of $3.50 applies to output of 1 unit).

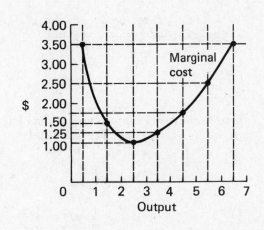

| Output | Total Cost | Average Total Cost |
|---|---|---|
| 1 | 3.5 | 3.5 |
| 2 | 5.0 | 2.5 |
| 3 | 6.0 | 2.0 |
| 4 | 7.25 | 1.81 |
| 5 | 9.00 | 1.80 |
| 6 | 11.50 | 1.92 |
| 7 | 15.00 | 2.14 |

(b) Calculate the average total cost schedule and plot this (approximately) on the graph at right.

(c) What is the capacity level of output?  5 units  of out put.

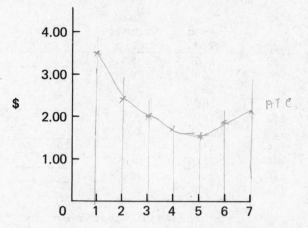

3. Suppose the following costs apply to a single flight from Toronto to Vancouver on a Boeing 707 with 180 seats.

| Depreciation | $1200 |
|---|---|
| Fuel | 2600 |
| Salary for crew | 3600 |
| Administration salaries | 2100 |
| Sales and publicity | 1100 |
| Office rent | 2800 |
| Interest on debt | 3500 |

(a) What are the average fixed costs (*AFC*) and average variable costs (*AVC*) for this flight (assume that fuel, crew salary, and depreciation are variable costs)?

$AFC = 52.78$

$AVC = 41.11$

(b) In establishing fares, the government regulation agency sets the price per seat at the level which allows the airline to cover *AFC* when operating at 50 percent of capacity. What will be the regular fare per person on this run?

$$\frac{52.78 \times 180}{90} = 105.56$$

(c) Given this price, what is the marginal cost to the airline of carrying the ninety-first passenger on the flight?

zero

(d) Should the airline agree to supply a charter flight for a group that offers to guarantee the sale of 140 tickets at $50 per seat? Explain.

Output $= 140 \times 50 = 7000$.
$+$
$40 \times 105.56 = 4222.4$

No. because the airline won't covered its input

4. A producer of a particular commodity finds that he has a total cost curve that can be described by the equation: $TC = \$50 + \$3Q + \$Q^2$.

   (a) Complete the columns below. [Hint: $(3Q + Q^2)$ is obviously variable costs, and \$50 is the fixed cost.]

| Q | FC | VC | TC | MC | AFC | AVC | ATC |
|---|----|----|----|----|-----|-----|-----|
| 0 | 50 | 0 | 50 | — | — | — | — |
| 1 | 50 | 4 | 54 | 4 | 50 | 4 | 54 |
| 2 | 50 | 10 | 60 | 6 | 25 | 5 | 30 |
| 3 | 50 | 18 | 68 | 8 | 16.67 | 6 | 22.67 |
| 4 | 50 | 28 | 78 | 10 | 12.5 | 7 | 19.50 |
| 5 | 50 | 40 | 90 | 12 | 10.0 | 8 | 18.00 |
| 6 | 50 | 54 | 104 | 14 | 8.33 | 9 | 17.33 |
| 7 | 50 | 70 | 120 | 16 | 7.14 | 10 | 17.14 |
| 8 | 50 | 88 | 138 | 18 | 6.25 | 11 | 17.25 |
| 9 | 50 | 108 | 158 | 20 | 5.56 | 12 | 17.56 |
| 10 | 50 | 130 | 180 | 22 | 5.00 | 13 | 18.00 |
| ... | | | | | | | |
| 20 | 50 | 460 | 510 | | 2.50 | 23 | 25.50 |

(b) At what output are total costs per unit (ATC) at a minimum?

   7

(c) What is the marginal cost at this output?

   16

(d) If, as shown above, there were only variable costs and no fixed costs, would MC be affected?

   No.

(e) By examining the table above, explain why ATC decreases to a minimum value and then starts to rise.

   It is because the average variable cost increases + offset the decreasing fixed average cost.

# PROBLEM

## THE RISING COST OF DRIVING AN AUTOMOBILE

On June 13, 1971, the *New York Times* reported that the American Automobile Association's "cost-of-driving index" had risen to \$1,550, an increase of \$102 over the 1969 level. The \$1,550 assumed 10,000 miles driven (the national average), made the calculations for full-sized Chevrolets (Impalas) with automatic transmission and power steering, and based the depreciation on a trade-in after four years.

   The average costs were as follows:

|  | Average per Mile (cents) | |
|---|---|---|
| Variable Costs | 1971 | 1969 |
| Gas and oil |  | 2.76 |
| Maintenance |  | .68 |
| Tires |  | .51 |
| Total per mile | 4.25 | 3.95 |

| Fixed Costs | Annually (dollars) | |
|---|---|---|
| Fire and theft insurance | $    62 | $    44 |
| Collision insurance | 125 | 102 |
| Liability insurance | 175 | 154 |
| License and registration | 25 | 24 |
| Depreciation | 738 | 729 |
| Total per year | $1,125 | $1,053 |

## Questions

1. Assuming that the total variable costs vary proportionally with output (this means that *AVC = MC*; why?), complete this cost output table for 1971.

| Output in Miles | TFC (dollars) | TVC | TTC | AFC | AVC = MC (cents) | ATC |
|---|---|---|---|---|---|---|
| 5,000 | $1,125 | 213 | 1338 | 22.5¢ | 4.25 | 26.75¢ |
| 10,000 | 1,125 | 425 | 1550 | 11.25¢ | 4.25 | 15.50¢ |
| 15,000 | 1,125 | 638 | 1763 | 7.50¢ | 4.25 | 11.75¢ |

2. Was it fair for firms to pay their employees 11 cents per mile for travel expenditures in 1971 in view of the average cost of driving?

yes

3. Assuming that gas and oil expenditures per mile had tripled by 1977 and all other costs had risen by 20 percent (over the 1971 figures), what would be a "fair" mileage compensation in 1977?

# 13

## Cost in the Long Run

1. In the long run, all factors are variable.
2. For two factors of production, the <u>cost-minimizing</u> use of these factors calls for a mix of factors such that the ratio of their marginal productivities equals the ratio of their prices.
3. It follows from 2 above that if <u>relative prices</u> of factors are altered, the method of production will change since factor inputs will have to be altered. This is known as the <u>principle of substitution</u>.
4. <u>Increasing returns</u>, where output expands faster than inputs as the scale of a plant is increased, is synonymous with decreasing costs where the <u>long-run average cost curve</u> is falling as the scale of the plant is increased. The long-run cost curve is horizontal when there are <u>constant returns</u>. Corresponding to increasing returns and decreasing costs are <u>decreasing returns</u> and <u>increasing costs</u>.
5. Shifts in the short-run average total cost curves are due to such things as changes in factor prices or technology.
6. An isoquant shows how two factors are combined to produce a given output. The rate at which one factor is substituted for another to maintain a constant output is the <u>marginal rate of substitution</u>, and it is equal to the ratios of the marginal products of the two factors.
7. Given factor prices and a fixed sum of money, an isocost line shows what amount of each of two factors can be used that will exhaust the fixed sum of money. The slope of that line will equal the relative prices of the two factors of production.
8. Cost minimization occurs at the tangency between an isoquant and isocost line, or where the ratio of the marginal products equals the ratio of the factor prices.
9. The notion of productivity or output per unit of input is an important factor in gauging technical change over time.
10. Long-run productivity increases stem from changes in factor proportions, new techniques of production, and improvements in factor input quality.

---

| CHECKLIST | Make certain that you also understand the following concepts: envelope cost curve; isoquant map; innovation; invention. |
|---|---|

# REVIEW QUESTIONS

1. The "long run" is defined as a situation in which _____all factors can be varied_____

2. A profit-maximizing firm will always try to choose the method of production of a given output that costs _____least_____. This means that it will equate the ratios of the marginal products of the factors of production to the ratio of _____prices of the factors_ of production_____

3. If the marginal product of capital rises, *ceteris paribus,* the firm will tend to use relatively (more/less) of it. If the price of labor rises, *ceteris paribus,* the firm will tend to substitute _____capital_____ for it.

4. The principle of substitution results in the greater use of factors that are (abundant/scarce) and therefore relatively (cheap/expensive). Thus the price system in a market economy acts to allocate factors so as to (waste/economize) scarce resources.

5. The long-run cost curve is determined by factor _____of (productions ) prices_____ and by the state of _____technology_____ in the industry.

6. Increasing returns mean that as output increases, long-run average costs are _____decreasing_____. This must be caused by either _____more efficient method_____ or _____lower factor prices_____, or both.

7. Decreasing returns mean that as output is increased, long-run average costs _____increase_____. This must be caused by _____rising factor prices_____, because no one would deliberately choose to expand with a less efficient plant that is already attainable.

8. If in the long run, with constant factor prices, output increases at exactly the same rate as inputs, average costs and returns will be _____constant returns_____.

9. Except for the point of tangency between them, the short-run average cost curve will be (above/below) the long-run average cost curve.

10. A rise in the price of any factor will shift all cost curves (upward/downward). Technological changes will shift cost curves (upward/downward).

---

If you have not answered all questions correctly, review the text in order to be sure that you have all of the important concepts clearly in mind before going on to the next chapter.

1. all factors can be varied  2. least; their prices  3. more; capital  4. abundant, cheap; economize  5. prices, technology  6. decreasing; more efficient methods of production, lower factor prices  7. increase; rising factor prices  8. constant  9. above  10. upward; downward

---

# MULTIPLE-CHOICE QUESTIONS

1. The long-run average cost curve
   (a) shows total output related to total input
   (b) assumes constant factor proportions throughout
   (c) reflects the least-cost production method for each output level
   (d) rises because of the "law" of diminishing returns

2. Constant long-run average costs for a firm mean that
   (a) there are greater advantages to small- rather than large-scale plants
   (b) an unlimited amount will be produced
   (c) any scale of production is as cheap per unit as any other
   (d) no addition of factors is taking place

3. Decreasing average costs for a firm as it expands plant size and output
    (a) result from decreasing returns to scale
    (b) results usually from the effects of increased mechanization and specialization
    (c) result from the increased complexity and confusion of rapid expansion
    (d) are a very rare case caused by exogenous events

4. If the marginal product of capital is six times that of labor and the price of capital is three times that of labor,
    (a) capital will be substituted for labor
    (b) labor will be substituted for capital
    (c) the price of capital will fall, of labor will rise
    (d) twice as much capital as labor will be employed

$$\frac{MP_k\ (6)}{MP_L} = \frac{P}{\ }$$

5. The long-run average cost curve is determined by
    (a) long-run demand
    (b) long-run supply
    (c) population growth and inflation
    (d) technology and input prices

6. Long-run decreasing returns are evidently the result of
    (a) rising factor prices
    (b) replication
    (c) "spreading the overhead"
    (d) incompetent management

7. A rise in labor cost relative to capital costs in an industry, *ceteris paribus*, will
    (a) lead to replacement of some workers by machines where possible
    (b) cause the industry to be unprofitable
    (c) necessarily increase long-run costs
    (d) tend to be offset by rising labor productivity

8. A firm facing long-run increasing returns should expand by
    (a) substituting labor for capital
    (b) replication
    (c) building smaller plants
    (d) building larger plants

9. An isocost line for two factors $C$ and $L$ (their respective prices are $P_C$ and $P_L$) could have which of the following equations?
    (a)   $LC = \$100$
    (b) $\$100 = P_C + P_L$
    (c) $\$100 = P_L L + P_C C$
    (d) $\$100 = P_L P_C$

10. If two factors $C$ and $L$ are graphed in the same unit scale with $C$ on the vertical axis and an isocost line has the slope = -2, then
    (a)   $P_L = 2P_C$
    (b) $P_C/P_L = 2$
    (c)   $C = 2L$
    (d)   $L = 2C$

11. At the point of tangency of this isocost line with an isoquant,
    (a) the desired factor combination has $2C$ for each $L$
    (b) the marginal product of labor is twice that of capital
    (c) the desired factor combination has $2L$ for each $C$
    (d) the marginal product of capital is twice that of labor

12. If firms are profit maximizers, we should not expect to find a competitive firm expanding
    its scale if it faces
    (a) increasing returns to scale
    (b) decreasing returns to scale
    (c) constant returns to scale
    (d) pecuniary returns to cost

---

Answers to multiple-choice questions: 1(c)   2(c)   3(b)   4(a)   5(d)   6(a)   7(a)   8(d)   9(c)
10(a)   11(b)   12(b)

---

# EXERCISES

1. At the beginning of some time period, it is observed that a firm producing 10,000 bottles
   of wine per month uses the following inputs of capital ($K$) and labor ($L$) per month:

   $K$ = 50 units
   $L$ = 1000 units

   The price of capital per unit is $20, and for labor the price is $4.
       As the firm increases its output over time, the following changes in the use of capi-
   tal and labor are observed:

   | Output per Month | $K$ | $L$ |
   |------------------|-----|-----|
   | 20,000 | 100 | 1800 |
   | 40,000 | 180 | 3000 |
   | 60,000 | 250 | 4000 |
   | 80,000 | 400 | 7200 |
   | 100,000 | 600 | 10000 |

   i) $\dfrac{MP_K}{MP_L} = \dfrac{50}{\frac{1000}{-70}} = \dfrac{20}{4} \cdot 5$

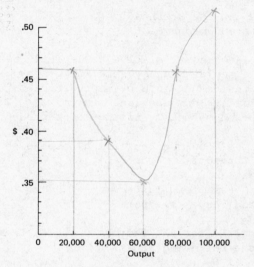

   (a) Calculate and graph the long-run average-cost curve.

   (b) At what output level do increasing returns come to an end?

   60,000.

   (c) What happens to the ratio of capital to labor inputs as output expands?

   $\dfrac{100}{1800} = \dfrac{1}{18}$

   (d) If the price of labor were increasing steadily over time, what might happen to the
       mix of labor and capital inputs as the firm expands? Justify your answer.

       The firm will use more capital relative to the use of
       the labour.

50/1000

50/1000 =

205/41

2. Below is a table showing hypothetical costs for a firm as it expands output and plant size.

| Output (units) | 100,000 | 200,000 | 300,000 | 400,000 | 500,000 |
|---|---|---|---|---|---|
| Materials | $ 50,000 | $100,000 | $150,000 | $200,000 | $250,000 |
| Labor | $100,000 | $180,000 | $260,000 | $340,000 | $440,000 |
| Capital (interest and depreciation) | $ 50,000 | $ 90,000 | $130,000 | $170,000 | $220,000 |
| Average cost | $2 | $1.85 | $1.80 | $1.98 | $1.82 |

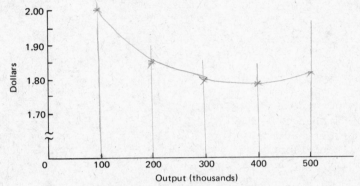

(a) Calculate the average cost for each level of output above and plot it on the graph.

(b) Returns to scale continue until what output is reached? ____400,000____

(c) Would you say that there seems to be substitution occurring or not? __No__

(d) Judging from these figures, what would you recommend that this firm do if it wants to produce output of 800,000 units? _Built two plant & produce 400,000 each._

3. The diagram to the right illustrates how various levels of output can be produced by different combinations of capital and labor

(a) If the ratio of the price of capital to that of labor were $L/K = 1/1$, how many units of capital and labor will the firm use to produce 100 units of output?

_( of capital & two of labor_

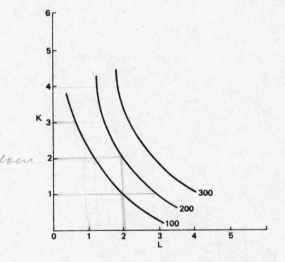

(b) If the price of capital per unit were to fall by 100 percent and the firm wished to produce 200 units of output, approximately how much capital and labor would it employ?

$\frac{L}{K} = \frac{2}{1}$     _Two units of each._

4. Suppose the input—output data for a firm are as shown in the table below.

|  | Labor Input | | | | |
|---|---|---|---|---|---|
|  | 1 | 2 | 3 | 4 | 5 |
| Capital Inputs 1 |  |  |  |  |  |
| 2 |  | 100* | 100 | 100 | 100 |
| 3 |  | 100 | 150 | 150 | 150 |
| 4 |  | 100 | 150 | 200 | 200 |
| 5 |  | 100 | 150 | 200 |  |

*Units of output.

(a) Draw the isoquant map for the three levels of output.

(b) What impact would a change in the relative factor prices have on the mix of capital and labor in the firm? Justify your answer.

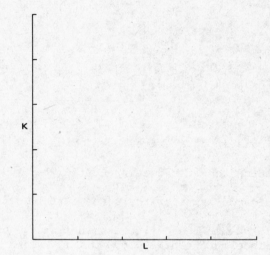

# 14

# Pricing in Competitive Markets

## KEY CONCEPTS AND DEFINITIONS

1. If the average revenue received from producing a certain output level does not at least equal the average variable cost at that level of output, the firm should not produce that output.
2. Marginal revenue is the addition to total revenue that occurs when one more unit of output is sold. If it is an advantage to produce at all, output should be expanded up to the level of output where marginal revenue equals marginal cost to maximize profits.
3. Under perfect competition, no firm can by itself influence the market price of the commodity which that firm produces. Thus the average revenue, a price of the product, must be assumed as given as far as the firm is concerned. The demand schedule for the firm is thus a horizontal line equal to the average revenue.
4. For the competitive firm, short-run equilibrium is achieved by adjusting output until the marginal cost equals the marginal revenue which is also the demand schedule to the firm. Thus the short-run supply curve for the firm is the marginal-cost curve or at least that portion above average variable cost (see 1 above).
5. By adding the supply schedules (curves) of each firm horizontally, we obtain the industry supply schedule (curve).
6. If a perfectly competitive industry generates profits, the ability of firms to enter the industry in response to profits will force prices down until profits are once again zero. If losses occur, some firms will leave the industry and the price will be forced up to a level sufficient to cover total costs.
7. In long-run equilibrium, profits cannot be increased through scale changes in plants, increasing the output of a given plant, or building more plants.
8. Changes in factor costs will influence the long-run industry supply curve. Rising supply price resulting in a rising-cost industry is often synonymous with rapid growth.

> | CHECKLIST | Make certain that you also understand the following concepts: market structure; equilibrium; price taker; freedom of entry and exit; competitive behavior; market; industry; total revenue; constant cost industry; declining industry. |

## REVIEW QUESTIONS

1. The number of firms in a market and the similarity of their products are two aspects of _market structure_ .

2. A behavioral rule for a profit-maximizing firm is that it should not produce at all unless total revenue exceeds or equals total _~~average~~ variable cost_.

3. A firm in perfect competition (~~has~~/has no) influence over the price it receives for its product; hence, it is called a _price taker_.

4. Such a firm can sell any amount of output, limited only by its capacity to produce, without lowering its price below the market price, but it will make no sales at all if it raises its price above the market, so its demand curve is _horizontal_ and its elasticity is, for all practical purposes, _infinity_. Its marginal revenue curve is the same as its _(price) demand curve_.

5. In most cases, beyond a certain output each additional unit adds more to costs than did the previous unit; in other words, _marginal_ cost is _rising_.

6. Therefore, if a firm wishes to maximize profits, it will expand or contract its output to the amount at which the marginal cost of that extra output _equals_ the price at which it can sell the extra output.

7. Whether or not the firm produces any output, it still has incurred _fixed_ costs. In deciding whether to produce at all in the short run, the profit-maximizing firm will (ignore/insist on covering) these costs. It will insist that its selling price at least covers average _variable_ cost.

8. If, for instance, production costs are $1 per unit in addition to the $1,000 of fixed costs already incurred, a selling price of _$1_ would be the minimum for which the firm should produce. If the firm did not produce, the total losses would be _$1,000_. If the market price were 80 cents and this firm produced 1,000 units, its total losses would be _1,200_. The firm would lose (more/less) by not producing at all.

9. The firm's short-run supply curve has the same shape as the firm's _marginal_ cost curve to the right of its intersection with the minimum of the average _variable_ cost curve.

10. If one store has much more business than another because it has a much better location, it incurs (more/less) rent than the other. If one firm has a manager more effective in keeping production costs down than has another firm, that manager will have a (higher/lower) salary. Thus, these factor advantages are costs to the advantaged firm, and we can therefore say that, according to this opportunity-cost principle, firms in a perfectly competitive industry will have (the same/~~differing~~) average costs.

11. In short-run equilibrium, with price = marginal cost, the firm will be making profits if market price exceeds average _total_ costs.

12. With such profits the _entry_ of new firms can be predicted until the price is driven down to the level of _average total_ costs. Short-run losses, on the other hand, should lead to the _exit_ of firms.

---

If you have not answered all questions correctly, review the text in order to be sure that you have all of the important concepts clearly in mind before going on to the next chapter.

1. market structure  2. variable cost  3. has no; price taker  4. horizontal, infinite; demand curve  5. marginal; rising  6. equals  7. fixed; ignore; variable  8. $1; $1,000; $1,200; less  9. marginal; variable  10. more; higher; the same  11. total  12. entry, average total; exit

# MULTIPLE-CHOICE QUESTIONS

1. A perfectly competitive firm does not try to sell more of its product by lowering its price below the market price because
   (a) this would be considered unethical price chiseling
   (b) its competitors will not permit it
   (c) its demand curve is inelastic, so total revenue will decline
   (d) it can sell all it wants to at the market price

2. If the market demand for wheat has an elasticity of 0.25,
   (a) an individual wheat farmer can increase his revenue by reducing output
   (b) nothing can be said about the elasticity of demand for a wheat farmer
   (c) revenue from wheat sales will rise with an increase of industry production
   (d) each wheat farmer, nevertheless, faces a highly elastic demand

3. Which is *not* a required characteristic of a perfectly competitive industry?
   (a) Consumers have no reason to prefer one firm's product to another.
   (b) There are enough firms so none can influence market price.
   (c) Any firm can enter or leave the industry.
   (d) Industry demand is highly elastic.

4. Long-run profits are incompatible with a perfectly competitive industry because
   (a) new firms will enter the industry and eliminate them
   (b) corporate income taxes eliminate such excess profits
   (c) competitive industries are too inefficient to be profitable
   (d) long-run increasing costs eliminate profits

5. In long-run equilibrium in an industry of perfectly competitive, profit-maximizing firms,
   (a) price will equal average variable cost
   (b) price will exceed marginal cost
   (c) price will equal average total cost
   (d) average fixed cost will be at a minimum

6. The conditions for long-run competitive equilibrium include all but one of the following for all firms:
   (a) $P = AVC$
   (b) $P = MC$
   (c) $P = AVC + AFC$
   (d) $P = LRATC$

7. If several firms in a competitive industry could achieve economies of large scale by doubling their outputs,
   (a) we predict that equilibrium will occur at double the present output
   (b) we predict there can be no equilibrium
   (c) we can say that the industry is not now in equilibrium and perhaps there will be no competitive equilibrium
   (d) we predict that the firms will prefer their present output rather than glut the market

8. In the short run, a profit-maximizing firm will produce additional units of a product as long as
   (a) price covers at least average fixed cost
   (b) additional revenue per unit exceeds additional cost per unit
   (c) total revenue is increasing
   (d) elasticity of demand is infinite

9. Equilibrium price and output in a market
   (a) are established where the amount people wish to buy equals the amount people wish to sell
   (b) depend entirely on cost
   (c) depend entirely on demand
   (d) are best described as the price existing at a particular time

---

Answers to multiple-choice questions: 1(d)   2(d)   3(d)   4(a)   5(c)   6(a)   7(c)   8(b)   9(a)

---

# EXERCISES

1. At present output levels, a competitive firm finds itself with the following:

   Output:        5,000 units      Fixed costs:       $2,000      Marginal cost: $1.25 and rising
   Market price:  $1.00            Variable costs:    $2,500

   (a) Is it maximizing profits? Why?
   (b) Should it produce more, produce less, or stay the same? _____

2. The graph shows the short-run cost situation of a hypothetical perfectly competitive, profit-maximizing firm. Fill in the blanks below.

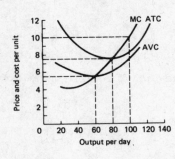

|  | If market price is | $10 | $7.50 | $5.50 |
|---|---|---|---|---|
| (a) | equilibrium output will be | ____ | ____ | ____ |
|  | At this output, | | | |
| (b) | total revenue is | ____ | ____ | ____ |
| (c) | total cost is | ____ | ____ | ____ |
| (d) | total profit is (+ or −) | ____ | ____ | ____ |
| (e) | marginal revenue is | ____ | ____ | ____ |
| (f) | marginal cost is | ____ | ____ | ____ |
| (g) | average total cost is | ____ | ____ | ____ |
| (h) | profit per unit is | ____ | ____ | ____ |

   (i) Why would we expect that neither $10 nor $5.50 will be the long-run market price?

3. Another competitive firm has the following:

   Output:        80 units
   Market price:  $10

   Average total costs are at minimum and are equal to $7.50.
   (a) What is marginal cost at this output? _____
   (b) Is the firm making profits? _____
   (c) Is it making maximum profits? _____
   (d) Should it change its output? _____
       (Refer to the diagram accompanying exercise 2.)

4. The diagram at the top of the next page illustrates the cost position of a firm operating in a perfectly competitive market, immediately following the introduction of a cost-saving innovation.
   (a) What initial advantage is this firm enjoying?


   (b) Can this advantage remain? Justify your answer by noting what will be taking place in the market as a whole.

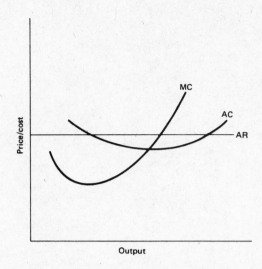

5. The supply (S) and demand (D) schedules for an industry are shown below in the figure on the left. The cost schedule for one firm in this industry is shown in the figure on the right.

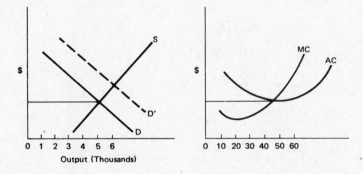

(a) Does the above information suggest that the industry is a perfectly competitive one? Give your reasons.

(b) If the market demand schedule were to shift to D', what is the initial impact on the price of output in this industry and on the profits of the firm?

(c) What change in the above diagram would be necessary to bring the firm back into a position of "normal profits?

# PROBLEM

## COMPETITION IN WORLD MARKETS

The "representative" Canadian firm in a perfectly competitive world market has the following cost and output schedule:

| Output | Total Cost | Average Cost | Marginal Cost | Average Cost (with tax) |
|--------|------------|--------------|---------------|-------------------------|
| 10,000 | $ 40,000 | $ | $ | $ |
| 20,000 | 60,000 | | | |
| 30,000 | 70,000 | | | |
| 40,000 | 80,000 | | | |
| 50,000 | 120,000 | | | |
| 60,000 | 180,000 | | | |

## Questions

1. Calculate the average- and marginal-cost schedules.

2. If the world price is roughly $2.25, what output would this firm produce?

3. Why would Canadian firms in this market strongly oppose a federal sales tax of 0.50 per unit of output?

Calculate the average-cost schedule that would occur if it were imposed.

# 15

## Pricing in Monopoly Markets

## KEY CONCEPTS AND DEFINITIONS

1. By definition, a <u>monopolist</u> is a single-seller market. Hence, the demand curve or average-revenue curve for the monopolist is the market-demand curve. The marginal revenue for the monopolist is always below the average revenue provided market demand is not infinitely elastic.
2. A monopolist will never set his price where marginal revenue is negative if he is a profit maximizer. Price will therefore be set on the elastic portion of the demand schedule.
3. Like selling in perfect competition, a monopolist will set a price where marginal cost equals marginal revenue. However, this is not likely to be where marginal cost equals average revenue.
4. The key to sustaining a monopoly is that there exist <u>barriers to entry</u> for new firms.
5. In actual fact, no firm is totally insulated from other products all the time, and this fact limits monopoly power. A measure of <u>monopoly power</u> is the degree to which one firm's decision on output-price affects the demand curve of other producers.
6. When different buyers pay different prices for the same commodity or when a single buyer pays different prices for different units of the commodity, <u>price discrimination</u> exists.
7. To be able to discriminate, a producer must be able to prevent the resale of his product and control the supply available to different buyers.
8. Price discrimination leads to specific predictions about total revenue to the producer but the overall consequences of price discrimination have complex positive and normative overtones.

| CHECKLIST | Make certain that you also understand the following concepts: collusion; equilibrium of a monopoly firm; concentration ratio; price discrimination; tacit collusion. |
|---|---|

## REVIEW QUESTIONS

1. The demand curve of a monopoly firm is the same as that of its ___industry___.
   Therefore, it must slope ___downward___.

2. If a monopoly firm aims to maximize its profits, its output will be set where its marginal ___cost revenue___ equals ___marginal___ cost.

3. The demand curve of a monopoly firm is the same as its ___*average*___ revenue curve. Its marginal-revenue curve will lie ___*below*___ the demand or average revenue curve.

4. Thus, at the price and output set by such a monopolist, the price will (⬭exceed⬭/equal/be less than) the marginal cost.

5. There (is only/is more than) one price and output at which a firm may be making some profit. If price exceeds ___*marginal average total*___ cost, the firm will be earning profits.

6. Because marginal cost cannot be negative, the most profitable output for a monopolist will be where marginal revenue is (positive/~~negative~~) and thus where demand is (elastic/~~inelastic~~).

7. Monopoly and monopoly profits can persist in the long run because of ___*barrier to entry*___ of new firms.

8. Monopoly power (varies in degree/~~means complete monopoly~~).

9. A firm's monopoly power will be greater, the (~~larger~~/smaller) the shifts in its demand caused by the actions of other sellers.

10. The share of total industry sales held by the four largest companies in an industry is called the ___*concentration ratio*___.

11. Two different prices charged for the same product do not constitute price discrimination if they are based on differences in ___*cost*___.

12. (a) The downward-sloping demand curve indicates that there are (⬭some⬭/no) buyers willing to pay more than the going market price for a commodity.
    (b) The fact that these buyers pay a lower price than they would be willing to gives them the benefit that is called the ___*consumer's surplus*___.
    (c) If a monopoly firm can sell some of its output at prices corresponding to what these buyers are willing to pay, total revenue can be ___*(maximize) increased*___

13. Two conditions are necessary for a firm to be able to practice price discrimination:
    (a) ___*control on the supply to particular buyer*___;
    (b) ___*can prevent resale*___.

14. *Ceteris paribus*, a monopoly firm charging a single price will, compared with a firm charging discriminatory prices, receive (more/⬭less⬭) revenue and produce a (larger/⬭smaller⬭) output.

15. If the monopolist were able to achieve perfect price discrimination, his marginal-revenue curve would become the same as his ___*demand*___ curve. His profit-maximizing output would as usual be where $MR =$ ___*MC*___, which in this case would be (less than/⬭the same as⬭/more than) the output of a perfect competitor.

---

If you have not answered all questions correctly, review the text in order to be sure that you have all of the important concepts clearly in mind before going on to the next chapter.

1. industry; downward  2. revenue; marginal  3. average; below  4. exceed  5. are more than; average total  6. positive; elastic  7. barriers to entry  8. varies in degree  9. smaller  10. concentration ratio  11. cost  12. some; consumer's surplus; increased  13. can control supply to particular buyer; can prevent resale  14. less; smaller  15. demand; *MC,* the same as

# MULTIPLE-CHOICE QUESTIONS

1. If profits are to be maximized by a firm, whether a monopolist or a competitor,
   (a) output should be increased whenever marginal cost is below average cost
   (b) output should be increased whenever marginal revenue is less than marginal cost
   (c) output should be set where unit costs are at a minimum
   (d) output should be increased whenever marginal revenue exceeds marginal cost

2. A monopolist has a downward-sloping demand curve
   (a) because it has an inelastic demand
   (b) because, typically, it sells only to a few large buyers
   (c) because it is the same as the industry
   (d) because consumers prefer that product

3. At the profit-maximizing output for a nondiscriminating monopolist,
   (a) price equals marginal cost
   (b) price exceeds marginal cost
   (c) price exceeds average total cost
   (d) price equals marginal revenue

4. In a monopolized industry,
   (a) other firms have no incentive to enter
   (b) profits are inevitable
   (c) there must be barriers to entry if the monopoly is to persist
   (d) there will be less incentive to lower costs than under competition

5. Monopoly power
   (a) can be measured quite precisely
   (b) varies inversely with the concentration ratio
   (c) implies a degree of control over price
   (d) is a term used only for complete monopolies

6. Concentration ratios have been found
   (a) to have considerable correlation with profit rates
   (b) to have little usefulness where there are more than two firms
   (c) to have little relevance in measuring the degree of monopoly power in an industry
   (d) to be very low in the great majority of manufacturing industries

7. Price discrimination is possible only
   (a) in the case of perfect monopoly
   (b) if it is possible to keep it a secret
   (c) if it is possible to conspire with competitors
   (d) if it is possible to separate the buyers or units that can be sold at different prices

8. A monopoly firm will not have more than normal profits unless
   (a) it practices price discrimination
   (b) its price exceeds average total cost
   (c) its marginal revenue exceeds marginal cost
   (d) it faces an inelastic demand curve

9. Which sentence below best describes the behaviour of a profit-maximizing monopolist?
   (a) He picks a price he knows will give him a profit and sells as much as he can.
   (b) He produces as much as he can and sets whatever price is necessary to sell it all.
   (c) He seeks to select a price at which the additional revenue associated with one more unit just equals the addition to cost.
   (d) He sets price equal to marginal cost at his most profitable output.

92    Chapter 15

10. Output under price discrimination will
    (a) generally be larger than under single-price monopoly
    (b) be produced at higher average cost than under single-price monopoly
    (c) usually be the same as under perfect competition
    (d) be indeterminate because we cannot know what prices can be charged

Answers to multiple-choice questions: 1(d)  2(c)  3(b)  4(c)  5(c)  6(a)  7(d)  8(b)  9(c)  10(a)

## EXERCISES

1. The diagram below shows the demand and average cost situation of a hypothetical monopoly firm.

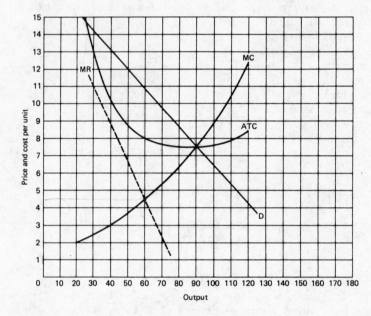

    (a) What is the output where the firm's profits will be at a maximum? _____ 60 _____
    (b) What will be the price at this output? _____ 11 _____
    (c) What will be the total revenue (at this output)? _____ 660 _____
    (d) What will be the total costs? _____ 480 _____
    (e) What will be the total profit? _____ 180 _____
    (f) Within what *range* of output and price will the firm also make at least *some* profit, though not maximum? _____ 25 to 90 _____
    (g) What price would limit the monopolist to competitive profits? _____ 7.50 _____

2. The data below relate to a pure monopolist and the product that he produces.

| Output | Total Cost | Price | Quantity Demanded |
|--------|-----------|-------|-------------------|
| 0 | $20 | $20 | 0 |
| 1 | 24 | 18 | 1 |
| 2 | 27 | 16 | 2 |
| 3 | 32 | 14 | 3 |
| 4 | 39 | 12 | 4 |
| 5 | 48 | 10 | 5 |
| 6 | 59 | 8 | 6 |

(a) What additional cost and demand information do you need before you can calculate the profit-maximizing output and price for the monopolist?

(b) Calculate these additional schedules and plot them (roughly) below.

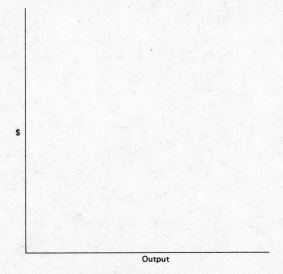

(c) What is the approximate profit-maximizing output?

(d) At what price will the monopolist sell his product?

(e) To calculate the monopolist's profits, what further cost schedule is necessary?

(f) Calculating this, what is the total monopoly profit in this case?

# PROBLEMS

## 1. THE NORTHERN DOCTOR

Dr. Lawrence practiced in a remote northern region over 50 miles from other medical services. To cover his family living expenditures and the fixed overhead expenses connected to his modest clinic required $20,000 gross income. (This amount was below the income he might command elsewhere but would be adequate.) In addition, he had expenses associated with visits estimated at $1.00 a visit. (This common unit, a visit, represents, of course, a considerable simplification of the variety of medical services he provided.)

The population of the area could be roughly divided into two groups. The first consisted of relatively prosperous oilmen, civil servants, merchants, and mining executives. The second, a lower-income group, included those whose employment was based on fishing, hunting, and trapping, as well as a few prospectors.

Assume that the demand for Dr. Lawrence's services is described by smoothly drawn curves through the points given in the table and that Dr. Lawrence can provide a maximum of 5,000 visits per year.

Hypothetical Demand Schedule for Dr. Lawrence's Services

| Fee | Group I Visits | Group II Visits | Total Visits |
|-----|-----|-----|-----|
| $25 | 300 | 0 | 300 |
| 20 | 500 | 0 | 500 |
| 15 | 700 | 200 | 900 |
| 10 | 900 | 800 | 1,700 |
| 5 | 1,100 | 2,000 | 3,100 |
| 0 | 1,300 | 3,700 | 5,000 |

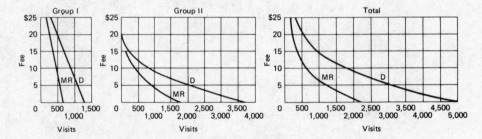

Note: The *MR* curves were plotted at interval midpoints as follows:
Group I: $12.50 at an output of 400, $2.50 at 600, -$7.50 at 800.
Group II: $15.00 at 100, $8.33 at 500, $1.67 at 1,400.
Total: $8.75 at 700, $4.38 at 1,300, -$1.07 at 2,400.

Interested students may wish to work out reasons for this.

## Questions

1. Evaluate the following pricing alternatives by the criteria below. To size up Dr. Lawrence's problem, draw the long-run average-cost curve on the "total" graph, and to help in the evaluations draw the *MC* curve on all three diagrams.

| | Price(s) | Output | TR | TVC | TC | TR - TC |
|-----|-----|-----|-----|-----|-----|-----|
| (a) One-price system | | | | | | |
| (b) Two-price system | | | | | | |
|    I | | | | | xx | xx |
|    II | | | | | xx | xx |
|       Total | xxx | | | | | |
| (c) Perfect price discrimination from | | | | | | |
|              to | | | | | | |

(approximate total revenue from areas on graph)

2. Recognizing that none of the alternatives above is fully possible [Dr. Lawrence would not have the perfect knowledge required for (c) and would find it professionally difficult to practice (a) and (b) without providing some free services and lower fees as well], what approach would you recommend?

3. Price discrimination in medical services probably has declined partly as influenced by government programs.

   (a) Some communities have subsidized the building of a clinic. How would this affect Dr. Lawrence's problem?

   (b) Would the provision of government payments of minimum fees under Medicare reduce discrimination?

## 2.  THE TELEPHONE COMPANY

In order to provide anywhere from 100,000 to 300,000 long-distance calls per month, Belle Canada must, it is assumed, commit a fixed amount of resources to this long-distance operation. In setting its price, then, the objective is to maximize total revenue.

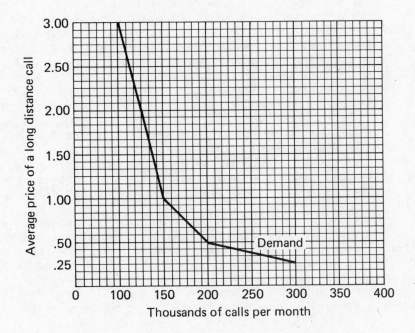

## Questions

1. Given the demand schedule above, if the present price of an "average" call is $.50, should Belle consider a reduced price of $.25 per call? Explain your answer.

2. Should Belle Canada try to persuade the Canadian Transport Commission (to which it is responsible) to allow a rate increase to $1.00? Why?

# Industrial Organization and Theories of Imperfect Competition

1. <u>Industrial concentration</u> refers to the degree to which a group of firms account for a large share of the total assets or sales of that industry.
2. Between perfect competition and monopoly, there are a number of industrial organization structures that have some of the characteristics of both extremes. <u>Oligopoly</u>, where average firms dominate the industry and where there are significant barriers to entry, and <u>monopolistic competition</u>, which is characterized by product differentiation and relative ease of entry, are two such structures.
3. Product differentiation between firms in the same industry gives individual firms market power such that their demand schedules are not perfectly elastic as in perfect competitions.
4. The equilibrium price under a regime of monopolistic competition is one that exceeds marginal cost and the lowest average total cost for the firm.
5. An industry characterized by oligopoly, or competition among the few, suggests that collusion among the firms to form a monopoly would maximize profits. Preventing this collusion, however, is the desire of each firm to maximize its <u>share</u> of total industry profits.
6. Oligopoly is a rather vague market structure, and predictions about price and output behavior will depend upon the growth of the industry, the actual number of firms, the degree of difference among the products, and possible response of one firm to another's actions, and barriers to entry.
7. The existence of a <u>kinked demand curve</u> in an industry suggests that there is price flexibility whereby a price increase by one firm would result in a drastic reduction in sales, and a price reduction would produce little increase in output.

| | |
|---|---|
| CHECKLIST | Make certain that you also understand the following concepts: nonprice competition; excess capacity theorem; atomistic competition; oligopoly; barriers to entry; limit price; joint profit maximization; minimum efficient scale. |

REVIEW QUESTIONS

1. Two crucial features of perfect competition affecting market behavior are
   _____ *price taking* _____ and _____ *free entry* _____ .

2. Except for the effect of extensive government intervention, agriculture most resembles the market structure of _perfect competition_.

3. A market structure where there are many sellers, free entry, but some control over price by each seller due to product differentiation is called _monopolistic_.

4. A market structure dominated by a few big firms, all aware of their possible effects on each other's sales, and to which entry is difficult, is called _Oligopoly_.

5. The firm in a perfectly competitive market sees its demand curve as _perfectly elastic_, whereas the firm in imperfectly competitive markets has a demand curve that is _sloping_.

6. The more a firm can differentiate its product from others and create a brand preference for its product, the (more/less) elastic its demand curve will be.

7. The most profitable output and price for a firm in monopolistic competition is where _marginal_ cost equals marginal _revenue_. Price at equilibrium will be (higher than/lower than/the same as) under perfect competition.

8. (a) In the long run, any profits over opportunity costs in a monopolistically competitive industy will be eliminated by what process? _entry of new firms_
   (b) Firm demand curves will be shifted to the (left/right) until just covers _Total average_ cost.
   (c) This point will occur at an output (below/beyond/at) the output where average costs are at a minimum.
   (d) Thus, the firms and the industry are producing below their most efficient level, and a condition of _excess_ capacity exists.
   (e) This inefficient situation has one possible advantage for the comsumer compared with perfect competition: _more choice of product_.

9. To increase its profits, a firm in imperfect competition must either lower its unit costs or increase its revenues by increasing its _share of market_. It attempts to do the latter not by changing its prices, but by _non-price competition_.

10. Profitable oligopolies do not turn into industries of monopolistic competition because of _barriers of entry_.

11. In addition to considering its marginal cost and revenues in setting price and output, an oligopoly firm must consider _reactions of its rival_.

12. There are several hypotheses about the conditions that will increase the tendency of oligopoly firms to attempt to maximize their combined or joint profits; for instance, the tendency is increased
    (a) the (smaller/larger) the number of sellers
    (b) the (more/less) similar are the rival products
    (c) the (greater/less) the barriers to new firms
    (d) when the industry or economy is (contracting/expanding)

13. In oligopolized industries, prices tend to be more inflexible
    (a) the (more/less) uncertainty exists as to rival reactions
    (b) the (more/less) effective is tacit agreement not to change them

14. Nonprice competition will tend to be more vigorous,
    (a) the (greater/less) the limitation on price competition
    (b) the (higher/lower) the other barriers to entry of new firms

15. Barriers to entry of new firms are greater,
    (a) the (smaller/larger) the minimum efficient scale of production
    (b) the (greater/less) the absolute cost advantage of existing firms over potential entrants

16. An oligopoly firm with a cost advantage could try to inhibit the entry of new firms by setting a price below the *limit price,* namely, below the entering firms' ___minimum___ ___average___ cost.

17. Firms with low minimum efficient scale can still create barriers to entry by increasing the number of the ___brands___ and the amount of ___advertisement___.

18. The possibility of a "kink" in an oligopoly firm's demand curve arises if the curve is elastic (upward/downward) and inelastic (upward/downward).
    (a) This would be the case if its rivals (do/do not) follow a price rise and (do/do not) follow a price reduction.
    (b) Such a firm has a strong incentive to (raise/lower/leave unchanged) its price.

19. Referring to the table of Concentration Ratios in Selected Manufacturing Industries in this chapter of the text, decide in what market structure you would classify the following industries.
    (a) cigarettes ___Oligopoly___
    (b) clothing ___monopolistic competition___
    (c) primary alimunum ___Oligopoly___
    (d) automobiles ___Oligopoly___
    (e) dairy products ___Monopolistic competition___
    (f) sawmills ___Monopolistic competition___

___

If you have not answered all questions correctly, review the text in order to be sure that you have all of the important concepts clearly in mind before going on to the next chapter.

1. price taking; free entry  2. perfect competition  3. monopolistic competition  4. oligopoly  5. horizontal; sloping  6. less  7. marginal, revenue; higher  8. entry of new firms; left, average; below; excess; wider choice of products  9. share of the market; nonprice competition (especially advertising)  10. natural or artificial barriers to entry  11. the reactions of its rivals  12. smaller; more; greater; expanding  13. more; more  14. greater; lower  15. larger; greater  16. minimum average  17. brands; advertising  18. upward, downward; do not, do; leave unchanged  19. oligopoly; monopolistic competition; oligopoly; oligopoly; monopolistic competition; monopolistic competition

___

# MULTIPLE-CHOICE QUESTIONS

1. Many small firms are typical of all but which one of the following industries?
   (a) agriculture
   (b) restaurant
   (c) primary aluminum
   (d) retail trade

2. The important difference between our assumptions for monopolistic competition and those for perfect competition is that monopolistic competitors
   (a) do not try to maximize profits
   (b) worry about their influence on the market
   (c) have an inelastic demand curve facing them
   (d) sell similar but not identical products

3. An important prediction of monopolistic competition is that the equilibrium output of the firm occurs at an output
   (a) where price exceeds average cost
   (b) less than the one at which average cost is at a minimum
   (c) less than the one at which average cost equals average revenue
   (d) less than the one at which marginal cost equals marginal revenue

4. Which of the following is *not* implied by the excess-capacity theorem for monopolistically competitive industries?
   (a) Prices and unit costs will be higher than they would have been under perfect competition.
   (b) Many firms will be operating at a loss.
   (c) The consumer pays for the privilege of having a wider choice.
   (d) The same total output could have been produced by fewer firms at a lower cost.

5. Which of the following is a seller *not* trying to do by giving out trading stamps?
   (a) shift his product's demand curve to the right
   (b) keep customers returning
   (c) reduce his total costs
   (d) increase his share of the market

6. According to the theory, temporary profits of a monopolistic competitor are eliminated primarily by
   (a) production where average costs are above the minimum
   (b) nonprice competition
   (c) entry of new firms
   (d) price reductions to meet new competition

7. Long-run profits are possible in an oligopolistic industry primarily because
   (a) firms can always set the profit-maximizing price and output
   (b) oligopolistic firms use the most efficient production methods
   (c) the demand is typically quite elastic
   (d) entry of new firms is difficult

8. In an oligopolistic industry, joint profit maximizing by setting prices through tacit agreement is
   (a) more likely the fewer the number of firms
   (b) more likely the less similar the products
   (c) more likely when prices are falling than when they are rising
   (d) invariably illegal under the anti-combines laws

9. According to our hypotheses, which of the following situations should give firms in an oligopolistic industry the best chance of reaching their profit-maximizing price and output?
   (a) a few firms, each with low minimum efficient scale
   (b) a few firms with similar products and very large fixed costs
   (c) a few firms, differing considerably in size and each with very unpredictable management
   (d) a few firms, one of which is managed by an aggressive price cutter

10. The "limit price" just below which an oligopolist might set his price to prevent new firms from entering is determined by
    (a) the oligopolist's lowest unit cost
    (b) the lowest price at which the oligopolist can still make a profit
    (c) the lowest price at which a new entrant could cover costs
    (d) the price that can be set where marginal revenue equals marginal cost

11. About what percent of total Canadian manufacturing output is produced by industries with four-firm concentration ratios of over 50 percent?
    (a) 50
    (b) 75
    (c) 10
    (d) 90

12. The price-quantity relationship cannot, in principle, be determined for an oligopolist
    (a) under the competitive *ceteris paribus* conditions
    (b) under any circumstances
    (c) because price is an unimportant factor in the oligopolist's sales
    (d) unless reactions by other firms in the industry are taken accurately into account

13. An industry frequently cited as an example of excess capacity because of monopolistic competition is
    (a) agriculture
    (b) gasoline retailing
    (c) steel
    (d) automobile manufacturing

---

Answers to multiple-choice questions: 1(c)  2(d)  3(b)  4(b)  5(c)  6(c)  7(d)  8(a)  9(b)
10(c)  11(a)  12(d)  13(b)

---

# EXERCISES

1. Below are hypothetical demand and cost curves for a monopolistic competitor.
   (a) What would be the profit-maximizing output? _____
       Price? _____
   (b) How much profit does the firm make at this position? _____
   (c) How can you tell that this is not a long-run equilibrium position for the industry?

   (d) Which curves will be affected, and in which direction, if the firm now increases its advertising budget by the given amount, with the desired results?

   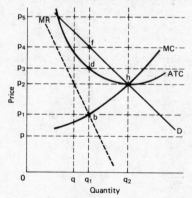

   (e) Suppose that new firms enter the industry. Show how the demand curve of this firm might appear in a long-run equilibrium position.

2. In the figure below, suppose that $D$ is the demand curve for an oligopoly firm if all the firms in the industry act together, and that $d$ is the demand curve for the firm when it along in the industry varies its price. Assume that price is now at $2.

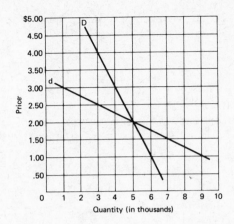

(a) If the firm lowers its price from $2 to $1.50 and no other firm does, its sales will go from _____ to _____, and total revenue will go from _____ to _____.

(b) If the firm lowers its price from $2 to $1.50 and every other firm does too, its sales will go from _____ to _____ and its total revenue from _____ to _____.

(c) If the firm raises its price from $2 to $2.50 and no other firm does, its sales will go from _____ to _____ and its total revenue from _____ to _____.

(d) If the firm raises its price from $2 to $2.50 and every other firm does too, its revenue will go from _____ to _____.

(e) Assuming that this firm has fairly constant variable costs of about 75 cents in the relevant range of output, under what circumstances, if any, would the manager consider raising his price? Lowering it?

(f) Does this situation encourage collusive action by the firms in the industry to raise prices together? _____ To lower prices together? _____

# PROBLEMS

## 1. SETTING THE PRICE OF FUEL OIL

In early 1974, the Nova Scotia Board of Commissioners of Public Utilities conducted hearings on fuel oil prices. An Imperial Oil executive told the hearings that, "Pricing is not a cost-plus formula. We don't determine in our pricing the cost of our products. We get what we can from the tone of the market at the time."

### Questions

1. Is such a pricing policy consistent with perfect competition? Justify your answer.

2. Why is such a pricing policy inconsistent with a profit-maximizing producer in a setting of monopolistic competition?

3. Under what conditions would such a pricing policy call for government control of the "industry"?

4. If Imperial Oil really does operate in this manner, what are they trying to maximize? What form of industrial organization might best be depicted by such behavior?

## 2.  COOPERATION IN THE PULP AND PAPER INDUSTRY

It was reported in early 1975 that Abitibi and Domtar pulp and paper producers closed their mills temporarily because of an inventory buildup. To continue producing would have necessitated lowering prices to eliminate excess inventories. The move to close the mills was hailed by the industry as a demonstration of price discipline in the industry.

### Questions

1. What type of market structure for the pulp and paper industry does this action (and the comments on it) tend to suggest? Why?

2. If the industry were marked by perfect competition, would such action occur? Explain. What do you think would occur under perfect competition?

3. Because the "industry" is unwilling to reduce prices to unload excess inventory, what might this suggest about the price elasticity of demand for pulp and paper?

# Price Theory in Action

## KEY CONCEPTS AND DEFINITIONS

1. Producers operating in a perfectly competitive market can increase profits by agreeing among themselves to restrict output. However, there is always an incentive to the individual firm to violate the agreement and expand output.
2. An effective agreement to limit output and raise prices above minimum average cost will generate excess profits which will attract new firms to the industry.
3. In a potentially competitive industry, even if there was an agreement to restrict output, the only way that earnings can be kept above the long-run competitive level would be to prevent the entry of new firms into the industry.

| CHECKLIST | Make certain that you also understand the following concepts: boycott, producers' association; cartel; patent monopoly. |
|---|---|

## REVIEW QUESTIONS

1. In theory, competitors can improve their profit position by jointly reducing (price/output) and increasing (price/output).

2. This will be particularly beneficial if market demand at competitive equilibrium is (elastic/inelastic).

3. By so doing, each firm will find its marginal-revenue curve (higher/lower). Although its marginal-cost curve is unchanged, the marginal cost of the last unit at the smaller output will be (less/greater) than before.

4. In a producers' organization like the Ontario Egg Marketing Board, voluntary quotas on output (to keep prices up) will not work because each producer can increase in revenue by _____increasing output_____.

5. Higher prices for haircuts in a town will not increase
   (a) barbers' revenues in the short run unless demand is _____inelastic_____.
   (b) barbers' profits in the long run unless _____entry_____ is limited.

6. The end result of higher prices is likely to be (more/fewer) barbers working (more/fewer) hours.

7. The recent trend toward much longer make hair would be diagrammed as a (shifting/elastic) demand curve for haircuts.

8. Heavy cigarette advertising seems to have two functions:
   (a) _____ nonprice competition _____
   (b) _____ barrier of entry _____

9. The electrical equipment companies set prices by (tacit/explicit) agreement. The agreement fell apart apparently partly because of excess (demand/capacity) in the industry.

10. In the ball-point pen case, the initial but ineffective barrier to entry of other firms was a _____ patent _____ .

___

If you have not answered all questions correctly, review the text in order to be sure that you have all of the important concepts clearly in mind before going on to the next chapter.

1. output; price  2. inelastic  3. higher; less  4. increasing his output  5. inelastic; entry of more barbers  6. more; fewer  7. shifting  8. nonprice competition; barriers to entry of new brands  9. explicit; capacity  10. patent

___

# MULTIPLE-CHOICE QUESTIONS

1. If entry to an industry cannot be limited, we would predict in the long run
   (a) that excess capacity will necessarily result
   (b) that economic profits will approach zero
   (c) that the price will necessarily be the perfectly competitive price
   (d) that a cartel will be formed

2. The Reynolds International Pen Company
   (a) was able to rely on a patent monopoly to prevent entry and maintain profits
   (b) found its patent protection ineffective but succeeded in making substantial innovation profits
   (c) clearly made a mistake in judgment by offering the ball-point pen at too high a price
   (d) definitely overestimated its elasticity of demand in cutting prices

3. Of greatest use for barbers interested in increasing all incomes in the profession would be legislation
   (a) fixing the minimum price of haircuts at $3
   (b) making strict licensing requirements for the industry
   (c) fixing the maximum price of haircuts at $3
   (d) eliminating licensing and price requirements for the industry

4. Which of these elements may have been significant in the great loss of market share suffered by the big three tobacco companies in the 1930s?
   (a) greater price consciousness by the consumer in a depression period
   (b) the large spread created between tobacco costs and cigarette prices in 1931
   (c) limited economies of scale, which had permitted the continued existence of small firms
   (d) all of the above

5. Oligopoly theory in the electrical equipment case is
   (a) most pertinent in explaining the formal price conspiracy in 1957
   (b) not useful at all because monopoly theory could predict the behavior of the 1950s
   (c) useful in understanding why joint profit maximization that worked in one period broke down in another
   (d) not at all necessary because the competitive model could predict the behavior of the 1950s

6. This chapter's examples of actual price and output behavior suggest that
   (a) there is a general preference among firms for strong price competition and expansion of output
   (b) agreements, whether tacit or explicit, to fix prices and divide markets are more apt to break down in good times than in bad
   (c) all firms in an industry can maximize profits by raising prices
   (d) raising prices in an industry, *ceteris paribus,* brings increased long-run profits only if entry can be restricted and output curtailed

Answers to multiple-choice questions: 1(b)   2(b)   3(b)   4(d)   5(c)   6(b)

# EXERCISE

Two firms within an oligopoly have revenue schedules $D_A$ and $D_B$ as shown below (at least they *believe* that the demand schedules are as shown). The agreement in this industry is such that firm A produces an output of $OQ_1$ and firm B produces an output of $OQ_2$.

This produces a "stable" price in the industry. After some calculations, the two firms become more aware of their cost schedules (which are also shown in the diagrams below).

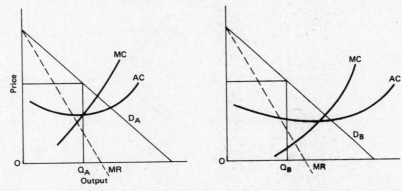

(a) Is there any incentive for the two firms to move away from the agreed-upon price and output? Why?

(b) Is there anything which might inhibit one or both of the firms from deviating from the agreed-upon price and output?

# PROBLEM

## WHY PRICES FALL

Four cases are presented in the chapter that involve price cuts or in one case an abortive attempt to raise prices:

1. the unsuccessful attempt in 1967 by the NFO to raise milk prices in the state of Wisconsin
2. the cutting of ball-point pen prices from mid-1946 to mid-1948

3. the price cuts by major cigarette companies following a raise in June 1931, which led led to the entry of the "10¢ brands"
4. the drastic price cuts in turbine generators starting in mid-1958

As a step in analyzing similarities and contrasts in these situations, fill in, from information available, the structural and performance characteristics listed below.

|  | Milk | Pen | Cigarette | Turbine |
|---|---|---|---|---|
| Number of sellers |  |  |  |  |
| Independence of sellers |  |  |  |  |
| Homogeneity of product |  |  |  |  |
| Entry possibilities |  |  |  |  |
| Ratio of sales to capacity |  |  |  |  |
| Ratio of price to costs |  |  |  |  |

## Questions

1. Are there common characteristics in each of the situations according to the information given?

2. What combination of characteristics in each case seemed to lead to effective downward pressure on prices?

# 18

# Monopoly Versus Competition

## Key Concepts and Definitions

1. In the event that the marginal cost of producing a good falls, the price and quantity response given perfect competition will be greater than in the case of a monopoly.
2. The case against monopoly can be demonstrated by the fact that if a competitive industry becomes a monopoly, price will rise and output fall if the monopoly maximizes profits.
3. Allocative efficiency occurs at that level of output where price equals marginal cost.
4. There are incentives to both perfectly competitive firms and monopolists to innovate and undertake research in order to lower costs. The incentive depends upon such theories as the cost of innovation, the chance of long-run profits, and government legislation.
5. Since there is no theoretical proof that a monopoly will not exist in the long run, the laws have been devised to prohibit the exercise of monopoly power.
6. Resale price maintenance and loss-leader selling are two areas of pricing policy which are felt to be detrimental to competition in the long run. The former involves the producer telling the retailer at what price the product must be sold while the latter is designed to attract customers by selling an item below cost.
7. Regulated industries such as natural monopolies are a unique blend of private sector/ government interaction. In exchange for being allowed to operate as the sole producer of a product, the firm relinquishes its power to set the price of its product. The government controls the price by establishing the fair rate of return the company can earn. This is achieved by applying a percentage figure to the rate base. The measurement of this latter concept is the subject of considerable debate.

| CHECKLIST | Make certain that you also understand the following concepts: pareto optimal, antitrust and anti-combines laws; rule of reason; merger; per se doctrine; Restrictive Trade Practices Commission; Research and Investigation Branch; private and social cost; principle of minimum differentiation. |
|---|---|

## Review Questions

1. Other things being equal, prices and quantities will change (less/more) in monopoly than in competition in response to a change in marginal costs.

2. According to classical analysis, if cost curves are the same under monopoly as under perfect competition, prices will be (higher/lower) and output will be (more/less).

3. This means an allocation of resources under monopoly that is considered (efficient/inefficient).

4. It is considered so because the monopoly price is (greater/less) than marginal cost, which means that the consumer is paying (more/less) for the last item purchased than the value of the additional resources being used.

5. If price exceeds marginal cost in all industries, it is theoretically (possible/impossible) to make some people better off without making others worse off, by changing some prices, outputs, and resource uses.

6. However, it is possible that, if a competitive industry is monopolized, economies of large scale will bring (lower/higher) unit costs, and price in the long run will be (higher/lower) and output (greater/less) than would have been possible under competition.

7. Unlike a competitive firm, a monopolist has a (long-run/short-run) incentive to innovate.

8. Providing temporary legal protection to the possible profits of a firm resulting from an innovating invention is one purpose of _____patent_____ laws.

9. Monopolistic competition provides (greater/less) product variety than does perfect competition at (the same/increased) costs.

10. The examples of British radio and television suggest that (more/less) variety of product might be produced by a monopoly than by an oligopoly.

11. Monopoly power is predicted to lead to the employment of (fewer/more) resources in the industry compared with those used under competitive conditions, and usually to a (greater/smaller) relative share of national income for the monopolistic firms.

12. Two contrasting policies toward monopolistic firms are those of the ___antitrust___ laws and public-utility ___regulations___.

13. However, attempts by labor and farmers to organize and acquire monopoly power (are/are not) generally illegal under the antitrust law.

14. The first antitrust law in the United States was the _____ Act in the year _____. This law prohibited _____ and _____.

15. Tying contracts and mergers were forbidden under the _____ Act if the effect might be to _____.

16. The prohibition of discriminatory pricing was brought into the Canadian _____ _____ Act in the year _____.

17. In the Canadian Breweries case, the charge was dropped because changes in (market shares/pricing) had not established that an offense had been committed.

18. In the Carnation case, the charge of price discrimination was dropped because the company claimed its different regional prices were defensible on grounds of (meeting competition/different costs).

19. A "natural" monopoly reaches lowest unit cost at a very (large/small) output relative to the market.

20. If average costs are declining with output, regulation that sets price equal to marginal cost will result in _____losses_____ for the firm.

21. Problems in regulating utility rates have included determination of the proper value of investment, or ___*rate bases*___, and a fair rate of ___*return*___ on investment.

---

If you have not answered all questions correctly, review the text in order to be sure that you have all of the important concepts clearly in mind before going on to the next chapter.

1. less  2. higher; less  3. inefficient  4. greater; more  5. possible  6. lower; lower; greater  7. long-run  8. patent  9. greater; increased  10. more  11. fewer; greater  12. antitrust; regulation  13. are not  14. Sherman, 1890; combination or conspiracy in restraint of trade, monopolizing or attempting to monopolize  15. Clayton; substantially lessen competition  16. Combines Investigation, 1935  17. market shares  18. meeting competition  19. large  20. losses  21. rate base; return

---

# MULTIPLE-CHOICE QUESTIONS

1. Classical economists preferred perfect competition to monopoly because it fulfilled all but which one of the following basic goals?
   (a) consumer sovereignty
   (b) dispersion of economic power
   (c) virtual equality in income distribution
   (d) efficiency of resource allocation

2. So far as it affects consumer welfare, monopoly is potentially objectionable because
   (a) price = marginal revenue
   (b) price > marginal cost
   (c) marginal cost = marginal revenue
   (d) marginal revenue > marginal cost

3. Assuming that cost curves would be the same in an industry under either monopoly or competition, a monopoly will produce at equilibrium at a point where, compared with the competitive equilibrium,
   (a) output is larger but price is higher
   (b) output is less but price is higher
   (c) output is less but price is the same
   (d) output is the same but price is higher

4. In order to have the consumer pay for the last unit just what it cost to produce the last unit,
   (a) price should equal average cost
   (b) average cost must be at a minimum
   (c) marginal cost should equal price
   (d) marginal revenue should equal price

5. One reason that we cannot say for sure that, given the technology and resources at hand, welfare is maximized when price equals marginal cost in all industries is that
   (a) there are still poor people
   (b) marginal cost does not include possible social costs that may be substantial
   (c) it is never impossible to make someone better off without making someone worse off
   (d) we cannot measure either welfare or marginal cost, so they are not useful concepts

6. A monopoly may produce more efficiently than the same industry in competitive form because
   (a) there may be economies of scale that would not be achieved by a number of small firms
   (b) monopolies typically have better management
   (c) a monopoly does not have to worry about what its rival may do
   (d) a monopoly can concentrate on production rather than profits

7. Anti-combines cases in Canada have been highlighted by all except one of the following:
   (a) low fines for the guilty
   (b) few merger cases
   (c) few convictions
   (d) consistent appeal to economic questions

8. Specialization agreements, proposed for a new competition law in Canada, would
   (a) allow firms to merge to lower costs
   (b) permit foreign companies to buy out domestic ones
   (c) allow firms in some industries to agree among themselves to limit the variety of products each firm produces
   (d) assist firms in developing, through government subsidies, those products that are in demand in foreign markets

9. The usual argument in favor of accepting a "natural" monopoly, if it is regulated, is that
   (a) regulation guarantees fair, low prices
   (b) more than one company would be obviously wasteful
   (c) it gives the same results as public ownership
   (d) regulation keeps it out of politics

10. Resale price maintenance was included in the Combines Investigation Act in
    (a) 1888
    (b) 1910
    (c) 1935
    (d) 1951

11. From the public's standpoint, a "fair rate of return" on a utility investment
    (a) should mean approximately the current rate on alternatives of similar risk
    (b) should be determined by historical costs
    (c) can always be earned, provided prices are set high enough
    (d) means what the stockholders think is fair

---

Answers to multiple-choice questions: 1(c)   2(b)   3(b)   4(c)   5(b)   6(a)   7(d)   8(c)   9(b)   10(d)   11(a)

---

# PROBLEMS

## 1.  THE COST OF A FREE PRESS

In 1974, the companies of K. C. Irving Ltd. and subsidiaries were convicted of operating a monopoly through their ownership of all English-language newspapers in the Province of New Brunswick. The companies were fined $160,000 and ordered to sell two of the five newspapers. K. C. Irving appealed the decision.

On June 4, 1975, the Court of Appeal overturned the Supreme Court decision. The Court of Appeal stated in his report:

> I differ from the trial judge, however, in his statement that when a monopoly as defined in the dictionary occurs, detriment in law results.

The Court of Appeal ruled that the conviction for monopoly must be based on evidence that the monopoly (in the dictionary sense) had harmed the public. As the Court decision stated:

> No evidence was adduced that any detriment to the public resulted. . . . The contention [that the five newspapers owned by one group was bad] was advanced . . . on a theoretical basis without supporting evidence of any actual lessening of competition.

What the Court of Appeal pointed out was that day-to-day control was in the hands of the publishers and editors and that they were as independent now as in the days before the takeover.

## Questions

1. Look up the definition of "monopoly in a dictionary.
2. What "evidence" would you look for to determine if the ownership of these five newspapers by one group was detrimental to the public?

3. If this decision is appealed again to the Supreme Court of Canada, regardless of the outcome, what recommendation could the Court make concerning the interpretation of monopoly?

## 2. LEGISLATION GOVERNING MONOPOLISTIC PRACTICES

Below is an excerpt from the *Combines Investigation Act*, Part V, Clause 33:

33A. (1) Every one engaged in a business who
   (a) is a party or privy to, or assists in, any sale that discriminates to his knowledge, directly or indirectly, against competitors of a purchaser of articles from him in that any discount, rebate, allowance, price concession or other advantage is granted to the purchaser over and above any discount, rebate, allowance, price concession or other advantage that, at the time the articles are sold to such purchaser, is available to such competitors in respect of a sale of articles of like quality and quantity;
   (b) engages in a policy of selling articles in any area of Canada at prices lower than those exacted by him elsewhere in Canada, having the effect or tendency of substantially lessening competition or eliminating a competitor in such part of Canada, or designed to have such effect; or
   (c) engages in a policy of selling articles at prices unreasonably low, having the effect or tendency of substantially lessening competition or eliminating a competitor, or designed to have such effect,
   is guilty of an indictable offence and is liable to imprisonment for two years.

## Questions

1. List several instances of pricing policies on the part of retailers that could, under the legislation, lead to an investigation by the government.

2. Why might prices differ across Canada for a given item, seemingly in contravention of 33A(b)?

3. Discuss the problem of obtaining a conviction against a company under 33A(c)?

# 19

## Who Runs the Firm, and for What Ends?

### KEY CONCEPTS AND DEFINITIONS

1. Firms do not operate in isolation from people. In many instances there is a clear distinction between the managers and the owners of a firm.
2. The hypothesis that the firms control the markets rests on the assumptions of the power of advertising, the lack of innovation, and a corporate-government alliance. The empirical evidence suggests that these conditions are not widely met throughout the economy and that changes in consumer tastes are often independent of advertising and have resulted in new products to satisfy those tastes.
3. If corporations "behave" in a way that is deemed to be socially detrimental, little will be accomplished by telling firms, individually and collectively, to behave. Public policy should be exercised through the enactment of appropriate legislation.
4. The control of the modern corporation is complex and no one "theory" is applicable to all forms of business. Minority stock control, holding companies, managerial power, and interlocking directorates are all forms of control leading to different conclusions about firms' behavior.
5. Modern theories of the firm suggest that such objectives as full-cost pricing, sales maximization, satisficing, and long-run profit maximization are alternatives to strict profit maximization in the short run. Although precise profit maximization may not be the objective of the firm, profits per se are an important motivating force in output and pricing decisions.

> **CHECKLIST** Make certain that you also understand the following concepts: proxy, holding company; proxy fight; interlocking directorships; full-cost pricing; markup; organization theory; profit constraint; satisficing; tender offer; takeover bid; consumerism.

### REVIEW QUESTIONS

1. Critics of the theory of behavior of firms question whether the goal of firms really is to _____.

2. U.S. ownership of Canadian industry is highest in the _____ industry and lowest in _____.

3. When one corporation controls another corporation by owning a controlling amount of its stock, it is called a _____.

4. The issue of ownership and control of firms affects the theory of the firm only if the firm's goals are thereby (different from/the same as) what the theory assumes.

5. If business managers do not know what marginal costs are, it is (impossible/still possible) for them to try to maximize their profits.

6. A producer is said to use full-cost pricing when he adds a _____ to his expected _____ costs.

7. (a) Under the theory of full-cost pricing, a decline in demand results in a price that (rises/falls/remains the same), sales will (fall/rise), inventories will (fall/rise), and production will probably be (increased/decreased).
   (b) However, if firms adjust their markup percentages downward or upward according to changes in (demand/supply), they must also adjust their (price/cost).

8. Some theorists believe that firms aim, not for maximum profits, but for _____ profits. This is (very/not) difficult to prove.

9. Another theory is that firms seek to maximize, not profits, but _____, assuming a minimum level of profits. This is more plausible if the firm is controlled by its (shareholders/managers).

10. Sales-maximizing behavior by a monopolistically competitive firm will result in (larger/smaller) output and (lower/higher) price than would its profit-maximizing behavior. It also implies setting price where demand elasticity is equal to _____.

11. Safarian and others feel that the major problem of Canadian industry is the _____ size of firms.

12. The application of U.S. laws to subsidiaries of U.S. companies in Canada is known as a problem of _____.

13. Two recent government reports dealing with foreign investment in Canada are the _____ and _____ reports.

---

If you have not answered all questions correctly, review the text in order to be sure that you have all of the important concepts clearly in mind before going on to the next chapter.

1. maximize profits  2. automobile; transportation and utilities  3. holding company  4. different from  5. still possible  6. markup; average  7. remains the same, fall, rise, reduced; demand, price  8. satisfactory; very  9. sales; managers  10. larger, lower; one  11. inefficient  12. extraterritoriality  13. Watkins; Grey

---

## MULTIPLE-CHOICE QUESTIONS

1. A characteristic of most modern large corporations is that
   (a) the stockholders really run the business
   (b) the board of directors really runs the business
   (c) hired managers run the business
   (d) the workers run the business

2. The full-cost pricing hypothesis
   (a) predicts market behavior and results better than the profit-maximizing hypothesis
   (b) means that the firm can never maximize profits
   (c) holds that the firm's pricing adjustments respond only to changes in costs
   (d) implies that firms will always be able to cover all their costs

3. If we find that one firm is content merely to make some level of satisfactory profits,
   (a) there is no specific prediction we can make about its equilibrium price and output
   (b) it is obviously a monopoly
   (c) it completely refutes our theory based on profit-maximizing assumptions
   (d) it will not long survive competition and change

4. If it would take ownership of 25 percent of the stock of Associated Gadgets to control it, and ownership of 20 percent of the holding company formed to hold the stock of Associated Gadgets to control that company, it would be necessary to have an amount of money equal to what percentage of the value of Associated Gadgets stock in order to control it? (Pick the minimum possible.)
   (a) 20
   (b) 25
   (c) 51
   (d) 5

5. The sales-maximizng hypothesis implies that
   (a) a firm will sell as many units as it can at a fixed price
   (b) firms are not interested in profits but only in growth
   (c) a firm will sell additional units by reducing price to the point where elasticity of demand is zero
   (d) a firm would reduce price so long as a minimum satisfactory level of profits were achieved

6. Which of the following predictions is *not* implied by any of the theories discussed in this chapter? If an industry's labor costs rise, *ceteris paribus*,
   (a) a profit-maximizing firm will raise its price and reduce output
   (b) a satisficing firm may or may not change its price and output
   (c) a sales-maximizing firm will raise price and reduce output
   (d) a full-cost-pricing firm will raise its price

7. The firm's goals, according to Simon's satisficing hypothesis, would not include
   (a) maintenance of market share
   (b) achievement of a specified gain in sales
   (c) attaining a target level of profits
   (d) maximization of profits

8. Which statement best describes Galbraith's "new industrial state":
   (a) The federal government now have a great deal of control over Canadian corporations.
   (b) Corporations are very responsive to the desires, needs, and best interests of the buying public.
   (c) Because of the power of unions and shareholders, industrial management has little real control.
   (d) The size and influence of large corporations give them too much power over government, consumers, markets, and other institutions.

9. The recommended approach in testing theories about firm behavior is to
   (a) ask business management whether they maximize profits, satisfice, or maximize sales
   (b) abstract from reality as much as possible
   (c) try to find evidence, facts, and figures to show what firms actually did in what circumstances
   (d) watch a business manager make a decision to see how he does it

---

Answers to multiple-choice questions: 1(c)    2(c)    3(a)    4(d)    5(d)    6(c)    7(d)    8(d)    9(c)

# Exercises

1. The diagram below represents demand and cost conditions for a firm.

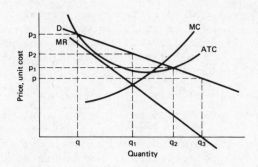

(a) What would be the choice of price and output for a profit maximizer?
_____

(b) What would be the range of price and output for a profit satisficer who is content to cover opportunity costs at a minimum? _____

(c) What would be the price and output of a sales maximizer who is willing to accept losses for short periods? _____

2. Given the following policy change, and the cost/revenue structure of a hypothetical firm, how would the firm respond in terms of price and output to the change in government policy under different assumptions about the firm's objectives?

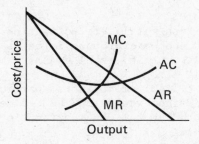

| Policy Change | Price and Output Response If the Firm Is | | |
| --- | --- | --- | --- |
| | Profit Maximizer | Sales Maximizer (Minimum Profit Required) | Full-Cost Pricing (Price = Average Minimum Cost) |
| (a) Increase in tax per unit of output | | | |
| (b) Increase in profits tax | | | |

# PROBLEM

## THE NONREFILLABLE CONTAINER

This problem is linked with the issue of private versus social cost mentioned in Chapter 18. Before answering the question, it would be useful to refresh your mind on this issue.

The *Solid Waste Task Force* (Ontario, 1974), from which the excerpt below is drawn, was established to examine all aspects of solid-waste disposal in Ontario and thus spent considerable time on the question of refillable versus nonrefillable containers. It summarized the debate as follows:

As non-refillable containers have become an important part of an increasingly convenience-oriented lifestyle, so have they also become one of the targets of a growing attack upon modern packaging methods by numerous environmental, conservation and consumer groups.

The basic argument against non-refillable containers centers about the fact that they replace refillable containers that can be re-used, up to 25 or more times depending on the exact nature of their use, whether for soft drinks, beer, or, for that matter, milk. From this, it is argued that non-refillable beverage containers create additional solid waste, use up more energy and raw materials, and, as they have no return value, increase the amount of litter stemming from beverage containers.

Accordingly, say their critics, they should be banned in Ontario, or their use drastically reduced in favour of a major swing back to refillable bottles.

These demands are supported by a number of soft drink bottlers who say they will be forced out of business if non-refillables, particularly cans, continue to increase their share of the market.

A consumer argument against non-refillables arises from the fact that a given soft drink often costs more in a non-refillable container than in a refillable container.

### The Counter Argument

Proposals to reduce the use of non-refillable soft drink containers by legislative means have been opposed primarily on economic grounds in terms of both lost capital investment, profits and job dislocation. In Ontario, as elsewhere, this opposition has primarily come from:

1. manufacturers of non-refillable containers, particularly those producing the can. (While the glass companies concerned would at least face some loss of employment, they would not be as severely affected as the can manufacturers because of the continued and increased use of refillable bottles.)

2. some soft drink companies with investments in canning systems.

3. vending companies that would have to convert existing machines or buy new equipment.

4. unions representing workers whose jobs might be affected.

5. many retailers for whom a greater use of refillable containers would mean additional handling and storage costs.

In addition to the economic aspect, proponents of the non-refillable container point out that it was readily accepted by the public when introduced and that its continued use has solely been the result of consumer demand. They maintain that increasing numbers of people have chosen the non-refillable for its convenience and are willing to pay the extra cost that may at times go with it.

### Questions

1. In producing the nonrefillable container, the firm must price such a container in line with the costs of production. Does such a price reflect all the costs associated with non-refillable container production?

2. Given the experience of most people, do you feel that consumers have had an adequate chance to illustrate their preference for one type of container over the other?

3. What would be a rough test to see whether or not consumers are willing to pay for the "convenience" of nonrefillable containers as compared with refillable or recycled containers?

4. Proponents of the nonrefillable container have suggested, according to the report, that its continued use has " . . . solely been the result of consumer demand." Can you think of additional reasons why it is in continued use?

# 20

# The Distribution of
# National Income

## KEY CONCEPTS AND DEFINITIONS

1. The functional distribution of income refers to the distribution of total national income among the major factors of production, labor, capital, and land. It focuses on sources of income.

2. The size distribution of income is the distribution of income between different households without reference to the social class to which they belong.

3. The inequality of income is depicted by the Lorenz curve which shows how much of total income is accounted for by given proportions of the nation's families.

4. The income of a factor of production has two elements: (a) the price paid per unit of the factor and (b) the quantity of the factor used. In competitive factor markets price is determined by the demand for and supply of the factor.

5. The demand for a factor is said to be a derived demand because a firm requires factors, not for their own sake, but in order to produce goods and services that the firm sells. The total demand for a factor is the sum of the derived demands for it in each productive activity.

6. The demand curve for a factor of production shows how the quantity demanded of that factor will vary as its price varies, the price of all other factors held constant.

7. As the price of the factor falls, the quantity demanded may rise for two reasons: (a) the reduction in the factor price will decrease the cost of production thus increasing the output of commodities, thereby increasing the quantity demanded of the factor. This effect will be larger the more elastic the demand for the goods that the factor helps to make and the more important the factor is in the total costs of producing the goods; (b) the factor price decrease will lead to the substitution of the now cheaper factors whose prices have not fallen. This effect will be larger the easier it is to substitute one factor for another in production.

8. In equilibrium, a profit-maximizing firm will hire units of any variable until the last unit hired adds as much to costs as it does to revenue. The addition to revenue of and additional unit of the variable factor is called the marginal-revenue product. In a competitive factor market, the addition to cost is the price per unit of the factor. Algebraically, this is given as $w$ = MRP.

9. In turn, the MRP is defined by the expression, MRP = MPP x MR where MPP stands for the marginal physical product and MR is the marginal revenue. MPP is defined as the physical increase in output that an additional unit of the variable factor makes possible.

10. The total supplies of most factors of production are variable over time. The total supply of labor depends on the size of the population willing to work (the participation rate), and the number of hours each individual is willing to work.

11. The hypothesis of <u>equal net advantage</u> is a theory of the supply of factors to particular uses. Owners of factors will choose the use that produces the greatest net advantage, allowing both for monetary and nonmonetary advantage of a particular employment.

12. If a factor of production moves easily between uses in response to small changes in incentives, it is said to be highly <u>mobile</u>. <u>Dynamic differentials</u>, temporary factor price differences, serve as signals of disequilibria and induce <u>factor mobility</u> which eventually removes the differentials.

13. The amount that a factor must earn in its present use to prevent it from transferring to another use is called its <u>transfer price</u>; any excess that it earns over this amount is called its <u>economic rent</u>. If the supply of a factor is completely inelastic, all of its earnings are rents, while if its supply is elastic, all earnings are transfer earnings.

## REVIEW QUESTIONS

1. The division of income among the three basic factors of production is called the
   _____*functional*_____ distribution of income.

2. A person who has a job, owns a house that he rents to another person, and owns a corporate bond receives three types of income: ____*labor*____, ____*capital*____, and ____*land*____.

3. The distribution of income according to the amount of income of households is called the
   _____*size*_____ distribution of income.

4. One indication of the inequality of income distribution in Canada is the fact that the lowest 20 percent of the population receive only about what percent of total income?
   *6 percent*

5. The functional distribution of income in Canada shows almost three-quarters of the total going to *employee's compensation*

6. Price theory states that the competitive market price of a factor of production is determined by *demand & supply.*

7. The demand for a factor of production will be more elastic
   (a) the (greater/~~lower~~) the elasticity of demand for the product it is used to make
   (b) the (~~larger~~/smaller) the proportion of total costs represented by payments to this factor
   (c) the (more/~~less~~) the substitutability of the factor for others in production

8. (a) The extra revenue a firm gains by using an additional unit of a factor is called its
      ____*marginal revenue product*____.
   (b) It consists of the extra output, or ____*marginal physical product*____ added by using the extra factor miltiplied by the value of the extra product, or
      ____*marginal revenue*____.

9. A profit-maximizing firm will hire an additional unit of a factor only up to the point at which the extra cost of the factor does not exceed its *marginal revenue product*.

10. The *MRP* curve of a factor slopes ____*downward*____ due to the effect of
    ____*diminishing marginal returns*____. Thus, a producer is willing to hire additional units of a factor only at a progressively (lower/~~higher~~) price, so that the demand curve for a factor slopes ____*downward*____ and can be represented by the ____*MRP*____ curve.

11. The prediction that owners of factors will wish to move them to use  the relative pay for which has (increased/~~decreased~~) results in factor supply curves that slope _____ _upward_ _____ .

12. The elasticity of supply of a factor will be greater the (~~shorter~~/longer) the length of time allowed and the (greater/~~less~~) the mobility of the factor from one use to another.

13. The supply of land in a particular geographic location is totally (elastic/inelastic). But agricultural land is quite (mobile/~~immobile~~) from one crop year to the next, and therefore relatively (elastic/~~inelastic~~) in supply for different crop uses.

14. Capital in money form is much (more/~~less~~) mobile than in the form of plant or machinery.

 15. If workers prefer more leisure time, a rise in wage rates may result in their supplying (~~more~~/fewer) hours of effort. As higher income taxes reduce people's net income, they may very likely want to work (more/(less)).

16. The productive factor most concerned about nonmonetary aspects of its uses is _____ _labor_ _____ .

17. If labor were fully mobile, workers would shift positions until the net advantage of one job over another is _____ _zero_ _____ .

18. To the extent that the relative pay differences between scientists and English teachers persuaded college students to switch to scientific careers, the differential would be considered a _____ _dynamic_ _____ one.

19. Skilled workers usually get paid more than unskilled because they are more (skilled/scarce), relatively.

20. The preference of professors for lower pay in academia than higher pay in industry is explained by what the text calls _____ _nonmonetary_ _____ advantages of the former. The pay differential would be considered a(n) _____ _equilibrium_ _____ one.

21. Ricardo said that high land rents ((caused)/were caused by) the high price of grain.

22. The steeper or more inelastic the supply curve of a factor, the ((greater)/less) the proportion of that factor income that will be economic rent rather than transfer earnings.

23. Assume that Jimmy Connors is willing to continue on the pro tennis circuit as long as he earns at least $100,000 per year. If in a particular year he earns $160,000, his economic rent is _____ _60,000_ _____ and his transfer earnings are _____ _100,000_ _____ .

24. The marginal-productivity theory predicts that each of identical factors in a competitive market would be paid according to the value of (its services/the services of the last unit of the factor hired).

---

If you have not answered all questions correctly, review the text in order to be sure that you have all of the important concepts clearly in mind before going on to the next chapter.

1. functional  2. wages; rent; interest  3. size  4. 6 percent  5. employee's compensation
6. demand and supply  7. greater; larger; more  8. marginal-revenue product; marginal-physical product, marginal revenue  9. marginal-revenue product  10. downward, diminishing marginal returns; lower, downward, *MRP*  11. increased, upward  12. longer; greater  13. inelastic; mobile, elastic  14, more  15. fewer; more  16. laboa  17. zero  18. dynamic
19. scarce  20. nonmonetary; equilibrium  21. were caused by  22. greater  23. $60,000;
$100,000  24. the services of the last unit of the factor hired

# MULTIPLE-CHOICE QUESTIONS

1. The theory of factor prices in competitive markets says that
   (a) factors are paid what they are worth
   (b) factor prices are determined by supply and demand
   (c) factor prices depend on their cost of production
   (d) factors are not paid what they are worth

2. Which of the following statements is *not* true about the demand for a factor of production?
   (a) It is more elastic the more elastic is the demand for the final product.
   (b) It is more elastic in cases where technology dictates its use in fixed proportions with other factors.
   (c) It is less elastic the smaller a part it is of the total cost of the product.
   (d) The quantity demanded varies inversely with its price.

3. The marginal-revenue product of a factor is
   (a) marginal revenue minus marginal cost
   (b) marginal physical product times the units of factors used
   (c) marginal revenue minus factor price
   (d) marginal physical product times marginal revenue

4. The marginal-revenue product of a factor is
   (a) the amount added to revenue by the last hired unit of a factor
   (b) total output divided by units of factors, multiplied by price
   (c) less under competition than under monopoly, *ceteris paribus*
   (d) always equal to its price

5. The quantity demanded of a factor, *ceteris paribus,* will vary inversely
   (a) with income
   (b) with the price of the factor
   (c) with the prices of other factors
   (d) with changes in demand for the product

6. Empirical evidence indicates that historically, as real wage rates have risen in North America,
   (a) workers have shown a willingness to work longer hours
   (b) business has shown no actual tendency to substitute capital for labor
   (c) the average work week has declined
   (d) the supply of effort has sloped upward to the right

7. If a firm is a price taker in factor markets, it means that
   (a) it is also a price taker in product markets
   (b) it can set the price it pays for factors
   (c) it pays the market rate for whatever quantities of factors it wishes
   (d) it is maximizing profits

8. Economic rent is
   (a) the income of a landlord
   (b) earned only by factors in completely inelastic supply
   (c) the excess of income over transfer earnings
   (d) usually taxable under the income tax, whereas transfer earnings are not

9. A dynamic differential in factor earnings
   (a) can exist in equilibrium
   (b) will be more quickly eliminated if factor supply is inelastic rather than elastic
   (c) will tend to cause movements of factors
   (d) is greater the greater is the mobility of the factor

10. The need for the physical presence of the owner of the labor factor (the worker)
    (a) is comparable to that of owners of capital and land
    (b) is not economically significant
    (c) makes nonmonetary factors much more important for it than for other factors
    (d) has not been fully demonstrated

11. Which of the following will *not* shift the supply curve of labor?
    (a) an increase in the population
    (b) an increase in the proportion of people going to college
    (c) an increase in the wage level
    (d) increased preferences for leisure activities

12. The marginal-revenue product of labor declines more rapidly for a monopoly firm than for a competitive firm because
    (a) workers are apt to be less productive when they work for a monopoly
    (b) the industry demand for the product is less elastic
    (c) the monopoly deliberately curtails output
    (d) with the monopoly firm, marginal revenue declines; with the competitive firm, it does not

---

Answers to multiple-choice questions: 1(b)  2(b)  3(d)  4(a)  5(b)  6(c)  7(c)  8(c)  9(c)
10(c)   11(c)   12(d)

---

# EXERCISES

1. Fill in the table below, and then answer the questions.
    Suppose a firm can vary its number of employees and output as shown. What will be the marginal physical product and the marginal-revenue product of each additional worker? Note difference between case (a) and case (b).

| Number of Workers | Units of Output per Day | MPP | Case (a) | | Case (b) | |
|---|---|---|---|---|---|---|
| | | | MR | MRP | MR | MRP |
| 0 | 0 | | $2 | | $2.00 | |
| 1 | 20 | | 2 | | 1.90 | |
| 2 | 40 | | 2 | | 1.80 | |
| 3 | 58 | | 2 | | 1.75 | |
| 4 | 74 | | 2 | | 1.70 | |
| 5 | 88 | | 2 | | 1.65 | |
| 6 | 100 | | 2 | | 1.60 | |
| 7 | 110 | | 2 | | 1.55 | |
| 8 | 118 | | 2 | | 1.50 | |
| 9 | 124 | | 2 | | 1.45 | |
| 10 | 128 | | 2 | | 1.40 | |

(a) If the market wage that this firm must pay is $20 per day, how many workers will the firm hire to maximize profits? Case (a) _____ Case (b) _____
(b) If the wage rises to $28 per day, how many will the firm hire?
    Case (a) _____ Case (b) _____
(c) If in case (a) the market price of the product rises to $3 and the wage is $28 per day, how many workers will be hired? _____
(d) Why does the *MPP* decline?

(e) In case (b), why does the *MR* decline?

2. Suppose there are three adult persons in a hypothetical economy. Each individual has his own preferences for working and consuming leisure time. We have portrayed the labor supply curve of each person. The labor-supply curve depicts the number of hours per time period which the individual is willing to offer to the labor market at various wage rates.

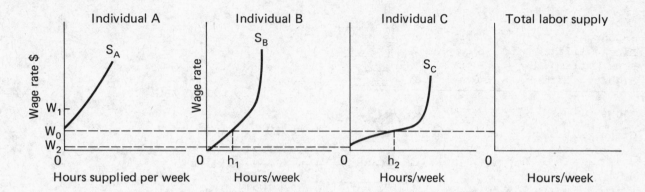

At wage rate $w_0$, A is not prepared to offer any hours per week, B is prepared to offer $Oh_1$, and C is willing to offer $Oh_2$ hours per week. Therefore, we can say that the total number of hours offered to the labor market is $Oh_1 + Oh_2$. Furthermore, two of the three members of population are willing to participate in the labor market. We say that the *participation* rate is two-thirds.

(a) Plot the total number of hours supplied per week at a wage rate of $w_0$.

(b) Taking a higher wage rate of $w_1$, determine the effect on the higher wage on hours supplied to the labor market. Has the number of hours increased? Why?

(c) What are your predictions regarding the magnitude of the participation rate at a wage rate of $w_2$?

# PROBLEM

## LORENZ CURVES AND INCOME DISTRIBUTIONS

The Lorenz curve is a graphical presentation permitting the comparison of income distributions (see text Figure 20-1). The vertical axis represents the cumulative percentage of total national income; the horizontal axis, the percentage of the population (here expressed as families) cumulated from the lowest to the highest income. Exact equality of income would be represented by the straight diagonal line running from the lower left (20 percent of the families would receive 20 percent of the income; 50 percent of the families, 50 percent of the income, etc.). The departure of the Lorenz curve from the diagonal is a measure of the inequality of income.

Table 20-3 of the test is the source of the figures in the table below.

| Family Income Rank | Income Share Canada, 1971 (percent) | Cumulative Percent of Income |
|---|---|---|
| Lowest fifth | 5.5 | _____ |
| Second fifth | 12.5 | _____ |
| Middle fifth | 17.8 | _____ |
| Fourth fifth | 23.8 | _____ |
| Highest fifth | 40.4 | _____ |

## Questions

1. Graph this distribution as a Lorenz curve.

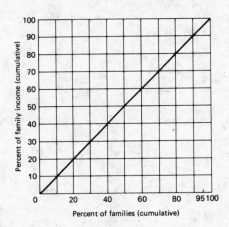

2. The following statistics were compiled by the World Bank for the year 1972.

Cumulative Percentage of World's

| GNP | Population |
|---|---|
| 7 | 53 |
| 10 | 62 |
| 15 | 70 |
| 31 | 81 |
| 51 | 90 |
| 100 | 100 |

Sketch a Lorenz curve for the world. Comparing the world's Lorenz curve with that of Canada, which one more closely approaches absolute equality of income? Explain.

# 21

# Labor Unions, Collective Bargaining, and the Determination of Wages

## KEY CONCEPTS AND DEFINITIONS

1. A wage-setting labor union entering a competitive market can raise wages but only at the expense of reducing employment and creating a pool of unemployed workers.
2. A monopsony means a single purchaser of labor. Even when a few firms exist, they may form an employer's association in order to act as a single unit. Whenever the supply curve of labor is upward sloping, the marginal cost of labor exceeds the average cost. The marginal cost exceeds the wage paid (the average cost) because the increased wage rate necessary to attract another worker must be paid to everyone already employed.
3. The profit-maximizing monopsonist will hire until the MC of labor is equal to MRP. Monopsonistic conditions in the factor market will result in a lower level of employment and a lower wage rate than would exist under competitive conditions.
4. A wage-setting labor union entering a monopsonistic market may increase both employment and wages. If, however, it sets the wage above the competitive level, unemployment will be created.
5. A union is an association of workers that speaks for workers in negotiations with their employers. Unions are subdivided into craft unions (workers with a common set of skills) and industrial unions (organized along industry lines).
6. In general, individual union members belong to a local union. The local union belongs to a national or an international union. A federation is a loose organization of unions; in Canada the principal federation is the Canadian Labour Congress (CLC).
7. Three kinds of bargaining arrangements are (a) the open shop, where, although a union represents its membership, union membership is not a condition for having a job in the firm; (b) the closed shop, where only workers who are already union members may be employed; and (c) the union shop, where the employer is free to hire whom he chooses, but where all new employees must join the recognized union within a specified period.
8. Unions must decide on their goals. One conflict in goals is between raising wages by restricting supply, thus reducing the union's employed membership, and preserving employment for its membership. Other trade-offs are wage and job security, and wage and fringe benefits.
9. Discrimination by sex and age has played a role in the labor market although the quantitative extent of wage and employment discrimination is a matter of continuing research. Economic discrimination, by changing supply, can decrease the wages and incomes of a group that is discriminated against.

> CHECKLIST    Make certain that you also understand the following concepts: jurisdictional
> disputes, strike, labor boycott, collective bargaining.

## REVIEW QUESTIONS

1. When a union can set a wage level for its members, this can be shown diagrammatically, by a supply curve of labor whose elasticity is _____ up to the maximum number willing to work at that wage.

2. If a union pushes wages above the competitive equilibrium wage, the quantity of labor hired will be (more/less) than the quantity of labor supplied. The result will be a (surplus/shortage) of workers available.

3. (a) For a monopsony firm, which can set the wages of unorganized workers, an upward-sloping labor supply means that, if it hires additional workers, it will have to (raise/lower) wages.
   (b) This wage increase will be paid to (all workers/the last worker hired only). The marginal labor cost will be (higher/lower) than the average labor cost or wages paid since increases in hirings push wages up.
   (c) This monopsony firm, if a profit maximizer, will hire workers up to the point at which marginal labor cost equals _____. Compared with the case of competitive demand for labor, this firm would therefore employ (more/fewer) workers at a (lower/higher) wage.

4. By forcing a profit-maximizing monopsonist to pay a higher wage than it otherwise would, a union can cause a (higher/lower) level of employment than would otherwise have occurred.

5. Unions of workers with similar skills are called _____ unions. A union of workers in a given industry, regardless of their different skills, is called a(n) _____ union.

6. Originally, the Trades and Labour Congress in Canada was based on _____ unions, while the Canadian Congress of Labour was formed on the basis of _____ unions. However, in 1956 the two groups amalgamated into a federation called the _____.

9. If a worker does not have to join the union at a plant in order to get or to keep his job, the firm is called a(n) _____.

10. If a new employee must join the union within a certain period after starting a job, the firm is called a(n) _____.

11. Federal government legislation in 1944 guaranteed workers _____ _____.

12. According to Table 21-1 in the text, the total number of union members in Canada is about _____ million. Referring to Figure 21-4 in the text, this number represents over _____ percent of nonagricultural employment.

13. Unions find it easier to gain wage increases under which conditions?
    (a) The industry or firm is (profitable/unprofitable).
    (b) Labor costs are a (small/large) part of total costs.
    (c) Firms are (competitive/monopolistic).
    (d) Demand for the product is (increasing/decreasing).
    (e) Labor supply is (elastic/inelastic).

14. If unions push wages up, *ceteris paribus,* unemployment is apt to increase if the employer is able to substitute _____ . Unions often try to protect their jobs from technological displacement by practices known as

_____ .

15. When workers combine to refuse to work, it is a _____ : when they combine to avoid buying the products of a particular firm, it is a _____ ; when they form a line outside a plant to try to prevent the entry of strikebreakers and/or customers, it is a _____ .

_____

If you have not answered all questions correctly, review the text in order to be sure that you have all of the important concepts clearly in mind before going on to the next chapter.

1. completely elastic or infinite  2. less; surplus  3. raise; all workers; higher; marginal-revenue product; fewer; lower  4. higher  5. craft; industrial  6. craft; industrial; Canadian Labour Congress  7. inelastic; smaller  8. supply of labor  9. open shop  10. union shop  11. the right to form a union and to elect an exclusive bargaining agent  12. 2-3; 30  13. profitable; small; monopolistic; increasing; inelastic  14. labor-saving equipment; featherbedding  15. strike; boycott; picket line

_____

# MULTIPLE-CHOICE QUESTIONS

1. If a group of workers or members of an occupation are able to reduce their numbers and prevent others from entering, in an otherwise competitive market,
   (a) it will still be necessary for them to bargain for any wage increases
   (b) the antitrust laws may be used against them
   (c) their wages will rise, *ceteris paribus*
   (d) the individual members will benefit only if the demand curve for their services is inelastic

2. The Canadian Union of Public Employees is an example of
   (a) a federation in Canada
   (b) an international union
   (c) a national union
   (d) a member of the Confederation of National Trade Unions

3. Pension rights for workers may help employers keep total costs down because
   (a) they are a form of incentive pay
   (b) many workers choose not to accept them
   (c) employers have ways of avoiding providing them
   (d) they may reduce labor turnover

4. An arrangement in which workers must join the union upon employment is called
   (a) a union shop
   (b) a closed shop
   (c) an open shop
   (d) a jurisdictional shop

5. Where the supply curve of labor up upward sloping, the marginal-cost curve of labor to the monopsonist
   (a) is the supply curve of labor
   (b) lies above the supply curve of labor
   (c) lies below and parallel to the supply curve of labor
   (d) lies above and parallel to the supply curve of labor

6. An employer may find the discrimination in employment against equally competent skilled minority groups is more profitable than nondiscrimination
   (a) because he has to pay nonminority groups more
   (b) if the majority of his workers and customers are prejudiced against minority groups
   (c) because nonminority groups are better workers
   (d) if he is the only employer practicing discrimination in a market of unprejudiced customers

7. It was quite common in the past for school boards to pay female teachers much lower salaries than males. This suggests all but one of the following possibilities:
   (a) Single women, with lower living expenses than men with families, were willing to work for less than men.
   (b) Women were not as productive teachers as men.
   (c) The supply curve of female teachers was separate from and to the right of that of male teachers.
   (d) There were far more women than men applying for teaching jobs.

---

Answers to multiple-choice questions: 1(c)   2(c)   3(d)   4(a)   5(b)   6(b)   7(b)

---

# EXERCISES

1. Columns 1 and 2 represent the supply-of-labor relationship for a monopsonist buyer. Fill in the values for total cost in column 3 and then calculate the marginal-cost values in column 4. This exercise should demonstrate to you that the marginal cost of labor lies above the supply curve of labor in a nonparallel fashion.

| (1) Quantity of Labor | (2) Wage Rate | (3) Total Cost | (4) Marginal Cost |
|---|---|---|---|
| 8 | $10.00 | $80.00 | — |
| 9 | 10.50 | | |
| 10 | 11.00 | | |
| 11 | 11.50 | | |
| 12 | 12.00 | | |
| 13 | 12.50 | | |
| 14 | 13.00 | | |

2. Referring to the diagram below, which represents the labor market in an industry, answer the questions below.

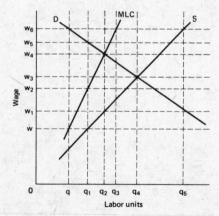

   (a) If a completely competitive market prevailed, the equilibrium wage would be _____, and the amount of employment would be _____.

(b) If a wage-setting union enters this market and sets the wage at $w_6$, the amount of employment would be _____, and the amount of surplus labor unemployed would be _____. How would the labor-supply curve look?

(c) Assume that this market consists of a single large firm hiring labor in a competitive labor market. If the firm hired $q_1$ workers, it would have to pay all workers the wage _____, but the marginal-labor cost of the last man hired would be _____. Because the marginal-revenue product of the last man hired is equal to the amount _____, there is an incentive for the firm to continue hiring to the amount _____, at which the wage will be _____, the marginal-labor cost will be _____, and the marginal-revenue product will be _____. Compare this with the result in (a): _____
_____.

(d) Suppose a union now organizes and sets a wage at $w_3$. The amount of employment will be _____. But if the monopsonist firm feels that it is as strong as the monopoly union, what is probably the only prediction we can make about wages and employment? _____

(e) Draw a new labor-supply curve showing what happens when a union organizes this labor market, but, instead of setting a high wage, excludes half the workers by a combination of stiff apprenticeship rules, high union dues, nepotism, and racial discrimination.

# PROBLEM

## TWO CASES ON MINIMUM WAGES

### A. The Case of the Rural Mill Owner

A traditional argument was that unionization (and/or a legal minimum wage) was necessary to prevent exploitation of labor by the monopsonistic firm—the only employer in an area, a fairly common situation. Not only would wages be raised, it was contended, but also employment would be *increased*.

Take the hypothetical case of Mr. Alfred Newman, whose mill was the only major employer in a rural county. Everyone available locally was on his payroll at the profit-maximizing wage ($1.20 per hour). He had decided not to expand output because he would have had to offer higher wages to attract workers from the next county. Then the United Textile Workers won a representation election and negotiated $1.50 as the minimum wage in the mill.

### Questions

1. Show on the diagram what happens to the supply curve of labor with the new minimum wage.
2. What happens to the marginal-cost-of-labor (*MLC*) curve?

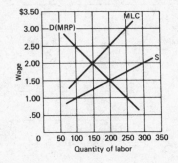

3. Where does the new *MLC* curve intersect the *D* curve for labor?

4. If Mr. Newman now wishes to maximize profits, how many people will he employ? _____

5. Assume that the union gets a further raise; at what level will it reduce employment below the original level? _____

## B. The Case of Ontario's Minimum Wage Increase

In January 1969, the minimum hourly wage rate was raised from $1.00 to $1.30 by the Province of Ontario. This was done to increase the income of workers who have relatively little bargaining power. However, some economists are skeptical about the use of minimum-wage laws to alleviate poverty because of the possibility of higher unemployment for those workers who are directly affected by minimum wage laws.

A study was conducted by Fantl and Whittingham* for the Research Department of the Ontario Department of Labour in order to investigate, among other matters, the *initial* employment effect of the 30-cent rise in the minimum wage. Five low-wage industries which would be relatively sensitive to the chance in the wage law were chosen for this investigation.

### Questions

1. Assuming that these industries can exert no monopoly power in buying labor, discuss the theoretical implications for the employment of workers of the 30-cent-per-hour increase.

2. If we assume that decreases in employment are likely, discuss the actions that firms might pursue to avoid layoffs.

3. During the period from November 1968 (just before the increase) to early January 1969, employers reported, only 25 workers (less than 10 percent of total layoffs) were dismissed because of the increase in the minimum wage.
   (a) According to marginal-productivity theory, what type of workers would be affected by the increase?

   (b) Consider the following information below, taken directly from the report. Given that females comprise about one-half of the labor force in these industries, what would your predictions be as to incidence of layoffs? Males or females?

Percentage Distribution of Non-Supervisory Employees by Sex and Wage Class for Selected Industries, Ontario, November 1968

| Wage Class | Shoe Factories | | | Luggage, Handbags, Small Leather Goods | | | Hosiery Mills | | |
|---|---|---|---|---|---|---|---|---|---|
| | Male | Female | Total | Male | Female | Total | Male | Female | Total |
| Under $1.10 | 0.5 | 4.3 | 3.0 | 1.0 | 2.9 | 2.2 | 0.8 | 4.6 | 3.8 |
| 1.10-1.19 | 1.4 | 7.5 | 5.4 | 0.6 | 9.0 | 6.2 | 1.6 | 11.6 | 9.4 |
| 1.20-1.29 | 2.3 | 13.2 | 9.4 | 2.6 | 13.0 | 9.5 | 3.5 | 14.9 | 12.4 |
| 1.30-1.39 | 2.6 | 11.9 | 8.6 | 1.3 | 6.7 | 11.5 | 2.6 | 13.6 | 11.2 |

Percentage Distribution . . . (continued)

| Wage Class | Children's Clothing | | | Foundation Garments | | |
|---|---|---|---|---|---|---|
| | Male | Female | Total | Male | Female | Total |
| Under $1.10 | 2.1 | 11.3 | 10.4 | — | 4.5 | 4.0 |
| 1.10-1.19 | 2.1 | 10.7 | 9.8 | — | 9.1 | 8.0 |
| 1.20-1.29 | 5.7 | 12.7 | 12.0 | 1.6 | 17.6 | 15.7 |
| 1.30-1.39 | 2.1 | 11.1 | 10.2 | 1.0 | 10.1 | 9.0 |

*Source:* Ontario Department of Labour, Research Branch, 1970.

*The Short-Run Impact of the Thirty Cent Revision in ontario's Minimum Wage on Five Industries, Ontario Department of Labour, Research Branch, September 1970.

# 22

# Interest and the Return on Capital

## KEY CONCEPTS AND DEFINITIONS

1. Capital is all man-made aids to production. When production with capital is more efficient than production without, capital is said to be productive. The difference between the two flows of output (one with capital and one without) is a measure of the productivity of capital.
2. The amount of revenue available to the owners of the firm's capital is the excess of a firm's revenue over the amount payable to factors of production other than capital, and after allowance for taxes and depreciation. This excess is called the return to capital.
3. Economists divide the gross return to capital into three parts: (a) the pure return (the amount that capital could earn in a riskless investment); (b) a risk premium (a return for risk taking); and (c) economic profits.
4. The capital stock refers to the total quantity of physical units of capital. The rate of return on the last dollar of capital employed is called the marginal efficiency of capital (MEC).
5. The schedule that relates the rate of return on each additional dollar of capital stock to the size of the capital stock is called the marginal-efficiency-of-capital schedule.
6. If the population is fixed and technology is constant, adding more capital increases the ratio of capital to labor. This increase is known as capital deepening.
7. Increasing the quantity of capital without affecting the capital-labor ratio (or the ratio with respect to other factors) is called capital widening.
8. Capital deepening decreases the marginal efficiency of capital because capital is assumed to be subject to diminishing returns.
9. Capital is valued because it promises an expected stream of future income to its owners. However, future incomes cannot be compared exactly with current incomes because of positive opportunity costs (usually considered to be the market rate of interest). The present value of income must be calculated. The PV refers to the value now of a payment, or payments, to be made in the future.
10. Present value depends directly on the income expected in the future and inversely on the rate of interest. The PV of a single payment of $x$ after $t$ years is given by the expression $x/(1 + i)^t$.
11. A profit-maximizing firm will invest in a machine whenever the PV of expected income (or the capitalized value of the machine) exceeds the current purchase price of the machine. Alternatively, we can say that a firm will invest in a machine if the MEC exceeds the interest rate that correctly reflects the opportunity cost of capital to the firm.
12. For the economy as a whole, competition among borrowers and lenders of funds for new investment will cause the rate of interest to move toward the MEC.

13. Other factors which affect the level of the interest rate are (a) expectations about future price changes, (b) expectations about future economic conditions, (c) other demands for funds other than for investment, (d) government policy, and (e) bank administration of interest rates.
14. At any moment in time there is a whole structure of interest rates. Individual rates depend on the riskiness, the asset's duration, liquidity, and the various costs of administering the loan.
15. Firms have three main sources for obtaining funds for investment: selling shares in the firm (equity); borrowing (debt); and reinvesting their own profits.
16. Securities (stock) markets allow firms to raise new capital from the sale of newly issued securities and allow the holders of existing securities to sell their securities to other investors.
17. The stockholders are the owners of the company and hence they share in its profits. Because stocks, unlike bonds, carry no promise to pay anything, they contain added elements of uncertainty particularly with respect to the firm's earnings.
18. The value of a stock is importantly determined by the expected income stream of the firm. The ratio of price to earnings, the price-earnings ratio, varies among companies because buyers have very different expectations of future earnings per dollar of present earnings.

---

CHECKLIST    Make certain that you also understand the following concepts: credit rationing; risk; real and money capital; common and preferred stock; bond; perpetuity; capital gains and losses; speculative swings; human capital; money and real rate of interest.

---

# REVIEW QUESTIONS

1. The difference between a flow of output in which part of a given amount of labor and raw materials is first used to produce capital goods and a flow in which the labor and raw materials are directly applied to producing consumption goods is a measure of the _____productivity_____ of capital.

2. In order to increase the production of capital goods, economic resources must be reallocated from the production of _____consumption_____ goods (assuming no unemployed resources exist). The current sacrifice should be more than offset by the future gain because of the (increase/decrease) in output.

3. Education may act as a source of _____human_____ capital. It is productive if the increase in the output of the trained worker over that of the untrained worker _____exceeds_____ the resources used in training him.

4. The gross return to capital is comprised of three elements: a _____risk_____ premium; the _____pure_____ rate of return on capital; and _____economic_____ profits, which may be negative.

5. The rate of return on the last dollar of capital employed is called the _____marginal efficiency of capital_____. The marginal-efficiency-of-capital schedule relates the rate of return on each additional dollar of the capital stock to the size of the _____capital stock_____.

6. Increasing the quantity of capital without changing the proportions of factors used is called _____capital widening_____.

7. Since funds earned in future periods have opportunity costs, future incomes must be _____discounted_____.

8. Future funds are discounted more heavily the (greater/~~lower~~) is the market rate of interest (opportunity cost of money).

9. The interest rate will tend in equilibrium to _____*equal*_____ the *MEC*.

10. In a world of static knowledge, the return on capital and the interest rate will _____*decrease*_____ as capital is accumulated.

11. If the money rate of interest is 8 percent and the price level is rising at 5 percent a year, the real rate of interest is _____*3%*_____.

12. If you are willing to swap $100 now for not less than $110 a year from now, you are discounting that future amount of money at an interest rate of _____*10*_____ percent. If, in addition, you were not very sure that you would get your money back at the end of the year, you would, no doubt, require another 1 percent or more to compensate for _____*risk*_____. If you also would have to go to considerable trouble in correspondence, telephone calls, or personal visits to get your money back, you would add another few percentages to cover _____*costs*_____. Thus, most interest rates charged on consumer borrowing consist of far more than what is called _____*pure*_____ interest.

13. Important sources of financing for a firm are _____*common*_____ or _____*(selling) preferred*_____ stock, borrowing from banks or through sale of _____*bonds*_____, and _____*reinvested*_____ profits.

14. The capitalized value of a perpetuity is found by dividing the current appropriate interest rate into the _____*annual income*_____.

15. If the market is paying 6 percent per year on similar alternate investments, then a building that brings in a net rental income of $3,000 per year should sell for about _____*50,000*_____. If market interest rates now fall, the value of this building will (rise/fall).

16. A rise in the rate of interest (~~raises~~/lowers) the capital value of any asset that yields a fixed future money income.

---

If you have not answered all questions correctly, review the text in order to be sure that you have all of the important concepts clearly in mind before going on to the next chapter.

1. productivity  2. consumption; increase  3. human; exceeds  4. rick, pure, economic
5. marginal efficiency of capita; capital stock  6. capital widening  7. discounted
8. greater  9. equal  10. decrease  11. 3 percent  12. 10; risk; costs; pure  13. common,
preferred, bonds, reinvested  14. annual income  15. $50,000; rise  16. lowers

---

## MULTIPLE-CHOICE QUESTIONS

1. When a firm uses its own funds instead of borrowing for investment purposes,
   (a) its economic costs are lower because it does not have to pay interest
   (b) it should impute an interest rate to get a true picture of cost
   (c) it means it cannot get a loan at the bank
   (d) it does not have to worry about the rate of return on the investment

2. Capital earns income because
   (a) it is productive
   (b) it is expensive
   (c) it is always cheaper to substitute capital for labor
   (d) it is technically more efficient

3. Profits of a particular business could be at a rate less than the pure return on capital
   (a) if economic profits were negative
   (b) if risks were unusually low
   (c) never
   (d) if most income had been paid out as dividends

4. The present value of $x$ dollars a year from now equals
   (a) $xi$
   (b) $x(1 + i)$
   (c) $x/(1 + i)$
   (d) $(1 + i)/x$

5. The higher the rate of interest, *ceteris paribus*,
   (a) the more investment opportunities will be profitable
   (b) the higher the necessary rate of return on any investment
   (c) the lower the amount of borrowing by the federal government
   (d) the greater the demand for investment funds

6. A rise in the interest rate on new debts is associated with
   (a) a fall in the price of old bonds
   (b) a fall in the income on old bonds
   (c) a rise in the price of old bonds
   (d) a rise in the income on old bonds

7. The value of an income-earning asset
   (a) is the sum of all its income payments
   (b) is the discounted present value of its expected income stream
   (c) is measured by its reproduction cost
   (d) rises as interest rates rise

8. Capital deepening occurs
   (a) whenever investment takes place
   (b) when a firm doubles output by replicating its existing facilities
   (c) when capital accumulation increases the proportion of capital to other factors
   (d) when a firm must go more deeply in debt

9. If you borrow $300 and pay it back in twelve equal monthly installments of $28, the true rate of interest is about
   (a) 12 percent
   (b) 6 percent
   (c) 24 percent
   (d) 10 percent

10. The *MEC* shifts to the right
    (a) as capital is accumulated
    (b) as the interest rate drops
    (c) as technical knowledge increases
    (d) as households save more

11. The advantage for shareholders of cumulative preferred stock over common stock is that
    (a) the dividends will be higher than those on common stock
    (b) the opportunity for capital gains is greater
    (c) the payment of dividends is certain
    (d) preferred dividends (including arrears) will be paid before common dividends

---

Answers to multiple-choice questions: 1(b)  2(a)  3(a)  4(c)  5(b)  6(a)  7(b)  8(c)  9(c)  10(c)  11(d)

# EXERCISES

1. Just for practice, fill in the following blanks using the present value (*PV*) table, Table 22-1.

|     | This many $ | in *t* years | has this *PV* | at *i* rate of interest |
|-----|-------------|--------------|---------------|-------------------------|
| (a) | 10          | 5            | _____     | 6%                      |
| (b) | 100         | 50           | $60.80        | _____               |
| (c) | 1,000       | _____    | 3.00          | 12                      |
| (d) | _____      | 6            | 4.56          | 14                      |

2. More practice, this time with the annuity table, Table 22-2.

|     | This many $ | received each year for *t* years | has this *PV* | at *i* rate of interest |
|-----|-------------|----------------------------------|---------------|-------------------------|
| (a) | 10          | 5                                | _____     | 6%                      |
| (b) | 100         | 50                               | $3,919.60     | _____               |
| (c) | 1,000       | _____                        | 8,304.00      | 12                      |
| (d) | _____      | 6                                | 38.89         | 14                      |

3. *Present-Value Calculations*

(a) *Dropping Out with Dad*. Business executive R. P. Squarehole, after a vigorous discussion with R. P., Jr., is considering whether he should drop out of the establishment. He is 50 years old and has $100,000 and adequate pension rights at age 60. Would a 6-percent, 10-year annuity yield him the $13,500 a year he feels would make it feasible? (Note that such an annuity would provide equal payments, pay 6 percent on the declining balance, and exhaust his capital at the end of 10 years.)

(b) *Calculating the Net Rate of Return*. The Acme Machine Shop is analyzing a proposal to purchase labor-saving equipment estimated to save $15,000 a year less $1,000 maintenance. It calculated a 10-year life and $10,000 salvage value for the $75,000 machine. It wishes a return of 14 percent per year before taxes. Should it invest?

(c) *My Son, the Doctor, Maybe*. The senior Schmidts were considering with son Hermann whether he should go on to medical school or enter the family business. They estimated that, if he went on to medical school (four years), internship (one year), and a residency for surgical training (four years), the opportunity cost would be $10,000 a year—mostly for reduced earnings for the nine years. It was esimated that, from the tenth to the fortieth year, his earnings in medicine would exceed his business earnings by $10,000 a year. Mother Schmidt argued for the prestige of the M.D., but Father wanted assurance that this investment in Hermann capital would yield at least 6 percent. Would it? What is it estimated to yield?

Table 22-1    Present Value of $1.00

$$PV = \left(\frac{1}{1+i}\right)^t$$

| Years hence (t) | 1% | 2% | 4% | 6% | 8% | 10% | 12% | 14% | 15% | 16% | 18% | 20% | 22% | 24% | 25% | 26% | 28% | 30% | 35% | 40% | 45% | 50% |
|---|---|---|---|---|---|---|---|---|---|---|---|---|---|---|---|---|---|---|---|---|---|---|
| 1 | 0.990 | 0.980 | 0.962 | 0.943 | 0.926 | 0.909 | 0.893 | 0.877 | 0.870 | 0.862 | 0.847 | 0.833 | 0.820 | 0.806 | 0.800 | 0.794 | 0.781 | 0.769 | 0.741 | 0.714 | 0.690 | 0.667 |
| 2 | 0.980 | 0.961 | 0.925 | 0.890 | 0.857 | 0.826 | 0.797 | 0.769 | 0.756 | 0.743 | 0.718 | 0.694 | 0.672 | 0.650 | 0.640 | 0.630 | 0.610 | 0.592 | 0.549 | 0.510 | 0.476 | 0.444 |
| 3 | 0.971 | 0.942 | 0.889 | 0.840 | 0.794 | 0.751 | 0.712 | 0.675 | 0.658 | 0.641 | 0.609 | 0.579 | 0.551 | 0.524 | 0.512 | 0.500 | 0.477 | 0.455 | 0.406 | 0.364 | 0.328 | 0.296 |
| 4 | 0.961 | 0.924 | 0.855 | 0.792 | 0.735 | 0.683 | 0.636 | 0.592 | 0.572 | 0.552 | 0.516 | 0.482 | 0.451 | 0.423 | 0.410 | 0.397 | 0.373 | 0.350 | 0.301 | 0.260 | 0.226 | 0.198 |
| 5 | 0.951 | 0.906 | 0.822 | 0.747 | 0.681 | 0.621 | 0.567 | 0.519 | 0.497 | 0.476 | 0.437 | 0.402 | 0.370 | 0.341 | 0.328 | 0.315 | 0.291 | 0.269 | 0.223 | 0.186 | 0.156 | 0.132 |
| 6 | 0.942 | 0.888 | 0.790 | 0.705 | 0.630 | 0.564 | 0.507 | 0.456 | 0.432 | 0.410 | 0.370 | 0.335 | 0.303 | 0.275 | 0.262 | 0.250 | 0.227 | 0.207 | 0.165 | 0.133 | 0.108 | 0.088 |
| 7 | 0.933 | 0.871 | 0.760 | 0.665 | 0.583 | 0.513 | 0.452 | 0.400 | 0.376 | 0.354 | 0.314 | 0.279 | 0.249 | 0.222 | 0.210 | 0.198 | 0.178 | 0.159 | 0.122 | 0.095 | 0.074 | 0.059 |
| 8 | 0.923 | 0.853 | 0.731 | 0.627 | 0.540 | 0.467 | 0.404 | 0.351 | 0.327 | 0.305 | 0.286 | 0.233 | 0.204 | 0.179 | 0.168 | 0.157 | 0.139 | 0.123 | 0.091 | 0.068 | 0.051 | 0.039 |
| 9 | 0.914 | 0.837 | 0.703 | 0.592 | 0.500 | 0.424 | 0.361 | 0.308 | 0.284 | 0.263 | 0.225 | 0.194 | 0.167 | 0.144 | 0.134 | 0.125 | 0.108 | 0.094 | 0.067 | 0.048 | 0.035 | 0.026 |
| 10 | 0.905 | 0.820 | 0.676 | 0.558 | 0.463 | 0.386 | 0.322 | 0.270 | 0.247 | 0.227 | 0.191 | 0.162 | 0.137 | 0.116 | 0.107 | 0.099 | 0.085 | 0.073 | 0.050 | 0.035 | 0.024 | 0.017 |
| 11 | 0.896 | 0.804 | 0.650 | 0.527 | 0.429 | 0.350 | 0.287 | 0.237 | 0.215 | 0.195 | 0.162 | 0.135 | 0.112 | 0.094 | 0.086 | 0.079 | 0.066 | 0.056 | 0.037 | 0.025 | 0.017 | 0.012 |
| 12 | 0.887 | 0.788 | 0.625 | 0.497 | 0.397 | 0.319 | 0.257 | 0.208 | 0.187 | 0.168 | 0.137 | 0.112 | 0.092 | 0.076 | 0.069 | 0.062 | 0.052 | 0.043 | 0.027 | 0.018 | 0.012 | 0.008 |
| 13 | 0.879 | 0.773 | 0.601 | 0.469 | 0.368 | 0.290 | 0.229 | 0.182 | 0.163 | 0.145 | 0.116 | 0.093 | 0.075 | 0.061 | 0.055 | 0.050 | 0.040 | 0.033 | 0.020 | 0.013 | 0.008 | 0.005 |
| 14 | 0.870 | 0.758 | 0.577 | 0.442 | 0.340 | 0.263 | 0.205 | 0.160 | 0.141 | 0.125 | 0.099 | 0.078 | 0.062 | 0.049 | 0.044 | 0.039 | 0.032 | 0.025 | 0.015 | 0.009 | 0.006 | 0.003 |
| 15 | 0.861 | 0.743 | 0.555 | 0.417 | 0.315 | 0.239 | 0.183 | 0.140 | 0.123 | 0.108 | 0.084 | 0.065 | 0.051 | 0.040 | 0.035 | 0.031 | 0.025 | 0.020 | 0.011 | 0.006 | 0.004 | 0.002 |
| 16 | 0.853 | 0.728 | 0.534 | 0.394 | 0.292 | 0.218 | 0.163 | 0.123 | 0.107 | 0.093 | 0.071 | 0.054 | 0.042 | 0.032 | 0.028 | 0.025 | 0.019 | 0.015 | 0.008 | 0.005 | 0.003 | 0.002 |
| 17 | 0.844 | 0.714 | 0.513 | 0.371 | 0.270 | 0.198 | 0.146 | 0.108 | 0.093 | 0.080 | 0.060 | 0.045 | 0.034 | 0.026 | 0.023 | 0.020 | 0.015 | 0.012 | 0.006 | 0.003 | 0.002 | 0.001 |
| 18 | 0.836 | 0.700 | 0.494 | 0.350 | 0.250 | 0.180 | 0.130 | 0.095 | 0.081 | 0.069 | 0.051 | 0.038 | 0.028 | 0.021 | 0.018 | 0.016 | 0.012 | 0.009 | 0.005 | 0.002 | 0.001 | 0.001 |
| 19 | 0.828 | 0.686 | 0.475 | 0.331 | 0.232 | 0.164 | 0.116 | 0.083 | 0.070 | 0.060 | 0.043 | 0.031 | 0.023 | 0.017 | 0.014 | 0.012 | 0.009 | 0.007 | 0.003 | 0.002 | 0.001 |  |
| 20 | 0.820 | 0.673 | 0.456 | 0.312 | 0.215 | 0.149 | 0.104 | 0.073 | 0.061 | 0.051 | 0.037 | 0.026 | 0.019 | 0.014 | 0.012 | 0.010 | 0.007 | 0.005 | 0.002 | 0.001 | 0.001 |  |
| 21 | 0.811 | 0.660 | 0.439 | 0.294 | 0.199 | 0.135 | 0.093 | 0.064 | 0.053 | 0.044 | 0.031 | 0.022 | 0.015 | 0.011 | 0.009 | 0.008 | 0.006 | 0.004 | 0.002 | 0.001 |  |  |
| 22 | 0.803 | 0.647 | 0.422 | 0.278 | 0.184 | 0.123 | 0.083 | 0.056 | 0.046 | 0.038 | 0.026 | 0.018 | 0.013 | 0.009 | 0.007 | 0.006 | 0.004 | 0.003 | 0.001 | 0.001 |  |  |
| 23 | 0.795 | 0.634 | 0.406 | 0.262 | 0.170 | 0.112 | 0.074 | 0.049 | 0.040 | 0.033 | 0.022 | 0.015 | 0.010 | 0.007 | 0.006 | 0.005 | 0.003 | 0.002 | 0.001 |  |  |  |
| 24 | 0.788 | 0.622 | 0.390 | 0.247 | 0.158 | 0.102 | 0.066 | 0.043 | 0.035 | 0.028 | 0.019 | 0.013 | 0.008 | 0.006 | 0.005 | 0.004 | 0.003 | 0.002 | 0.001 |  |  |  |
| 25 | 0.780 | 0.610 | 0.375 | 0.233 | 0.146 | 0.092 | 0.059 | 0.038 | 0.030 | 0.024 | 0.016 | 0.010 | 0.007 | 0.005 | 0.004 | 0.003 | 0.002 | 0.001 | 0.001 |  |  |  |
| 26 | 0.772 | 0.598 | 0.361 | 0.220 | 0.135 | 0.084 | 0.053 | 0.033 | 0.026 | 0.021 | 0.014 | 0.009 | 0.006 | 0.004 | 0.003 | 0.002 | 0.002 | 0.001 |  |  |  |  |
| 27 | 0.764 | 0.586 | 0.347 | 0.207 | 0.125 | 0.076 | 0.047 | 0.029 | 0.023 | 0.018 | 0.011 | 0.007 | 0.005 | 0.003 | 0.002 | 0.002 | 0.001 | 0.001 |  |  |  |  |
| 28 | 0.757 | 0.574 | 0.333 | 0.196 | 0.116 | 0.069 | 0.042 | 0.026 | 0.020 | 0.016 | 0.010 | 0.006 | 0.004 | 0.002 | 0.002 | 0.002 | 0.001 | 0.001 |  |  |  |  |
| 29 | 0.749 | 0.563 | 0.321 | 0.185 | 0.107 | 0.063 | 0.037 | 0.022 | 0.017 | 0.014 | 0.008 | 0.005 | 0.003 | 0.002 | 0.002 | 0.001 | 0.001 | 0.001 |  |  |  |  |
| 30 | 0.742 | 0.552 | 0.308 | 0.174 | 0.099 | 0.057 | 0.033 | 0.020 | 0.015 | 0.012 | 0.007 | 0.004 | 0.003 | 0.002 | 0.001 | 0.001 | 0.001 | 0.001 |  |  |  |  |
| 40 | 0.672 | 0.453 | 0.208 | 0.097 | 0.046 | 0.022 | 0.011 | 0.005 | 0.004 | 0.003 | 0.001 | 0.001 |  |  |  |  |  |  |  |  |  |  |
| 50 | 0.608 | 0.372 | 0.141 | 0.054 | 0.021 | 0.009 | 0.003 | 0.001 | 0.001 | 0.001 |  |  |  |  |  |  |  |  |  |  |  |  |

Table 22-2    Present Value of $1.00 Received Annually for t Years

$$PV = \left(\frac{1}{1+i}\right)^1 + \left(\frac{1}{1+i}\right)^2 + \cdots + \left(\frac{1}{1+i}\right)^t$$

| Years (t) | 1% | 2% | 4% | 6% | 8% | 10% | 12% | 14% | 15% | 16% | 18% | 20% | 22% | 24% | 25% | 26% | 28% | 30% | 35% | 40% | 45% | 50% |
|---|---|---|---|---|---|---|---|---|---|---|---|---|---|---|---|---|---|---|---|---|---|---|
| 1 | 0.990 | 0.980 | 0.962 | 0.943 | 0.926 | 0.909 | 0.893 | 0.877 | 0.870 | 0.862 | 0.847 | 0.833 | 0.820 | 0.806 | 0.800 | 0.794 | 0.781 | 0.769 | 0.741 | 0.714 | 0.690 | 0.667 |
| 2 | 1.970 | 1.942 | 1.886 | 1.833 | 1.783 | 1.736 | 1.690 | 1.647 | 1.626 | 1.605 | 1.566 | 1.528 | 1.492 | 1.457 | 1.440 | 1.424 | 1.392 | 1.361 | 1.289 | 1.224 | 1.165 | 1.111 |
| 3 | 2.941 | 2.884 | 2.775 | 2.673 | 2.577 | 2.487 | 2.402 | 2.322 | 2.283 | 2.246 | 2.174 | 2.106 | 2.042 | 1.981 | 1.952 | 1.923 | 1.868 | 1.816 | 1.696 | 1.589 | 1.493 | 1.407 |
| 4 | 3.902 | 3.808 | 3.630 | 3.465 | 3.312 | 3.170 | 3.037 | 2.914 | 2.855 | 2.798 | 2.690 | 2.589 | 2.494 | 2.404 | 2.362 | 2.320 | 2.241 | 2.166 | 1.997 | 1.849 | 1.720 | 1.605 |
| 5 | 4.853 | 4.713 | 4.452 | 4.212 | 3.993 | 3.791 | 3.605 | 3.433 | 3.352 | 3.274 | 3.127 | 2.991 | 2.864 | 2.745 | 2.689 | 2.635 | 2.532 | 2.436 | 2.220 | 2.035 | 1.876 | 1.737 |
| 6 | 5.795 | 5.601 | 5.242 | 4.917 | 4.623 | 4.355 | 4.111 | 3.889 | 3.784 | 3.685 | 3.498 | 3.326 | 3.167 | 3.020 | 2.951 | 2.885 | 2.759 | 2.643 | 2.385 | 2.168 | 1.983 | 1.824 |
| 7 | 6.728 | 6.472 | 6.002 | 5.582 | 5.206 | 4.868 | 4.564 | 4.288 | 4.160 | 4.039 | 3.812 | 3.605 | 3.416 | 3.242 | 3.161 | 3.083 | 2.937 | 2.802 | 2.508 | 2.263 | 2.057 | 1.883 |
| 8 | 7.652 | 7.325 | 6.733 | 6.210 | 5.747 | 5.335 | 4.968 | 4.639 | 4.487 | 4.344 | 4.078 | 3.837 | 3.619 | 3.421 | 3.329 | 3.241 | 3.076 | 2.925 | 2.598 | 2.331 | 2.108 | 1.922 |
| 9 | 8.566 | 8.162 | 7.435 | 6.802 | 6.247 | 5.759 | 5.328 | 4.946 | 4.772 | 4.607 | 4.303 | 4.031 | 3.786 | 3.566 | 3.463 | 3.366 | 3.184 | 3.019 | 2.665 | 2.379 | 2.144 | 1.948 |
| 10 | 9.714 | 8.983 | 8.111 | 7.360 | 6.710 | 6.145 | 5.650 | 5.216 | 5.019 | 4.833 | 4.494 | 4.192 | 3.923 | 3.682 | 3.571 | 3.465 | 3.269 | 3.092 | 2.715 | 2.414 | 2.168 | 1.965 |
| 11 | 10.368 | 9.787 | 8.760 | 7.877 | 7.139 | 6.495 | 5.988 | 5.453 | 5.234 | 5.029 | 4.656 | 4.327 | 4.035 | 3.776 | 3.656 | 3.544 | 3.335 | 3.147 | 2.757 | 2.438 | 2.185 | 1.977 |
| 12 | 11.255 | 10.575 | 9.385 | 8.384 | 7.536 | 6.814 | 6.194 | 5.660 | 5.421 | 5.197 | 4.793 | 4.439 | 4.127 | 3.851 | 3.725 | 3.606 | 3.387 | 3.190 | 2.779 | 2.456 | 2.196 | 1.985 |
| 13 | 12.134 | 11.343 | 9.986 | 8.853 | 7.904 | 7.103 | 6.424 | 5.842 | 5.583 | 5.342 | 4.910 | 4.533 | 4.203 | 3.912 | 3.780 | 3.656 | 3.427 | 3.223 | 2.799 | 2.468 | 2.204 | 1.990 |
| 14 | 13.004 | 12.106 | 10.563 | 9.295 | 8.244 | 7.367 | 6.628 | 6.002 | 5.724 | 5.468 | 5.008 | 4.611 | 4.265 | 3.962 | 3.824 | 3.695 | 3.459 | 3.249 | 2.814 | 2.477 | 2.210 | 1.993 |
| 15 | 13.865 | 12.849 | 11.118 | 9.712 | 8.559 | 7.606 | 6.811 | 6.142 | 5.847 | 5.575 | 5.092 | 4.675 | 4.315 | 4.001 | 3.859 | 3.726 | 3.483 | 3.268 | 2.825 | 2.484 | 2.214 | 1.995 |
| 16 | 14.718 | 13.578 | 11.652 | 10.106 | 8.851 | 7.824 | 6.974 | 6.265 | 5.954 | 5.669 | 5.162 | 4.730 | 4.357 | 4.033 | 3.887 | 3.751 | 3.503 | 3.283 | 2.834 | 2.489 | 2.216 | 1.997 |
| 17 | 15.562 | 14.292 | 12.166 | 10.477 | 9.122 | 8.022 | 7.120 | 6.373 | 6.047 | 5.749 | 5.222 | 4.775 | 4.391 | 4.059 | 3.910 | 3.771 | 3.518 | 3.295 | 2.840 | 2.492 | 2.218 | 1.998 |
| 18 | 16.398 | 14.992 | 12.659 | 10.828 | 9.372 | 8.201 | 7.250 | 6.467 | 6.128 | 5.818 | 5.273 | 4.812 | 4.419 | 4.080 | 3.928 | 3.786 | 3.529 | 3.304 | 2.844 | 2.494 | 2.219 | 1.999 |
| 19 | 17.226 | 15.678 | 13.134 | 11.158 | 9.604 | 8.365 | 7.366 | 6.550 | 6.198 | 5.877 | 5.316 | 4.844 | 4.442 | 4.097 | 3.942 | 3.799 | 3.539 | 3.311 | 2.848 | 2.496 | 2.220 | 1.999 |
| 20 | 18.046 | 16.351 | 13.590 | 11.470 | 9.818 | 8.514 | 7.469 | 6.623 | 6.259 | 5.929 | 5.353 | 4.870 | 4.460 | 4.110 | 3.954 | 3.808 | 3.546 | 3.316 | 2.850 | 2.497 | 2.221 | 1.999 |
| 21 | 18.857 | 17.011 | 14.029 | 11.764 | 10.017 | 8.649 | 7.562 | 6.687 | 6.312 | 5.973 | 5.384 | 4.891 | 4.476 | 4.121 | 3.963 | 3.816 | 3.551 | 3.320 | 2.852 | 2.498 | 2.221 | 2.000 |
| 22 | 19.660 | 17.658 | 14.451 | 12.042 | 10.201 | 8.772 | 7.645 | 6.743 | 6.359 | 6.011 | 5.410 | 4.909 | 4.488 | 4.130 | 3.970 | 3.822 | 3.556 | 3.323 | 2.853 | 2.498 | 2.222 | 2.000 |
| 23 | 20.456 | 18.292 | 14.857 | 12.303 | 10.371 | 8.883 | 7.718 | 6.792 | 6.399 | 6.044 | 5.432 | 4.925 | 4.499 | 4.137 | 3.976 | 3.827 | 3.559 | 3.325 | 2.854 | 2.499 | 2.222 | 2.000 |
| 24 | 21.243 | 18.914 | 15.247 | 12.550 | 10.529 | 8.985 | 7.784 | 6.835 | 6.434 | 6.073 | 5.451 | 4.937 | 4.507 | 4.143 | 3.981 | 3.831 | 3.562 | 3.327 | 2.855 | 2.499 | 2.222 | 2.000 |
| 25 | 22.023 | 19.523 | 15.622 | 12.783 | 10.675 | 9.077 | 7.843 | 6.873 | 6.464 | 6.097 | 5.467 | 4.948 | 4.514 | 4.147 | 3.985 | 3.834 | 3.564 | 3.329 | 2.856 | 2.499 | 2.222 | 2.000 |
| 26 | 22.795 | 20.121 | 15.983 | 13.003 | 10.810 | 9.161 | 7.896 | 6.906 | 6.491 | 6.118 | 5.480 | 4.956 | 4.520 | 4.151 | 3.988 | 3.837 | 3.566 | 3.330 | 2.856 | 2.500 | 2.222 | 2.000 |
| 27 | 23.560 | 20.707 | 16.330 | 13.211 | 10.935 | 9.237 | 7.943 | 6.935 | 6.514 | 6.136 | 5.492 | 4.964 | 4.524 | 4.154 | 3.990 | 3.839 | 3.567 | 3.331 | 2.856 | 2.500 | 2.222 | 2.000 |
| 28 | 24.316 | 21.281 | 16.663 | 13.406 | 11.051 | 9.307 | 7.984 | 6.961 | 6.534 | 6.152 | 5.502 | 4.970 | 4.528 | 4.157 | 3.992 | 3.840 | 3.568 | 3.331 | 2.857 | 2.500 | 2.222 | 2.000 |
| 29 | 25.066 | 21.844 | 16.984 | 13.591 | 11.158 | 9.370 | 8.022 | 6.983 | 6.551 | 6.166 | 5.510 | 4.975 | 4.531 | 4.159 | 3.994 | 3.841 | 3.569 | 3.332 | 2.857 | 2.500 | 2.222 | 2.000 |
| 30 | 25.808 | 22.306 | 17.292 | 13.765 | 11.258 | 9.427 | 8.055 | 7.003 | 6.566 | 6.177 | 5.517 | 4.979 | 4.534 | 4.160 | 3.995 | 3.842 | 3.569 | 3.332 | 2.857 | 2.500 | 2.222 | 2.000 |
| 40 | 32.835 | 27.355 | 19.793 | 15.046 | 11.925 | 9.779 | 8.244 | 7.105 | 6.642 | 6.234 | 5.548 | 4.997 | 4.544 | 4.166 | 3.999 | 3.846 | 3.571 | 3.333 | 2.857 | 2.500 | 2.222 | 2.000 |
| 50 | 39.196 | 31.424 | 21.482 | 15.762 | 12.234 | 9.915 | 8.304 | 7.133 | 6.661 | 6.246 | 5.554 | 4.999 | 4.545 | 4.167 | 4.000 | 3.846 | 3.571 | 3.333 | 2.857 | 2.500 | 2.222 | 2.000 |

(d) A. E. Ames & Co. report in their August 9, 1974, edition of *Money and World Markets* that the ask price of a $100 Bell Canada bond maturing in June 1979 with a coupon rate of 9.75% was $99. Using the present-value tables, prove that the ask price is equal to the capitalized value of the bond.

4. *Marginal Efficiency of Capital Calculations.* Suppose that a firm currently maximizes profits with a capital stock of $10,000. The *MEC* of this capital stock is 10 percent and this is shown in the diagram below.

Now assume that the market rate of interest falls to 8 percent and the firm reassesses the level of the capital stock. It is possible to invest in a machine costing $1,000, which when added to the current capital stock, yields $1,080 in additional net revenue for one year. Thereafter it yields nothing and has no scrappage value.

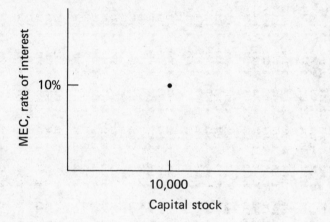

(a) Before the interest rate changed, what must have been the level of the market rate of interest?

(b) Calculate the *MEC* of the $1,000 machine. Show this value with the associated level of the capital stock in the diagram.

(c) Should the firm buy this machine?

# PROBLEM

## CASH BONUSES ON CANADA SAVINGS BONDS (CSB)

Canada savings bonds have been one of the major sources of cash for the federal government for many years. They were first issued to the public in November 1946. They represent a contractual agreement between the government and the original buyer who must be a bona-fide Canadian resident. Canada savings bonds are not transferable; that is, the original buyer cannot sell his CSBs to anyone else. However, CSBs can be cashed in at any time.

There are at least three types or CSBs. The "coupon" variety is the most common. If a bond has a maturity of five yeras, there may be five coupons attached, which indicate the annual interest payment which is to be paid. One coupon is detached each November, and the holder receives a cash payment from the government. Often there will be additional coupons. These will be bonuses paid to the holder if he holds the bond to its maturity date.

During 1973 and 1974, the number of redemptions (the number of bonds sold back to the government) increased substantially and hence the cash position of the federal government became serious. Therefore, the Minister of Finance introduced a system of additional cash bonuses which would become effective on September 1, 1974. The bonuses depended on the date of purchase and the date of maturity of the CSB. For the bonds maturing on or before November 1, 1979, a cash bonus would be paid if they were held to maturity. There were two additional cash bonuses for bonds maturing after November 1, 1979, one in November 1979 and one at the date of maturity. Some of the economic facts during this period are outlined in the table below.

| Year | Average CSB Rate (December observation)* | Annual Inflation Rate | Rate of 5-Year Trust Company Investment Certificates (December observation) |
|---|---|---|---|
| 1971 | 7.13% | 2.85% | 7.14% |
| 1972 | 7.18 | 4.80 | 7.57 |
| 1973 | 7.58 | 7.58 | 8.61 |

*L. N. Christofides, *Aspects of the Canada Savings Bond Market,* Special Study for the Economic Council of Canada, September 1974.

## Questions

1. Why do you think that the number of redemptions increased in 1973 and 1974 (the 1974 inflation rate was about 11 percent, and the CSB rate some time before September 1974 was probably less than 8 percent)?

2. Why was it necessary for the Minister of Finance to introduce the special cash bonus system? Why were bonuses paid only if the bond was held to maturity? What effect would this change have on the CSB rate?

# Poverty, Inequality, and Mobility

## KEY CONCEPTS AND DEFINITIONS

1. The concept of <u>poverty</u> involves relative and absolute levels of income. A minimum amount of income needed by a family is defined as the <u>poverty line</u> below which a family is said to be poor. Roughly 20 percent of Canadians are classified as living in poverty.
2. The <u>incidence of poverty</u> is higher in rural areas, in the Atlantic provinces, and among those who are old, have limited education, or are unemployed.
3. Antipoverty programs have included retraining programs to improve job opportunities, <u>social insurance</u> (old-age pensions, Canada Pension Plan, unemployment insurance), and other welfare programs.
4. Market conditions exercise a powerful influence on factor earnings particularly for nonhuman factors such as land and raw materials. For labor, the influence of nonmonetary factors is important. Nevertheless, market forces exert powerful influences on earnings of labor.
5. In the case of nonhuman factors, there is strong evidence that mobility is high in response to changes in earnings. Nonhuman factor mobility is higher than for labor.
6. Marginal productivity theory of distribution successfully predicts changes in factor earnings that occur for particular groups in response to changes in market conditions. It has little to say about changes in the <u>functional distribution</u> of income among labor, land, and capital.

---

CHECKLIST　　Make certain that you also understand the following concepts: regional economic policy; criticisms of distribution theory.

---

## REVIEW QUESTIONS

1. Marginal-productivity theory explains the (demand for/supply of) factors of production. Profit-maximizing firms will hire units of a factor to the point at which its marginal _____revenue product_____ equals its _____price_____.

2. The theory of supply of factors asserts that factors will move between uses in search of the _____highest_____ net advantage.

3. Labor markets differ from other factor markets in that they are often (more/less) competitive, and differences in money earnings alone (are/are not) enough to make factors move.

4. This chapter suggests that (lower/higher) wages or incomes and (lower/higher) unemployment rates may persuade labor to move from one region to another. The relative of one over the other is an empirical question.

5. In order to explain the (rise/fall) in the wages of coal miners in the face of (declining/ rising) demand for their labor, the monopoly power of _____union_____ must be recognized. Employment, however, has _____fallen_____ in this industry.

6. Functional distribution of income refers to the distribution among such categories as rent, interest, profits, and _____wages + salaries_____.

7. According to two studies by the Economic Council of Canada and Statistics Canada, the percentage of the population classified below the poverty standard of income is approximately _____20%_____ percent.

8. According to the data given in the text, the chances of being poor are greater for people who live in (rural/urban) areas and who work on a (full-time/part-time) basis.

___

If you have not answered all questions correctly, review the text in order to be sure that you have all of the important concepts clearly in mind before going on to the next chapter.

1. demand for; revenue product, price  2. highest  3. less; are not  4. higher; lower
5. rise, declining; unions; fallen  6. wages and salaries  7. 20  8. rural; part-time

___

## MULTIPLE-CHOICE QUESTIONS

1. The condition that firms equate a factor's marginal-revenue product to that factor's price
   (a) is true only in the short run
   (b) is true for all firms, industries, and market structures
   (c) is true only for monopolistic firms
   (d) assumes profit maximization and competition in factor markets

2. Which of the following statements is not true of the marginal-productivity theory?
   (a) It requires competition in all markets.
   (b) It requires that employees be numerous enough to be competitors in factor markets.
   (c) It permits employers to be monopolists.
   (d) It is a theory of demand.

3. To test the theory of distribution, one question which must be answered is
   (a) whether an employer knows the marginal-revenue product of a factor
   (b) whether factors do in fact move to other occupations in response to higher earnings
   (c) whether factor owners have complete knowledge of all opportunities
   (d) whether each factor is being paid the value of its own contribution to production

4. One reason why income differentials do not set up movements of the labor factor as readily as they stimulate movements of nonhuman factors is that
   (a) labor is made less mobile because of nonpecuniary considerations
   (b) people do not really care much about making money
   (c) nonhuman factors are typically small and easily shipped around the country
   (d) nonhuman factors are owned by profit-maximizing people

5. The Canadian government in 1968 established the Department of Regional Economic Expansion, which
   (a) uses compulsion as a means of reallocating labor
   (b) introduces nonmarket policies designed in part to compensate for the immobility of labor
   (c) shifts the demand curve for labor to the left
   (d) has brought unemployment rates in the Atlantic Provinces to the national average

6. The poverty level established by Statistics Canada is the level of a family which spends on the basic necessities of food, clothing, and shelter
   (a) 50 percent of income
   (b) 70 percent or more of income
   (c) 30 percent of income
   (d) less than 50 percent of income

7. The poverty level for a family of five or more in Canada in 1975 is calculated to be
   (a) $5000
   (b) $7200
   (c) $9000
   (d) $4500

8. The highest incidence of poverty occurs in
   (a) the Maritime Provinces
   (b) British Columbia
   (c) Quebec
   (d) the Prairie Provinces

Answers to multiple-choice questions: 1(d)  2(a)  3(b)  4(a)  5(a)  6(b)  7(b)  8(a)

# EXERCISE

The following exercise combines your knowledge of the theories of human capital and net advantage.

Suppose that John Smith, who currently lives in Nova Scotia, conducts some job and information search in the labor markets in Nova Scotia and Ontario. John is assumed to be an income maximizer in the sense that nonmonetary considerations do not influence his locational choice of employment.

He estimates that he will receive $8000 per year for the next thirty years if he works in Nova Scotia. If he moves to Ontario his income flow is estimated to be $8500 per year for the next thirty years. However, his total moving costs are estimated to be $1000 over the first year in Ontario. Moving is a risky business and so John decides to use a 10 percent discount rate when computing the present value of both income streams.

Should John move to Ontario? Use the *PV* tables in Chapter 22 for your analysis.

# PROBLEMS

## 1. THE TREND OF DISTRIBUTIVE SHARES IN CANADA

In what proportions is income distributed between the function of furnishing current labor services and the function of furnishing properties in Canada?

Have these relative shares of income changed over time?

The table below suggests some clues to the answer to these questions. However, the text makes the point that the traditional theory of distribution has not done well in explaining why the shares are as they are.

We have grouped the various components of the Net National Income at Factor Cost into three categories. *Employee Compensation* involves wages, salaries, and supplementary income. *Property Income* includes corporation profits before taxes (but net of dividends paid to nonresidents and inventory valuation adjustment) *plus* interest and miscellaneous investment income. *Entrepreneurial Income* includes net income of farm operators *plus* net income of nonincorporated businesses. This last group also includes rent income, which might more suitably be classified as property income, but we are unable to separate it out of entrepreneurial income.

Distributive Shares in Canada's National Income, 1926-1970, in Percentages*

| Period | Employee Compensation | Property Income | Entrepreneurial Income |
|--------|----------------------|-----------------|------------------------|
| 1926-1930 | 60.3 | 11.8 | 27.7 |
| 1931-1935 | 72.8 | 8.3 | 20.0 |
| 1936-1940 | 63.9 | 12.1 | 22.9 |
| 1941-1945 | 54.6 | 14.3 | 21.5 |
| 1946-1950 | 61.8 | 13.2 | 23.6 |
| 1951-1955 | 62.7 | 16.2 | 19.4 |
| 1956-1960 | 66.4 | 16.3 | 15.6 |
| 1961-1965 | 67.7 | 16.6 | 13.9 |
| 1966-1970 | 70.8 | 16.5 | 11.4 |
| 1971-1975 | 71.5 | 17.4 | 10.0 |

*Compiled from data in *Revised Estimates of Income and Expenditures*, Statistics Canada, 1972, and *Canadian Statistical Review*. Omitted are military salaries and allowances.

Questions

1. Check those generalizations that seem true from the table above.
   (a) The share of employee compensation in national income has remained stable since 1945.

   _____
   (b) The share of employee compensation rose drastically during the depression years, fell during war years, and since then has risen steadily. _____
   (c) The property share declined during depression years but has risen steadily since then.

   _____
   (d) The property share has remained relatively constant since the end of World War II.

   _____
   (e) The entrepreneurial income share has fallen steadily since the depression years.

   _____

2. Many factors have contributed to the fall in the entrepreneurial share of national income. However, given that a large majority of entrepreneurs have been farmers or small retailers, what is one obvious reason why the share of entrepreneurial income has declined?

3. If we neglect the element of rent included in entrepreneurial income, is it reasonable to argue that entrepreneurial income may itself be divided between labor and a return to capital (property income)? Explain.

## 2.  THE INCIDENCE OF POVERTY ACCORDING TO OCCUPATIONS IN CANADA

Table 23-2 in the text illustrated some of the major characteristics of families whose income was below some cutoff point called the *poverty line*. We now consider an additional characteristic: the main occupation of the head of the family. In the table below we have shown the incidence of low income according to the main occupation of the head of the family. These figures give rough indications of the chances or "probabilities" of poverty according to various occupations. For example, we can say that there is about a 3-percent probability of being poor if you have a professional or technical occupation.

Incidence of Low Income, Canada, 1967*

| Occupation of Head | Percentage |
|---|---|
| Managerial | 6.7 |
| Professional and technical | 3.3 |
| Clerical | 5.6 |
| Sales | 7.2 |
| Service and recreation | 16.7 |
| Transportation and communication | 14.9 |
| Farmers and farm workers | 52.8 |
| Loggers and fishermen | 42.3 |
| Miners | 8.9 |
| Craftsmen | 9.6 |
| Laborers | 21.4 |

*Statistics on Low Income in Canada, 1967,
Statistics Canada, 1971.

## Questions

1. In Chapter 22 you were introduced to the concept of investments in human capital. Specifically, academic and vocational education along with apprenticeship programs are examples of investments in human capital that improve individual skills and crafts. In turn, higher income is obtained for the improvement in skills. By inspecting the table above, select those occupations that most likely involve the greatest amounts of investments in human capital. Are the probabilities of poverty relatively high or low for these occupations?

2. If an individual finds himself continually unemployed and/or hired for particular seasons, his income is likely to be low. In your opinion, which of the above occupations tends to have the highest levels of unemployment and/or seasonality? Give reasons for your choices. What relationship exists between your choices and the incidence of poverty?

# The Price System: Market Success and Market Failure

## KEY CONCEPTS AND DEFINITIONS

1. The main advantage of the price system is that it provides a signal to alter levels and the composition of output in response to consumer preferences. Without markets and a price system, decisions on output levels must be made by administrative structures. In a complex economy, such bureaucracies are themselves expensive.

2. In a market system, unfettered by government, pricing policies are ultimately based on costs as determined by the producer. Such private costs reflect the best alternative of any resource to the producer. However, this cost may not reflect the best alternative use to society as a whole. A cost which measures the value of a resource to society is known as social cost.

3. The market system equates private benefits and private costs. Should these be different from social benefits and social costs, then the market system fails from the viewpoint of society in allocating resources in the best possible way. A divergence between social and private benefits or costs may be generated by what is called an externality.

4. Markets do not function independently. In some instances, the interaction is small while in others it is highly significant. The study of markets and their interaction is called general equilibrium analysis and is the study of the operation of a single market.

5. When markets fail to allocate resources and distribute the economy's wealth in accordance with social objectives, governments may be asked to intervene in a market. A market failure may result due to the presence of externalities, the existence of collective consumption goods, value judgments on the part of society and ignorance.

6. Pollution of air and water is the classic case of an externality. Government interference with those markets which contribute to pollution may involve rules of behavior or the imposition of taxes or effluent charges to internalize the external effects of production. Such market intervention is costly and the costs of interference must be carefully weighed against the benefits.

> **CHECKLIST**  Make certain that you also understand the following concepts: laissez-faire; collective consumption goods; net private benefit; net social benefit.

# REVIEW QUESTIONS

1. One of the features of a market economy is that centralized planning is not necessary for allocating resources. Private enterprise responds to signals, such as
_____ , _____ , and
_____ that result from interaction of supply and demand.

2. A market that is working most efficiently is one where marginal net private benefits _____ marginal net social benefits.

3. The more efficient the market in allocating and producing, the (greater/less) the net social benefit.

4. A policy of least possible governmental interference in the market is called one of
_____ . Such a policy is apt to be abandoned if net social benefits are greatly (in excess of/exceeded by) net private benefits.

5. Because of the interdependence of markets, a change in one area of the economy produces a series of three effects: _____ , _____ , and
_____ . Where feedback is noticeable, _____
equilibrium analysis is important.

6. *Externalities* discussed in this chapter result when social costs (exceed/are less than)
_____ .

7. Markets often fail to perform efficiently because of so-called market imperfections, such as (name several): _____ , _____ ,
_____ , _____ .

8. Goods and services that, if provided at all, benefit simultaneously a large group of people are called _____ . Local roads are financed by
_____ rather than by private enterprise, because there is generally no practical way to collect payment directly from users.

9. By *internalizing* externalities, we mean that the producer is required to
_____ .

10. If a particular polluting activity is causing $1 million of damage to the environment and would cost $3 million to prevent, the economic cost of the pollution is _____ .

11. One way for society to induce a polluting firm to adopt antipollution devices is by providing incentives such as _____ .

12. If anti-air-pollution regulations cause a firm to close down because of the cost, there may be a conflict between the goals of cleaner air and _____ .

13. Governmental intervention is more likely when the difference between private and social costs is (large/small).

14. In deciding how many resources to put into the fight against pollution, the economic answer would be to compare the benefits to be gained with the _____
of the action.

---

If you have not answered all questions correctly, review the text in order to be sure that you have all of the important concepts clearly in mind before going on to the next chapter.

1. prices, cost profits  2. equal  3. greater  4. laissez-faire; in excess of  5. impact, spillout, feedback, general  6. exceed, private costs  7. factor immobility, ignorance, monopoly, externalities  8. collective consumption goods  9. pay the total cost  10. $1 million  11. effluent charges  12. employment  13. large  14. costs

# MULTIPLE-CHOICE QUESTIONS

1. A market is operating most efficiently if
   (a) total social cost is minimized
   (b) total private benefit is maximized
   (c) net social benefit is maximized
   (d) the excess of private benefits over social cost is maximized

2. General-equilibrium analysis as compared with partial-equilibrium analysis
   (a) is necessarily more comprehensive
   (b) is more dependent on *ceteris paribus* assumptions
   (c) is not concerned with relative prices
   (d) includes feedback effects

3. A collective consumption good is
   (a) the same as a free good
   (b) goods provided to union members
   (c) a good which, if it is provided at all, automatically is provided to many
   (d) a consumption good produced by a co-operative

4. A firm would have no incentive to internalize its externalities if
   (a) it is penalized by a fine
   (b) its pollution is subject to tax
   (c) its stockholders are environmentalists
   (d) the cost of the externalities is borne by others

5. From the point of view of those who favor a market economy, government intervention would be least justifiable to
   (a) protect the health and safety of the public
   (b) guarantee profits to businessmen
   (c) ensure correct information to consumers
   (d) provide needed public services that private enterprise finds unprofitable

6. All but which of the following are market imperfections that could be alleviated by government intervention?
   (a) nonmonetary preferences of labor that reduce mobility
   (b) lack of knowledge of the market by consumers and workers
   (c) monopoly power
   (d) artificial barriers to entry

7. A tax on the effluent that a firm in a competitive industry places in a river would likely
   (a) cause the firm to raise its price
   (b) change the level of production in the firm
   (c) induce the firm to seek methods of reducing its effluent
   (d) affect the market demand schedule in the industry

Answers to multiple-choice questions: 1(c)   2(d)   3(c)   4(d)   5(b)   6(a)   7(c)

# EXERCISES

1. Suppose that installing an antipollution device adds $10 to the cost of making each unit of a product at every level of output. *Ceteris paribus:*
   (a) marginal cost will _____.
   (b) average cost will _____.
   (c) the supply curve will _____.
   (d) short-run equilibrium price will _____ but by less than _____.
   (e) short-run equilibrium output will _____.

2. Suppose that all firms in an industry must install an antipollution device at $10,000 regardless of the level of output. *Ceteris paribus:*
   (a) marginal cost will _____.
   (b) average cost will _____.
   (c) variable cost will _____.
   (d) short-run equilibrium price will _____.
   (e) short-run equilibrium output will _____.
   (f) long-run equilibrium price will _____.

3. The following are examples of possible government intervention in the economy. In a word or two, predict the effect on relative profitability of indicated industries or relative desirability of indicated activity.
   (a) The Province of Ontario passes new laws reducing allowed length and weight of trucks on provincial highways. Effect on:
      trucking _____
      railroads _____
   (b) The government of Canada imposes a tax on gasoline which applies only to individuals who use gasoline for noncommercial purposes. Effect on:
      private gasoline consumption _____
      trucking _____
      private transportation _____
   (c) The Federal Department of Transport announces a new policy of letting aviation pay its own way; federal aid to airport construction and air-traffic control will be financed from higher taxes on airline fares, aviation gasoline, and airport taxes, instead of from general taxation revenues. Effect on:
      airlines _____
      railroads _____
   (d) Parliament legislates new laws that disallow tax advantages which various U.S. magazines (*Reader's Digest* and *Time*) had in Canada and gives subsidies to Canadian publications. Effect on:
      foreign publishers _____
      Canadian publishers _____

4. The following schedule shows (a) how the cost of resources increases as a pulp and paper firm expands output and (b) the effect of pollution from the firm on commercial fishing in the area.

| Output (tons/wk) | Total Private Cost | Dollar Value of Fishing Loss Due to Pollution |
|---|---|---|
| 0 | 0 | 0 |
| 1 | 500 | 100 |
| 2 | 550 | 225 |
| 3 | 620 | 365 |
| 4 | 710 | 515 |
| 5 | 820 | 675 |
| 6 | 1050 | 845 |
| 7 | 1350 | 1025 |

(a) Complete the table below and graph your results.

| Average Private Cost (*APC*) | Marginal Private Cost (*MC*) | Average Social Cost (*ASC*) | Marginal Social Cost (*MSC*) |
|---|---|---|---|
| _____ | _____ | _____ | _____ |
| _____ | _____ | _____ | _____ |
| _____ | _____ | _____ | _____ |
| _____ | _____ | _____ | _____ |
| _____ | _____ | _____ | _____ |
| _____ | _____ | _____ | _____ |
| _____ | _____ | _____ | _____ |

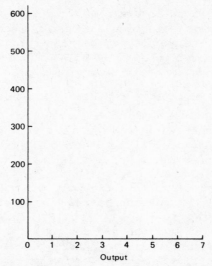

(b) If the firm were producing four tons of output per week, what price would they require to cover their private cost? What price would they require to cover the social cost?

(c) If pricing were based on the average costs and *all* costs of producing pulp and paper were considered, then the price of pulp and paper would always be _____ than the case where only private costs are considered.

# PROBLEMS

## 1. THE ECONOMICS OF POLLUTION

### A. The Canada Water Act

In 1970, the Federal Government of Canada passed legislation that established the Canada Water Act. The following remarks are by the Honorable J. J. Greene, Minister of Energy, Mines and Resources, delivered during the second reading of the Bill in 1969.*

> Waste disposal is not necessarily an illegitimate use for water and it does not necessarily interfere with other uses for water because our waterways, if not overloaded, can purify themselves. It is only when the natural ability of water to cleanse itself is surpassed that we find this use of water interfering with other uses of that precious resource.
> All of this makes one point very clear. Our water must be so used as to ensure the maximum stream of benefits to all of the users for all of the purposes for which water is required. This optimization can only occur if we have comprehensive planning to achieve our goal of multi-purpose use. We must look at each basin as an integrated whole. We must examine all the uses which can be made of each basin. We must plan for the future so as to achieve the greatest long-term net social benefit of our water resources. The Canada water bill will allow us to do this—to plan together with the provinces firstly the optimum utilization of our water resources, taking into account all the uses which can be made of our water; and secondly, the re-establishment of water quality to preserve the best balance among these uses.
> . . . we are facing a costly problem and we shall not avoid it. It will cost Canadian society some billions of dollars over a period of time to deal with its water resources in

a rational way, and to undo the damage we have done in the last hundred years. But let us think of the alternate cost, that of doing nothing. To begin with, doing nothing is a threat to our entire way of life, and, yes, perhaps to life itself. Eventually, if we do not act to clean up air and water pollution, if we allow our environment to run down further we may upset the ecological and climatological balances of nature upon which life itself depends.

But even if the problem we face has not yet reached this peak, there are huge social costs involved. It is not heard to imagine the day—not far off if we do not act—when there will be no place within easy range of our cities where a person can go to swim in a natural river or lake, or any accessible place where fish can still live, or any place to just walk beside a pleasant stream. Our society will have its two cars in every garage but there will be no fit outdoor place in which to drive them. Yes, we will have our superclean, automatically washed clothes, but will there be any place fit to walk in these snow white garments? These are staggering social costs, costs that neither we nor our children will have to pay, if we act now.

Then, too, there are the purely monetary costs. Water despoiled by man must be cleaned again for his own use. The cost of purifying the water we have first made dirty is high. How much better to clean up our effluents before we put them into our rivers. For we then have the double benefit of clean water while it is in the stream, and drastically lowered purification costs when we want to use it again.

There are other monetary costs as well. The salmon run in certain maritime rivers may by dying because of our pollution. With it would die a source of revenue as well as of pleasure. Our other fisheries are also threatened by pollution, and with them would go the livelihood and the way of life of thousands of Canadians. Our tourist industry depends on no small part on the cleanliness of our stresms, rivers and lakes . . . Without the use of our most important single resource, water, the future of the industry would be a bleak one indeed!

The problem has arisen from the unwise use of resources that come to us free of charge. The lesson which we can learn from the past is a vital one. It is simply this, that the unplanned and uncontrolled use of our resources, even of the Canada water bill, and the thinking of experts of all persuasions across Canada, is that no longer can we afford the unplanned and uncontrolled use of our water resources. No longer can each individual, each industry, each municipality, use our water resources as each sees fit. In that absolute and laissez-faire freedom lies the mistake of the past, and the disaster of the future. Those who use our waters must pay for that use, either by cleaning up what they discharge into our river basins, or by paying others to clean it up for them. This is the very gist of the Canada Water Act and the essence of its structure, that the user must pay for cleaning the water, for putting it back into the condition in which he found it and for improving it if indeed it requires improvement. The result, it is true, may be higher direct costs for certain goods and services. But as we look at these costs, we must remember that there will be savings to other users of the water who also have a right to expect that the water they receive will be clean and in good condition when it reaches them. We must remember, too, that there is no way we can avoid these costs and still maintain the quality of life. Everyone in society must eventually pay; this is the thing we must remember, and all society will thereby gain.

## Questions

1. Why is it that the "social costs" referred to by Mr. Greene cannot normally be considered part of the total production costs of any polluting activity?

2. Why do you think man uses "free" resources unwisely?

## B. Effluent Charges

Section 13(1) subsection (c)(iv) of the Canada Water Act reads that water quality management agencies will recommend " . . . as to the appropriate effluent discharge fees to be paid by persons for the deposit of waste in those waters. . . . "

### Questions

1. What factors do you feel should be considered in setting the amount of the fee?

2. What problems do you envisage in making these fees workable?

## 2.  THE NOISY FACTORY

Consider a factory which is causing such excessive noise that it seriously affects the enjoyment of living for residents in three houses nearby. The residents file a complaints, and, in the hearing which follows, the following information is revealed:

1. The cost to the factory to reduce the noise would be $150,000.
2. The expense of relocating the three homes would be $100,000.

### Questions

1. If you have to decide on efficiency grounds *alone,* what should be done? What would you recommend? Why?

2. If the law were such that it was a person's "right" to have a quiet place of residence, why would the factory probably pay for the relocation of the homes?

# 25

## Public Finance and Public Expenditure

Key Concepts and Definitions

1. The effect that various taxes have on taxable income are often described as progressive, proportional, or regressive, dependong on the change in the ratio of tax revenue to taxable income as income rises.
2. Government expenditures can be similarly classified depending on the ratio of the benefit bestowed by some public expenditure to taxable income as income increases.
3. Although a given tax may be levied upon a specific tax base, those who initially bear the tax may <u>shift</u> the burden of the tax to others so thatthe ultimate <u>incidence</u> of the tax may be quite removed from the person(s) who inistially made the payment to the government.
4. Taxes will affect prices, output levels, and incomes to factors of production, thereby exerting allocative effects in the economy through changing the net rewards to factors of production.
5. Government spending can be classified into two broad categories, transfer payments, and expenditure on goods and services. Only the latter represents a direct or indirect purchase of factors of production from the economy.
6. Within a federation, the central government may adopt policies to redistribute wealth on a geographical basis from wealthy to less wealthy jurisdictions in the country. Such payments take the form in Canada of <u>equalization payments</u>. An additional, <u>conditional grant</u> may be used to encourage particular kinds of expenditure by provincial or local governments.
7. The debate over the relative size of government spending depends very much upon individual marginal evaluations of additional monies being spent on public projects versus the value of leaving the money in private households.

---

CHECKLIST    Make certain that you also understand the following concepts: excise; marginal tax rate; negative income tax; ad valorem tax.

---

Review Questions

1. When a tax takes an increasing proportion of income as income increases, it is termed *progressive* _____*proportional*_____. If it takes a decreasing proportion of income as income increases, it is termed _____*regressive*_____ .

2. Sales taxes on such commodities as tobacco and gasoline are generally _regressive_ _____. Most studies have shown property taxes to be somewhat _____ _regressive_ _____. The federal income tax is _progressive_ _____ both in structure and effect.

3. Negative income taxes are _____ _payments_ _____ to people whose income falls below a certain level.

4. Answering the question of who really bears the burden of a tax involves analysis of the _____ _incidence_ _____ of a tax.

5. As long as the demand curve for a commodity slopes downward and the supply curve upward, the incidence of an excise on that commodity falls on (the sellers/the buyers/~~both~~).

6. In general, the greater the elasticity of demand with a given elasticity of supply, the (greater/~~less~~) the rise of price following the imposition of a specific excise.

7. In general, the greater the elasticity of supply with a given elasticity of demand, the (greater/~~less~~) the rise of price following the imposition of a specific excise.

8. A tax on pure profits (~~will~~/will not) affect price and output and thus the incidence will fall on (producers/~~consumers~~).

9. Payments by government to individuals for no productive service are called _____ _transfer_ _____ payments. Such payments constitute about __1/3_____ of total federal expenditures; the rest consists of purchases of __goods + services_ Federal conditional grants to provinces are primarily for two main purposes: _____ _health_ _____ and _____ _education_ _____.

10. Indicate the major source or sources of tax revenue for the following levels of government:
    (a) federal—_income_
    (b) municipal—_property_
    (c) provincial—_sales + income_

11. Increasing tax rates and public expenditures in North American cities result primarily from a combination of circumstances:
    (a) (high/~~low~~) income elasticity of demand for certain public services
    (b) departures of the (wealthy/~~poor~~) to the suburbs
    (c) tax revenues that rise (more slowly/~~faster~~) than income
    (d) government pay that has risen (faster/~~more slowly~~) than productivity in these jobs
    (e) relocation of industry and jobs in the (~~cities~~/suburbs)

---

If you have not answered all questions correctly, review the text in order to be sure that you have all of the important concepts clearly in mind before going on to the next chapter.

1. progressive; regressive  2. regressive; regressive; progressive  3. payments  4. incidence  5. both  6. less  7. greater  8. will not, producers  9. transfer; one-third, goods and services; health, education  10. income, property, sales and income  11. high, wealthy, more slowly, faster, suburbs

---

## MULTIPLE-CHOICE QUESTIONS

1. A 10-percent surtax on income taxes all across the board raises the tax rate in each bracket by 10 percent of itself. This meant that the income tax
   (a) became slightly more progressive than before
   (b) became slightly closer to proportional than before
   (c) required an equal absolute increase from everyone
   (d) even affected those with no taxable income

2. A tax that takes the same amount from everyone, regardless of income, is
   (a) regressive
   (b) progressive
   (c) not fair at all
   (d) proportional to the benefit received

3. The text suggests that personal income taxes are progressive, while sales taxes are apt to be
   (a) proportional
   (b) intolerable
   (c) about the same as federal
   (d) regressive

4. A negative income tax of the type described in the text would have the advantage of
   (a) eliminating all need for welfare or relief programs
   (b) guaranteeing a minimum income to the poor with less red tape and with increased work incentives
   (c) penalizing those with large families
   (d) keeping recipients out of the labor force where they would cause unemployment

5. The marginal rate (1972) of 50 percent on a taxable income of $24,000
   (a) meant that the average person with $24,000 of income paid $12,000 in taxes
   (b) had no effect whatever because of exemptions, deductions, and tax avoidance
   (c) signified the collection of 50 cents on each additional dollar of income
   (d) applied to capital gains as well as ordinary income

6. The more elastic the demand for a commodity on which a specific excise was levied, *ceteris paribus*,
   (a) the greater the after-tax price increase
   (b) the less the reduction in the quantity produced
   (c) the more elastic the associated supply curve
   (d) the less the after-tax price increase

7. Property taxes generally
   (a) fall entirely on the home-owner or landlord
   (b) are less likely to be shifted in the long run than in the short run
   (c) fall on renters as well as home-owners and landlords
   (d) are borne entirely by the occupany of a house

8. Which of the following has *not* been a significant reason for the financial difficulties of local governments over the last decade?
   (a) tax revenues that do not respond relatively to growth in income
   (b) lower local tax rates
   (c) rising demands for government services
   (d) rising unit costs of providing government services

9. Decentralization of government economic activity can be justified by all but which of the following?
   (a) regional preferences
   (b) income redistribution
   (c) particular local needs for public expenditure
   (d) cultural differences within the country

10. Increasing amounts of tax revenue have been transferred to the provincial and municipal governments for all except which of the following reasons?
    (a) expenditure needs of urban areas are rapidly growing
    (b) municipal revenue sources have been growing slowly
    (c) provincial and municipal governments don't collect tax revenue
    (d) the federal government has access to the high-growth tax sources

Answers to multiple-choice questions:  1(a)    2(a)    3(d)    4(b)    5(c)    6(d)    7(c)    8(b)    9(b)
10(c)

# EXERCISES

1. Assume that an excise of one-fifth of $P$ is imposed on each of the commodities for which demand and supply curves are given below.

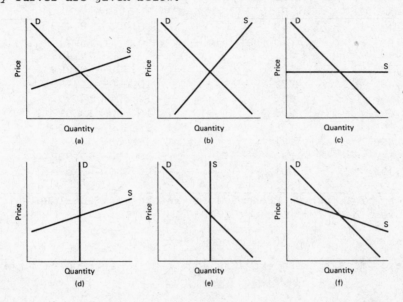

(a) In which cases is the price predicted to rise by at least the full amount of the tax?
_____ _____ _____

(b) In which case is the price unaffected? _____

(c) Is the price rise greater in case a or case b? _____ Why?

(d) Is the price rise greater in case a or case d? _____ Why?

# PROBLEM

## THE PROPERTY TAX IN ONTARIO

A study by the Province of Ontario in Guelph, Ontario, produced the following table illustrating the relationship between household income and property taxes in 1968.

| Household Income (class) | Average Property Tax Paid | Household Income (class) | Average Property Tax Paid |
|---|---|---|---|
| Less than $ 2,500 | $268 | $ 8,000-  8,499 | $317 |
| $ 2,500-  2,999 | 276 | 8,500-  8,999 | 319 |
| 3,000-  3,499 | 261 | 9,000-  9,499 | 330 |
| 3,500-  3,999 | 276 | 9,500-  9,999 | 342 |
| 4,000-  4,499 | 278 | 10,000- 11,999 | 355 |
| 4,500-  4,999 | 285 | 12,000- 14,999 | 417 |
| 5,000-  5,499 | 275 | 15,000- 19,999 | 495 |
| 5,500-  5,999 | 268 | 20,000- 24,999 | 581 |
| 6,000-  6,499 | 281 | 25,000- 49,999 | 650 |
| 6,500-  6,599 | 290 | 50,000- 99,999 | 836 |
| 7,000-  7,499 | 301 | 100,000 and over | — |
| 7,500-  7,999 | 302 | | |

*Source:* Ministry of Treasury, Economics and Intergovernmental Relations; *Analysis of Property Taxes in Guelph,* October 1972.

## Questions

1. Given these data, does the property tax appear to be regressive or progressive? Why?

2. To make a tax a proportional one, at a tax rate roughly equal to 8 percent, what kind of subsidies and additional taxes would the government need to impose at each household income level?

# 26

# Tariff Policy and the Gains from Trade

## KEY CONCEPTS AND DEFINITIONS

1. Tariffs are a tax placed on imported goods and can be used as a source of revenue or as a tool of protection to restrict or to prevent the importation of certain goods.
2. Free trade exists when no tariffs and/or no restrictions of any kind are put on imports and exports.
3. The advantages that may be realized as a result of trade between any two groups, be they individuals, regions, or nations, are usually referred to as the gains from trade.
4. The source of such gains is that trade stimulates people (nations) to specialize in production.
5. The gains from specialization are clear if both nations have an absolute advantage in producing one good. Absolute advantage relates to the quantities of a single product that can be produced with the same quantity of resources in two different regions. One region is said to have an absolute advantage over another in the production of good X if an equal quantity of resources can produce more X in the first region than in the second.
6. In the case of absolute advantage, the gains from specialization generate gains from trade.
7. However, the gains from trade do not require absolute advantage on the part of each country, only comparative advantage. Comparative advantage refers to the relative advantage one country enjoys over another in various commodities.
8. World production of all commodities can be increased if each country transfers resources into the production of the commodities in which it has a comparative advantage.
9. The theory of the gains to trade may be stated in terms of opportunity costs. Trade allows all countries to obtain goods in which they do not have a comparative advantage at a lower opportunity cost (in terms of units sacrificed of the commodities in which they do have a comparative advantage) than they would have to accept if they were to produce all commodities for themselves.
10. Other gains from trade are learning by doing (greater efficiency) and economies of scale (large-scale production causes reductions in cost).
11. The terms of trade refer to the quantity of imported goods that can be obtained per unit of goods exported. They therefore measure the opportunity cost of obtaining goods by trade.
12. Free trade allows world output of all commodities to be higher than when protectionism restricts regional specialization. Ignoring the case for world output increases, protectionism is advanced as a means of reducing fluctuations in national income, retaining national traditions, and to improving national defense.

13. Protection can also be urged on grounds that it may lead to a higher living standard for the protectionist country. This may come about if (a) there are monopoly gains to be made, and (b) industries which are inexperienced or small scale may become efficient eventually. This latter consideration is referred to as the <u>infant-industry argument</u> for tariffs.

14. Virtually everyone would agree that free trade should be chosen if the only choice were between free trade and no trade. But the choice between <u>a little more trade</u> (caused by a lowering of tariffs) and <u>a little less trade</u> (raising tariffs) is less clear. The potential gain from small reductions in tariffs must be balanced against other objectives and other effects.

---

| CHECKLIST | Make certain that you also understand the following concepts: fallacious pro-tariff and antitariff arguments; ad valorem tariff. |

## REVIEW QUESTIONS

1. Tariffs are used for two different and opposite purposes: _protection_ and _revenue_. A tariff makes imported goods (cheaper/**more expensive**).

2. Free trade is said to exist when tariffs and/or trade restrictions (are/**are not**) imposed on imports and exports.

3. Gains from trade between nations are (~~unlike~~/similar) to those from trade between individuals and regions. Trade allows _specialization_ to occur; otherwise a nation, a region, or an individual must be _self-sufficient_. Trade (raises/~~lowers~~) living standards, because a (**greater**/~~smaller~~) total output may thus be produced.

4. If an equal quantity of resources can produce more of product X in country A than in country B, A is said to have a(n) _absolute_ advantage over B in the production of X. For trade to take place, it is a (~~necessary but not sufficient~~/sufficient but not necessary) condition for B to have an absolute advantage in the production of some other commodity.

5. The gains from specialization and trade depend on the existence of _comparative advantage_. Gains from trade are (**possible**/~~impossible~~) if one country can produce all commodities more efficiently than the other.

6. Suppose that country A is 10 times more efficient than country B in producing watches, and 5 times more efficient than B in producing dairy products. A has a comparative advantage in _producing watches_, and B in _producing dairy products_. A should specialize in and export _watches_ to B; B should specialize in and export _dairy products_ to A.

7. Comparative advantage can be restated in terms of _opportunity_ costs. This avoids the problem of comparing real resource costs, because it expresses costs in terms of the _output otherwise could be produced_.

8. Opportunity costs depend on (~~absolute~~/relative) costs. Differing opportunity costs in two countries result in (~~absolute~~/comparative) advantage for one country.

9. Specialization may permit further gains from trade to occur if it results in the producers of a product becoming more _efficient_, or if there are economies of _scale_. As production expands, opportunity costs will (**rise**/fall) and gains from trade will (rise/~~fall~~).

10. If expanding production of a good with a comparative advantage results in long-run increasing costs in a country, opportunity cost of that good will (rise/~~fall~~) and comparative advantage will (~~increase~~/decrease).

11. The division of the gains from trade between nations depends on the so-called terms of _____*trade*_____. These are defined as the quantity of _____*domestic good*_____ that must be given up to obtain a unit of _____*imports*_____, in other words, the _____*opportunity*_____ cost of obtaining imports. If the opportunity cost of obtaining imports is less than that of producing the same goods at home, it makes sense to (import them/~~produce them at home~~).

12. As with other prices, the terms of trade are determined by conditions of _____*demand*_____ and _____*demand*_____ in the markets of the products concerned.

13. National defense is used as an argument for a protectionist policy in such industries as _____*shipping*_____ and _____*oil*_____.

14. A developing country might justify tariffs to protect its _*infant industries*_. This is a valid argument only if expanded production results in _*economies of scale*_.

---

If you have not answered all questions correctly, review the text in order to be sure that you have all of the important concepts clearly in mind before going on to the next chapter.

1. revenue; protection  2. are not  3. similar; specialization, self-sufficient; raises, greater  4. absolute; sufficient but not necessary  5. comparative advantage; possible  6. watches, dairy products; watches, dairy products  7. opportunity; output that otherwise could be produced  8. relative; comparative  9. skilled, scale; fall, rise  10. rise, decrease  11. trade; domestic goods, imports, opportunity; import them  12. demand, supply  13. shipping, oil  14. infant industries; economies of scale

---

## MULTIPLE-CHOICE QUESTIONS

1. The doctrine of comparative advantage says that there are gains from international trade
   (a) only if both comparative and absolute advantage are present
   (b) if opportunity costs are the same in the countries involved
   (c) only if there are economies of scale available
   (d) if countries specialize in the production of goods in which they are *relatively* more efficient

2. A country is relatively more efficient than another in producing a good if
   (a) it produces it more cheaply in terms of alternate goods not produced
   (b) it produces it at lower money cost
   (c) it has lower wage levels
   (d) there are economies of scale available

3. Nations through trade
   (a) may consume at levels beyond their production-possibilities frontiers
   (b) will be limited in their consumption to points on the production-possibilities frontier
   (c) will not alter their previous production patterns
   (d) are more likely to be confined to choices inside their production-possibilities frontiers

4. Tweedledum has a comparative advantage over Tweedledee in planting as compared with harvesting.
   (a) Tweedledum must have an absolute advantage over Tweedledee in planting.
   (b) Tweedledum must have a comparative advantage over Tweedledee in harvesting.
   (c) Tweedledee must have an absolute advantage over Tweedledum in planting.
   (d) Tweedledee must have a comparative advantage over Tweedledum in harvesting.

5. A country would welcome an improvement in its terms of trade because
   (a) it can then export more
   (b) its exchange rate will rise
   (c) the cost of its imports will fall in terms of what it must give up to get them
   (d) it now becomes cheaper to produce the same goods at home instead of importing them

6. In the case of a country with one important exported commodity (like oil) and fixed ex-change rates
   (a) a rise in its price in international markets will improve the country's terms of trade
   (b) a fall in its price will improve the terms of trade
   (c) its terms of trade will be unaffected by a chance in its price, because of fixed ex-change rates
   (d) a rise in its price will be helpful to the terms of trade and balance of payments only if world demand for it is elastic

7. From the point of view of the domestic standard of living, a country should
   (a) welcome cheap imports
   (b) impose quotas on imports
   (c) impose tariffs to keep out foreign competition
   (d) try to be self-sufficient

8. Lower wages in other countries than in Canada
   (a) create unfair competition for Canadian labor
   (b) mean that those countries cannot gain from trade with Canada
   (c) mean that Canadian costs are bound to be higher
   (d) may reflect lower labor productivity and higher unit costs abroad

9. Which of the following would *not* be a valid reason for imposing a tariff?
   (a) to protect an infant industry that will eventually be competitive
   (b) to diversify the economy
   (c) to maximize real income
   (d) to maintain a vital but high-cost defense industry

10. The gains from the removal of tariff barriers within the Common Market have been estimated to be
    (a) very large
    (b) negative
    (c) significant but fairly small
    (d) zero

11. The "Buy Canadian" argument for tariffs
    (a) is economically valid
    (b) states that dollars spent on foreign goods will be used for Canadian exports
    (c) should be recognized as usually being fallacious
    (d) is a defense of tariffs as revenue-raising measures

12. A general increase of import duties by a nation during a time of unemployment
    (a) is unlikely to produce any short-run increase of income and employment
    (b) should prove a very substantial stimulus to employment
    (c) would have the same effect on the allocation of resources as an export subsidy
    (d) would have a mild expansionary effect on the economy provided others do not fully re-taliate

13. If Japan became able to undersell Canada on all commodities at existing exchange rates,
    (a) Japan would continue to export to Canada but receive no imports
    (b) either the dollar would depreciate in terms of the yen or trade would very soon cease
    (c) Japan would continue to import from Canada but send no exports
    (d) Japan's exports to and imports from Canada would balance every year

Answers to multiple-choice questions: 1(d)   2(a)   3(a)   4(d)   5(c)   6(a)   7(a)   8(d)   9(c)
10(c)   11(c)   12(d)   13(b)

## EXERCISES

1. For each of the situations below, determine which commodity each country should specialize in and trade:

   (a) One unit of resources can produce:

   |  | Wheat (hundred bushels) | Beef (hundredweight) |
   |---|---|---|
   | Canada | 2 | 4 |
   | Argentina | 3 | 1 |

   The opportunity costs are:

   |  | Wheat/100 bushels | Beef/hundredweight |
   |---|---|---|
   | Canada | 2 | 0.5 |
   | Argentina | 1/3 | 3 |

   Canada should specialize in the production of ___Beef___.
   Argentina should specialize in the production of ___Wheat___.

   (b) One unit of resources can produce:

   |  | Wheat (hundred bushels) | Beef (hundredweight) |
   |---|---|---|
   | Canada | 2 | 4 |
   | Argentina | 1 | 3 |

   The opportunity costs are:

   |  | Wheat/100 bushels | Beef/hundredweight |
   |---|---|---|
   | Canada | 2 Beef | 0.5 wheat |
   | Argentina | 3 Beef | 1/3 Wheat |

   Canada should specialize in the production of ___Wheat___.
   Argentina should specialize in the production of ___Beef___.

   (c) One unit of resources can produce:

   |  | Wheat (hundred bushels) | Beef (hundredweight) |
   |---|---|---|
   | Canada | 2 | 4 |
   | Argentina | 1 | 2 |

   The opportunity costs are:

   |  | Wheat/100 bushels | Beef/hundredweight |
   |---|---|---|
   | Canada | 2 | 0.5 |
   | Argentina | 2 | 0.5 |

   Canada should specialize in the production of _____. _no gain from_
   Argentina should specialize in the production of _____. _trade._

2. If country A gives up the opportunity to produce 100 pounds of dairy products for each watch it makes, and B could produce 1 watch for each 200 pounds of dairy products it produces:

   (a) the opportunity cost of making watches (in terms of dairy products) is lower in country _____.

   (b) the opportunity cost of making dairy products (in terms of watches) is lower in country _____.

   (c) So country B should specialize in _____ and let country A produce _____.

   (d) The terms of trade (the price of one product in terms of the other) would be somewhere between _____ and _____ pounds of dairy products for 1 watch.

3. The *Economic Review* of the Department of Finance measures terms of trade by means of an index calculated by dividing the price index of exports by the price index of imports.
   (a) If the price index of Canadian exports in 1972 was 126.8 and the price index of imports was 127.9, what was the index of the terms of trade? _____
   (b) In 1973 there was a sudden sharp rise in the price of agricultural products and raw materials, major export products. *Ceteris paribus*, would you expect the terms of trade to become more or less favorable? _____ In fact, in 1973 the export price index rose from 126.8 to 145.0 while the import index rose from 127.9 to 139.3, an increase in the terms of trade index from _____ to _____.

4. Listed below are short paraphrases of pro- or anti-tariff arguments that the text suggests are fallacious. Give a brief refutation. (Your choice may not necessarily be the same as the suggested answers.)
   (a) Trade is exploitation.

   (b) Buy Canadian and keep the money here.

   (c) Protect Canadians against sweatshop labor.

   (d) A tariff for infant industries is forever.

   (e) Imports lower national income.

# PROBLEMS

## 1.  BREAKING THROUGH THE PRODUCTION-POSSIBILITIES FRONTIER WITH TRADE

In each of the cases below, assume a two-nation, two-product model in which no trade is taking place. The two nations, Austerity and Bacchanalia, henceforth referred to as A and B, make their production and consumption choices between products X and Y. Assume that both nations have identical patterns of tastes and preferences and that they are such that, when the products are equal in price, equal quantities will be consumed. In each case, after trade commences, assume that the prices are equal and that the consumption of X and the consumption of Y will be equal in each country. Perfect competition is assumed in product markets.

   In each of the graphs below, you are given the production-possibilities frontier and the price and quantity produced and consumed before trade (indicated by the dots). The before-trade relative prices ($P_X/P_Y$) are given by the slope of the production-possibilities curve. Show the amount that will be produced and consumed by each after trade when $P_X = P_Y$. Note that when trade does take place, each nation in its consumption will have broken through its production-possibilities frontier. For questions on absolute advantage you should assume the same quantities of factors in each country.

Complete the table below on the before-trade conditions as you work with each case.

| Before-Trade Conditions | 1 | 2 (and) 2a | 3 | 4 | 5 |
|---|---|---|---|---|---|
| Opportunity cost of X (in terms of Y) in country A[a] | _____ | _____ | _____ | _____ | 25/36 |
| Opportunity cost of X (in terms of Y) in country B[a] | _____ | _____ | _____ | _____ | 36/25 |
| $P_X/P_Y$ in country A | _____ | _____ | _____ | _____ | _____ |
| $P_X/P_Y$ in country B | _____ | _____ | _____ | _____ | _____ |

[a]At existing production levels.

## Case 1

(a) A has an absolute advantage in the production of _____. B has an absolute advantage in the production of _____. Therefore, A has a comparative advantage in the production of _____ and is at a comparative disadvantage in the production of _____.

(b) With the opening of trade, A will produce _____ of product _____; B will produce _____ of product _____. With $P_X = P_Y$, A will export _____ units of product _____ and import _____ units of product _____.

(c) Both countries will have gained because A can now consume _____ more units of _____ and B _____ more units of _____, while maintaining its consumption of the other product. $P_X/P_Y$ is greater than before in country _____ and less than before in country _____.

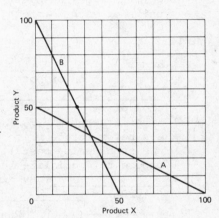

## Cases 2 and 2a

(a) In case 2, there (is/is not) an absolute advantage for either; there (is/is not) a comparative advantage for either.

(b) In case 2a, country A has a(n) _____ advantage in both products. It has no _____ advantage because opportunity costs are the _____ as reflected in relative prices of the products, which are _____. There (will/will not) be trade.

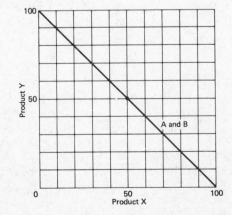

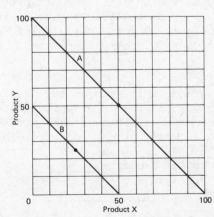

## Case 3

Again, in this case there is apparently no absolute advantage or comparative advantage.

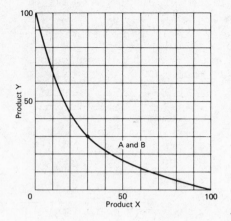

  (a) This case differs from case 2, where opportunity costs were constant, since when either country expands its production of X or Y units it encounters _____ opportunity costs for that production in terms of the other. If trade is opened up, it therefore will pay one country, say A, to _____ in the output of X, and the other country, say, B, to _____ in the output of Y.
  (b) With such specialization, A will establish a comparative advantage in X and B in Y, and with $P_X = P_Y$, A will export _____ of X in exchange for _____ of Y. Both countries will have gained by trade _____ units of each commodity.

## Case 4

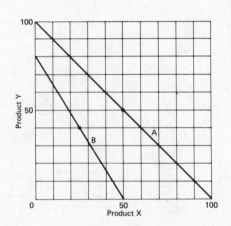

  (a) A has _____ advantages in production of both X and Y, but B has a(n) _____ advantage in the production of Y.
  (b) At an after-trade $P_X/P_Y$ of 1, which is less than B's before-trade price ratio of 8/5 (reflecting the opportunity costs), the producers in B will choose to specialize in the production of _____. By exporting 40 units of Y in return for _____ units of X, B can consume _____ X and _____ Y, a gain of _____ X.
  (c) If country A chooses to produce 90 of X and 10 of Y, it will be able to (increase/maintain) its before-trade consumption.

## Note

You may be concerned about why the gains of trade go entirely to B. This reflects the assumption both of perfect competition and of the particular demand conditions that allowed $P_Y$ to continue to equal $P_X$. For A to gain, it would be necessary that the after-trade price ratio be more favorable for product X, in which it has the comparative advantage. The complexities of this problem of price determination belong in a more advanced course in international trade, but the student should recognize this much: If country A can keep the price ratio of X:Y just below 8:5, B's producers will still find it profitable to offer Y in trade because trading for X will be cheaper than producing it. One way of accomplishing this would be for A to place a tariff on product Y of almost 60 percent ($37\frac{1}{2}/62\frac{1}{2}$). B could then get only $.62\frac{1}{2}X$ instead of $1X$ for each unit of Y, and most of the gains of trade would go to A.

## Case 5

Refer to the graph at the top of the next page.

  (a) In this case, the opportunity costs vary with the production level. In each country, the opportunity cost of each product becomes _____, the more that is produced. For any given production level, the opportunity costs in A are less for product _____ and in B for product _____. Thus, the comparative advantage in A is for product _____ and in B for product _____.
  (b) Even with trade complete, specialization will not occur because the opportunity costs become very _____ as all resources are devoted to the output of one good.

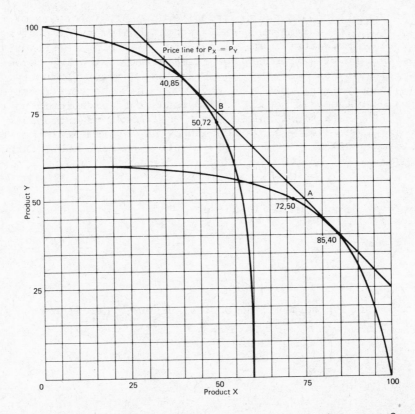

Cases 1, 2, and 4 can be termed as cases of constant costs, case 3 as one of decreasing costs, and this case as one of _____ costs.

(c) Trade can take place at $P_X = P_Y$ because in country A at before-trade consumption levels the opportunity cost of producing more X is _____ than 1Y, and in country B the opportunity cost of producing more Y is _____ than 1X. Thus, A will _____ its production of X from 72 yo 85, where the opportunity cost is _____ Y, and B will increase its production of Y from 72 to 85, where the opportunity cost is _____ X.

(d) Total production of X for both countries together is now _____, instead of the before-trade _____. Total production of Y is likewise _____, instead of the before-trade _____.

(e) To achieve the equal consumption of both commodities called for by the demand assumptions, A will export _____ in return for _____. This new consumption point can be found on the graph on the price line with the slope of 1, which is _____ to the production-possibilities frontiers at the points of after-trade _____.

## 2.  DUMPING AND REQUESTS FOR ADDITIONAL EXCISE TAXES

The following excerpt is taken from the Toronto *Globe and Mail*, August 12, 1975.

*Ottawa Finds Dumping of Color Television Sets*
   The Department of National Revenue has issued a preliminary finding of dumping involving color television sets made by about 20 companies in the United States, Japan, Taiwan, and Singapore.
   Dumping is selling a foreign market at prices less than those charged in the home market.
   The finding follows intensive lobbying by the Electronic Industries Association of Canada, which represents domestic producers, and likely will mean higher prices for consumers.

A department spokesman said that, effective July 31, importers of the television sets with screens 16 inches or larger must pay a provisional duty or post a bond to cover the amount by which the manufacturers are alleged to be dumping the televisions.

The federal Anti-Dumping Tribunal now has started an inquiry to decide whether the dumping of imported TVs has harmed or may harm, the domestic industry. . . .

If it rules that no injury has occurred, then the importers' posted bonds or any additional duties paid will be refunded. If it decides the domestic industry has been harmed, the department will make a final ruling about the amount of extra duty to be paid.

The Electronic Industries Association asked the Government in May to restrict imports of color TVs claiming 46% of the one million sets with screens 16 inches or larger sold in Canada last year were imported.

## Questions

1. Why would foreign producers "dump" in Canada?

2. In what sense does dumping harm the domestic industry? What might the Anti-Dumping Tribunal look for?

3. If dumping has been proven and a duty imposed, how would the costs and benefits of this additional protection be distributed in Canada? (In fact, the Tribunal subsequently found no cases of dumping.)

# Canada's Trade and Tariff Policy

## KEY CONCEPTS AND DEFINITIONS

1. Canada is very much involved with the world economy. The financial transactions between Canada and the rest of the world are recorded regularly in the <u>balance-of-payments ac-counts</u>. A transaction that involves an inflow of foreign exchanges is a receipt whereas a loss of foreign exchange is a payment.

2. The balance of payments is broken into two components: the <u>current account</u> and the <u>capital account</u>. <u>The former records, mainly, transactions involving goods and services whereas the latter records largely flows of financial payments</u>.

3. A deficit/surplus on current account must be balanced by a surplus/deficit on capital account or a change in holdings of <u>foreign-exchange</u> reserves.

4. Although tariffs can be imposed unilaterally, they may invite retaliation by other countries. International agreements and institutions attempt to prevent tariff wars and have promoted a general reduction in tariffs in the period since 1945.

5. Free trade, through the removal of all tariffs in Canada and elsewhere would subject all Canadian enterprise to international competition. While it is clear that this would give Canada greater access to world markets in some sectors, other sectors would find it difficult to compete internationally.

6. Foreign ownership is highly concentrated in some industrial sectors of Canada but there is no evidence that economic performance varies between domestic and foreign-owned firms. Problems may arise in foreign-owned industries where laws imposed by the country of the parent company may result in managerial decisions not in keeping with Canadian policy. This is known as the problem of <u>extraterritoriality</u>.

## REVIEW QUESTIONS

1. The record of transactions between a nation and foreign countries is called its ___balance of payment___. A transaction that typically leads to the purchase of a foreign currency is recorded as a ___debit___, and a transaction that typically gives rise to the sale of a foreign currency is recorded as a ___credit___. Canadian exports, therefore, are ___credit___, and Canadian imports are ___debit___. A debit transaction for Canada is a ___credit___ transaction for the foreign country.

2. The balance of payments always balances, but particular categories may show a deficit if _____*debits*_____ are greater than _____*credits*_____. Similarly, a surplus may result if _____*credits*_____ are greater than _____*debits*_____. The most important division in the balance-of-payments account is between the _____*current*_____ account and the _____*capital*_____ account.

3. A deficit on the current account must be matched either by a _____*surplus*_____ in the capital account, which means borrowing from abroad, or by a _____*reduction*_____ in the foreign exchange and gold held by domestic central authorities, or by a combination of both.

4. A surplus on the current account must be matched either by a _____*deficit*_____ on the capital account, which means loans or gifts to foreigners, or by a reduction of the _____*reserves*_____ of gold and foreign exchange held by the foreign central authorities, or by a combination of both.

5. The current account is usually divided into visibles and invisibles, a distinction corresponding to the division of commodities into _____*goods*_____ and _____*services*_____.

6. Classify the following transactions by Canadians as debits (−) or credits (+) in the current account:
   (a) the importation of a Volkswagen  *−*
   (b) the purchase of insurance from Lloyds of London  *−*
   (c) the hotel bill of a Canadian tourist in Fort Lauderdale, Florida  *−*
   (d) dividends received from foreign stocks  *+*

7. The capital account consists of long- and short-term _____*capital*_____. Purchases of foreign securities would appear as a (debit/~~credit~~) in the balance of payments. Shifts of bank deposits from Canadian to foreign banks in other countries would appear as a (debit/credit). Both of these transactions create a (demand for/~~supply of~~) foreign currencies or a (~~demand for~~/supply of) Canadian dollars.

8. A balance-of-payments surplus or deficit refers to the balance of the current account plus the capital account. A deficit in the Canadian balance of payments means that the total amount Canadians are trying to pay to foreigners (exceeds/~~is less than~~) the amount foreigners are trying to pay Canadians; the difference is financed by reductions in gold and _____*foreign exchange*_____ reserves.

9. An overall surplus on the balance of payments will result in a (~~reduction~~/increase) in a country's _____*gold & foreign exchange reserves*_____.

10. Since 1945, Canada has (~~always~~/not always) had a surplus on merchandise trade.

---

If you have not answered all questions correctly, review the text in order to be sure that you have all of the important concepts clearly in mind before going on to the next chapter.

1. balance of payments; debit, credit; credits, debits; credit  2. debits, credits; credits, debits; current, capital  3. surplus, reduction  4. deficit, reserves  5. goods, services  6. −, −, −, +  7. capital; debit; debit; demand for, supply of  8. exceeds, foreign exchange  9. increase, gold and foreign-exchange reserves  10. not always

---

# MULTIPLE-CHOICE QUESTIONS

1. An excess of exports over imports in a given year would be recorded as
   (a) a payment on the current account
   (b) a receipt of short-term capital
   (c) a receipt in the current account
   (d) net invisible trade

2. If there is a current account deficit, the sale of government bonds to U.S. citizens will
   (a) guarantee a balance on the balance of payments
   (b) increase the likelihood of an overall deficit on the balance of payments
   (c) be recorded as a payment on the capital account
   (d) offset the deficit on the current account

3. Which of the following statements is true about the balance of payments?
   (a) Current-account debits must equal current-account credits.
   (b) Visibles must equal invisibles.
   (c) Total debits must equal total credits.
   (d) Desired payments must equal actual payments.

4. Exports of Canadian goods are on the same side (credit) of the Canadian accounts as
   (a) Canadian investment abroad
   (b) Canadian government aid to underdeveloped countries
   (c) the money spent on travel in Europe by Canadians
   (d) investment by British people in Canadian stocks

5. The General Agreement on Tariffs and Trade
   (a) requires countries to specialize in producing certain commodities
   (b) permits a fixed set of tariffs to remain in place for a specified time
   (c) encourages the bilateral reduction in tariffs
   (d) has not been a success

6. Freer trade between Canada and the rest of the world would
   (a) lower national income in Canada
   (b) cause the Canadian dollar to depreciate
   (c) alter Canada's industrial structure
   (d) broaden Canada's industrial output

7. By restricting the export of Canadian oil,
   (a) the price of oil in the world will rise
   (b) exploration for oil in Canada will be encouraged
   (c) the balance of payments will be affected
   (d) the price of oil in Canada will necessarily by lower

Answers to multiple-choice questions: 1(b)    2(d)    3(c)    4(d)    5(c)    6(c)    7(c)

# EXERCISE

Arrange the following balance-of-payments items into current-account, capital-account, and official-reserve-account groupings. Compute the balance-of-payments deficit, surplus, or equilibrium position. (Figures are in millions of dollars.)

| | | |
|---|---|---|
| (a) | Long-term capital receipts | $ 1,305 |
| (b) | Merchandise exports | 17,785 |
| (c) | Freight and shipping receipts | 1,170 |
| (d) | Freight and shipping payments | 1,147 |
| (e) | Short-term capital receipts | 1,182 |
| (f) | Changes in official reserves | + 777 |
| (g) | Merchandise imports | 15,556 |
| (h) | Long-term capital payments | 814 |
| (i) | Short-term capital payments | 1,158 |
| (j) | Interest and dividend receipts | 545 |
| (k) | Interest and dividend payments | 1,613 |
| (l) | Other current-account payments | 721 |
| (m) | Net travel payments | 201 |

# PROBLEM

## CANADIAN TRADE AND GATT

In 1978, Canada, along with other nations, took part in discussions associated with GATT (General Agreement on Tariffs and Trade). The objective of these talks is a worldwide reduction in tariffs as a means of stimulating trade among countries of the world.

Lower Canadian tariffs means more goods can enter Canada; lower world tariffs would mean that we would likely be able to ship more exports to the rest of the world.

## Questions

1. Why are some people very concerned that a reduction in tariffs will lead to unemployment?

2. Suppose lower tariffs lead to greater exports. Will export industries be able to find labor to meet the increased demand? Do you foresee any particular regional problems in this regard?

3. The shoe and textile industry in Canada are in part protected by the tariff. If world tariffs (Canada included) are lowered on these goods, what is likely to happen to prices and why?

# 28

# National Income

1. National income refers to the total market value of goods and services produced in the economy during a year. The notion of market value incorporates both the prices as well as thephysical output of goods and services.

2. National income may be calculated either by the output-expenditure approach (gross national expenditure) or by the factor-income approach (gross national product). GNE is made equivalent to GNP by counting all output including that which is added to inventories.

3. The value of output of final goods and services can be found by taking the sum of the values added. Value added is the market value of the firm's output minus the cost of purchases of intermediate goods and services from other firms. Therefore, the value added approach avoids double-counting of output.

4. GNE equals the sum of consumption expenditures by households, gross investment in capital goods and changes in inventory levels, government expenditures on goods and services, and exports minus imports.

5. Gross investment can be split into replacement investment (necessary to keep the stock of capital intact) and net investment (net additions to the capital stock).

6. The factor-income approach (GNP) divides the same total (obtained by the output-expenditures approach) according to payments to factors of production. Wages, interest, rents, profits, taxes, and depreciation allowance are the major categories. Saving is income not spent on goods and services for current consumption. Both households and firms can save.

7. Other related measures of national income are net national product (NNP) which measures total output after deducting an allowance for output needed to keep the capital stock intact; personal income (PI) which is the income earned by individuals, before allowance for personal income taxes; and disposable income (DI) which is GNP minus any part of it that is not actually paid over to households, minus personal income taxes, plus transfer payments received by households.

8. It is often useful to compute real or constant-dollar values of national income. This is accomplished by dividing the nominal value of national income by some price deflator.

| CHECKLIST | Make certain that you also understand the following concepts: undistributed profits; fixed capital formation; capital consumption allowances; depreciation; transfer payments; net exports; base year; omissions from measured income; closed economy; open economy. |
|---|---|

# REVIEW QUESTIONS

1. The total market value of all goods and services produced for final use in an economy in a given period of time is called the ___national income___.

2. There are two approaches to measuring GNP: the ___output-expenditure___ approach and the ___factor-income___ approach.

3. Adding up the value of output produced by *all* firms in the country would not give the correct value for GNP because of ___double counting___. To eliminate this problem it is necessary to arrive at a figure for the firm's ___intermediate goods___ in production. The firm's value added is found by subtracting from its total revenues ___the purchases from other firms___

4. The factor-income approach adds up four types of income: ___wages___, ___profit___, ___interest___, and ___rents___.

5. The value of the factor-income approach must be ___equal___ to the value of output-expenditure approach.

6. Income not spent or paid in taxes is ___saving___. Gross business savings are of two categories: ___depreciation___ and ___distributed profits___.

7. To the economist, *investment* means production of goods for ___future production___. Gross business investment falls into two general categories: ___inventories___ and ___machines + equipment___.

8. Net investment equals gross investment minus ___depreciation___.

9. In an economy without government or foreign trade, the sum of the values of consumption and gross investment is called the ___GNE___.

10. The accounting definition of the sum of factor-income payments is the ___Gross national product___. Its value must be equal to the value of GNE.

11. One type of government expenditure not included in GNE is ___transfer payments___. This is because such payments are not for ___productive services___

12. Total income received by households is less than national income not only because of business savings but also because of ___income tax___. The amount of income remaining to households after payment of personal income taxes is called ___Disposable___ income; this includes not only earned income but also ___transfer earnings___.

13. For an economy with international trade, calculating the value of total output produced domestically (or, alternatively, the value of expenditures on domestically produced goods and services) requires subtracting ___imports___ and adding ___exports___.

14. An economy which is engaged in foreign trade is called a(n) (~~closed~~/open) economy.

15. The equation for calculating national income by the expenditure approach is:
GNE = consumption + ___Investment___ + ___Government___ + ___X − M (net exports.)___

16. National income deflated for price-level changes is GNP or GNE expressed in ___constant___ dollars; when not deflated, it is in ___current___ dollars.

17. National income which has been deflated by a price index is called ___real___ income.

18. GNP per capita is not a good measure of human welfare because it includes such things as (give several) ___pollution, crimes, costs of illness etc___. An approach to measuring household welfare emphasizes not production but is by opportunity cost, which means valuing it according to ___consumption___.

19. Which of the following expenditures by a firm would be termed a final good in the definition of national income? (a) a new machine for production; (b) raw materials for further processing; (c) the manager's salary; (d) a newly constructed executive office; (e) indirect business taxes.

20. New housing construction is included under (consumption/investment) in the GNE. Housing services provided by owner-occupied dwellings are (ignored/given an imputed value).

21. The largest component of national income measured by the factor-income approach or GNP is ___wages + other labour income___.

22. The largest component of national income measured by the expenditure approach or GNE is ___consumption___.

23. "Net change in inventories" for a period equals inventories at the (beginning/end) minus inventories at the (beginning/end). This item will appear in the (GNP/GNE) account.

24. Purchases of foreign cars by Canadians are considered (imports/exports). Spending by foreign tourists in Canada is treated as an (export/import).

25. Transfer payments such as social insurance payments, ___pensions___, relief payments, and ___unemployment insurance___ are excluded from national income.

26. Indirect business taxes are (included/excluded) in the measurement of (GNE/GNP).

27. Corporate profits before taxes are (included/excluded) in the measurement of (GNE/GNP).

---

If you have not answered all questions correctly, review the text in order to be sure that you have all of the important concepts clearly in mind before going on to the next chapter.

1. national income  2. output-expenditure, factor-income  3. double counting; intermediate goods; purchases of goods and services from other firms  4. rents, wages, interest, profits  5. equal  6. saving; depreciation, undistributed profits  7. future production; machines and equipment, changes in inventories  8. depreciation or capital consumption allowances  9. gross national expenditures (GNE)  10. gross national product (GNP)  11. transfer payments; productive services  12. income taxes; disposable, transfer payments from the government  13. imports, exports  14. open  15. gross investment, government expenditures, net exports (X - M)  16. constant, current  17. real  18. arms, costs of illness, pollution, crime; consumption; income or commodities sacrificed by not working  19. (a), (d)  20. investment; given an imputed value  21. wages and other labor income  22. consumption  23. beginning, end; GNE  23. imports; export  25. unemployment insurance, pensions  26. included, GNP  27. included, GNP

## MULTIPLE-CHOICE QUESTIONS

1. We define the circular flow of income as
   (a) the sum of all the withdrawals from the system
   (b) the flow of income from domestic households to domestic firms and back again
   (c) the amount of money in the economy at any one point of time
   (d) all of the above

2. Value added in production is equal to
   (a) purchases from other firms
   (b) profits
   (c) total sales revenue
   (d) total sales revenue minus purchases from other firms

3. Which of the following about savings is *not* true?
   (a) It is the same as investing.
   (b) It is the result of not spending all of one's income.
   (c) It is often used to finance investment by business firms.
   (d) It is done by businesses as well as households.

4. Mass marriages of men to housekeepers
   (a) would reduce national income as now measured
   (b) would increase national income as now measured
   (c) would leave national income the same
   (d) cannot tell the effect on GNP

5. National income can be measured in all but which of the following ways?
   (a) by the flow of goods and services produced for final demand
   (b) by the payments made to purchase this flow of goods and services
   (c) by adding all money transactions in the economy
   (d) by the value of payments made to factors of production which have been used to produce final goods and services

6. Which of the following is *not* part of the total of final goods and services included in the national income?
   (a) transfer items
   (b) goods sold to government and foreign countries
   (c) increases in purchases of business equipment
   (d) additions to inventories

7. The difference between GNP and net national product is
   (a) depreciation or capital consumption allowances
   (b) total taxes paid to governments
   (c) net exports
   (d) personal savings

8. Personal disposable income is
   (a) the same as personal income
   (b) income that is used for consumption
   (c) income remaining after personal income taxes
   (d) exclusive of social insurance payments or welfare

9. If there is unintentional investment in inventory,
   (a) inventories have declined
   (b) the rate of sales is less than the rate of production
   (c) total investment falls
   (d) GNE will not be affected

10. If GNP in current pesetas in 1970 was 500 billion while GNP in constant (1960) pesetas was 200 billion in 1970
    (a) real GNP doubled over the decade 1960-1970
    (b) the price level more than doubled over the decade
    (c) real income declined slightly over the decade
    (d) it is impossible to estimate what happened to prices over the decade; more information is needed

11. If actual GNP rises from $100 billion to $115 billion and the GNP deflator rises from 125 to 150,
    (a) real GNP has risen
    (b) real GNP has fallen
    (c) real GNP is unchanged
    (d) it is impossible to tell the change in real GNP

---

Answers to multiple-choice questions: 1(b)  2(d)  3(a)  4(a)  5(c)  6(a)  7(a)  8(c)  9(b)  10(b)  11(b)

---

# Exercises

1. Suppose that the following items represent the expenditures and factor incomes for an economy in 1973. By selecting the appropriate items, calculate the values for GNP and GNE. Prove that GNE = GNP. (Figures are in billions of dollars.)

| | |
|---|---|
| Government purchases of goods and services | $277.1 |
| Wages and employee compensation | 785.3 |
| Net exports of goods and services | 4.6 |
| Income of proprietors | 84.3 |
| Indirect business taxes | 117.8 |
| Gross private investment | 201.5 |
| Capital consumption allowances | 109.6 |
| Corporate profits | 126.4 |
| Personal consumption expenditures | 805.0 |
| Rental and interest income | 75.5 |
| Adjustments on GNP account | -10.7 |

$GNE = 1288.2$

$GNP = 1288.2$

2. You are given the following national income accounting items for the Canadian economy in 1975. (Figures are in billions of dollars.)

| | |
|---|---|
| Gross national product at market prices | $161.1 |
| Indirect taxes less subsidies | 17.5 |
| Capital consumption allowances and miscellaneous valuation adjustments | 17.5 |
| Residual error of estimate | .1 |
| Government transfers and interest on public debt | 25.3 |
| Earnings not paid out to persons | 18.3 |
| Personal direct taxes and other current transfers to the government | 25.2 |
| Personal expenditure and current transfers to corporations and nonresidents | 96.9 |

(a) Calculate NNP at market prices and net national income at factor cost.

$161.1 - 125 = 143.6$

$143.6 - 125 = 126.1$

(b) Using the value for net national income at factor cost, calculate personal income and personal disposable income.

$P.I = 126.1 - 18.3 + 25.2$
$= 133$

$PDI = 133 - 25.2 = 107.8$

(c) What was the magnitude of personal saving in 1975?

$$107.8 - 96.9 = 10.9$$

3. From the figures given, calculate the 1929 GNP in 1961 dollars and the implicit price deflator that converts current 1970 GNP to constant (1961 dollars) GNP.

| Year | GNP, 1961 Dollars (billions) | GNP, Current Dollars (billions) | Implicit Price Deflator (1961 = 100) |
|------|------|------|------|
| 1929 | _____ | 6.16 | 50.2 |
| 1961 | 39.65 | 39.65 | 100.0 |
| 1970 | 64.01 | 85.69 | _____ |
| 1974 | 79.20 | 139.49 | 176.1 |

(a) What was the percentage increase in current-dollar GNP between 1961 and 1970?

(b) What was the percentage increase in the price level, as measured by the implicit price deflator, between 1961 and 1970? Between 1970 and 1974?

(c) What was the percentage change in real GNP between 1961 and 1970?

(d) What was the percentage change in real GNP between 1970 and 1974?

4. From 1950 to 1970, personal disposable income in Canada rose from $12.69 billion to $53.60 billion. Population increased from 13.71 million to 21.41 million in the same period. The consumer price index increased from approximately 100.0 to 142.2. What was the total percentage increase in the per capita standard of living as measured by per capita real personal disposable income from 1950 to 1970?

5. The following values for the GNP deflator (1971 base year) between 1971 and 1975 are given below. Calculate the annual inflation rates and fill in the table.

| Year | GNP Deflator | Inflation Rate/Year |
|------|------|------|
| 1971 | 1.00 (or 100) | _____ |
| 1972 | 1.050 | _____ |
| 1973 | 1.147 | _____ |
| 1974 | 1.311 | _____ |
| 1975 | 1.452 | _____ |

6. (a) Identify the items below according to the following code:

C    Consumption               $S_p$    Savings of persons or households
C  I    Investment               M    Imports
   G    Government spending on goods    X    Exports
         and services            F    Factor-income payments
   T    Taxes                    N    None of the above
   $S_b$    Savings of business

__C + F__ (1) A student gets a haircut from a self-employed barber.
__I  I  F__ (2) The barber buys some clippers from the Short-Cut Clipper Company.
__$S_p$__ (3) Out of each day's revenue, the barber sets aside $5 in his piggybank.
__N__ (4) When he has enough set aside, he buys a share of Royal Bank of Canada stock.
__I__ (5) The Royal Bank expands its computer facilities in its head office.
__T__ (6) The Royal Bank pays municipal taxes to the City of Montreal.
__$S_b$ F__ (7) The Royal Bank sets aside some of its income as depreciation reserves.
  (8) The Short-Cut Clipper Company has profits of $50,000 after paying provincial and municipal taxes.
     __T__ (a) It pays $17,500 in corporate profits taxes to the federal government.
     __I__ (b) It pays dividends of $20,000.
     __$S_b$__ (c) It retains the rest and adds it to its surplus.
__M + C__ (9) Canadians go to London, England, and stay at the Savoy Hotel. (Two answers.)
__X__ (10) Russia buys beef cattle from Ontario beef cattle farmers.
__I__ (11) Acme Construction Company builds 1,000 new houses to put on the market.
__G__ (12) The Province of Saskatchewan builds a new highway.

(b) Which of the above would be included in the output-expenditure approach to measuring national income?

# PROBLEMS

## 1.  NATIONAL INCOME ACCOUNTING: EXPENDITURE OR INCOME APPROACH?

$G \quad I \quad C \quad X - M$

National income can, as we have seen, be measured by aggregating expenditures by consumers, business, government, and foreigners or by aggregating the payments made to the factors of production or resources used to produce goods and services.

Below is a list of items that may or may not enter national income. Place them under the factor-payments-approach or expenditures-approach account, and justify your reason for doing so. If you do not place them in one of the accounts, explain.

|  | Account | | Reason |
|---|---|---|---|
|  | Factor Payment | Expenditure |  |
| 1. Increase in business inventory |  | ✓ | Part of Investment |
| 2. Purchases of steel by General Motors |  |  | Intermediate good to GM |
| 3. Rent received by apartment building owners | ✓ |  | Payment to owner of factor |
| 4. Capital consumption allowances | ✓ |  |  |
| 5. Wages received by doctors | ✓ |  |  |
| 6. Sales of snowmobiles to foreigners |  | ✓ |  |
| 7. Expenditures on school construction |  | ✓ |  |

## 2.  CONSTRUCTION OF A LASPEYRES INDEX

One of the most frequently used types of indices is called the Laspeyres index. This index assumes that the quantity of purchases in some base year remain the same for all other years.

Suppose that the government's data collection agency has calculated that consumers spend in the following proportions:

| | |
|---|---|
| Shelter | 30% |
| Food | 25 |
| Transportation | 15 |
| Clothing | 10 |
| Entertainment | 10 |
| Other | 10 |

The average prices of these consumer items for two years are as follows:

| | Base Year | Next Year |
|---|---|---|
| Shelter | $3000 | $3300 |
| Food | 2500 | 2500 |
| Transportation | 500 | 500 |
| Clothing | 100 | 100 |
| Entertainment | 60 | 60 |
| Other | 300 | 330 |

## Questions

1. The index for the base year, by definition, is 1.00 or 100. Compute the index for the next year assuming that the consumer spending proportions remain constant.

2. You may have noticed that the prices of shelter, clothing, and other goods increased by 10% each. Does your answer in question 1 indicate a 10% rate of inflation in the next year? Why or why not?

3. If the oil-producing countries substantially increased the prices of home fuel oil and gasoline, what commodity prices are most seriously affected? If the oil price increase was a permanent one, what might happen to the consumer spending proportions?

# What Determines National Income?

## Key Concepts and Definitions

1. <u>Potential</u> or <u>full-employment</u> GNP is the level of national income that could have been produced if the economy had been kept at full employment. This occurs when approximately 4 to 5 percent of the labor force is unemployed.

2. National income is said to be in <u>equilibrium</u> when there is no tendency for it either to increase or decrease. The national income achieved at that point is referred to as the <u>equilibrium national income</u>.

3. Households spend only part of their income on <u>consumption</u> and they save the rest. Firms <u>produce</u> goods and services and invest in capital equipment.

4. The <u>consumption function</u> is the relationship between consumption expenditures and all other factors that determine it. The most important determinant of consumption is income.

5. The <u>savings function</u> is the relationship between savings and all the factors that determine it. Since households divide their income between consumption and savings and consumption is a function of income, it follows that saving is determined by income.

6. Two technical terms are used to describe the relationship between consumption and income. The <u>marginal propensity to consume</u> relates the <u>change</u> in consumption to the <u>change</u> in income that brought it about. The <u>average propensity to consume</u> is total consumption divided by total income.

7. The <u>marginal propensity to save</u> refers to the change in savings given a <u>change</u> in income; the <u>average propensity to save</u> is total saving divided by total income.

8. The <u>aggregate demand function</u> relates the level of desired expenditures to the level of income. In the frugal economy, the aggregate demand function is the sum of the consumption function and the <u>investment function</u>.

9. Equilibrium income, according to the <u>income-expenditure approach</u>, is where aggregate demand is exactly equal to total output. If aggregate demand is greater than total output, there will be a strong tendency for national income to rise. If aggregate demand is less than total output, national income will tend to fall.

10. Equilibrium income in a frugal economy, according to the saving-investment approach, is where total saving equals total investment. If saving is greater than investment, national income will fall.

11. The generalization of the theory of equilibrium national income involves introducing other aspects of macroeconomic behavior such as <u>exports</u>, <u>imports</u>, <u>government expenditures</u>, <u>taxes</u>, and <u>business saving</u>.

12. In terms of the income-expenditure approach, equilibrium national income is where total output equals <u>C</u> + <u>I</u> + <u>G</u> + <u>(X - M)</u>.

13. A <u>withdrawal</u> is any income received by a household not passed on through spending to firms and any income received by firms not passed on through income payments to households. Withdrawals exert a contractionary force on the circular flow of income.

14. An <u>injection</u> is income received by either a firm or a household that does not arise out of spending of the other group. Injections exert an expansionary force on the circular flow of income.

15. In terms of the <u>withdrawal-injection approach</u>, equilibrium national income is where total withdrawals equal total injections. Injections include government expenditures, exports, and investment. Withdrawals include total saving, imports, and taxes.

| CHECKLIST | Make certain that you also understand the following concepts: short-run consumption function; long-run consumption function; dissavings; break-even level of national income. |
|---|---|

# REVIEW QUESTIONS

1. Potential GNP is total output that would be produced with _full employment_. If the unemployment rate were 6 percent, potential GNP would be (less/greater) than actual GNP. In a dynamic fluctuating economy, potential, actual, and equilibrium GNP are (usually/rarely) the same.

2. Total consumption spending is a function of _income_. Income changes therefore affect the _consumption_ component of aggregate demand.

3. The ratio of the change in consumption to the related change in income is called the _marginal propensity to consume_.

4. The ratio of total level of consumption to the related level of income is called the _average propensity to consume_.

5. The ratio of the change in savings to the related change in income is called the _marginal propensity to save_.

6. In terms of the aggregate-expenditure approach, equilibrium national income or GNP is where desired total spending equals _total output_. This is shown on the diagram where the _aggregate demand_ intersects the 45-degree line.

7. If desired total spending exceeds actual output, inventories will _decrease_ unexpectedly. Given the assumptions of the chapter, businessmen will react by expanding production; therefore employment will _increase_ and income will _rise (increase)_. Diagrammatically this situation is shown where the level of desired spending (which is a point on the aggregate-expenditure function) is (above/below) the 45-degree line and to the (right/left) of the equilibrium level of national income.

8. If desired total spending is less than actual output, inventories will _increase_. With the assumption of constant prices, businessmen will react by cutting production; therefore employment will _fall_ and income will _fall_. Diagrammatically this situation is shown where the level of desired spending (which is a point on the aggregate-expenditure function) is (above/below) the 45-degree line and to the (right/left) of the equilibrium level of national income.

9. Aggregate expenditures on GNP in an open, governed economy consist of the spending of four sectors: consumption, _government_, _investment_, and _exports minus import_.

10. Equilibrium national income is defined as an income level in which $C + I + G + (X - M)$ equals ___*actual output*___.

11. Withdrawals from the circular flow consist of ___*saving*___, ___*imports*___, and ___*taxes*___. They tend to rise and fall with ___*income*___.

12. Injections into the circular flow are the expenditures for ___*Government*___, ___*investments*___, and exports.

13. Other things being equal, an increase in injections causes national income to ___*expand*___; a decrease causes it to ___*fall*___.

14. In terms of the injections-withdrawals approach, equilibrium national income occurs where desired withdrawals equal ___*desired injections*___. If net exports are zero and taxes equal government spending, an excess of investment over desired savings will cause national income to ___*rise*___.

15. If net exports are zero and desired savings equals investment, an excess of government expenditures over taxes will cause GNP to ___*rise*___.

---

If you have not answered all questions correctly, review the text in order to be sure that you have all of the important concepts clearly in mind before going on to the next chapter.

1. full employment; greater; rarely  2. income; consumption  3. marginal propensity to consume  4. average propensity to consume  5. marginal propensity to save  6. total output; aggregate demand  7. decrease; increase; rise; above; left  8. increase; fall; fall; below; right  9. investment; government expenditures, exports minus imports  10. actual output  11. savings, imports, taxes; income  12. investment, exports, government expenditures  13. rise; fall  14. desired injections; rise  15. rise

---

## MULTIPLE-CHOICE QUESTIONS

1. Investment, government expenditures, and exports are
   (a) withdrawals from the circular flow
   (b) of minor importance to the determination of income
   (c) too unpredictable to study usefully
   (d) injections of spending into the circular flow

2. If aggregate expenditures (demand) exceed actual output,
   (a) withdrawals must exceed injections
   (b) GNP is less than the equilibrium level and will tend to rise
   (c) inventories will rise and employment and income will fall
   (d) a rise in the price level is inevitable

3. The first symptom of a reduction in aggregate spending will probably be
   (a) a tendency for prices to rise as sellers try to make up for losses
   (b) an increase in overtime work as firms try to sell more to make up for losses
   (c) an increase in unintended inventory
   (d) a decrease in unintended inventory

4. Government expenditure and imports are, respectively,
   (a) an injection and a withdrawal
   (b) a withdrawal and an injection
   (c) both withdrawals
   (d) both injections

5. Which of the following is *not* an injection into the circular flow of income?
   (a) The Province of Saskatchewan builds a road.
   (b) Molson's Brewery sells beer to foreign customers.
   (c) Stelco builds a new plant in Quebec.
   (d) General Motors buys an already operating ball-bearing plant in Ontario.

6. The level of GNP will be in equilibrium
   (a) when prices are stable
   (b) when injections equal desired withdrawals
   (c) only when there is full employment
   (d) always since GNP = GNE

7. We hypothesize that consumption
   (a) is a function of income, like withdrawals
   (b) is exogenous, like injections
   (c) is an independent variable, so we cannot predict it
   (d) is a relatively unimportant fraction of aggregate expenditure

8. The aggregate-expenditure function has an upward slope because we assume that
   (a) government spending increases as employment and income rise
   (b) business investment is the main component of aggregate spending
   (c) prices are rising as full employment is approached
   (d) components of aggregate demand depend positively on levels of income

Answers to multiple-choice questions: 1(d)  2(b)  3(c)  4(a)  5(d)  6(b)  7(a)  8(d)

# EXERCISES

1. Suppose we have the following hypothetical consumption schedule. You may assume that there are no business savings, no personal income taxes, and no government transfers.

| Consumption Expenditures (constant dollars) | GNP (National Income) (constant dollars) |
|---|---|
| 100 | 0 |
| 180 | 100 |
| 260 | 200 |
| 340 | 300 |
| 420 | 400 |
| 500 | 500 |
| 580 | 600 |
| 660 | 700 |
| 740 | 800 |

(a) Plot the consumption function on the graph.
(b) What is the break-even level of income?

(c) Calculate the marginal propensity to consume. Is it constant?

(d) What happens to the value of the average propensity to consume as national income rises?

(e) Since savings are defined as national income minus consumption expenditure, calculate the saving schedule. Plot this function.

(f) Prove that $S = 0$ at the break-even level of national income.

2. The aggregate-expenditure schedule below shows what the various components of intended spending would be at each income level. Fill in the blanks in the table and plot the aggregate demand curve on the graph. Assume that all taxes are zero throughout and that all government expenditures are on goods and services.

| Level of GNP = Y | C | I | G | (X − M) | Aggregate Expenditures | J | Y − C = W |
|---|---|---|---|---|---|---|---|
| 0 | 90 | 10 | 30 | 10 | 140 | 50 | −90 |
| 50 | 120 | 10 | 30 | 10 | 170 | 50 | −70 |
| 100 | 150 | 10 | 30 | 10 | 200 | 50 | −50 |
| 150 | 180 | 10 | 30 | 10 | 230 | 50 | −30 |
| 200 | 210 | 10 | 30 | 10 | 260 | 50 | −10 |
| 250 | 240 | 10 | 30 | 10 | 290 | 50 | 10 |
| 300 | 270 | 10 | 30 | 10 | 320 | 50 | 30 |
| 350 | 300 | 10 | 30 | 10 | 350 | 50 | 50 |
| 400 | 330 | 10 | 30 | 10 | 380 | 50 | 70 |
| 450 | 360 | 10 | 30 | 10 | 410 | 50 | 90 |
| 500 | 390 | 10 | 30 | 10 | 440 | 50 | 110 |

(a) GNP is at equilibrium level at _____ 350 _____.
    At this level, expenditures = _____ 350 _____. W = _____ 50 _____.
                                                        J = _____ 50 _____.

(b) Write the equation for the consumption schedule and for the W schedule. (Hint: These are linear equations of the form a + bx.)

$$C = 90 + 0.6Y \qquad W = -90 + 0.4Y$$

(c) The *C* and *W* equations added together should equal _____ $C+W=Y$ _____ .

(d) Calculate the value of the marginal propensity to consume.

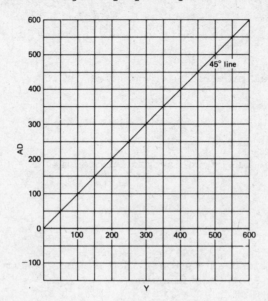

3. *Inventory Adjustment Model*. Suppose that the following diagram depicts the economic situation of a particular country.

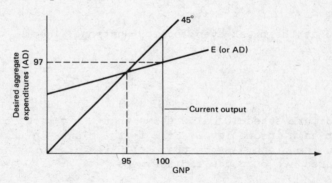

(a) Does this situation represent overproduction or underproduction? What is happening to inventory investment?

(b) Assuming that prices are constant, what changes in production would occur?

(c) As production is altered, employment and factor payments are affected. Would income rise or fall?

(d) Since consumption expenditures depend on the level of national income, would consumption rise or fall?

(e) Adjustment continues until aggregate expenditures equal _____.

4. Consumption expenditures are a function of disposable income. Suppose that consumption is a function of disposable income (income minus personal taxes). Furthermore assume that tax payments are equal to 10 at each level of income.

(a) Fill in the following table and draw a rough diagram of consumption on the vertical axis and disposable income on the horizontal axis.

| Consumption | Income | Personal Taxes | Disposable Income |
|---|---|---|---|
| 100 | 0 | 0 | _____ |
| 150 | 110 | 10 | _____ |
| 200 | 210 | 10 | _____ |
| 250 | 310 | 10 | _____ |
| 300 | 410 | 10 | _____ |
| — | 510 | 10 | _____ |

(b) Calculate the marginal propensity to consume out of disposable income.

(c) Calculate the value of savings at each level of disposable income. (The definition of savings is now disposable income minus consumption.)

# PROBLEM

## AN ALGEBRAIC DETERMINATION OF EQUILIBRIUM NATIONAL INCOME

You are given the following information about behavior in an economy:

Equation 1: the consumption function
$C = 100 + .7YD$, where $YD$ is disposable income
Equation 2: the tax function
$T = 20$
Equation 3: the investment function
$I = 50$
Equation 4: the export function
$X = 20$
Equation 5: the government expenditure function
$G = 50$
Equation 6: the import function
$M = 10 + .1Y$, where $Y$ is national income

## Questions

1. Referring to the consumption function, what does the term 100 mean?

2. Plot the tax function with taxes on the vertical axis and income ($Y$) on the horizontal axis. What is the slope of this function? What does this imply about the relationship between taxes and income?

3. Plot the import function with imports on the vertical axis and national income ($Y$) on the horizontal axis. What is the slope of this function? What does this imply about the relationship between imports and national income?

4. Calculate the algebraic expression for disposable income ($YD$). Call this function equation 7.

5. Substitute equation 7 into equation 1 and call this new expression equation 8.

6. Aggregate demand equals the sum of all components of aggregate expenditures: $AD = C + I + G + (X - M)$. Derive the algebraic expression for $AD$ by substituting equations 3, 4, 5, 6, and 8 into the above expression for $AD$.

7. Equilibrium national income is where $AD$ equals $Y$. Using your answer to question 6, calculate the equilibrium value of $Y$.

8. Using the definition of savings, $YD - C = S$, derive the algebraic expression for the saving function. *Hint:* Use equations 7 and 8.

9. The withdrawals-injection approach defines equilibrium national income where $S + T + M = X + G + I$. Using the various equations you have been given and those which you have solved for, prove that the equilibrium level of national income obtained from the withdrawals-injection approach is exactly equal to that obtained by the income-expenditure approach (your answer to question 7).

# 30

# Changes in National Income

## Key Concepts and Definitions

1. The response of injections, consumption, and withdrawals to a change in income is indicated by a <u>movement along</u> the injection, consumption, and withdrawals schedule and is shown graphically by the slope of the relevant curve.
2. The response of any flow to a change in income is called a <u>marginal propensity</u>. For example, the response of consumption to a change in national income is called the <u>marginal propensity</u> to consume.
3. Changes in injections, irrespective of income changes, cause <u>shifts</u> in the injection schedule.
4. Changes in withdrawals, with a given level of income, cause the withdrawal function to <u>shift</u>.
5. The <u>paradox of thrift</u> says that an increase in savings shifts the withdrawal function and thereby decreases the equilibrium level of national income.
6. If one injection decrease is matched by an equal injection increase, equilibrium national income is unaffected. This is an example of <u>compensating shifts</u> in injections.
7. The <u>multiplier</u> measures the magnitude of changes in income should the withdrawal, injection, and consumption schedules <u>shift</u>. The multiplier is defined as the ratio of the change in national income to the <u>initial</u> change in injections or withdrawals.
8. An increase in injections will increase national income by a <u>multiple</u> amount. An increase in withdrawals will decrease national income by a <u>multiple</u> amount.
9. The slope of the withdrawals function is called the <u>marginal propensity to withdraw</u>. The <u>marginal propensity to spend</u> is one minus the marginal propensity to withdraw. The reciprocal of the marginal propensity to withdraw is the value of the <u>multiplier</u>.
10. The larger the value of the marginal propensity to withdraw, the lower the value of the multiplier.
11. Equilibrium national income may not coincide with potential GNP. If the equilibrium national income is less than potential, a <u>deflationary gap</u> situation exists. The magnitude of the deflationary gap is equal to the amount that the injection function, or alternatively, the aggregate-demand curve, must be <u>shifted up</u> to produce full-employment GNP.
12. If current equilibrium GNP is greater than potential, prices are rising. This is known as an <u>inflationary gap</u> situation. The magnitude of the inflationary gap is equal to the amount that the injection function, or alternatively, the aggregate demand curve, must be <u>shifted down</u> to produce full-employment <u>and</u> no inflation.

| CHECKLIST | Make certain that you also understand the following concepts: L-shaped relationship between output levels and changes in prices; budget deficit; budget surplus. |

# REVIEW QUESTIONS

1. The response of any flow, such as consumption or saving, to a change in income is called a ___marginal propensity___ .

2. The consumption function shows how desired consumption spending varies with ___income___ . If the marginal propensity to consume is .60, a rise of $10 billion in incomes will cause consumption to rise by ___$ 6 billion___ . This describes a (movement along/~~shift of~~) the consumption schedule.

3. If the marginal propensity to consume rises from .60 to .66, we would call it a (~~movement along~~/shift of) the consumption schedule. This would have the same effect on equilibrium GNP as an increase in (injections/~~withdrawals~~).

4. If 60 percent of an increase in national income is respent, the marginal propensity to make withdrawals is ___40 %___ . The marginal propensity to make withdrawals includes the marginal propensities to ___save___ , ___taxes___ , and ___imports___ .

5. An increase in investment spending is an example of a(n) ___injection___ . Ceteris paribus, this would cause total income to ___rise___ , and desired and actual withdrawals would ___rise___ to equal ___injections___ at equilibrium GNP.

6. A rise in tax rates causes withdrawals to ___increase___ and causes spending to ___fall___ ; ceteris paribus, total output and income would ___fall___ .

7. In addition to shifts in C and I schedules, the level of national income will be changed by changes in the amount of injections for ___government___ and ___exports___ .

8. The level of national income will rise if there is a (fall/~~rise~~) in tax rates, savings, or import schedules, ceteris paribus.

9. An attempt to increase the rate of aggregate savings, ceteris paribus, will (~~raise~~/lower) the level of national income; this unexpected conclusion is called the ___paradox___ ___of thrift___ .

10. An increase in the rate of saving will not result in a fall in national income if offset by an increase in ___injection___ .

11. A rise in tax rates will not cause national income to fall if offset by an increase in government ___spending___ . If a government spends more than it collects in taxes, there is a budget ___deficit___ ; if tax receipts exceed government spending, there is a budget ___surplus___ . The government finances a deficit by ___borrowing___ ; it uses a surplus to ___reduce debt___ .

12. If government wishes to maintain a given level of income in the face of a fall in business investment, it can either increase its ___spending___ or decrease ___taxes___ .

13. The *multiplier* is the ratio of the change in _____*injection*_____ to the change in _____*income*_____. The formula is the reciprocal of the marginal propensity to _____*withdrawal*_____.    $1/w = \frac{1}{1-b}$

14. If the marginal propensity to spend is .50, the marginal propensity to withdraw is _____*.5*_____, and the multiplier is _____*2*_____. As long as part of all increases in income is respent, the multiplier is greater than (0̸/1).

15. If the multiplier is 3, an increase of injections of $10 billion will cause national income to rise by _____*$30 billion*_____.

16. Suppose that actual equilibrium GNP is $500 million and full-employment GNP is estimated to be $600 million, with a multiplier of 2.5; the size of the injection needed to reach full employment is _____*40 million*_____. The deflationary gap is _____*40*_____.

17. A country with heavy taxes and much saving will have a relatively (low/~~high~~) multiplier. A reduction in tax rates causes the multiplier to (rise/~~fall~~).

18. The L-shaped relation is the relation between output and ___*change in price level*___ It assumes that, until full employment is reached, prices ___*are stable*___.

19. Statistically, actual *J* equals actual _____*W*_____. In equilibrium, actual *J* equals _____*desired*_____ *W*. If actual *X* equals *M*, *I* plus *G* must equal actual *S+T* ___*withdrawal*___. If either *I* or *G* is increased, *ceteris paribus*, income will _____*increase*_____ so that both _____*Saving*_____ and _____*Taxes*_____ will rise until actual *J* equals both desired and actual _____*withdrawal*_____.

20. Suppose that *X* equals *M*, *G* equals *T*, and *I* equals desired *S*, but there is considerable unemployment. The government therefore increases *G*. *G* is now greater than *T*, so there is a budget _____*deficit*_____. More *G* spending causes income to _____*rise*_____, and *S* to _____*rise*_____, so that the government can finance the deficit by _____*borrowing the S*_____. Because *T* will also rise with income, the final deficit will be (~~greater~~/less) than the original.

---

If you have not answered all questions correctly, review the text in order to be sure that you have all of the important concepts clearly in mind before going on to the next chapter.

1. marginal propensity  2. income; $6 billion; movement along  3. shift of; injections 4. .40; save, pay taxes, import  5. injection; rise, rise, injections 6. rise, fall, fall 7. government, exports  8. fall  9. lower, paradox of thrift  10. investment or other injections 11. spending; deficit, surplus; borrowing, reduce the national debt  12. spending, taxes  13. income, injections that caused the change in income; make withdrawals or 1/w 14. .50, 2; 1  15. 30  16. $49 million ($100 million ÷ 2.5); $40 million  17. low; rise 18. *changes* in the price level; are stable  19. *W*; desired; *S* plus *T*; rise *S, T, W*  20. deficit, rise, rise, borrowing the increased *S*; less

---

# MULTIPLE-CHOICE QUESTIONS

1. Increases in national income are predicted to be caused by increases in all but which of the following, *ceteris paribus*?
   (a) taxes
   (b) exports
   (c) government spending
   (d) investment spending

2. Increases in national income are predicted to be caused by decreases in all but which of the following, *ceteris paribus*,
   (a) exports
   (b) the savings schedule
   (c) tax rates
   (d) imports

3. If $G$, $I$, and $X$ are not related to changes in $Y$, then
   (a) the $AD$ schedule is horizontal
   (b) equilibrium income cannot be determined
   (c) the slope of $AD$ will be the same as the consumption function
   (d) shifts in injections will not affect the $AD$ schedule or $Y$

4. The effect on GNP of a fall in $I$ could be offset by
   (a) a rise in taxes
   (b) a rise in savings
   (c) a rise in $G$
   (d) a fall in exports

5. A deflationary gap of $10 billion means that
   (a) actual GNP is $10 billion below full-employment GNP
   (b) prices will fall until GNP falls by $10 billion
   (c) an increase in injections of $10 billion is needed, which when multiplied will attain full-employment GNP
   (d) deflation is needed; spending must be reduced by $10 billion

6. The multiplier measures
   (a) the rise in injections resulting from an increase in income
   (b) the number of steps it takes to move from one equilibrium to another
   (c) the marginal propensity to invest or export
   (d) the extent by which income will change as a result of a shift in the aggregate-demand schedule

7. The size of the multiplier varies inversely with
   (a) the marginal propensity to withdraw
   (b) firms' attitudes toward investment
   (c) the level of unemployment
   (d) the level of government spending

8. If the withdrawals schedule has a slope of 0.33, the multiplier is
   (a) 1/3
   (b) 2/3
   (c) 3
   (d) 3/2

9. The message of the "paradox of thrift" is that
   (a) saving causes depressions
   (b) individuals who try to save cannot succeed
   (c) increased total saving may, *ceteris paribus*, have a contractionary effect on the economy
   (d) thrift is never a virtue

10. If all of any increase in income were saved, spent on imports, or taxed away, the multiplier would be
    (a) infinity
    (b) 1
    (c) 0
    (d) -1

11. Which of the following is basic to the hypothesis of the L-shaped aggregate-supply curve?
   (a) Output increases because the supply of labor is increasing along with population.
   (b) There is always full employment of resources.
   (c) As output increases, prices do not begin to rise until full employment is reached.
   (d) As output increases toward capacity, firms produce more efficiently.

12. One implication of the L-shaped aggregate-supply curve is that
   (a) output can be increased only with rising unit costs
   (b) output can be increased with no increase in the amount of inputs
   (c) changes in aggregate demand could affect the quantity of employment without affecting factor prices
   (d) unemployment cannot be reduced without prices beginning to rise gradually

13. An inflationary gap exists if, at the full-employment level of national income,
   (a) the aggregate-demand schedule intersects the 45-degree line
   (b) aggregate withdrawals exceed aggregate injections
   (c) aggregate demand is less than potential GNP
   (d) aggregate demand exceeds potential GNP

Answers to multiple-choice questions: 1(a)   2(a)   3(c)   4(c)   5(c)   6(d)   7(a)   8(c)   9(c)
10(b)   11(c)   12(c)   13(d)

# EXERCISES

1. The income-expenditure and withdrawal-injection diagrams below depict the current situation in an economy. Suppose that investment expenditures increase by 20.

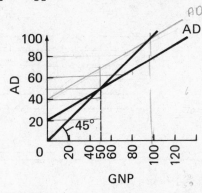
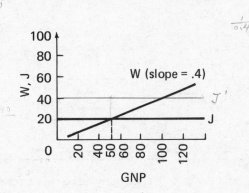

(a) What is the slope of the *AD* curve?   0.6

(b) Illustrate the increase in investment in both diagrams.
(c) Given the increase in investment, what is the relationship between injections and withdrawals at an income level of 50?

   J > W   By 20

(d) Given your answer to (c), what is happening to inventory levels?

   Inventory declining

(e) Assuming the existence of the L-shaped relationship mentioned in this chapter, what do you think will happen to output and employment in the economy? As this adjustment occurs, what will happen to the level of expenditures? To the level of withdrawals?

*output & employment increase.*

(f) According to the diagram, what is the new equilibrium level of GNP?

*100.*

(g) Does the formula, $\Delta Y = (1/w)\Delta J$, yield the same answer for the increase in income that you obtained in part (f)?

*Yes.*    $\dfrac{1}{0.4} \times 20 = 50.$

2. Suppose that there is a very simple evonomy in which only consumption expenditures and savings are influenced by the level of national income. Furthermore, business savings are zero and no government exists. The marginal propensity to consume is .8.

We assume that the economy begins initially at an equilibrium level of 100 in period 0 but that in period 1 investment increases by 10 and stays at the level of 30 permanently.

Furthermore, for expositional purposes, assume that consumption expenditures in period $t$ depend on the income level one period in the past, e.g., $t - 1$. Fill in the table below.

| Spending Period | Consumption | $\Delta C$ | Investment | $\Delta I$ | Income | $\Delta Y$ ($\Delta$ in income) |
|---|---|---|---|---|---|---|
| 0 | 80 | 0 | 20 | 10 | 100 | 0 |
| 1 | 80 | 0 | 30 | 10 | 110 | 10 |
| 2 | 88 | 8 | 30 | 0 | 118 | 8 |
| 3 | 94.4 | 6.4 | 30 | 0 | 124.4 | 6.4 |
| 4 | 99.52 | 5.1 | 30 | 0 | 129.52 | 5.12 |
| 5 | 103.6 | 4.1 | 30 | 0 | 133.6 | 4.1 |
| 6 | 106.9 | 3.3 | 30 | 0 | 136.9 | 3.3 |
| 7 | 109.5 | 2.6 | 30 | 0 | 139.5 | 2.6 |
| Total change or level | 120.0 | 0 | 30 | 0 | 150.0 | 0 |

(a) Why are the values of $\Delta C$ becoming progressively smaller?

(b) Will the economy reach a new equilibrium? Why?

(c) What is the value of the multiplier?

(d) What will the total change in savings be when the new equilibrium level is reached? Prove that total withdrawals are equal to 30 at the new equilibrium level.

3. Suppose that there is a more complicated economy than before. You may continue to assume that there is no business saving. The consumption function is given by the equation $C = .6Y_{t-1}$, with $.4Y_{t-1}$ going to $S$, $T$, and $M$. Fill in the following table to show the final effect on national income ($Y$) of a permanent decrease in exports of 5 millions. (Round off to one decimal place.)

| Spending Round | $\Delta X$ | $\Delta C$ | $\Delta W$ | $\Delta Y$ |
|---|---|---|---|---|
| 0 | -5 | — | — | -5 |
| 1 | — | -3.0 | -2.0 | -3 |
| 2 | | | | |
| 3 | | | | |
| 4 | | | | |
| 5 | | | | |
| 6 | | | | |
| Total change | | | | |

The multiplier = $\Delta Y/\Delta J$ _____ ; also it = $1/(\Delta W/\Delta Y)$ = _____ . Since $w$ (the marginal propensity to withdraw) is .4, prove that the value of the multiplier is 2.5 by using the formula $1/w$.

4. You are told that the actual equilibrium value of national income of an economy is $90 billion but that potential income has been estimated at $98 billion. Economic advisors have estimated that the marginal propensity to withdraw for this economy has the value .5.
   (a) Using an injection-withdrawal diagram, sketch the situation described above.
   (b) What is the size of the multiplier for this economy?

   (c) What type of gap exists? What is its magnitude? Show this on your diagram.

   (d) Would an increase in investment of $3.5 billion close the gap? Explain.

   (e) Would an increase in government expenditure of $4 billion close the gap?

5. Indicate in the table below if the following events cause a change in the slope of either the injection or withdrawal function *or* whether they cause a parallel shift in the injection or withdrawal function. Answer by inserting a yes or no and the direction of the change (+ for shift up and - for shift down).

| Event | Injections Curve | | Withdrawal Curve | |
|---|---|---|---|---|
| | Slope Change | Parallel Shift | Slope Change | Parallel Shift |
| (a) Marginal tax rate increase | | | | |
| (b) More government expenditures | | | | |
| (c) An increae in the marginal propensity to save | | | | |
| (d) Less imports because of crop failures abroad | | | | |

# PROBLEM

## MULTIPLIERS AND WITHDRAWALS

The multiplier can be defined in terms of withdrawals from the circular flow, or specifically as the reciprocal of $\Delta W/\Delta Y$, that is: $\Delta Y/\Delta W$. Students sometimes have difficulty with the discrepancy between a multiplier of 10 that is indicated by a consumer's marginal propensity to save of .1 and that of less than 2 which has been found to apply to many empirical studies of our complex economy. This problem seeks to show how the apparent multiplier of 10 is diminished to about 2 as the economic model takes on greater realism, with an increase in withdrawals related to income.

## Economy A: Closed, Ungoverned, Without Business Savings

In this economy all income is disposable ($Y = Y_d$), and the only withdrawal is personal saving. Assuming that $.1Y_d$ is saved, then $S_p = .1Y_d = .1Y$. (Remember, $\Delta W/\Delta Y$ = the sum of the coefficients in the various withdrawal functions.)

$Kd = (1 - b_i)$   $\Delta W/\Delta Y =$ _____0.1_____ , and the multiplier is _____10_____ .

## Economy B: Closed, Ungoverned, with Business Savings

In this economy it is assumed that firms do not distribute all of their income. Assume that business savings ($S_b$) = $.1Y$ and only $.9Y$ is disposable income to households.  Then $S_p = .1$ = $(.1)(.9Y) = .09Y$.

$\Delta W/\Delta Y =$ _____0.19_____ , and the multiplier is _____5.26_____ .

## Economy C: Closed, Governed, with Business Savings

With government, another withdrawal in the form of taxes is introduced. It is conceivable that such taxes could be unrelated to $Y$, for example, head taxes so that $T = \$100$ billion. Would the multiplier be affected in this case? Why?

No

It is more realistic to assume that taxes will be related to income and that the government will be concerned with transferring income to the old and the poor. With such transfers treated as negative taxes, assume $T_n = .3Y - 75$. $Y_d$ now equals $Y - .1Y - .3Y + 75$, and $S_p = .1(.6Y + 75)$.

$\Delta W/\Delta Y =$ _____0.46_____, and the multiplier is _____2.17_____.

## Economy D: Open, Governed, with Business Savings

With trade opened up to foreign countries, not all expenditures will be made domestically and thus in the economy's circular flow. Assume that imports $(M) = .04Y$ and that other withdrawals have the same relationship to $Y$ as in economy C.

$\Delta W/\Delta Y =$ _____0.5_____, and the multiplier is _____2_____.

# 31

# Cycles and Fluctuations in National Income

## KEY CONCEPTS AND DEFINITIONS

1. Short-term fluctuations in GNP are often caused by variations in aggregate demand. Thus fluctuations are often referred to as business cycles. Past evidence indicates that the cycles are irregular in amplitude, in timing, in duration, and in the way they affect various sectors of the economy.

2. Although changes in government expenditures and exports can cause cycles, the major fluctuations are explained in terms of changes in consumption and investment expenditures.

3. Shifts in the consumption function may generate business cycles. Shifts are caused by changes in income distribution, availability of credit, stocks of durable goods, and price expectations.

4. Ceteris paribus, if households expect inflation, they may purchase nondurable goods they would otherwise purchase at some time in the future.

5. The government can shift the consumption function related to GNP by changing personal tax rates. An increase in personal taxes lowers disposable income relative to GNP and can decrease consumption at every level of GNP.

6. Most economists regard shifts in investment as a major cause of business fluctuations. Changes in business inventories are very volatile and often account for an important fraction of the year-to-year changes in investment. They respond directly to changes in the level of production and sales and inversely to the interest rate.

7. Residential construction, a major component of investment, is one that shows a wavelike motion of its own. Residential construction is directly related to GNP and inversely to the rate of interest. The interest rate importantly determines residential construction because interest payments are a large fraction of mortgage payments which affect the household's ability to buy a house.

8. Business fixed investment in the form of machinery, equipment, and nonresidential construction, is the largest component of domestic investment. It depends upon innovation, changes in the level of national income, expectations about future profits, current profits, and the rate of interest.

9. A decrease in the rate of interest increases the desired stock of capital. However, investment may not expand immediately because of supply constraints in the capital-goods-producing firms.

10. The accelerator theory relates net investment to changes in the level of national income on the assumption of a fixed capital-output ratio.

11. The chief prediction of the accelerator theory is that rising income is required to maintain a positive level of investment. The accelerator theory is not without its

limitations. It ignores capital deepening and the influence of other economic variables, and assumes a constant capital-output ratio.

12. Economists have developed a vocabulary to denote the different stages of a business cycle: <u>trough</u> (the bottom), <u>expansion</u>, <u>peak</u> (upper turning point), and <u>recession</u> (downward turn).

13. The combination of the <u>multiplier</u> and the <u>accelerator</u> can cause upward or downward movements in the economy to be cumulative.

---

**CHECKLIST** — Make certain that you also understand the following concepts: seasonally adjusted; intended and unintended inventory investment; disequilibrium; capital widening; capital deepening; depression; upper and lower turning points; cumulative movements; inventory cycles; building cycle.

---

# REVIEW QUESTIONS

1. The condition of actual GNP below potential GNP is an example of (~~long-term~~/short-term) fluctuations of income.

2. Macroeconomic theory sees the primary cause of fluctuations of actual from potential GNP to be changes in ___*aggregate expenditure*___. It is possible that output, employment, and income could also be depressed by shortages of important inputs such as ___*energy sources*___.

3. That part of the business cycle characterized by substantial unemployment, losses for many firms, and downward trends in prices is called the ___*trough*___. The last example of this occurred during ___*1930's depression*___

4. In a severe depression, the amount of investment may be insufficient to replace worn-out capital, so that net investment is ___*zero negative*___. This means that the total capital stock of the country is ___*decreasing*___.

5. A period of labor and other shortages, rising costs, prices, interest rates, and investment suggests the part of the cycle called the ___*peak*___.

6. In this century, large rapid increases in federal spending and resulting periods of boom and inflation have invariably resulted from events occurring during ___*wars*___

7. We distinguish three categories of investment: ___*business investment*___ (*Inventories*), ___*Residential*___, and ___*Business fixed*___. Of these three the smallest but most volatile is ___*business investment*___.

8. Intended inventories are usually related to a firm's volume of ___*sales*___. An increase in unintended inventories means that sales are (exceeding/~~less than~~) output; to correct the inventory/sales ratio, a firm would (reduce/~~increase~~) output. Firms may want to reduce their inventories if interest rates (rise/~~fall~~).

9. In addition to income changes, the main economic influence on investment in residential housing is the cost and availability of ___*credit mortgages*___. Thus housing construction tends to vary inversely with ___*interest rates*___.

10. Business fixed investment is influenced by several major variables: opportunities for new ___*products*___, changes in aggregate ___*demand expenditure*___, expectations of ___*profit*___, rate of deterioration or obsolescence of ___*old equipment*___, and the rate of ___*interest*___. A firm that wishes to invest in new facilities or equipment without borrowing or selling shares may finance it out of either ___*profit*___ or ___*investment*___. *(depreciation reserves)*

11. The act of investment is a *flow* of spending; the total amount of capital in existence is a _____*stock*_____. Investment adds to the capital stock only if *net* investment is _____*positive*_____. If gross investment is less than the amount estimated for depreciation in a period, net investment would be _____*negative*_____.

12. It is predicted that, *ceteris paribus,* a fall in the rate of interest will (increase/decrease) the desired capital stock, and will therefore (increase/decrease) the amount of investment in a given period. However, regardless of the rate of interest and profit expectations, the amount of investment in a period is limited by _____*capacity of*_____ *capital - good industry*_____.

13. Suppose that, with a multiplier of 2 and some unemployed productive capacity, investment rises from $8 billion to $8½ billion per year, for one year: *ceteris paribus,* GNP would rise by _____*1 billion*_____. Suppose that the following year, after the desired amount of capital stock has been attained, investment returns to $8 billion; *ceteris paribus,* GNP will fall by _____*1 billion*_____.

14. The marginal-efficiency-of-investment schedule slopes downward to indicate that additional investment spending will be undertaken only if there is a fall in the _____*rate of interest*_____. The steeper or less elastic the schedule, the (greater/smaller) the change in investment with a change in the _____*rate of interest*_____.

15. The accelerator theory predicts that net investment is related also to changes in _____*income*_____, expressed as *I* (net) = a∆ *Y*_____. The accelerator coefficient a represents the ratio of capital needed per unit of new *output existing stock*_____. The theory points out that net investment occurs when desired capital stock differs from _____*existing capital stock*_____.

16. The effect of the accelerator is to (widen/narrow) the amplitude of cyclical fluctuations in total spending. If the rate of increase in national income declines, the accelerator theory holds that investment spending will (decrease/remain constant/increase at a declining rate).

17. Peaks or ceilings to economic expansions are eventually reached because of points of recessions or depressions are reached when there is a sufficient revival of spending for replacement of _____.

---

If you have not answered all questions correctly, review the text in order to be sure that you have all of the important concepts clearly in mind before going on to the next chapter.

1. short-term  2. aggregate expenditure or demand; energy sources  3. trough; the depression of the 1930s  4. negative; decreasing  5. peak  6. wars  7. inventories, business fixed investment, residential construction; inventories  8. sales; less than; reduce; rise  9. mortgages, interest rates  10. products or techniques, expenditure, profit, old equipment, interest; depreciation reserves, retained profits  11. stock; positive; negative  12. increase, increase; capacity of capital-goods industry  13. $1 billion; $1 billion  14. rate of interest; smaller, rate of interest  15. income, *Y*; output; existing capital stock  16. widen; decrease  17. bottlenecks, shortages, no unused capacity to produce; worn-out capital goods

---

# MULTIPLE-CHOICE QUESTIONS

1. The demographic variable that most affects housing sales in a particular year is
    (a) the death rate
    (b) the birth rate
    (c) the marriage rate
    (d) the adjusted fertility rate

2. Investment in inventory in a year is measured by
   (a) the inventory/sales ratio
   (b) the level of inventory
   (c) year-end inventory minus beginning inventory
   (d) beginning inventory minus year-end inventory

3. If you were determining the total of investment spending, which would you *not* include?
   (a) changes in inventories
   (b) purchases of stocks and bonds
   (c) new residential construction
   (d) new plant and equipment

4. History shows that investment in Canada
   (a) has been quite a stable but small fraction of GNP
   (b) has fluctuated a great deal
   (c) has usually been about 30 percent of GNP
   (d) has never fallen below the amount needed for replacement

5. The marginal-efficiency-of-capital schedule relates
   (a) the amount of investment to GNP
   (b) the size of the capital stock to equipment prices
   (c) the size of the capital stock to the interest rate
   (d) the amount of investment to interest rates

6. Inventories tend to vary
   (a) directly with the level of sales, inversely with the rate of interest
   (b) inversely with sales, directly with interest rates
   (c) directly with sales and interest rates
   (d) inversely with sales and interest rates

7. A shift in the *MEC* schedule upward implies
   (a) interest rates have fallen
   (b) the price of capital goods has risen
   (c) aggregate consumption has fallen
   (d) the marginal return on each unit of capital has increased

8. Which of the following would have the effect of shifting the consumption function upward?
   (a) Borrowing rates increase.
   (b) Prices are expected to fall in the future.
   (c) Income is redistributed from households with high marginal propensities to consume to households with low ones.
   (d) Government policies lower income tax rates.

9. The amount of investment spending by firms
   (a) is influenced by profit expectations and interest rates
   (b) seems to be entirely random
   (c) has little effect on the economy
   (d) is quite stable and predictable

10. According to the accelerator theory, investment in a function of
    (a) the level of income
    (b) profits
    (c) changes in income
    (d) savings

11. The kind of borrowing most discouraged by high interest rates is
    (a) corporate borrowing
    (b) residential mortgages
    (c) consumer credit
    (d) government borrowing

12. The multiplier and accelerator effects operating together
    (a) tend to cancel out
    (b) help to explain why recoveries, once started, continue upward
    (c) make the amplitude of cycles less than they otherwise would be
    (d) tend to keep growth going perpetually

---

Answers to multiple-choice questions: 1(c)   2(c)   3(b)   4(b)   5(c)   6(a)   7(d)   8(d)   9(a)
10(c)   11(b)   12(b)

---

# EXERCISES

1. *Illustrating the Accelerator Principle.* The table below shows the hypothetical situation
   for a firm that requires 1 machine for every 1,000 units of product it turns out annually.
   As it increases its output and sales in response to changing demand, show how its investment will be affected. Replacement for depreciation is 1 machine per year throughout.

| Year | Annual Output (units) | Units of Capital Needed | New Machines Required | Replace- ment Machines | New Machines to Be Purchased |
|------|------|------|------|------|------|
| 1 | 10,000 | 10 | 0 | 1 | 1 |
| 2 | 10,000 | | | | |
| 3 | 11,000 | | | | |
| 4 | 12,000 | | | | |
| 5 | 15,000 | | | | |
| 6 | 17,000 | | | | |
| 7 | 18,000 | | | | |
| 8 | 18,000 | | | | |

(a) Between year 2 and year 5, output increased by what percent? _____

(b) In the same period, total investment spending by this firm increased by what percent?

_____

2. A seller of shirts has had weekly sales of 100 and tries to keep inventory on his shelves
   equal to twice his weekly sales, adjusting his weekly orders from the jobber according to
   the current week's sales. Fill out the rest of the table, showing how his actual inventory
   and orders from his supplier would change as his weekly sales change.

| Week | Weekly Sales | Actual Inventory, End of Week | Inventory/ Sales Ratio | Desired Inventory | Desired Inventory plus Expected Sales | Weekly Orders for Next Week |
|------|------|------|------|------|------|------|
| 1 | 100 | 200 | 2 | 200 | 300 | 100 |
| 2 | 100 | 200 | 2 | 200 | 300 | 100 |
| 3 | 110 | 190 | | 200 | 300 | 140 |
| 4 | 110 | 220 | | | | 110 |
| 5 | 120 | | | | | |
| 6 | 120 | | | | | |
| 7 | 110 | | | | | |
| 8 | 110 | | | | | |
| 9 | 110 | | | | | |

(a) The range of weekly sales was from _____ to _____ .

(b) The range of weekly orders was from _____ to _____ .

(c) How do these findings help to explain the cause of economic fluctuations?

3. *Changes in Desired Capital Stocks*. You are given two *MEC* schedules.

| Schedule A | | Schedule B | |
|---|---|---|---|
| Capital Stock | MEC (%) | Capital Stock | MEC (%) |
| 100 | 20 | 100 | 22 |
| 200 | 18 | 200 | 20 |
| 300 | 14 | 300 | 16 |
| 400 | 8 | 400 | 10 |
| 500 | 1 | 500 | 3 |

(a) Suppose that the interest rate was 14% and the economy had reached its desired level of capital stock. From Schedule A, determine the magnitude of the capital stock and the implied level of desired investment.

(b) Suppose that the rise of interest fell to 8%. According to Schedule A, what is the new level of desired capital stock? What is the desired level of investment? Would businessmen necessarily be able to achieve this investment in the current period?

(c) Suppose that the *MEC* schedule given by A suddenly changed to that given by Schedule B. With an interest rate of 14%, what is the approximate magnitude of the desired capital stock? Does the change in the *MEC* schedule imply new investment activity? Indicate two factors that may have caused the *MEC* schedule to change.

4. *Shifts in the Consumption Function*. The table below depicts the relationships between consumption and income and taxes and income.

| Consumption | Income | Tax Payments | Disposable Income |
|---|---|---|---|
| 200 | 0 | 0 | _____ |
| 240 | 100 | 20 | _____ |
| 280 | 200 | 40 | _____ |
| 320 | 300 | 60 | _____ |
| 360 | 400 | 80 | _____ |
| 400 | 500 | 100 | _____ |

(a) Calculate the level of disposable income for each level of total income and fill in these values in the table.
(b) What is the magnitude of autonomous consumption expenditures?

(c) What is the *tax rate* at each level of income? Is it constant?

(d) Calculate the marginal propensity to consume out of disposable income. Is it constant?

(e) Plot the relationship between consumption and total income on the graph below.

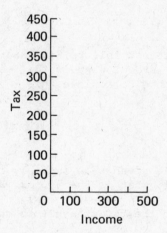

(f) Suppose the tax rate was a constant 10%. Recalculate the disposable income levels and tax payments.

(g) Assuming that the *mpc* out of disposable income had not changed from your answer to part (d), recalculate consumption expenditure levels for each level of disposable income.

(h) Plot the new consumption—total-income relationship on the graph above.

# Problems

## 1. POTENTIAL VERSUS ACTUAL GNP

Earlier you were introduced to the idea of deflationary and inflationary gaps, the amount by which aggregate demand differs from the amount necessary to produce a full-employment equilibrium. The GNP gap differs from this in two respects:

1. It is the difference between "potential," or full-employment, GNP and actual GNP. As indicated in Figure 31-1, it is measured horizontally along the axis rather than vertically. (When, as in Figure 31-2, the horizontal axis is time, then the difference between potential and actual GNP is measured vertically.)
2. The actual GNP may differ from the equilibrium GNP discussed in earlier chapters.

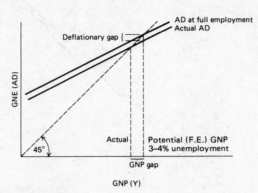

Figure 31-1

You are asked in this problem to investigate the relationship of changes in investment and changes in the GNP gap. Because investment is an important injection, the hypothesis to be tested is that substantial year-to-year increases in investment will reduce the gap of potential minus actual GNP, whereas reductions will increase the gap.

First, examine the problem of measuring the gap, which is primarily a problem of measuring potential GNP.

In its report, *Performance and Potential, mid-1950s to mid-1970s,* the Economic Council of Canada defined the concept of potential GNP as the volume of goods and services that the economy would ordinarily produce at an unemployment rate of 3.8 percent. The measurement of potential GNP incorporates the effects of higher productivity, a larger labor force, and a fuller work schedule. As a consequence, potential GNP does not stand still. Over time, population trends add to the number of persons in the labor force. Furthermore, increases in the quantity and quality of capital, advances in technology, and improvements in the quality of labor raise the potential productivity of the labor force.

In Canada, between 1956 and 1969, the increase in the labor force was about 41 percent. In addition, between 1956 and 1961, real output per employed person grew at 1.3 percent per year; from 1961 to 1966 at the rate of 3.1 percent per year; and from 1966 to 1969 at 1.6 percent per year. Taking all of these factors into consideration, the annual growth rate in potential GNP was about 5.2 percent.

Comparing actual and potential output, the Council computed that in 1971 the Canadian economy was operating about 3 to 4 percent *below* its potential, or at about a $3 billion loss on an annual basis. This is a considerable loss to Canadian society.

The size of the GNP "gap" between actual and potential output between 1956 and 1974 is shown at the top of the next page.

## Questions

1. What relationship exists between the size of the "gap" and the percentage change in real output per employed workers?

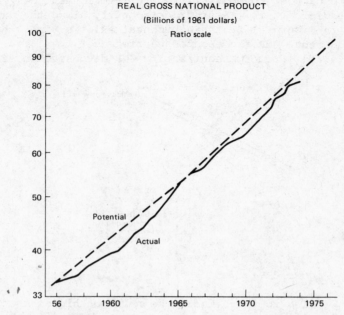

ACTUAL AND POTENTIAL LEVELS OF
REAL GROSS NATIONAL PRODUCT

(Billions of 1961 dollars)

Ratio scale

Figure 31-2. *Sources: The Tenth Annual Review,*
Economic Council of Canada, p. 78; *Economic Re-*
*view,* Department of Finance, pp. 29-30.

2. We have displayed data on the percentage change in real private investment (excluding
   residential construction) expenditures in Canada between the years 1956 and 1974:

   | | | | |
   |---|---|---|---|
   | 1956-1961 | - 1.5% per year | 1966-1974 | + 7.5% per year |
   | 1961-1966 | +13.9% per year | 1966-1971 | + 1.3% per year |
   | 1966-1969 | - 0.5% per year | 1971-1974 | + 9.1% per year |

   What relationship exists between the size of the gap and investment expenditures? Why would
   you expect this?

3. What effect might the size of the GNP gap in the United States have on the size of Canada's
   GNP gap? Explain.

## 2.   THE MULTIPLIER-ACCELERATOR INTERACTION MODEL

The multiplier when combined with the accelerator may generate fluctuation in national income.
For this model we have assumed: (1) the marginal propensity to consume is .5, (2) consumption
in time period $t$ depends on the level of income one period past ($t - 1$), (3) the capital-output
ratio or what is often referred to as the accelerator coefficient, is 1, and (4) investment in
time period $t$ depends on an autonomous amount, 100, plus the difference in income between $t - 1$
and $t - 2$.

These assumptions are expressed by the following equations:

$$C_t = .5Y_{t-1}$$
$$I_t = 100 + 1(Y_{t-1} - Y_{t-2})$$
$$Y_t = .5Y_{t-1} + 100 + 1(Y_{t-1} - Y_{t-2})$$

The economy is assumed to be at an equilibrium level of income of 200 in the current time period 0 and has been at that level for two previous periods, -2 and -1. In period 1 autonomous investment increases from 100 to 200 and stays at that level permanently.

The effect of this increase shows up in national income in period 1 as simply an increase of 100. Why? Since consumption depends on last period's income (period 0) and income is 200, the consumption level remains at a level of 100. Furthermore, there is no accelerator effect in period 1 since the difference between income in period 0 and period -1 (one period and two periods removed from period 1, respectively) is zero.

However, interesting things start to occur to national income thereafter. We have started the process by completing the entries for period 2.

| Period | Consumption $C_t = .5Y_{t-1}$ | Investment ($I_t$) Autonomous | Accelerator $1(Y_{t-1} - Y_{t-2})$ | National Income $Y_t = C_t + I_t$ |
|---|---|---|---|---|
| -2 | 100 | 100 | 0 | 200 |
| -1 | 100 | 100 | 0 | 200 |
| 0 | 100 | 100 | 0 | 200 |
| 1 | 100 | 200 | 0 | 300 |
| 2 | 150 | 200 | 100 | 450 |
| 3 | 225 | 200 | 150 | 575 |
| 4 | 287.5 | 200 | 125.5 | 612.5 |
| 5 | 306.25 | 200 | 37.5 | 543.75 |
| 6 | 271.90 | 200 | -68.7 | 403.2 |
| 7 | 201.6 | 200 | -140.6 | 261.0 |
| 8 | 130.5 | 200 | -142.2 | 188.3 |
| 9 | 94.15 | 200 | 72.7 | 221.45 |
| 10 | 110.7 | 200 | 33.2 | 343.9 |

## Questions

1. Fill in the missing values for periods 3 through 10.

2. Identify by period(s) the trough of the cycle, the peak, the expansion phase, and the recession phase.

3. Assume that the autonomous element of investment is sensitive to the rate of interest. What changes in the level of the rate of interest might the government of this economy pursue in periods 2 to 4 and periods 5 to 8 to "smooth out" this business cycle?

# 32

# Fiscal Policy

## KEY CONCEPTS AND DEFINITIONS

1. In any given period of time, the impact of the government's fiscal policy will result in either a balanced budget, a budget surplus, or a budget deficit. Raising expenditure without changing tax rates is known as deficit financing.
2. To remove an inflationary gap, the appropriate fiscal policy would be to change expenditures and/or taxes so as to move the budget toward a surplus. The reverse procedures would be followed in an attempt to remove a deflationary gap.
3. Government expenditure and tax charges of equal absolute magnitude have different effects on national income. The expenditure change is more "powerful" than a tax change.
4. As long as tax revenue depends upon the level of national income, an initial deficit resulting from an increase in expenditure will be reduced as national income increases toward its new equilibrium level.
5. The full-employment deficit or surplus is the potential budget balance that would result if (a) the economy were at full employment and (b) all policies related to expenditure and taxation were unchanged.
6. A simultaneous and equal increase in both government spending and taxation will raise the level of national income. The ratio of the change in income that results to the charge in expenditure (that was tax financed) is the balanced budget multiplier. A similar multiplier works for a balanced reduction in expenditure and tax revenue.
7. Built-in stabilizers may be present on both the expenditure and tax side of the budget. They operate in such a manner to dampen an expansion in income and cushion a decline without the need for the government to make a policy change. Discretionary fiscal policy refers to the decision by the government to change a tax rate or level of expenditure through legislative action.
8. The efficacy with which discretionary fiscal tax policy works may depend upon the specific relationship between consumption and disposable income. Consumption behavior based on a permanent income concept may be less responsive to short-term tax changes than one based on changes in current absolute income.
9. In addition to raising taxes, an expenditure increase can be financed by borrowing money from persons and corporations, at home and abroad or through the creation of new money.
10. The burden of financing a deficit will depend not just on the method used, but the economic conditions prevailing at the time of the deficit financing. The major difference between borrowing "at home" and "abroad" is that in the case of the latter paying back the loan implies a flight of financial resources out of the country and the burden of the present deficit financing is shifted to future generations.

| CHECKLIST | Make certain that you also understand the following concepts: treasury bill, crowding-out; pump priming; fiscal drag; stagflation; lags of fiscal policy, opportunity cost of government. |
|---|---|

## Review Questions

1. The use of taxing and spending by government to promote certain macroeconomic goals is called _____ *fiscal policy* _____.

2. When government expenditures exceed taxes, the government has a (deficit/~~surplus~~). When the government has a deficit, it gets the money it needs by _____ *borrowing* _____. If the money it borrows would not otherwise have been spent, the budget deficit will cause aggregate demand to _____ ~~fall~~ *rise* _____.

3. Government can close a deflationary gap and move the economy toward the full-employment level by (cutting/~~raising~~) tax rates or (~~decreasing~~/increasing) expenditures, or a combination of the two. When the government spends money on goods and services, (all of it/ ~~only part of~~ it) is added to aggregate demand on the first round of spending. If the multiplier is 2, $1 million of government spending not financed by additional taxes will, *ceteris paribus*, increase GNP by _____ *2* _____. If the government lowers tax rates in order to reduce personal income tax payments by $1 million, disposable income will rise by _____ *1* _____. If *MPC* out of $Y_d$ = 0.9, first-round spending out of the tax cut will amount to _____ *0.9* _____. If the multiplier is 2, GNP will rise, *ceteris paribus*, by _____ *1.8* _____. Thus, to achieve an equivalent change in GNP with one method or the other, a (smaller/~~larger~~) change in tax revenues is required than in government spending.

4. A rise in GNP can thus be caused by a deliberate initial increase in the government deficit or a reduction in the _____ *surplus* _____. The initial rise in the deficit will be (reduced/~~increased~~) as income rises and tax collections (rise/~~fall~~).

5. If the economy is booming in an inflationary manner, the government can reduce aggregate demand by raising _____ *taxes* _____ and/or lowering _____ *expenditure* _____. The cut in *G* spending necessary to remove a given inflationary gap will be (more/~~less~~) than the rise in tax revenue necessary to do the same job.

6. At given tax rates, rising incomes produce _____ *rising* _____ tax revenues. Thus, if the government has a deficit, *ceteris paribus*, it will grow (smaller/~~larger~~) as incomes rise. For given tax rates and a constant level of government spending, the surplus or deficit which it is calculated that the government would experience at full employment is called the _____ *full-employment-surplus* _____. It is (possible/ ~~not possible~~) for a government to have simultaneously an actual budget deficit and a full-employment surplus. The analysis suggests that to reach full employment in this case, taxes should be (cut/~~raised~~) and/or government expenditures (~~reduced~~/increased).

7. If the government increases its expenditures and increases its taxes by the same amount, there will be (an increase/~~no increase~~) in aggregate demand and therefore (also/~~not~~) in income. This is because (~~all~~/not all) of the increased taxes would _____ *saving* _____ and _____ *imports* _____. If 10 percent of the increased personal income taxes of $1 million had been saved or spent on imports, and if government had spent all of the increased tax revenues at home, aggregate demand would have increased initially by $ _____ *0.1* _____. If the multiplier is 2, $w$ = _____ *0.5* _____; the increase in GNP would be $ _____ *0.2* _____, and the balanced budget multiplier would be 10 percent/$w$, or _____ *0.2* _____. We would thus expect that a reduction in government spending of $2 million, matched by an equal reduction in taxes, would usually have, *ceteris paribus*, a total effect of reducing income by (the same or a lesser amount/~~a greater amount~~).

8. "Stabilizing" the economy means (narrowing/~~widening~~) the range of fluctuations in production, employment, and prices.

9. A built-in stabilizer is any feature of the government's fiscal structure that automatically in booms tends to (~~decrease~~/increase) taxes relative to government spending, and in slumps tends to (decrease/~~increase~~) them relative to government spending. Such a stabilizer makes withdrawals (rise/~~fall~~) in good times and (~~rise~~/fall) in poor times, relative to injections.

10. The higher and more progressive the tax structure, the (more/~~less~~) stabilizing its effects will be, *ceteris paribus*.

11. Government expenditures will have a greater stabilizing effect the (~~less~~/more) they fall as income rises and the (~~less~~/more) they rise as incomes fall.

12. Fiscal drag occurs when the tax structure is overstabilizing and thus prevents an upswing in the economy from reaching _____ inflation full-employment level.

13. The chief built-in stabilizers are agricultural support policies, social security and unemployment insurance, and above all _____ taxes (income) _____. The original purpose of these measures (~~was~~/was not) to stabilize the economy. Since World War II, they have been (partially/~~entirely~~) successful in limiting economic fluctuations.

14. The choice of what fiscal policy "mix" to adopt is (affected/~~not affected~~) by attitudes toward government. If expansion in the economy is needed, those who wish to limit the growth of the government would usually favor _____ tax cuts _____.

15. The decisions lag in Canada is _____ much shorter _____ than in the United States. In both countries, however, these lags make it (easy/~~difficult~~) to time tax changes and government spending in order to counteract the business cycle rather than to intensify it.

16. The 10 percent reduction in income taxes voted in 1965 by Parliament is an example of a(n) (~~automatic~~/discretionary) tool of fiscal policy.

17. In relying on pump priming in the 1930s, the government used deficits that proved too (small/~~large~~) to bring the economy close to full employment. The depression was finally ended with enormous _____ war _____ expenditures.

18. The milestone legislation for conscious use of fiscal policy to influence the Canadian economy was the _____ white paper of 1945 _____.

19. Fiscal policy was not really used as a means of achieving full employment in the United States until _____ 1964 _____.

20. One method of offsetting "fiscal drag" (as in 1965) is to _____ lower _____ taxes.

21. A cyclically balanced budget implies (surpluses/~~deficits~~) in booms and (~~surpluses~~/deficits) in recessions. It will not work if there is a chronic tendency for saving to exceed _____ investment _____ at full-employment levels. The appropriate response to this situation, which is called secular _____ stagnation _____, is a policy of continuing budget _____ deficits _____.

22. The opposite situation of secular boom in which full-employment investment exceeds full-employment _____ saving _____ would call for a continuing _____ surplus _____ in the federal budget.

23. The opportunity cost of a given government expenditure (~~is the same regardless of~~/varies according to) how it is financed. If government expenditures take resources away from consumer-goods production, the opportunity cost is borne in the (present/~~future~~). If government expenditures take resources from capital-goods production, the opportunity costs will

be borne in the _____*future*_____, in the form of (fewer/more) consumer goods produced than otherwise. If government expenditures used unemployed resources, the opportunity cost would be _____*zero*_____.

24. If the government borrows from the private sector to finance expenditures, the opportunity cost is borne by the _____*lenders*_____. The latter will be rewarded by _____*interest*_____ paid by the taxpayers. When the government pays interest to domestic holders of the debt, it usually pays it with money raised by _____*taxes*_____; this is called a _____*transfer*_____ payment and does not affect total income. Government debt can be a burden to future generations if it is owed to _____*foreigners*_____.

25. Referring to Figure 32-3 in the text, in what year was the national debt actually larger than the GNP? _____ Since 1949, the debt as a percentage of GNP has been (falling steadily/rising steadily).

26. As measured by the ratio of debt to GNP, the national debt since 1950 has been a(n) (increasing/constant/declining) burden. As measured by the ratios of interest on debt to GNP or to taxes, the burden has for the most part been (increasing/constant/declining).

---

If you have not answered all questions correctly, review the text in order to be sure that you have all of the important concepts clearly in mind before going on to the next chapter.

1. fiscal policy  2. deficit; borrowing; rise  3. cutting, increasing; all of it; $2 million; $1 million; $0.9 million; $1.8 million; larger  4. surplus; reduced, rise  5. tax rates, expenditures; less  6. rising; smaller; full-employment surplus, deficit, or balance; possible; cut, increased  7. an increase, also; not all; saving, imports; $0.1 million; 0.5; $0.2 million; 0.2; the same or a lesser amount  8. narrowing  9. increase; decrease; rise; fall  10. more  11. more; more  12. full-employment levels  13. taxes, especially on income; was not; partially  14. affected; tax cuts  15. shorter; shorter; difficult  16. discretionary  17. small, war  18. White Paper of 1945  19. 1964  20. lower  21. surpluses, deficits; investment; stagnation, deficits  22. savings; surplus  23. varies according to; present; future, fewer; zero  24. lenders; interest; taxes, transfer, foreigners  25. 1944-1947; falling steadily  26. declining; constant

---

## MULTIPLE-CHOICE QUESTIONS

1. Government spending will increase incomes only if
   (a) it is spent on capital goods
   (b) it is spent on transfer payments
   (c) it is in addition to what would otherwise have been spent by households and firms
   (d) it is spent out of taxation

2. It is possible that government spending, even if financed wholly out of taxes, will increase incomes if
   (a) taxpayers would have saved some of the money they had to pay in taxes
   (b) only high-income levels are taxed
   (c) prices rise as a result
   (d) investment declines by an equivalent amount

3. If the government spends more than it receives in taxes and other revenues,
   (a) it is obviously spending too much
   (b) national income will surely rise
   (c) there will be a surplus in the budget
   (d) there will be a deficit in the budget

4. A budget deficit will increase GNP only if
   (a) the government borrows money that otherwise would have been spent on investment
   (b) the government borrows money that otherwise would not have been spent at all
   (c) the government borrows from households money that otherwise would have been lent to firms
   (d) the government spends the money abroad rather than at home

5. Which of the following is not a built-in stabilizer?
   (a) a change in tax rates
   (b) unemployment insurance payments
   (c) the corporate income tax
   (d) agricultural subsidies

6. A "full-employment surplus" means that
   (a) a countercyclical fiscal policy is being followed
   (b) the budget will be in surplus at all levels of GNP
   (c) government spending must have declined
   (d) there may be fiscal drag in the tax structure

7. The balanced-budget multiplier
   (a) applies only when government expenditures are equal to taxes
   (b) is larger than the multiplier for government expenditures
   (c) applies when additional tax receipts are equal to additional government expenditures
   (d) is the same as the multiplier for government expenditures

8. With an exogenous expenditure multiplier of 2, a personal income tax cut of $2 million will raise GNP
   (a) by $4 million
   (b) by $2 million only
   (c) by somewhat less than $4 million, depending on the *MPC* out of $Y_d$
   (d) totally by less than $2 million because of withdrawals

9. All but which one of the following are practical problems connected with successful use of fiscal policy to stabilize the economy?
   (a) It is hard politically to get rapid action on proposed tax changes.
   (b) Forecasting is sometimes inaccurate, so the right policy measures may not be taken, or taken soon enough.
   (c) Time lags are too great both in decision making and action taking.
   (d) There is no evidence that lower taxes will actually increase consumption.

10. Stagflation
    (a) implies that fiscal policy will not work
    (b) refers to the coexistence of inflation and high unemployment
    (c) inflation cannot be cured by fiscal policy
    (d) economic growth is the economy's major problem

11. Interest on the federal debt
    (a) has risen in relation to GNP since 1945
    (b) represents a transfer from taxpayers to bondholders
    (c) is less of a burden when paid to foreigners
    (d) is included in our aggregate of government purchases of goods and services

12. The burden of the economic cost of a war
    (a) is borne mainly by future generations
    (b) is the current and future consumption that is forgone
    (c) is borne only by the losers
    (d) is almost always less than the economic benefits

13. Fiscal policy in the 1930s was one of
    (a) pump priming
    (b) compensatory fiscal policy
    (c) cyclically balanced budgets
    (d) annually balanced budgets

14. The Finance Minister stated in the February 1973 Budget Speech that by concentrating the personal income tax reduction in the lower income strata the most expansion would be attained. This implies
    (a) that high income earners don't know how to spend their money wisely
    (b) a belief that the marginal propensity to consume rises as incomes fall
    (c) a value judgment about income redistribution
    (d) none of the above

---

Answers to multiple-choice questions:  1(c)   2(a)   3(d)   4(b)   5(a)   6(d)   7(c)   8(b)   9(d)
10(b)   11(b)   12(b)   13(a)   14(b)

---

# EXERCISES

1. Say that, for all levels of income, $G$ will be $100 million and net taxes (taxes minus transfer payments) will be $0.25Y$. Plot $G$ and $T_n$ on the graph below, and answer the questions. Suppose that the full-employment level of GNP is $500 million.

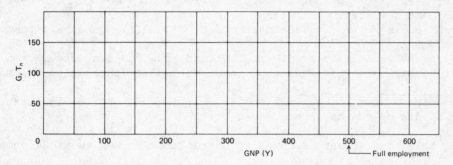

(a) The budget will be balanced at a GNP of _____.
(b) At GNP of $200 million, the budget will show a (deficit/surplus) of _____.
(c) At full-employment GNP, the budget will show a (deficit/surplus) of _____.
(d) Suppose that at full-employment GNP, $I$ equals $S$ and $X$ equals $M$. Can this economy ever reach full employment with the fiscal policy depicted here? _____
(e) Show on the graph what two moves fiscal policy could make in this situation if full employment were the goal, and explain briefly.

2. At the top of the next page is an aggregate-demand schedule for a hypothetical economy, showing an estimated full-employment level of 40 GNP.
(a) What will be the *actual* GNP level in equilibrium? _____
(b) How big is the gap between actual and potential, or full-employment, GNP. (*Hint:* Measure along the horizontal axis.) _____
(c) How much of an increase in aggregate demand would be needed to move GNP from actual to full-employment GNP? (*Hint:* Measure along the vertical axis.) _____
(d) Explain in a few words why your answer to (c) is different from your answer to (b).

(e) What fiscal policy measures would be appropriate in this situation?

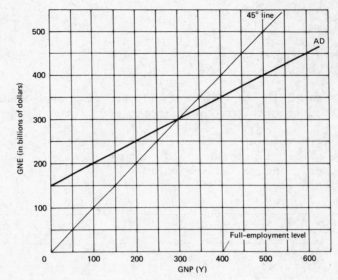

(f) Draw in the new *AD* curve, showing the elimination of the deflationary gap (assuming no change in slope).

3. Suppose that the government increases total spending by $10 million per year and at the same time increases taxes so that it collects $10 million more in tax revenues. Assume that $C = 0.60Y$ and $K = 2.5$.
   (a) The *G* spending increases aggregate demand by $10 million and, via the multiplier, *increases* GNP by _____.
   (b) The tax increase reduces *Y* by $10 million and thus reduces consumption spending by 0.60*Y*, or $6 million. This reduction in *C*, multiplied through the economy, *reduces* GNP by _____.
   (c) *Net change* in GNP is _____. (This exercise illustrates, but does not prove, the idea of the balanced-budget multiplier.)

4. The following relationships are assumed to characterize a hypothetical economy:

   $C = 5 + 0.80(Y - T)$
   $I = 5$
   $G = 5$
   $Y = C + I + G$

   where *C* = consumer expenditure; *Y* = national income; *I* = planned investment; *G* = planned government expenditure, and *T* = tax revenue, all in billions of dollars.
   (a) What is the equilibrium level of national income, assuming that the government budget is balanced?

   (b) If the full-employment level of national income is $65 billion, what income tax policy is needed to achieve the full-employment income level? (Indicate both the direction and the magnitude of the policy.)

(c) What will happen to the original balanced budget position after the execution of the tax policy in (b)?

## PROBLEMS

### 1. THE FULL-EMPLOYMENT BUDGET SURPLUS AND CANADIAN FISCAL POLICY

The concept of the full-employment budget surplus (FEBS) is one of the tools that can be used to analyze fiscal policy. In the chart below, the actual federal deficit/surplus and the FEBS result for the recession period 1957-1963 are shown.

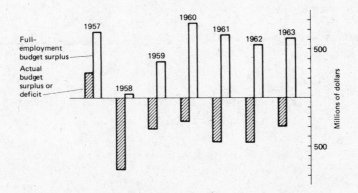

Source: R. M. Will, *Canadian Fiscal Policy, 1945-63,* Study no. 17, Royal Commission on Taxation, Queen's Printer, Ottawa, 1967.

## Questions

1. From this chart, what can you suggest about the adequacy of fiscal policy during this period?

2. Following a substantial increase in federal spending in 1958, tax revenue increased the following year without there being any major tax changes. The economy was still performing below its potential. Describe what was occurring and its probable effect on unemployment in the absence of any discretionary policy changes.

## 2.  WAS THE 1965 TAX CUT INFLATIONARY?

In the text, it is suggested that fiscal policy makers, in retrospect, misjudged the situation in 1965 when they reduced taxes. What evidence, however, did the government have at that time with respect to the overall economic situation?

In the table below, some basic statistics, taken from the *Budget Papers* that accompanied the 1965 Budget, are shown. Given this information, the Minister of Finance, the Hon. Walter Gordon, announced a reduction in federal tax payable equal to 10 percent of the basic tax payable subject to a maximum reduction of $600 per year.

In making this tax cut, the Minister said, "I believe this budget should be an expansionary one."

| Selected Economic Indicators | 1963-1964 | 1963 | 1964 |
|---|---|---|---|
| Percentage change in consumer price index | 1.8% | | |
| Unemployment (percent of labor force) | | 5.5% | 4.7% |
| Percentage change in real GNP | 5.0 | | |
| Percentage change in average weekly wages and salaries | 3.7 | | |
| Gross private investment (real 1957 dollars) | | $6.97 | $7.85 |

*Source:* Statistics Canada.

## Questions

1. Would this tax proposal be expansionary? If so, how would it generate increases in income and employment?

2. In view of the statistics and goals of economic policy, do you think that this policy was the right one for the time? Justify your answer with reference to the information given in the table.

## 3.  A TURNING POINT IN FISCAL POLICY

In the Budget Speech of February 19, 1973, the Hon. John Turner proposed a reduction in personal income taxes, higher personal exemptions, and a reduction in sales taxes and tariffs on certain consumer goods. Mr. Turner stated, "We shall be attacked in some quarters for still not doing enough to stimulate the economy. Others will say that we are doing too much and that by overshooting the target we will aggravate inflation. We recognize that we are running a risk, and . . . that is a risk worth taking at this time in the interests of dealing more effectively with unemployment." Regarding the sales tax reductions specifically, he said, "This action should help to moderate prices. . . . "

Use the table at the top of the next page to answer the questions below.

## Questions

1. Explain how Mr. Turner's proposals are expected to operate to reduce unemployment and moderate price inflation.

| Quarterly Period and Year | GNP (real 1961 dollars) | Gross Private Fixed Investment (real 1961 dollars) | Consumer Price Index (1961 = 100.0) | Unemployment Rate | Average Weekly Wages in Industry |
|---|---|---|---|---|---|
| 1971 | | | | | |
| Q1 | $65.8 billion | $15.5 billion | | | $134.75 |
| Q2 | 66.6 billion | 16.3 billion | | | 138.06 |
| Q3 | 68.4 billion | 16.8 billion | 134.7 | 6.9% | 140.99 |
| Q4 | 68.9 billion | 17.2 billion | 136.3 | 6.3 | 140.90 |
| 1972 | | | | | |
| Q1 | 69.6 billion | 17.8 billion | 137.4 | 6.0 | 145.88 |
| Q2 | 71.0 billion | 18.3 billion | 138.5 | 6.2 | 148.03 |
| Q3 | 70.5 billion | 18.5 billion | 141.8 | 7.1 | 152.61 |
| Q4 | | | 142.8 | 6.8 | |

*Source:* Statistics Canada.

2. On February 20, the spending estimates were tabled in the House of Commons. These estimates called for a 17-percent rise in federal spending which, when coupled with the tax revenues, would result in a deficit of almost a billion dollars.

   (a) Given these spending estimates, tax proposals, and other budgetary changes such as increased old-age pensions, do you think the federal government was running a risk of overstimulating the economy? (Some key economic statistics are presented in the table above.)

   (b) Traditional antiinflationary policy calls for higher taxes. Why do you think that the government is reducing taxes to combat inflation?

# 33

## The Nature
## and Importance of Money

### KEY CONCEPTS AND DEFINITIONS

1. <u>Money</u> is defined as any generally accepted medium of exchange. It has three main functions: to act as a <u>medium of exchange</u>, a <u>store of value</u>, and as a <u>unit of account</u>.
2. An important function of money is to facilitate <u>exchange</u>. With money as a medium of exchange, everyone is free to specialize in the <u>direction</u> of one's natural abilities, and hence the product of all commodities increases.
3. As a <u>store of value</u>, money is a convenient way of storing purchasing power.
4. As a <u>unit of account</u>, money is used to measure the value of goods and services.
5. Money has evolved from metallic coins, to paper money <u>convertible</u> to precious metal, to token coinage and <u>paper money</u> fractionally backed by previous metals, to <u>fiat</u> money, and to <u>deposit money</u>.
6. <u>Deposit money</u>, a liability of a bank, can be in the form of <u>demand deposits</u> and/or <u>notice deposits</u>. A demand deposit is one which a customer can withdraw his money on demand.
7. <u>Near money</u> is assets which serve as a store of value and are readily converted into a medium of exchange but are not themselves a medium of exchange.
8. <u>Money substitutes</u> are things that serve as a temporary medium of exchange but are not a store of value.
9. Early economic theory regarded the economy as being divided into a <u>real</u> part and a <u>money</u> part. The monetary part determined the absolute <u>level</u> of <u>prices</u> at which the real transactions (production, resources allocation, distribution) took place. This was determined by the <u>quantity</u> of <u>money</u>. Increasing the quantity of money causes inflation of the price levels leaving the real part unchanged.
10. The <u>quantity theory of money</u> provided early economists with a link between the money supply and the price level. They assumed that the <u>transactions motive</u> was the sole source of the demand for money—and that the demand was directly proportional to the level of national income.
11. The need to finance transactions forces firms and households to hold money balances called <u>transactions balances</u>. The level of transactions balances is directly related to the amount of transactions or the level of national income.
12. The quantity theory of money is represented by the expressions $\underline{M} = \underline{kPY}$ or $\underline{MV} = \underline{PY}$, where V is the <u>velocity of circulation</u>. Furthermore, $\underline{V} = 1/\underline{k}$.
13. Given full employment, the quantity theory of money predicts that changes in the money supply lead to proportional changes in the price level with no changes in real output.
14. However, if unemployed resources are present, the quantity theory predicts that changes in the money supply lead to changes in real income.

| CHECKLIST | Make certain that you also understand the following concepts: Gresham's law; gold standard; legal tender; neutrality of money; unanticipated inflation; anticipated inflation; the modified quantity theory of money. |
| --- | --- |

## REVIEW QUESTIONS

1. The function served by money in making possible specialization and the division of labor is its use as a _medium of exchange_. If there were no form of money, trade in goods and services would have to be conducted by _barter_.

2. The function served by money in making easier the saving of claims on someone else to use at a later date is its use as _store of value_. This use of money is not very satisfactory unless its value is _stable_.

3. The function served by money in providing a monetary value to goods and services is its use as a _unit of account_.

4. Before the days of paper money, debasing the coinage had the effect of (increasing/~~decreasing~~) the money supply and causing prices to (rise/~~fall~~).

5. Originally, the earliest paper money usually represented a claim on a deposit of _gold_. When a country's money is thus convertible into gold, the country is said to be on a _gold_ standard.

6. In nineteenth-century Canada, private banks were allowed to issue their own bank notes. These were promises to pay in _gold_. Typically, banks kept enough gold to pay off (~~all~~/only a fraction) of these claims at any one time.

7. Fiat currency has value because it is (~~backed by gold~~/declared to be legal tender).

8. Canada's paper money is now issued by the _Bank of Canada_

9. The majority of Canada's money supply consists of _demand deposits_ in the chartered banks. These are (~~assets~~/liabilities) to the banks but (assets/~~liabilities~~) to the public.

10. Only (demand/~~notice~~) deposits are totally transferable by cheque.

11. As the authors of the text indicate, the distinction between money and near money is difficult in Canada. However, one type of near money is an account in a (trust company/~~chartered bank~~).

12. Unanticipated inflation causes a redistribution of wealth from _lenders_ to _borrowers_.

13. Whether inflation is anticipated or unanticipated, the living standards of those on _fixed_ money incomes is reduced.

14. If creditors anticipate inflation, they will (increase/~~decrease~~) the nominal rate of interest by the amount of the future expected inflation.

15. The transactions demand for money depends (directly/~~inversely~~) with the money level of transactions.

16. According to the quantity theory of money, the demand for money is a (constant/~~variable~~) proportion of money income. Furthermore, the supply of money is (controllable/~~uncontrollable~~) by the central bank.

17. Assuming full employment, the quantity theory of money predicts that the price level changed proportionally with increases in the _money supply_ .

18. Because of the existence of strong self-correcting adjustments, (full employment/~~unemployment~~) is the natural state of an economy.

19. Should short-term unemployment exist and price levels are fixed, a(n) (~~decrease~~/increase) in the money supply would increase the real level of national income.

---

If you have not answered all questions correctly, review the text in order to be sure that you have all of the important concepts clearly in mind before going on to the next chapter.

1. medium of exchange; barter  2. store of wealth (value); stable  3. unit of account  4. increasing; rise  5. gold; gold  6. gold; only a fraction  7. declared to be legal tender  8. Bank of Canada  9. deposits; liabilities; assets  10. demand  11. trust company  12. lenders; borrowers  13. fixed  14. increase  15. directly  16. constant; controllable  17. money supply  18. full employment  19. increase

---

## MULTIPLE-CHOICE QUESTIONS

1. For money to serve as an efficient medium of exchange, it must have all but which one of the following characteristics?
   (a) general acceptability
   (b) convertibility into gold
   (c) high value for its weight
   (d) divisibility

2. A requirement for the gold standard was that
   (a) the price level be stable
   (b) there be no paper money
   (c) the paper money be convertible into gold
   (d) gold coinage by 100 percent of the money supply

3. The value of money depends primarily on
   (a) the gold backing of the currency
   (b) the gold backing of both currency and deposits
   (c) its purchasing power
   (d) who issues it

4. A government bond could fill one function of money by acting as a
   (a) medium of exchange
   (b) store of wealth
   (c) unit of account
   (d) hedge against inflation

5. Which one of the following is *not* an assumption of the simple quantity theory of money?
   (a) The economy is at full employment except for very temporary lapses.
   (b) People try to hold a fairly constant fraction of their income in money form.
   (c) Changes in this fraction caused by changes in the supply of money result in changes in spending.
   (d) The supply of money is a function of the price level.

6. The amount of money held for transactions balances
   (a) will vary in the same direction as income
   (b) will vary in the same direction as interest rates
   (c) will be larger the shorter the interval between paydays
   (d) none of the above

7. If the public finds ways of making the same amount of money achieve a larger amount of transactions than before
   (a) $K$ must have risen
   (b) velocity must have risen
   (c) incomes and prices must have fallen
   (d) interest rates will rise

8. Assuming full employment exists, the quantity theory of money predicts that a doubling of the money supply will cause
   (a) prices to fall
   (b) price levels to double
   (c) real income levels to double
   (d) the demand for money to fall

Answers to multiple-choice questions: 1(b)   2(c)   3(c)   4(b)   5(d)   6(a)   7(b)   8(b)

# EXERCISES

1. Indicate which of the three functions of money is demonstrated in each of the following transactions. Use the appropriate letter: (a) medium of exchange; (b) store of wealth; (c) unit of account; (d) none.

   _____ 1. Farmer Brown puts cash in his mattress.
   _____ 2. Storekeeper Brown adds up his total sales for the day.
   _____ 3. Banker Brown uses some of his bank's reserves to buy government bonds.
   _____ 4. Traveling salesman Brown uses his credit card to buy gas for his car.
   _____ 5. Mrs. Brown buys a good oriental rug with the thought that it will keep its value for a long time.

2. If $k$ = .20, price level is unit, real income is $100 billion, and potential GNP is $100 billion, what will be the desired or equilibrium amount of the money supply? What is the income velocity of money? _____ Suppose that the actual money supply if $25 billion. Outline the expected reactions in the economy and the likely final effects in the economy.

3. Suppose that a household is paid $1000 at the beginning of each month. The household spends all of its income on the purchase of goods and services each month. Furthermore, assume that these purchases are at a constant rate throughout the month.
   (a) What is the value of cash holdings at the beginning of the month? At the end of the first week? At the end of the third week? At the end of the month?

   (b) What is the magnitude of the *average* cash holdings over the month?

(c) Suppose that the household's income increases to $1200 and purchases of goods and services during a month are equal to this amount. What is the *average* cash holding?

(d) Suppose that the household is paid $1000 over the month but in installments of $500 at the beginning of the month and $500 at the beginning of the third week. What is the magnitude of the *average* cash holdings per month?

4. Indicate whether the probable effect of unanticipated inflation for the following will be favorable, unfavorable, or neutral:
   (a) A tenant who signs a three-year lease on an apartment for $300 per month _____
   (b) The landlord in the above agreement _____
   (c) A university student receives a provincial scholarship for $2500 per year over the next four years. _____
   (d) A graduate student who receives a three-year award which is adjusted for the annual rate of inflation per year. _____
   (e) Quebec government tax revenue from a provincial sales tax on consumer goods _____
   (f) A Toronto Blue Jay baseball player receives $300,000 for the next five years. _____
   (g) A retired person whose primary source of income is from a portfolio of bonds _____
   (h) A real estate salesman's income from commissions _____

# PROBLEMS

## 1. OLYMPIC COINS

The Olympic Committee announced early in 1973 that they intended to finance the 1976 Olympic Games in Montreal partly by the sale of about $240 million in special Olympic coins. A similar scheme had been successfully used by the Munich Olympic Committee in 1972.

The federal government agreed to instruct the Mint in Ottawa to produce the coins in various face values. The coins were sold to the Olympic Committee at cost, which was well below the total face value of the coins. The Olympic Committee then sold the coins to the public at their *face value*.

Furthermore, the coins were declared legal tender by the federal government.

## Questions

1. If the Olympic Committee sold all of the coins, would the money supply increase? Explain.

2. According to the details you have been given, does it appear that the value of the coins depended on the value of their metallic content? What did their value depend upon?

3. Suppose that these coins became valuable collector items so that their market price (the price determined on the coin collectors' market) doubled. Would the money supply double?

4. Suppose that the price of the metals used to produce these coins increased tenfold, so that the metallic price of the coins became greater than their face value. How do you think the holders of these coins would react?

## 2.  CANADA'S INCOME VELOCITY OF MONEY

Below are some relevant data for recent years. $M_1$ is a narrow measure of the money supply: currency and demand deposits. $M_2$ is the definition of the money supply as suggested by the authors of the text: currency plus private dollar deposits in the chartered banks. The velocity here is *income velocity* (GNP/M).

| Year | $M_1$ | $M_2$ | GNP | $V_{M_1}$ | $V_{M_2}$ |
|------|------|------|------|------|------|
|  | (billions of dollars) | | | | |
| 1950 | 4.0 | 8.5 | 18.5 | 4.6 | 2.2 |
| 1955 | 4.8 | 10.8 | 28.5 | 5.9 | 2.6 |
| 1960 | 5.5 | 13.2 | 38.4 | 7.0 | 2.9 |
| 1961 | 5.9 | 14.4 | 39.6 | 6.7 | 2.8 |
| 1962 | 6.1 | 14.9 | 42.9 | 7.0 | 2.9 |
| 1963 | 6.3 | 15.9 | 46.0 | 7.3 | 2.9 |
| 1964 | 6.7 | 17.0 | 50.3 | 7.5 | 3.0 |
| 1965 | 7.2 | 19.1 | 55.4 | 7.7 | 2.9 |
| 1966 | 7.7 | 20.3 | 61.8 | 8.0 | 3.0 |
| 1967 | 8.3 | 23.6 | 66.4 | 8.0 | 2.8 |
| 1968 | 8.9 | 26.7 | 72.7 | _____ | _____ |
| 1969 | 9.2 | 27.7 | 79.7 | _____ | _____ |
| 1970 | 9.7 | 30.7 | 85.7 | _____ | _____ |
| 1971 | 11.4 | 35.3 | 94.5 | _____ | _____ |
| 1972 | 12.9 | 40.9 | 105.2 | _____ | _____ |
| 1973 | 14.4 | 48.4 | 123.6 | _____ | _____ |
| 1974 | 15.3 | 56.5 | 147.2 | _____ | _____ |
| 1975 | 18.8 | 66.3 | 165.4 | _____ | _____ |
| 1976 | 19.1 | 78.0 | 190.0 | _____ | _____ |

*Source:* Statistics Canada, *Canadian Statistical Review,* various issues.

## Questions

1. Which concept of the supply of money generally gives a more stable value for velocity?

2. For a velocity of 3, what is the fraction of income held in money balances, on the average?

3. Do the figures seem to suggest a substantial change over the last twenty years in the desire to hold balances in the form of $M_1$?

4. What role might higher interest rates on notice deposits, wider use of credit cards, and price inflation in the late 1960s and 1970s have played in the higher $V_{M_1}$?

# 34

# The Banking System
# and the Supply of Money

## KEY CONCEPTS AND DEFINITIONS

1.  The total stock of money in the economy at any moment of time is called the money supply.
2.  Two definitions of the money supply are: $M_1$ = currency (Bank of Canada notes and coins) plus demand deposits in the chartered banks, and $M_2$ = currency plus total privately held bank deposits.
3.  $M_1$ concentrates on the medium-of-exchange function of money while $M_2$ also includes savings deposits which serve as a temporary store-of-value function.
4.  The banking system in Canada consists of 10 chartered banks. The central bank in Canada which regulates the activities of the banks is the Bank of Canada.
5.  The chartered banks are profit-seeking institutions that allow the customers to transfer deposits from one bank to another by means of cheques. They create and destroy money as a by-product of their operations.
6.  The principal assets of the banks are securities, loans, and cash reserves. Cash reserves include vault cash and deposits with the Bank of Canada. Because of the Bank of Canada's policy, banks must hold a certain fraction of their deposits in reserves. This fraction is called the cash reserve ratio.
7.  Those reserves which the banks are required to hold under the Bank Act are called required reserves. Any reserves that a bank holds over and above required reserves are called excess cash reserves.
8.  The major liabilities of the chartered banks are the public's deposits (demand and notice).
9.  Because most customers of the banks are content to pay their transactions by cheques rather than by currency, the bank need only keep a small cash reserve against their deposit liabilities. Because of this, when banks receive new deposits, the banking system will end up creating new deposits by some multiple of the initial increase in deposits.
10. The amount of new deposits created depends on the cash reserve ratio, the currency drain to the public, and whether the banks are motivated to hold excess reserves.
11. Assuming no cash drain or excess reserve holdings, the money creation multiplier is $1/r$ where r is the cash reserve ratio.
12. If banks lose deposits, there will be a multiple contraction of the money supply.
13. One of the major functions of the central bank is to control the money supply. The major technique of monetary policy to affect the money supply is open-market operations.
14. Open-market operations involve purchases and sales by the central bank of government securities in financial markets. If the central bank purchases securities on the open market, this increases the reserves of the chartered banks and permits them to expand deposits by a multiple, thereby increasing the money supply by a multiple.

15. If the central bank <u>sells</u> securities on the open market, it decreases the reserves of the banks and forces them to <u>contract</u> loans. This causes a <u>multiple contraction</u> of the money supply.

---

| CHECKLIST | Make certain that you also understand the following concepts: clearinghouse, functions of a central bank. |

---

# REVIEW QUESTIONS

1. The narrow definition of the money supply ($M_1$) includes currency (coins and Bank of Canada notes) and _demand deposit_ at the chartered banks. The broad definition of the money supply ($M_2$) includes currency and all _private held deposit_ at the chartered banks.

2. As contrasted to the U.S. banking system, Canada's banking system is characterized by a (large/small) number of banks which have (many/few) branches throughout Canada.

3. Most of a bank's income comes from _interest on loans & security_

4. *Assets* are property or claims (owned by/owed to) a person or firm.

5. A bank's reserves are listed as (assets/liabilities). But the major part of total bank assets consists of _loans & securities_. Most of a bank's liabilities consist of _deposits_. The larger these are, the (larger/smaller) the amount of loans a bank can make.

6. The fraction of total deposits that a bank is required to keep in reserves is called the _cash reserves ratio_. If the cash reserve ratio required by the Bank of Canada is 0.12, a bank with demand deposits of $12 million must have reserves of at least _$ 1.44 million_. These reserves must be in the form of either _currency_ or _deposits in bank of canada_   12 × 0.12   1.44

7. Bank reserves beyond the amount legally required are called _excess_ reserves.

8. If a bank gains deposits from another bank, the receiving bank's reserves will _increase_ and the other bank's reserves and deposits will _decrease_. If banks gain deposits from outside the system, total reserves and deposits will _rise_.

9. *Ceteris paribus,* banks will not want to keep their excess reserves low if possible because reserves do not _earn interest_. So they will prefer to change these assets into another form, namely _loans & securities_.

10. (a) When a bank makes a loan, the borrower takes the money in the form of either _currency_ or a _deposit_. Thus, the money supply is immediately _increased_; the bank has created _money_.
    (b) When the borrower spends the borrowed money, and the recipient puts it in his bank account elsewhere, the second bank gains deposits and excess reserves from the first bank; it now has excess reserves and will similarly wish to _make loans or buy securities_.

11. Thus, an increase in total bank reserves can result in a much (larger/smaller) increase in the money supply.

12. (a) An equal reduction in a bank's reserves and deposits when the bank has no excess reserves will leave the bank short of _required reserves_. To restore them it may temporarily borrow reserves, but in the longer run it will have to sell _securities_ or reduce its _loans_.

(b) This, in turn, draws deposits and reserves from other banks. The process causes the money supply to _____*fall*_____ by (more/<u>less</u>) than the original loss of reserves; the banks have destroyed _____*money*_____.

13. As bank loans increase, deposits _____*increase*_____: as loans decrease, deposits _____*decrease*_____.

14. The size of the change in the money supply associated with a change in bank reserves depends on the *cash reserve ratio*. If $r = 1/5$, the effect on the money supply of an increase in bank reserves could be _____*5*_____ times the change in reserves.

15. There are two main reasons why the expansion of the money supply for a given increase in reserves will probably not be as large as the maximum amount indicated by the reciprocal of the required reserve ratio:
    (a) Some of an increase in bank reserves may be needed by the public as _____*cash*_____.
    (b) The banks may not find a sufficient amount of worthy *(loans) borrowers*.

16. The central bank of Canada is the *Bank of Canada*. Its three major functions are: to serve as a bank for *chartered banks*: to perform banking services for the _____*government*_____; and to control the supply of _____*money*_____ and influence rates of _____*interest*_____, for certain policy goals.

17. As banker for banks, it holds chartered banks' reserves as _____*deposit*_____.

18. The two largest and most important liabilities of the Bank of Canada are _____*chartered bank deposits*_____ and _____*Bank of Canada notes*_____. The amount of currency in circulation depends on the amount (of gold backing/<u>that people need for use</u>).

19. Bank reserves and currency in circulation (<u>used to be</u>/are) required to be backed by gold reserves. The major asset item on the Bank of Canada's balance sheet is *government securities*.

20. The federal government can make payments to the public out of deposits at the *Bank of Canada*.

21. When the Bank of Canada buys bonds in the open market, the deposits of the sellers at the chartered banks (<u>rise</u>/fall) and the reserves of the banks (<u>rise</u>/fall) as the payment is cleared. If the banks now have excess reserves, they can buy assets and create _____*loans*_____. It becomes (<u>easier</u>/harder) to get a loan. Also, as the price of bonds rises as a result, interest rates will (<u>fall</u>/rise).

22. When the central bank sells government bonds from its holdings to the public, deposits and reserves will (rise/<u>fall</u>), and interest rates will tend to (<u>rise</u>/fall). The ratio of reserves to deposits will also have (risen/<u>fallen</u>); if it has (<u>fallen too much</u>/risen enough), the banks will (<u>have to reduce</u>/be able to increase) their loans and investments.

---

If you have not answered all questions correctly, review the text in order to be sure that you have all of the important concepts clearly in mind before going on to the next chapter.

1. demand deposits; privately held deposits  2. small; many  3. interest on loans and securities  4. owned by  5. assets; loans and securities; deposits; larger  6. cash reserve ratio; $1.44 million; currency, deposits in the Bank of Canada  7. excess  8. rise, fall; rise  9. earn interest; loans and securities  10. currency, deposit; increased, money; make loans or buy securities  11. larger  12. required reserves; securities, loans; fall, more, money  13. increase; decrease  14. cash reserve ratio; five  15. cash; borrowers  16. Bank of Canada; banks; government; money; interest  17. deposits  18. chartered bank deposits; Bank of Canada notes; that people need for use  19. used to be; government securities  20. Bank of Canada  21. rise; rise; deposits and loans; easier; fall  22. fall; rise; fallen; fallen too much; have to reduce

# MULTIPLE-CHOICE QUESTIONS

1. A bank is able to create money
    (a) by printing it
    (b) by creating a deposit as it extends a new loan
    (c) by maintaining reserves
    (d) by issuing cheques to its depositors

2. The required reserves of a bank
    (a) are listed among its liabilities
    (b) consist of currency
    (c) are kept at other banks
    (d) consist of currency and its deposits at the Bank of Canada

3. The process of creation of deposit money by banks
    (a) is possible because of the fractional-reserve requirement
    (b) is consciously undertaken by each bank
    (c) always occurs if there are excess reserves
    (d) permits only small, gradual changes in the supply of money

4. A reduction in bank reserves, say, by payments to foreigners,
    (a) will always cause a multiple contraction in deposits
    (b) will cause a multiple contraction in deposits only if there are no excess reserves
    (c) will not affect domestic deposits
    (d) will not affect the availability of domestic credit

5. If you withdraw $100 at your bank,
    (a) deposits fall by a multiple of $100
    (b) deposits and bank reserves fall by $100
    (c) currency in circulation is unaffected
    (d) the money supply is increased

6. A bank that has insufficient reserves
    (a) may borrow from the Bank of Canada
    (b) may call in loans
    (c) may sell securities to other banks or to the public
    (d) may do all of the above

7. If $1 is added to a bank's reserves, and the required reserve ratio is .20, the money supply can be increased by several dollars because
    (a) the bank can use its new reserves to purchase government bonds that it can then sell to the public for a profit
    (b) the bank can make $.80 in new loans; this will create new reserves of $.80 in another bank, which in turn can lend $.64, and so on
    (c) the bank can create $4 of new deposits by making loans
    (d) the bank can issue new loans of $5, which creates excess reserves for other banks, and so on

8. Which one of the following is *not* one of the functions of a central bank?
    (a) to provide banking services for the government
    (b) to act as lender of last resort to banks
    (c) to lend to business
    (d) to control the supply of money and credit

9. Which one of the following is an important function of chartered bank deposits in the Bank of Canada?
   (a) to settle accounts with foreign banks
   (b) to use for loans
   (c) to provide an easy way for banks to transfer funds among themselves
   (d) to earn interest for the banks

10. Purchase and resale agreements involve
    (a) sales and purchases of securities between the chartered banks
    (b) sales and purchases of securities between the chartered banks and the Bank of Canada
    (c) sales of securities by investment dealers to the Bank of Canada
    (d) sales of securities by investment dealers to the Bank of Canada with agreement to re-purchase at a later date

11. Open-market operations are
    (a) used by the Bank of Canada regularly to meet seasonal, cyclical, and erratic fluctuations in the banks' need for reserves
    (b) used only sparingly by the Bank of Canada in order not to upset the government bond market
    (c) conducted primarily in order to make a profit for the Bank of Canada
    (d) not very effective as a means of influencing the supply of money and credit

12. Open-market purchases of securities will tend to
    (a) lower the price of bonds
    (b) lower interest rates
    (c) raise interest rates
    (d) reduce bank reserves and deposits

---

Answers to multiple-choice questions: 1(b)  2(d)  3(a)  4(b)  5(b)  6(d)  7(b)  8(c)  9(c)  10(d)  11(a)  12(b)

---

# EXERCISES

Exercises 1 through 4 involve banking problems in the absence of Bank of Canada policies, and Exercises 5 through 8 involve open-market operations and the Bank of Canada.

1. From the data below, calculate the magnitudes of the narrow definition of the supply of money ($M_1$) and the broad definition of the supply of money ($M_2$).

| Financial Statistics, December 1977 (in millions of dollars) | |
|---|---|
| Currency outside the banks | $ 7,972 |
| Chartered bank deposits | |
| Demand | 13,566 |
| Personal savings | 44,578 |
| Nonpersonal term and notice | 22,541 |
| Government of Canada | 4,747 |

*Source: Bank of Canada Review*, March 1978, Tables 14 and 6.

$M_1$ = _____21,538_____ .    $M_2$ = _____88,657_____ .

2. Arrange the following items on the proper side of a bank's balance sheet:
   (a) Demand deposits                                             $5,000,000
   (b) Notice deposits                                               1,000,000
   (c) Currency in vaults                                              60,000
   (d) Deposits in the Bank of Canada                               1,000,000
   (e) Loans to public                                              4,000,000
   (f) Security holdings, Canadian government,
       provincial, municipal, and other                            1,500,000
   (g) Banking building and fixtures                                  360,000
   (h) Capital and surplus                                            920,000

| Assets | | Liabilities | |
|---|---|---|---|
| Currency in vaults | 60,000 | Demand deposits | 5,000,000 |
| Deposits in B. of C. | 1,000,000 | Notice deposits | 1,000,000 |
| Loans to public | 4,000,000 | | |
| Security holdings | 1,500,000 | | |
| Banking buildings fixtures | 360,000 | Capital + surplus | 920,000 |

3. We use "T-account," abbreviated balance sheets, for a bank to show changes in bank re-serves, loans, and deposits. Make the entries on the T-accounts below, using + and - signs to show increase or decrease, for each of the following independent events. (Remember that all changes must balance.)

| | Assets | Liabilities |
|---|---|---|
| (a) You deposit your pay cheque of $100 at your bank | Reserves: +100 <br> Loans and Securities: | Deposits: + 100 |
| (b) A bank sells $10,000 of government bonds in the market to replenish its reserves. | Reserves: +10,000 <br> Loans and Securities: -10,000 | Deposits: |
| (c) A bank makes a loan of $5,000 to a local businessman and credits it to his chequing account. | Reserves: <br> Loans and +5,000 <br> Securities: | Deposits: +5,000 |
| (d) A bank sells $50,000 of securities to the Bank of Canada and receives deposits in the Bank of Canada. | Reserves: +50,000 <br> Loans and Securities: -50,000 | Deposits: |
| (e) A businessman uses $5,000 of his demand deposit to pay off a loan from the same bank. | Reserves: <br> Loans and -5,000 <br> Securities: | Deposits: -5,000 |
| (f) A bank orders $5,000 in currency from the Bank of Canada. | Reserves: <br> Loans and Securities: | Deposits: |

4. Suppose that bank A, a Canadian bank, begins with the following T-account. The cash reserve ratio is assumed to be 10 percent. Joe Doe, a holder of a deposit in bank A, withdraws $1000 and deposits this amount in a commercial bank in a foreign country. Thus, $1000 has been taken out of the Canadian banking system.

| Bank A (initial situation) | | Bank A (after the withdrawal) | |
|---|---|---|---|
| Reserves: $ 10,000 | Deposits: $100,000 | Reserves: $ 9,000 | Deposits: $ 99,000 |
| Loans: 90,000 | | Loans: 9,000 | |

(a) What were bank A's required reserves? Did it have excess reserves initially?

*R. reserves = 10,000.        No excess*

(b) Show the immediate effect of the withdrawal from bank A.

*Reserves – 1,000        Deposit – 1,000*
*99,000*

(c) What is the magnitude of bank A's reserve deficiency?

*99,000 × 0.1 = 9,900*
*Reserve deficiency = 900*

(d) Bank A reacts by calling in a loan, equal to the amount of its reserve deficiency, which it had made to Mary Smith. Mary repays the loan by writing a cheque on her account in bank B, another Canadian bank. Bank B's initial T-account is shown below. Fill in the T-accounts below for the effects of bank A's receiving the payment from Mary and of bank B's losing Mary's deposit.

**Bank B**
**(initial situation)**

| Reserves: | $ 5,000 | Deposits: | $50,000 |
|---|---|---|---|
| Loans: | 45,000 | | |

**Bank B**
**(after losing Mary's deposit)**

| Reserves: | $ *4,100* | Deposits: | $ *49,100* |
|---|---|---|---|
| Loans: | *45,000* | | |

**Bank A**
**(after receiving loan repayment)**

| Reserves: | $ *9900* | Deposits: | $ *99,000* |
|---|---|---|---|
| Loans: | *8100* | | |

(e) After this transaction, does bank A have deficit reserves? Bank B?

*No        but Bank B has a deficit of $810*

(f) In fact, bank B has a deficiency of reserves. It reacts by calling in a loan, equal to the amount of the deficiency, made to Peter Piper. Peter cashes in a savings deposit that he held in bank C; that is, bank C loses a deposit and Peter repays bank B. Bank C's initial situation is shown below. Fill in the T-accounts for the effects of bank B's receiving the loan repayment and bank C's losing Peter's savings deposit.

**Bank C**
**(initial situation)**

| Reserves: | $ 7,000 | Deposits: | $70,000 |
|---|---|---|---|
| Loans: | 63,000 | | |

**Bank C**
**(after loss of deposit)**

| Reserves: | $ *6,190* | Deposits: | $ *69,190* |
|---|---|---|---|
| Loans: | *63,000* | | |

**Bank B**
**(after receiving loan repayment)**

| Reserves: | $ *4910* | Deposits: | $ *49,100* |
|---|---|---|---|
| Loans: | *44,190* | | |

(g) After this transaction, does bank B have deficient reserves? Bank C?

*No        Bank C has a deficient reserves of $729*

(h) After this transaction, the reduction in the money supply has been Joe's original withdrawal plus $_____ in other deposits. Loans have been reduced by $_____.

(i) The process will continue until the total reduction in the money supply will be $_____. The total reduction in loans will be $_____.

5. Indicate on which side of the Bank of Canada's balance sheet the following items should go.
   (a) Chartered bank reserves
   (b) Currency in circulation
   (c) Canadian government deposits
   (d) Government securities
   (e) Foreign currency assets
   (f) Advances to chartered banks

| Bank of Canada | |
|---|---|
| Assets | Liabilities |

6. The Bank of Canada decides to purchase $100 million of Canadian government securities from the nonbank public for open-market operations. Show the effect on the banking system of this first step. (Be sure to use + and - to indicate changes, not totals.) Assume that the public holds all their money in bank deposits.

(a)

| Bank of Canada | | | All Banks | |
|---|---|---|---|---|
| Securities: | Bank reserves: | | Reserves: | Demand deposits: |

(b) If the reserve ratio is 20 percent, it now is possible for deposits to increase by a total of _____ (including the original increase).

(c) What is likely to happen to the level of interest rates?

7. Suppose the Bank of Canada purchases $150 million of Canadian government securities from the chartered banks. Show the immediate effect of this transaction in the balance sheets below. The case reserve ratio is assumed to be .10.

| Bank of Canada | | | Banking System | |
|---|---|---|---|---|
| Securities | Bank reserves: | | Reserves: | Deposits: |
| | | | Loans: | |
| | | | Securities: | |

(a) Is the money supply immediately changed? Why or why not?

(b) After this transaction, what is the level of excess reserves in the banking system? What is the total amount of loans that can be extended initially?

(c) What will be the final change in the money supply?

8. Suppose that the economy is experiencing inflationary tendencies and the Bank of Canada decides to conduct open-market operations. It possesses new $100 Government of Canada one-year bonds with a coupon rate of 5%. Suppose also that the current market rate of interest is 7%.

   (a) If the Bank of Canada wishes to maintain the current rate of interest, at what price should it sell the bonds to the public and to the banks? (Check the present-value table in Chapter 22.)

   (b) If the Bank of Canada announced a selling price of $92.60 per bond, what is the effective rate of interest for these bonds?

   (c) What might the effect of this policy change have on the level of all interest rates?

## PROBLEM

### PENNIES FROM HEAVEN

Suppose that a shower of Mint-fresh Canadian pennies falls from the sky onto the property of Joe Farmer. Joe, bewildered but delighted, collects all of them, worth the sum of $100, and takes them to his branch of the Bank of Nova Scotia. The manager of the bank, also bewildered, is skeptical. After making several calls to other bank managers, the manager of Joe's bank is convinced that the pennies have not been withdrawn from any other bank. In addition, the Mint in Ottawa cannot explain the shower of pennies, but assures the manager that the pennies are not counterfeit.

    Asking no further questions, the manager accepts the $100 worth of pennies and Joe is given a deposit of $100.

### Questions

1. Show the effect of this transaction on the balance sheet of the Bank of Nova Scotia.

| Assets | Liabilities |
|---|---|
| (Reserves) | |
| Currency _____ | Deposits _____ |

2. If the cash reserve ratio is .2, what is the magnitude of the new loans that can be created by the Bank of Nova Scotia?

3. Fill in the table below for the various other generation banks.

| Bank | New Deposits | Additions to Reserves | New Loans |
|------|--------------|-----------------------|-----------|
| Second generation | _____ | _____ | _____ |
| Third generation | _____ | _____ | _____ |
| Fourth generation | _____ | _____ | _____ |

4. What is your prediction for the *final* change in the money supply as a result of the shower of pennies? State the necessary assumptions.

5. If the Bank of Canada had not deemed this increase in the money supply to be beneficial, what type of open-market operation could it have conducted to prevent the money supply from increasing?

# 35

## Monetary Policy

### KEY CONCEPTS AND DEFINITIONS

1. This chapter deals with the links between the money supply and the interest rate and that between the interest rate and aggregate demand. This is the modern Keynesian theory. It emphasizes the function of money as a store of wealth.

2. The demand for money, according to the Keynesian theory, has three components: the transaction demand, precautionary demand, and the speculative demand.

3. The transactions demand is directly related to the level of national income and inversely with the rate of interest. Since wealth held as money is not earning interest, an increase in interest rates increases the opportunity cost of holding money and hence money balances will be reduced.

4. Precautionary balances are held if there is uncertainty about the exact timing of receipts and payments. The magnitude of precautionary balances are also directly related to national income and inversely related to the rate of interest.

5. The speculative motive stresses the role of money as a store of value. If there were perfect certainty that the price of bonds would never change, people would never hold money as a store of value since money yields no interest payment. If bond prices are high and are expected to fall, people will hold their wealth in the form of speculative balances.

6. Since an inverse relationship between the price of bonds and the interest rate exists, it follows that the speculative demand for money is inversely related to the rate of interest.

7. Liquidity preference refers to the total demand for money. The schedule relating the demand for money to the interest rate is called the liquidity-preference schedule.

8. An increase in the money supply causes the interest rate to fall. The quantity demand of money will increase. The extend to which the interest rate falls depends on the elasticity of the LP schedule. The less interest elastic the LP schedule, the greater the decline in the rate of interest.

9. A given decrease in the interest rate should increase investment expenditures. The schedule relating investment to the interest rate is called the marginal-efficiency-of-investment schedule. The more elastic the MEI schedule, the greater the increase in investment given a decrease in the interest rate.

10. The greater the increase in investment, the greater the increase in national income.

11. The instruments of monetary policy include open-market operations, the bank rate, secondary reserve requirements, and moral suasion.

12. The bank rate is the rate of interest charged to banks that borrow funds from the central bank. To discourage borrowing, the central bank will increase the bank rate.

13. Two target variables are the money supply and the interest rate. The money supply target involves some desired growth rate in $M_1$. An interest rate target involves maintaining some desired level of the interest rate.

## APPENDIX

1. The IS curve relates all combinations of national income and the rate of interest for which withdrawals (savings, taxes, imports) equal injections (investment, government expenditures, exports).
2. The IS curve slopes downward because income and the interest rate must vary in opposite directions if withdrawals are to be held equal to injections.
3. The LM curve relates the combinations of national income and the rate of interest for which the demand for money is equal to the supply of money.
4. The LM curve slopes upward because income and the interest rate must vary in the same direction if the demand for money is to be held equal to a constant supply of money.
5. The equilibrium levels of income and the rate of interest are established by the intersection of the LM and IS curves. Shifts in the one or both of the curves will alter the equilibrium levels of income and interest rates.
6. An increase in the stock of money will shift the LM curve to the right.
7. An increase in government expenditure will shift the IS curve to the right.

| CHECKLIST | Make certain that you also understand the following concepts: secondary reserve requirements; moral suasion; policy variables; relationship between bond prices and interest rates. |
| --- | --- |

## REVIEW QUESTIONS

1. The modern theory of how monetary policy operates involves three separate links which connect policy actions by the central bank to aggregate demand. The first link, one which was reviewed in the last chapter, is between central bank policy instruments such as open-market operations and the _____money supply_____.

2. The second link is between the money supply and the _____interest rate_____.

3. The third link is between the interest rate and _____aggregate demand_____.

4. The Keynesian theory emphasizes the function of money as a _____store of wealth_____. According to the Keynesian theory, there are three motives for holding money: the transaction motive, the _____speculative_____ motive, and the _____precautionary_____ motive.

5. The transactions demand for money depends (directly/~~inversely~~) on the level of national income and (~~directly~~/inversely) with the rate of interest.

6. The precautionary demand arises because of the _____uncertainty_____ of payments and receipts. This demand tends to be (directly/~~inversely~~) related to the size of income and (~~directly~~/inversely) related to the opportunity cost of funds, or the _____interest rate_____.

7. Whereas the transactions and precautionary motives emphasize money's role as a _____medium of exchange_____ the speculative motive emphasizes its role as a _____store of wealth_____.

8. The speculative motive arises because the future price of _____bonds_____ is uncertain. Hence, households tend to speculate about future movements in prices of bonds. If the price of bonds is very high in relation to what people think is the normal price, people speculate that the price will _____fall_____ and hence tend to sell bonds now in order to avoid future capital (~~gains~~/losses). The speculation that bond prices are likely to fall implies that interest rates are expected to _____rise_____.

9. If bond prices are currently low (relative to some normal level), households will (buy/
~~sell~~) bonds on the speculation that prices will _____rise_____, thus achieving (avoiding) capital (gains/~~losses~~). Accordingly, interest rates are expected to ___fall_____.
Therefore, when interest rates are currently high, the demand for money tends to be
_____low_____.

10. When households and firms decide how much of their monetary assets they will hold as money
rather than as bonds, they are said to be exercising their preference for _liquidity_.

11. Economists hypothesize that there is a (~~direct~~/inverse) relation between the rate of interest and the quantity of investment. The schedule that summarizes the relationship between investment and the rate of interest is called the _marginal efficiency_ _of investment_ schedule.
The steeper this schedule (interest on the vertical axis), the (smaller/~~larger~~) will be
the change in investment in response to a given change in interest rates. Under this situation, the schedule is said to be relatively (~~elastic~~/inelastic) with respect to interest
rates.

12. A change in the money supply will have a larger effect on interest rates the (steeper/
~~flatter~~) the liquidity preference schedule. In other words, the more (~~elastic~~/inelastic)
is the *LP* schedule, the more effective is monetary policy in changing the interest rate.

13. A change in the rate of interest will have a larger effect on investment, and hence on national income, the more (~~inelastic~~/elastic) the *MEI* schedule.

14. Other than for open-market operations, the Bank of Canada has four other instruments. They
are _changing the reserve ratio_, secondary reserve requirements, change in the bank
rate, and _moral suasion_.

15. The bank rate refers to the rate of interest at which the _Bank of Canada_ makes
advances to the _Chartered Bank_. An increase in the bank rate acts as a signal that the Bank of Canada wishes interest rates to (rise/~~fall~~) and its intentions to
pursue (tight/~~easy~~) monetary policy.

16. If an inflationary situation exists and the Bank of Canada wishes to slow down the rate of
price increases, it should (sell/~~buy~~) bonds in the open market. This action tends to
(reduce/~~increase~~) the price of bonds and hence cause interest rates to (~~fall~~/rise). Banks
will tend to (lose/~~gain~~) reserves, hence (~~expand~~/reduce) loans, and hence interest rates
will tend to (~~fall~~/rise) even further. Providing aggregate expenditures are sensitive to
the interest rate change, investment and perhaps consumption expenditures should (fall/
~~rise~~) and given the multiplier process, national income should (fall/~~rise~~) by a multiplied
amount.

17. Both the money supply and the level of _interest rate_ may be targets of monetary policy. The money supply target normally refers to a certain _growth rate_
in the money supply. Prior to the early 1970s, monetary policy in Canada was formulated
primarily in terms of target levels of _interest rate_. In 1975, the Bank announced target ranges for the growth rate of ($M_1$/~~$M_2$~~).

# APPENDIX

18. The *IS* curve relates all combinations of national income and the _interest rate_
for which _withdrawal_ equal _injection_.

19. The *IS* curve slopes (downward/upward) because income and the interest rate must vary in
(opposite/~~the same~~) direction(s) if savings, taxes, and imports are to be held equal to
_investment_, _G_, and _X_.

20. The *LM* curve relates all combinations of national income and the interest rate for which
the _supply of money_ is equal to the _demand of money_. The *LM* curve slopes
(upward/~~downward~~).

21. The equilibrium levels of income and the ____*interest rate*____ are established by the ____*intersection*____ of the two curves.

22. An increase in the money supply shifts the (~~IS~~/LM) curve to the (~~left~~/right) and causes national income to (rise/~~fall~~) and the interest rate to (~~rise~~/fall).

23. An increase in government expenditures shifts the (IS/~~LM~~) curve to the ~~(left~~/right) and causes national income to (rise/~~fall~~) and the interest rate to (rise/~~fall~~).

---

If you have not answered all questions correctly, review the text in order to be sure that you have all of the important concepts clearly in mind before going on to the next chapter.

1. money supply  2. interest rate  3. aggregate demand  4. store of wealth; precautionary; speculative  5. directly; inversely  6. uncertainty; directly; inversely; interest rate  7. medium of exchange; store of wealth  8. bonds; fall; losses; rise  9. buy; rise; gains; fall; low  10. liquidity  11. inverse; marginal efficiency of investment; smaller; inelastic  12. steeper; inelastic  13. elastic  14. changing the reserve ratio; moral suation  15. Bank of Canada; chartered banks; rise; tight  16. sell; reduce; rise; lose; reduce; rise; fall; fall  17. interest rates; growth rate; interest rates; $M_1$  18. interest rate; injections; withdrawals  19. downward; opposite; $G$; $X$; $I$  20. supply of money; demand for money; upward  21. interest rate  22. *LM*; right; rise; fall  23. *IS*; right; rise; rise

---

# MULTIPLE-CHOICE QUESTIONS

1. Which one of the following is *not* an instrument of monetary policy?
   (a) open-market operations
   (b) changes in the bank rate
   (c) changes in the required secondary reserve ratio
   (d) changes in tax rates

2. Open-market sales of securities will tend to
   (a) lower the price of bonds
   (b) lower interest rates
   (c) increase the price of bonds
   (d) increase bank reserves and deposits

3. An increase in the bank rate signals the Bank of Canada's intentions to
   (c) conduct expansionary monetary policy
   (b) lower the general level of interest rates and encourage more borrowing
   (c) conduct contractionary monetary policy
   (d) conduct open-market purchases of government securities

4. *Ceteris paribus,* an increase in the interest rate will
   (a) increase the quantity demanded for cash balances
   (b) increase investment expenditures
   (c) decrease the quantity demanded for cash balances
   (d) none of the above

5. If the price of bonds is expected to fall, households and firms are likely to
   (a) reduce their holdings of money and buy bonds
   (b) increase their holdings of money and sell bonds
   (c) speculate that interest rates will also fall
   (d) anticipate capital gains in the future

6. If a 6% decrease in interest rates generates a 15% increase in investment expenditure, the *MEI* schedule has
   (a) an elasticity of 2/5
   (b) an elasticity of 5/2
   (c) an elasticity of 90
   (d) a completely vertical shape

7. If the *LP* schedule is perfectly elastic, changes in the money supply will
   (a) have a large effect on the interest rate
   (b) have no influence on the demand for money
   (c) have a small effect on the interest rate
   (d) have no effect on the interest rate

8. The Bank of Canada could attempt to remove a deflationary gap by
   (a) selling government securities to the public
   (b) raising the bank rate
   (c) purchasing government securities from the banks
   (d) requiring higher secondary reserve requirements

9. In order to induce the public to purchase bonds, the Bank of Canada should
   (a) increase the price of bonds
   (b) decrease the price of bonds
   (c) reduce the yield on bonds
   (d) lower the coupon rate on bonds

10. An increase in the money supply should reduce interest rates providing that the following does not occur:
   (a) the demand for money decreases substantially
   (b) the demand for money increases substantially
   (c) banks expend loans at lower loan rates
   (d) the *IS* curve is vertical

---

Answers to multiple-choice questions: 1(d)   2(a)   3(c)   4(c)   5(b)   6(b)   7(d)   8(c)   9(b)
10(b)

---

# EXERCISES

1. Suppose that the Bank of Canada sells 1 million dollars of securities to the public. You may assume that the cash reserve ratio is 10% and that all the assumptions involved in the money process hold.
   (a) What will be the final change in the money supply?




   (b) What will be the final change in the quantity of money demanded? What factors explain the change?




   (c) What will tend to happen to the level of interest rates? Explain carefully.

2. The liquidity-preference schedule below depicts the attitude of households and firms to holding cash at various interest rates. Using the theories of the transactions and speculative motives for money explain

   (a) Why the demand for cash is low at high interest rates

   (b) Why the quantity demanded for money is inelastic at interest rates above 15%

   (c) Why the quantity demanded for money is high at low interest rates

   (d) Why the quantity demanded for money is completely elastic at a 2% interest rate

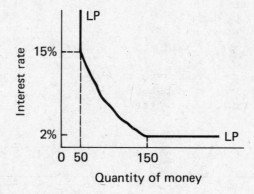

   (e) What is the effect on interest rates of increasing the supply of money from 150 to 160? Explain.

# PROBLEM

## THE EFFECTIVENESS OF MONETARY POLICY

> The general conclusion we draw from our research is that the effect of monetary policy on the Canadian economy is *imprecise, slow,* and *variable;* there is a relationship present, but it is extremely hazy. This conclusion has important implications for the use of monetary policy as a short-run stabilizing instrument.*

This was the comment of Professor H. G. Johnson upon the results of research that he and Professor John Winder conducted for the Canadian Royal Commission on Banking and Finance. In their

*H. G. Johnson, *The Canadian Quandary* (Toronto: McGraw-Hill, 1963), p. 187.

investigation, they distinguished between *inside* and *outside* lags. The inside lag was defined to be the lag between the appearance of a need for a change in monetary policy in the economy and the corresponding change in policy; the outside lag was the lag between the change in monetary policy and the appearance of a response in the economy. Both lags were found to be quantitatively large.

The impreciseness and variability of monetary policy stems from the fact that it is difficult to predict the behavior of businessmen, banks, and consumers. If individuals react differently from what has been assumed in a model, then the predictions of the model are no longer likely to hold. Slowness of monetary policy may result if individuals and firms do not react immediately to changes in economic variables. For example, the uncertainty about future events, the costs of adjusting plans, and various institutional constraints might outweigh the effects of changes in the money supply and the market rate of interest.

Let us suppose that the Bank of Canada wishes to counteract rising unemployment. We shall use a Keynesian approach (described in Chapter 35) to explain the course of events of the change in monetary policy and the change in employment and output. Hence we concentrate on the *outside lag*. If a link in a chain is weak, then the chain is weak. Similarly, if the assumptions about behavior do not hold, then the effectiveness of monetary policy is reduced.

## Questions

1. Should the Bank of Canada buy or sell bonds in the open market in order to counteract unemployment?

2. Because of the policy outlined in Question 1, the banks will find that reserves have (increased/decreased). As a result, a multiple (expansion/reduction) in the money supply is possible. Whether this multiple change in the money supply *actually* occurs depends on the behavior of the banks and the public. Explain the behavior that must exist in order for there to be a multiple change in the money supply. Why might banks or the public not react immediately?

3. If the money supply does change, the interest rate may be affected. What would be your prediction about the direction of the change in the interest rate as a result of the change in monetary policy? Whether the interest rate *actually* changes depends on events in the money market. In particular, the behavior of holders of cash balances with respect to the interest rate is critical. Under what conditions would the interest rate not change?

4. (a) If the interest rate does change, economic theory tells us that investment expenditures (and possibly consumption) might change. Discuss some factors that might cause businessmen not to invest in new machines and equipment in the current time period even though the interest rate changed. In your analysis distinguish between movements along and shifts in the marginal-efficiency-of-capital schedule.

   (b) What effect might the existence of excess capacity have on the decision to invest?

5.  (a)  If investment changes, national income should change by a multiple. However, what assumption concerning the marginal propensity to spend does the multiplier analysis depend upon?

    (b)  If individuals did not spend immediately on each round of expenditures in the multiplier process, what implications would this have for the time taken to change national income by a multiple?

# 36

## The International Monetary System

### KEY CONCEPTS AND DEFINITIONS

1. Under the gold standard, the central authorities of each country kept their paper currency convertible into gold at a fixed rate, and the "gold content" of each currency established fixed rates of exchange between all the currencies. Because all currencies were freely convertible into gold, they were also freely convertible into each other.

2. A country having balance-of-payment deficits would lose gold, thereby shrinking its money supply and causing domestic prices to fall. This in turn would stimulate the country's exports and reduce imports. A country experiencing surpluses in the balance of payments would receive gold and increase its money supply, causing prices to rise. In both cases, the relationship between gold and prices is called the gold flow, price level mechanism.

3. In the 1920s, the gold standard failed because price level adjustments could not take place fast enough and because governments were unwilling to allow their price levels to change solely because of the balance of payments.

4. The gold standard was abandoned and many experiments were tried throughout the 1920s. One policy, the beggar-my-neighbor policy, involved attempting to reduce exports in order to reduce imports. This had the effect of shifting unemployment onto another country.

5. From 1944 to the early 1970s, the international monetary system was the Bretton Woods system. It put the world on an adjustable peg (pegged against short-term fluctuations but adjusted from time to time), gold exchange standard (reserves of gold, pound sterling, and U.S. dollars). To fix their exchange rates relative to the U.S. dollar, foreign monetary authorities held reserved of gold, pounds, and U.S. dollars.

6. Exchange rates were only to be changed in the face of a fundamental disequilibrium (a persistent, long-run problem) in the balance of payments.

7. The International Monetary Fund (IMF) was the major institution of the Bretton Woods system.

8. Three major problems with any adjustable peg system are (1) to provide sufficient international reserves both for short-run and long-run needs, (2) to handle periodic speculative crises, and (3) to adjust to long-term trends in receipts and payments.

9. The Bretton Woods system broke down under a series of speculative crises that stemmed from the failure of the system to provide sufficient international reserves and to accommodate devaluations of the U.S. dollar, which was the currency to which all other countries pegged their exchange rates.

10. The two major events in the transition from the Bretton Woods system to the present one were the abandonment of gold convertibility of dollars held by central banks in 1971 and the drift toward managed flexibility of exchange rates.

11. The present system is a <u>dollar standard</u> (foreign countries held U.S. dollars as reserves but the dollar itself is not convertible into gold) with managed flexibility of exchange rates. This system is under heavy strains because of the current-account deficits of the oil-importing countries and because of the enormous supplies of short-term foreign investment held by the oil exporters.

---

| CHECKLIST | Make certain that you also understand the following concepts: SDRs; Smithsonian agreements; managed float or dirty float. |
|---|---|

## REVIEW QUESTIONS

1. The gold standard relied on _____*fixed*_____ exchange rates with adjustments brought about in domestic _____*price levels*_____. If a country bought more goods from other countries than it sold to them, demand for _____*foreign exchange*_____ would exceed the supply at the fixed rates; the excess demand would be met by shipments of _____*gold*_____. The loss of gold in a deficit country would _____*decrease*_____ its money supply, while the gain in gold in the _____*surplus*_____ country would _____*increase*_____ its money supply. The changes in money supply would result in _____*lower*_____ prices in deficit countries and _____*higher*_____ prices in surplus countries. The change in price level would increase exports of _____*deficit*_____ countries and would _____*decrease*_____ exports of surplus countries, and thus move them both toward equilibrium in their _____*balance of payment*_____.

2. A difficult test for the gold standard came after World War I, when exchange rates were (~~close to~~/far from) equilibrium rates. Price levels adjusted slowly, and the gold standard was _____*abandoned*_____ in the 1930s when unemployment was widespread. Efforts made to _____*restrict*_____ imports while maintaining exports (~~worked~~/did not work), and the volume of trade _____*fell*_____.

3. The Bretton Woods Conference in 1944 results in the creation of the _____*International Monetary Fund*_____. The Fund could lend nations _____*foreign exchange*_____ in the face of temporary balance-of-payments deficits. It sought to prohibit the competitive devaluation of the 1930s by providing that changes in excess of _____*10*_____ percent be made only after consultation with officials of the Fund.

4. The postwar gold-exchange standard used U.S. dollars, convertible into _____ at approximately _____ an ounce, as international monetary reserves. Other currencies, including the British pound, also used as a reserve currency, were convertible into dollars, and therefore into _____, at _____ rates.

5. After the heavy gold speculation in early 1968, the United States maintained the $35 gold price for _____ only. The _____ market price for gold was allowed to fluctuate. In 1971, the United States suspended the _____ of the dollar reserves into gold.

6. Three major problems confronted the gold-exchange standard: the provision of _____ _____ to iron out short-term fluctuations in international receipts and payments, making adjustments to _____ trends in payments balances, and meeting _____ crises. It seems likely that to meet short-term fluctuations, _____ reserves will be needed as trade grows.

7. A new form of exchange reserve was created in 1970, the _____ _____ (SDR) administered by the International Monetary Fund. Creation of SDRs represents an alternative method of increasing reserves to that of _____ the dollar price of the gold.

8. A solution to long-run disequilibria envisioned at Bretton Woods was the occasional modification of _____. Two major rounds of devaluation, in 1949-1950 and 1967-1968, were led by the _____. In 1971, after Germany and the Netherlands had allowed their currencies to float upward in value, the United States encouraged further upward revaluations by _____ gold payments for dollars. One alternative to exchange-rate changes is changes in _____ price levels; such changes are accomplished (easily/with difficulty). Restrictions on trade and foreign exchange frequently have been used by nations to meet _____ in the balance of payments. In 1971, the United States inaugurated a temporary _____ surcharge of 10 percent.

9. Speculation is likely if expectations are high that there will be a change in _____ _____. In early 1968, many speculators expected that the official dollar price of _____ would be raised, and the gold (inflow/outflow) from the United States resulting from the speculation led to the two-tier system of gold prices.

10. Flexible exchange rates are predicted to (reduce/increase) greatly the need for international liquidity, or reserves. Instead of meeting the problem of long-run disequilibria by delayed and politically difficult _____ revisions, difficult domestic price changes, or protectionism, a free market would make gradual _____ adjustments.

11. Objections to flexible rates, particularly strong among the world's bankers, are that such a system will increase the _____ of exporters and importers and will thus _____ trade and lead to _____ speculation. Such speculation in the face of a depreciating exchange rate could lead to (a decrease/an increase) rather than (an increase/a decrease) in the quantity of that currency demanded and to (an increase/a decrease) rather than (a decrease/an increase) in the quantity supplied. Under such circumstances, the price of this currency would _____ further.

---

If you have not answered all questions correctly, review the text in order to be sure that you have all of the important concepts clearly in mind before going on to the next chapter.

1. fixed, price levels; foreign exchange, gold; reduce, surplus, increase; lower, higher; deficit, reduce, balance of payments  2. far from; abandoned; restrict, did not work, fell  3. International Monetary Fund; foreign exchange; 10  4. gold, $35; gold, fixed  5. official transactions (central banks); private or free; convertibility  6. reserves, long-term, speculative; increased  7. special drawing rights; increasing  8. exchange rates; British pound; suspending; domestic, with difficulty; deficits; import  9. exchange rates (gold price); gold, outflow  10. reduce; exchange-rate, price (exchange rate)  11. uncertainty, reduce, destabilizing; a decrease, an increase, an increase, a decrease; decline

## MULTIPLE-CHOICE QUESTIONS

1. Under the gold standard
   (a) exchange rates fluctuated frequently
   (b) equilibrium was produced by changes in fixed exchange rates
   (c) crises of confidence were met quickly despite the small amount of gold relative to claims on it
   (d) equilibrium was supposed to be reached by changes in domestic price levels

2. During the monetary crisis and the depression of the 1930s
   (a) most countries stayed on the gold standard despite the difficulties
   (b) competitive currency devaluations were frequent
   (c) U.S. tariff policy became less protectionist
   (d) international trade was stimulated because of the low prices of goods

3. Under the Bretton Woods agreement
   (a) most countries returned to the gold standard
   (b) countries were given almost complete freedom to let their currencies float
   (c) all exchange rates were tied to the U.S. dollar
   (d) gold was completely abandoned as an international means of payment

4. Among postwar international developments were all except
   (a) the dollar shortage confronting war-torn countries which needed U.S. goods
   (b) the dollar surplus Europe and Japan accumulated as they recovered
   (c) prompt upward adjustments of undervalued currencies
   (d) considerable international cooperation to maintain stable exchange rates

5. The International Monetary Fund
   (a) is a fund for long-term development projects
   (b) was designed to assist in making exchange rates more readily flexible
   (c) was designed to help maintain fixed exchange rates in the face of short-term fluctuations
   (d) was abandoned after the dollar shortage of the early postwar years

6. Destabilizing speculation occurs when
   (a) lower exchange rates increase the quantity of a currency demanded
   (b) higher exchange rates increase the quantity of a currency supplied
   (c) there is no expectation that fixed exchange rates will be changed
   (d) a change in exchange rates leads to expectation of further changes in the same direction

7. Floating exchange rates
   (a) are the same as fixed rates
   (b) describe the fluctuations around fixed rates permitted by IMF rules
   (c) are necessarily destabilizing
   (d) are determined in international exchange markets by competitive demand and supply conditions

8. Special drawing rights are
   (a) supplementary reserves with the IMF which member countries can use to finance balance-of-payments deficits
   (b) demand deposits that central banks hold in the World Bank
   (c) special credit given to importers in IMF countries
   (d) long-term reserves available to member countries in return for gold

9. The "dirty" float of currencies means that
   (a) currencies are officially pegged but a large black market exists
   (b) the official price at which gold is being sold is allowed to fluctuate
   (c) currencies are officially floating but are being influenced unofficially by central bank policies
   (d) none of the above

10. A workable international monetary system must be able to deal with all but which one of the following?
    (a) short-term fluctuations in trade and capital movements
    (b) long-term changes in trade and payments patterns
    (c) the necessity of gold as a source of confidence in the value of currencies
    (d) speculative crises

Answers to multiple-choice questions: 1(d)   2(b)   3(c)   4(c)   5(c)   6(d)   7(d)   8(a)   9(c)
10(c)

# EXERCISES

1. Indicate which characteristics apply to each of the following monetary arrangements:

| | Gold Standard | Bretton Woods System | Current Monetary Arrangements |
|---|---|---|---|
| International Monetary Fund | | | |
| Effective fixed gold content for U.S. dollar | | | |
| Fluctuating exchange rate | | | |
| Special drawing rights | | | |
| Dollar convertible to gold domestically | | | |
| Adjustable peg | | | |
| "Dirty" float | | | |
| Free market for gold | | | |
| Fixed exchange rates | | | |

2. During the late 1977 and early 1978 period, the U.S. price of the Canadian dollar fell dramatically, reaching a low of $80.80. This low had not been experienced since September 1931.

   Several factors have contributed to this decline, including increased unemployment, the national unity crisis, poor domestic inflation experience, low forecasts of domestic investment in 1978, adverse speculation, and a poor trade sale performance.

   (a) As a Canadian who is engaged in importing goods from abroad, what guarantees might you try to obtain concerning the goods which you are planning to buy during 1978 and early 1979? Why might you wish such guarantees?

   (b) As a speculator in the foreign-exchange market, what activity might you become engaged in if you anticipated a worsening in Canadian economic activity and export sales and a growing dependence on foreign oil? If your behavior was a general tendency, what would happen to the price of the Canadian dollar?

# PROBLEM

## OIL PRICE INCREASES AND RECYCLING OPEC DOLLARS

The foreign-exchange reserve position of a number of countries is shown below. (Figures are in billions of U.S. dollars.)

| | 1973 | 1974 | 1975 |
|---|---|---|---|
| Canada | $ 5.8 | $ 5.8 | $ 5.3 |
| United States | 14.4 | 16.1 | 15.9 |
| United Kingdom | 6.5 | 6.9 | 5.3 |
| Japan | 12.2 | 13.5 | 12.8 |
| Oil-exporting countries (mostly OPEC countries) | 14.5 | 46.4 | 55.4 |

In addition, the trade deficit between Canada and the OPEC countries and that trade between the United States and the OPEC countries widened substantially during this period.

## Questions

1. Explain why the rise in the price of oil imposed by the OPEC countries during this period contributed to the significant difference in the reserve positions of the first four countries in the table and the OPEC countries.

2. Describe the adjustment process that would have occurred over this period if the world had operated under the gold standard, with the free convertibility of currencies into gold and fixed rates with each other.

3. In the text, the authors point out that these reserves or "OPEC dollars" will eventually be recycled by the way of trade and investment between the OPEC and other countries. Some OPEC countries are interested in investing substantial amounts in Canada. If this were to occur, how might it affect:
   (a) Canada's employment situation?



   (b) Canada's foreign-reserve position?



4. Some of the OPEC dollar investments in Canada may be in the form of short-term capital, including deposits in Canadian banks. If this were to occur and the OPEC countries suddenly withdrew their OPEC dollar investments from Canada, what would happen to the price of Canadian dollars under the current international monetary system? What type of foreign-exchange speculation might occur as a result of the withdrawal of OPEC dollars?

# Monetarist Versus
# Neo-Keynesian Views of Policy

1. There are two extreme views of macroeconomic policy. The <u>monetarist</u> view is that the economy tends to be relatively self-regulating and that monetary policy is much more potent than fiscal policy. Monetarists maintain that if a satisfactory general climate is maintained, the economy will naturally tend toward <u>full employment</u> and a relatively <u>stable price level</u>.

2. The <u>neo-Keynesian</u> view is that the economy cannot be relied on to produce full employment if left to itself. Monetary and fiscal policies are both useful instruments to eliminate unemployment although fiscal policy is generally the more potent of the two.

3. Monetarists hold that changes in the money supply cause major fluctuations in national income. Major recessions are associated with absolute declines in the money supply and minor recessions with the <u>slowing</u> down of the rate of increase in the money supply.

4. Neo-Keynesians emphasize variations in investment as a cause of business cycles and stress nonmonetary causes of these variations.

5. Keynesian theory demonstrated that an economy might achieve an <u>underemployment equilibrium</u>: a situation in which the economy comes to rest with substantial unemployment and without any significant forces operating to push the economy back to full-employment equilibrium.

6. Neo-Keynesians reject the monetarist position that only money matters in explaining cyclical fluctuations. They believe that both monetary and nonmonetary factors are important in explaining the behavior of the economy. They accept the correlation between changes in the money supply and changes in national income, but their explanation reverses the causality suggested by the monetarists.

7. Since the neo-Keynesians argue that the monetary authorities tend to stabilize interest rates, they tend to increase the money supply when the demand for money increases due to an expansion in economic activity.

8. Neo-Keynesians also suggest that the money supply is not completely controlled by the monetary authority since banks vary their quantities of excess reserves over the business cycle. During expansions, banks tend to reduce their excess reserve positions and in recessionary periods they increase their excess reserve holdings. Thus, the money supply tends to be positively correlated with the business cycle.

9. Monetarists blame persistent inflationary gaps on excessive increases in the money supply. Neo-Keynesians believe that monetary expansions as well as increases in real factors such as investment expenditures can cause inflation.

10. Monetarists and neo-Keynesians disagree on the relative potency of fiscal and monetary policy. Monetarists believe that monetary policy exerts a major influence on the economy

whereas fiscal policy is relatively powerless. Neo-Keynesians accept both instruments for stabilization policies but tend to place more emphasis on fiscal policy.

11. These divergent views regarding the relative potency of monetary and fiscal policy arise from different views of the quantitative values of the <u>interest elasticity of the demand for money</u> and the <u>interest elasticity of aggregate demand</u>.

12. The <u>interest elasticity of the demand for money</u> is defined as the percentage change in the quantity of money demanded given a particular percentage change in the interest rate. The monetarists hold that the demand for money is interest inelastic; the most important determinant is income. Neo-Keynesians believe that the demand for money is highly sensitive to the rate of interest.

13. The <u>interest elasticity of aggregate demand</u> is defined as the percentage change in the amount of desired expenditure given a particular percentage change in the interest rate. Monetarists believe that the aggregate-demand schedule is very interest elastic; neo-Keynesians believe that most components of aggregate expenditures, including private investment, are insensitive to the rate of interest.

14. These views regarding interest elasticities suggest that monetary policy is considered very effective by the monetarists but potentially ineffective by neo-Keynesians.

15. Furthermore, the divergent views regarding interest-elasticities imply that fiscal policy is ineffective according to the monetarists. This is because of the <u>crowding-out effect</u>.

16. The <u>crowding-out effect</u> arises when expansions in government expenditures, given an inelastic demand for money schedule, causes an increase in interest rates which in turn causes private investment expenditures to fall. Thus, the increase in government expenditures crowds out private investment expenditures. Neo-Keynesians believe the crowding-out effect is quantitatively small and hence fiscal policy is relatively effective in changing national income.

17. Monetarists argue that money is so powerful an influence on the short-run behavior of the economy that monetary policy is too dangerous a tool to be used as an anticyclical device. Since they believe that the <u>lags</u> involved in monetary policy are long and variable and that previous monetary management has proven unenlightened, monetary policy should be restricted to a more or less automatic policy in which the money supply is expanded at some small constant rate.

18. Since neo-Keynesians believe that an economy can persist at an <u>underemployment equilibrium</u> situation, active stabilization policy is called for with an emphasis on fiscal policy and with monetary policy playing a supporting role.

## APPENDIX

1. Since monetarists believe that the interest elasticity of aggregate demand is high, the <u>IS</u> curve becomes relatively flat. The <u>IS</u> curve is relatively steep according to neo-Keynesians.

2. According to the monetarists, the <u>LM</u> curve is steep whereas neo-Keynesians believe that it is relatively flat.

3. The different views regarding the shapes of the <u>IS</u> and <u>LM</u> curves generate different views concerning the efficacy of monetary policy. Given the neo-Keynesian views, the effects of <u>fiscal policy</u> are mainly felt in relatively large changes in national income and relatively small changes in the interest rate. The monetarists believe that fiscal policy has a large effect on interest rates with little change in national income.

4. Given the monetarists' views regarding the shapes of the two curves, the effects of <u>monetary</u> policy are mainly felt in large changes in national income and small changes in the interest rate. Neo-Keynesians believe that monetary policy has a large effect on the interest rate but only small effects on national income.

## REVIEW QUESTIONS

1. By "stabilization policy" we mean trying to maintain the economy at satisfactory levels of ____employment____, without ____inflation____.

2. The monetarists believe that monetary policy is a very (weak/strong) tool of stabilization and that fiscal policy is usually (effective/ineffective).

3. That the economy has adequate self-correcting tendencies is believed by the _____monetarists_____ group. That the economy probably cannot correct its tendencies toward unemployment unaided is the opinion of most _____Neo-keynesian_____; they believe that fiscal policy is (more/less) potent than monetary/policy.

4. Monetarists believe that changes in the money supply (cause/are caused by) changes in national income and, especially, inflation. Neo-Keynesians suggest instead that changes in the money supply are often the (result/cause) of changes in national income and inflation.

5. Neo-Keynesians believe that cyclical fluctuations are caused by changes in spending, especially for _____investment_____. Keynes's theory was new in showing that the economy could be in equilibrium with a situation of _____underemployment_____.

6. Neo-Keynesians argue that banks (increase/decrease) loans and therefore deposits (money supply) in response to good times, and (contract/expand) loans and deposits in response to depressed times. Thus changes in national income (cause/are caused by) changes in the money supply.

7. Monetarists believe that changes in interest rates affect the demand for and supply of money (much/little) but affect spending (much/little). But they believe that changes in the money supply have (much/little) effect on interest rates. Thus in their view monetary policy has a (powerful/weak) influence on spending.

8. Monetarists believe that fiscal policy is rather ineffective, because a rise in government spending causes interest rates to (rise/fall), thus "crowding out" _____private spending_____. Also, the effect of government spending may be confused with the effect of increasing the money supply if it is financed indirectly by open-market (purchases/sales) of government bonds.

9. Neo-Keynesians believe that the demand for and the supply of money are (sensitive/insensitive) to changes in interest rates, but that aggregate expenditure is interest (elastic/inelastic). Thus monetary policy achieves (small/large) changes in interest rates and (small/large) changes in spending. The use of fiscal policy, in their view, causes (small/large) changes in interest rates and therefore a (small/large) "crowding-out" effect.

10. The monetarists favor a neutral monetary policy in which the money supply is allowed to _____increase_____ at about the same rate as _____inflation  GNP_____. Neo-Keynesians believe in using (only fiscal/only monetary/both fiscal and monetary) policy. They are, however, concerned about the uneven effect of _____monetary_____ policy on small businesses and housing construction.

11. A decision to use monetary policy can be made (faster/more slowly) than a decision about fiscal policy, but the effects of the former operate with (more/less) uncertainty and (longer/shorter) time lags.

## APPENDIX

12. The monetarists believe that the *IS* curve is relatively (steep/flat). This implies that small changes in the rate of interest will generate (small/large) changes in aggregate demand, hence making monetary policy potentially very (effective/ineffective).

13. Neo-Keynesians believe that during unemployment situations, the interest elasticity of aggregate expenditures is (low/high), thus causing the *IS* curve to be (steep/flat). Hence, the effectiveness of monetary policy is (increased/reduced).

14. According to the monetarists, the *LM* curve is (steep/flat) whereas neo-Keynesians believe that it is relatively (steep/flat). Increases in government expenditures will cause the interest rate to (increase/decrease) because the transactions demand for money has (increased/decreased). If the *LM* curve is steep, the increase in government expenditures causes the interest rate to (increase/decrease) by a (small/large) amount.

15. Monetarists believe that monetary policy has a (large/small) effect on interest rates and a (small/large) effect on national income. By way of contrast, neo-Keynesians believe that monetary policy has a (large/small) effect on interest rates and a (small/large) effect on national income.

16. Monetarists believe that fiscal policy has a (large/small) effect on interest rates and a (small/large) effect on national income. On the other hand, neo-Keynesians believe that fiscal policy has a (large/small) effect on interest rates and a (small/large) effect on national income.

---

If you have not answered all questions correctly, review the text in order to be sure that you have all of the important concepts clearly in mind before going on to the next chapter.

1. employment, inflation  2. strong, ineffective  3. monetarist; neo-Keynesians, more  4. cause; result  5. investment; underemployment  6. increase, contract; cause  7. little, much; much; powerful  8. rise, private spending; purchases  9. sensitive, inelastic; small, small; small, small  10. increase, real GNP1 both fiscal and monetary; monetary  11. faster, more, longer  12. flat, large, effective  13. low, steep, reduced  14. steep, flat, increase, increased, increase, large  15. small, large, large, small  16. large, small, small, large

---

## MULTIPLE-CHOICE QUESTIONS

1. In the view of the monetarist group of economists,
   (a) changes in the money supply should be used often as a countercyclical tool
   (b) interest rates have very little effect on spending
   (c) the economy will not recover by itself from recessions
   (d) inflation is caused by excessive increases in the supply of money

2. The economists called neo-Keynesians in this chapter
   (a) do not agree with Keynes that investment spending is important in causing a rise in national income
   (b) believe that fiscal policy is a more effective stabilization tool than monetary policy
   (c) are opposed entirely to the use of monetary policy
   (d) believe that investment spending is very interest elastic

3. The monetary policy advocated by the monetarists
   (a) is one of growth in the money supply at about the rate of growth of real GNP
   (b) would use controls on and changes in interest rates to affect NGP
   (c) would be determined primarily by Parliament
   (d) includes the active use of fiscal policy as well

4. As compared with fiscal policy, monetary policy
   (a) can be decided quickly but may have a longer time lag in its effects
   (b) takes longer to put into operation, but the effects are quicker
   (c) is subject to more political obstacles in its formulation
   (d) is made by the Economic Council of Canada

5. Neo-Keynesians have little faith in expansionary monetary policy because
   (a) they feel that the government is ill equipped to predict future economic conditions
   (b) they believe that the interest-elastic demand and supply of money will offset the effect of open-market policy on the rate of interest, and hence national income
   (c) commercial banks will usually maintain only required reserves and thus are responsive to Bank of Canada policy changes
   (d) they believe that since the demand for money is highly interest elastic and aggregate expenditure is interest inelastic, the Bank of Canada can induce only small changes in the interest rate which, in turn, will have a small effect on aggregate expenditure

6. The permanent-income hypothesis is used by the monetarists in their arguments against the effectiveness of fiscal policy
   (a) in that they expect temporary tax changes to have large effects on households' view of their permanent income
   (b) in that they believe the effect of a temporary tax change will be mostly absorbed by changes in savings rather than consumption
   (c) through their feeling that tax and government expenditure changes always have large effects on consumers' permanent income
   (d) none of the above

---

Answers to multiple-choice questions: 1(d)   2(b)   3(a)   4(a)   5(d)   6(b)

# EXERCISES

1. Insert an *M* for monetarist or a *K* for neo-Keynesian after the statements below.
   (a) The demand for money, especially for the speculative motive, can be quite sensitive to interest rates. _K_
   (b) The demand for money is quite insensitive to interest rates but depends mostly on income and the demand for transactions balances. _M_
   (c) The cause of inflation and changes in national income is found primarily in changes in the supply of money. _M_
   (d) Investment spending is much more responsive to profit expectations than to changes in interest rates. _K_
   (e) Changes in the money supply may be a response to, rather than the cause of, changes in GNP and the price level. _K_
   (f) Expansionary fiscal policy only works to the extent that it is financed by monetary expansion. _M_
   (g) Because the crowding-out effect is large, fiscal policy is relatively ineffective in changing thelevel of real GNP. _M_
   (h) Contraction of the money supply raises interest rates, but the small rise in interest rates does not do very much to discourage expenditures. _K_
   (i) Monetary policy is uncertain, variable, powerful, and lagged in its effects; therefore it should be as neutral as possible. _M_
   (j) Fiscal policy has more general effects on the economy, whereas monetary policy affects primarily interest rates and therefore has too much effect on housing and small businesses. _K_

2. *The Crowding-out Effect.* Suppose that the federal government decides to increase its expenditures by 500 million dollars permanently. Prices and the exchange rates are assumed constant. The marginal propensity to withdraw is .5, potential GNP is 151 billion dollars, and current equilibrium GNP is 150 billions.
   (a) What type of gap exists and what is its magnitude?

(b) The government assumes that the interest rate will not change due to its policy change. If this assumption is correct, will the increase in $G$ solve the gap problem?

(c) In fact, suppose that the demand for money equation is given by the expression $D_m = .8Y - 2i$, where $Y$ stands for GNP and $i$ represents the level of the interest rate in percentage terms. If the current money supply is 100 billion, solve for the current level of $i$.

(d) If the government's policy raised real GNP to 151 billion, what would be the effect on the level of the interest rate?

(e) Suppose that you know that every increase in the interest rate of .1% decreased investment expenditures by 125 million dollars. Given your answer to part (d), what is the total effect on investment expenditures?

(f) What is the extent of the crowding-out effect in this problem?

3. *Fiscal Policy and Permanent Income*. The monetarists stress that consumption is a function of permanent income and that tax changes which are considered transitory (or temporary) do not have much effect on consumption spending and hence on national income.

Suppose that a family has a stream of income for the next five years given by column 2 of the table below. Also assume that the tax rate per year is 20% of income and that the marginal propensity to consume out of disposable permanent income is .8.

| Period | Actual Income | Tax Payments | Disposable $Y$ | Disposable Permanent $Y$ |
|--------|---------------|--------------|----------------|--------------------------|
| 1      | 100           |              |                |                          |
| 2      | 120           |              |                |                          |
| 3      | 140           |              |                |                          |
| 4      | 160           |              |                |                          |
| 5      | 180           |              |                |                          |

(a) Calculate the tax payments and disposable income for each year and fill in the table with these values.
(b) Suppose that disposable income per year is computed by adding the five values of disposable income and dividing by 5. We have therefore ignored the problem of discounting for interest rates. What is the constant value of disposable permanent income per year? What is the value of consumption per year? What is the value of savings per year?

(c) Suppose the government cuts the tax rate to 15% in year 1 but restores the 20% tax rate thereafter. What effect does this have on disposable income in period 1? If the *mpc* out of current disposable income was .8, what would be the effect on consumption?

(d) However, the monetarists stress that consumption per year depends on disposable permanent income. Fir the tax change described in part (c), recompute the annual level of disposable permanent income, consumption per year, and saving per year. What was the increase in consumption per year? Over the five years?

(What you have learned in answering parts (c) and (d) is that the total change in consumption using the current income model and the permanent income model are the same. However, the permanent income model indicates that it will take a long time achieving this total increase in consumption.

(e) Instead of the policy change described in parts (c) and (d), suppose that the government decided to lower tax payments by $5 in period 2 but that the family anticipates a tax increased of $5 some time in the future. What will be the effect on disposable permanent income? Consumption per year? Saving per year? What do your answers imply about the effectiveness of fiscal policy to change spending?

# PROBLEM

## INFLATION AND THE NOMINAL RATE OF INTEREST

The previous chapters have stressed the analysis that increases in the money supply should lead to decreases in the interest rate. However, monetarists stress that the nominal rate of interest depends positively on the real rate of interest and the rate of price inflation. Excessive expansion in the money supply, as is argued by the monetarists, is a key determinant of price inflation.

Canada's inflationary experience in the 1970s has been an unhappy one, even though the inflation rates in most western European countries and Japan have been higher than that of Canada.

Professors Harry Johnson and Thomas Courchene* were critical of the Bank of Canada's overly expansionary monetary policy and its reluctance to allow the price of the Canadian dollar to appreciate on the world market during the 1973-1975 period. It is argued that both of these policies contributed significantly to the rate of inflation in Canada. The "dirty float" policy (the Bank of Canada's unwillingness to allow the dollar to appreciate) meant that Canada "imports" more inflation from abroad than would be the case under a flexible exchange-rate policy.

The following table provides some of the evidence for Canada during the 1970s.

---

*Harry G. Johnson, "Inflation, Unemployment, and the Floating Rate," *Canadian Public Policy,* Spring 1975; Thomas Courchene, "Canadian Monetary Policy Under Fixed and Floating Exchange Rates: The 1969-74 Experience," unpublished monograph, delivered at the Conference on Canadian Monetary Issues, Queens University, August 1975.

| Year | Percent Change in the Money Supply | | Percent Change in the Consumer Price Index | Long-Term Canadian Bond Rate |
|------|------|------|------|------|
|      | $M_1$ | $M_2$ | | |
| 1971 | 12.7 | 12.3 | 2.8 | 6.95 |
| 1972 | 14.2 | 10.5 | 4.8 | 7.23 |
| 1973 | 14.5 | 14.2 | 7.6 | 7.55 |
| 1974 | 9.4 | 20.1 | 10.9 | 8.87 |
| 1975 | 13.7 | 15.0 | 10.8 | 9.00 |
| 1976 | 8.0 | 12.6 | 7.5 | 9.22 |

Professor Courchene also stresses that the relevant money supply magnitude is $M_2$ rather than $M_1$. This is closely in tune with the monetarist's position.

## Questions

1. Why would the monetarists prefer $M_2$ as the relevant definition of the money supply? (Review your answer to part (1), *Canada's Income Velocity of Money,* problem, Chapter 33.)

2. From the evidence provided, is there a relationship between changes in $M_2$ and changes in the price level?

3. What relationship exists between changes in the price index and the nominal rate of interest?

4. Calculate the "real" rate of interest between 1971 and 1975. (See Chapter 22 for this discussion.)

5. If you have been a holder of bonds in 1974 and 1975, what would you have done?

6. Why would allowing the price of Canadian dollars to appreciate have helped to prevent the importation of inflation from abroad during 1973-1975?

# 38

# The Nature of Unemployment and Inflation

## KEY CONCEPTS AND DEFINITIONS

1. <u>Voluntary unemployment</u> occurs when there is a job available but the unemployed person is not willing to accept it at the going wage rate for persons now employed.
2. <u>Involuntary unemployment</u> occurs when a person is willing to accept a job at the going wage rate but no such job can be found.
3. There are four major types of unemployment: <u>frictional</u>, <u>structural</u>, <u>deficient-demand</u>, and <u>search</u>.
4. <u>Frictional unemployment</u> is associated with the normal turnover of labor. Persons are frictionally unemployed in the course of finding new jobs.
5. <u>Structural unemployment</u> is said to exist when there is a mismatching between the unemployed and the available jobs. In a sense, structural unemployment is really <u>long-term</u> frictional unemployment.
6. <u>Deficient-demand unemployment</u> occurs because there is insufficient aggregate demand to purchase full-employment output. A useful measure of this is the difference between the number of persons seeking jobs and the number of <u>unfilled job vacancies</u>.
7. <u>Search unemployment</u> occurs when a person who could find work remains unemployed in order to search for a better offer than he or she has so far received. The basic cause of search unemployment is <u>imperfect information</u> about job opportunities.
8. There are five major causes of inflation: <u>demand-pull</u>, <u>cost-push</u>, <u>price-push</u>, <u>structural rigidity</u>, and <u>expectations</u>.
9. The <u>demand-pull inflation</u> theory says that changes in prices are caused by changes in aggregate demand. An increase in aggregate demand in a situation of full employment will create excess demand and prices will rise.
10. The <u>cost-push</u> theory says that rises in costs, not themselves associated with excess demand, cause prices to rise.
11. The <u>price-push</u> theory suggests that firms with monopoly powers may be able to increase their profit margins by increasing prices.
12. The <u>structural rigidity</u> theory assumes that resources do not move quickly from one use to another. When patterns of demand and costs change, real adjustments occur very slowly and shortages appear in expanding sectors, causing prices to rise.
13. The <u>expectational</u> theory of inflation says that if decision makers expect a certain future inflation they will use this value as a base from which to negotiate price and wage increases.
14. When cost-push, price-push, or expectational inflation is allowed to persist because the government permits the money supply to expand at the same rate as the inflation, economists speak of the inflation as being <u>validated</u> by increases in the money supply. A continuing inflation that is <u>not validated</u> must sooner or later produce ever-falling levels of output and ever-rising levels of unemployment.

255

# REVIEW QUESTIONS

1. When a person is not willing to accept a job at the going wage rate, he is said to be ___voluntary___ unemployed.

2. When a person is willing to accept a job at the going wage rate but no such job can be found, he is said to be ___involuntary___ unemployed.

3. There are two main reasons for worrying about unemployment: it produces ___waste___ and it causes ___human suffering___

4. The amount of unemployment that is associated with normal turnover of labor is called ___frictional unemployment___. When there is a mismatching between the unemployed and available jobs, ___structural___ unemployment is said to exist.

5. Deficient-demand unemployment occurs when aggregate demand is (less/~~greater~~) than full-employment output. A useful measure of this type of unemployment is the difference between the number of persons seeking jobs and the number of ___unfilled vacancies___

6. When a person who could find work but remains unemployed in order to search for a better offer, ___search___ unemployment is said to exist. The basic cause of search unemployment is ___uncertainty___ about job opportunities.

7. Measured unemployment may understate involuntary unemployment by omitting people who ___would accept a job if one were available___

8. A program designed to improve ___information___ and/or (reduce/~~increase~~) moving costs might reduce the level of frictional unemployment. Structural unemployment might be attacked by policies for ___retraining___ labor. Expansionary fiscal and monetary policies could reduce the level of ___deficit-demand___ unemployment.

9. The demand-pull theory of inflation is associated with increases in ___aggregate demand___ In the absence of excess demand, the ___cost-push___ theory of inflation says that price level rises are associated with rises in costs, particularly wage costs.

10. In a (competitive/~~monopoly~~) market, firms may be able to increase their prices and hence profits even in the absence of excess demand. This is called the ___price-push___ theory of inflation.

11. The structural rigidity theory of inflation assumes that ___resources___ do not move quickly from one use to another. When patterns of demand and costs change, real adjustments occur (very slowly/~~quickly~~) and (shortages/~~excess supply~~) appear in expanding sectors, causing prices to rise.

12. If decision makers expect some level of future price inflation, they will tend to negotiate factor price increases starting from a base of the expected inflation rate. This is called the ___expectational___ theory of inflation. This type of inflation often follows ___demand-pull___ inflation and hence tends to prolong inflationary periods even when excess demand has been eliminated.

13. One of the most important propositions in the theory of inflation is that inflations cannot long persist, whatever their initiating causes, unless the inflations are ___validated___ by (increases/~~decreases~~) in the money supply. For example, cost-push, price-push, or expectational inflation tend to reduce real income on average and hence unemployment would (increase/~~decrease~~). To prevent this occurrence, the government will (increase/~~decrease~~) the money supply and this action validates the inflationary cause.

If you have not answered all questions correctly, review the text in order to be sure that you have all of the important concepts clearly in mind before going on to the next chapter.

1. voluntarily  2. involuntarily  3. waste; human suffering  4. frictional unemployment; structural  5. less; unfilled vacancies  6. search; uncertainty  7. would accept a job if one were available  8. information; reduce; retraining and relocating; deficient-demand  9. aggregate demand; cost-push  10. monopoly; price-push  11. resources; very slowly; shortages  12. expectational; demand-pull  13. validated; increases; increase; increase

## MULTIPLE-CHOICE QUESTIONS

1. Voluntary unemployment
   (a) occurs when there is a job available at the going wage but the unemployed person is unwilling to accept it
   (b) is of more concern to policy makers than involuntary unemployment
   (c) increases substantially during a deep recession
   (d) occurs when a person is willing to accept a job at the going wage rate but no such job can be found

2. Unemployment that occurs as a result of the normal turnover of the labor force as people move from job to job is called
   (a) involuntary unemployment
   (b) structural unemployment
   (c) search unemployment
   (d) frictional unemployment

3. Structural unemployment means that
   (a) there is an inadequate number of jobs in the economy
   (b) there are not enough employees
   (c) the building trades workers are suffering from high unemployment rates
   (d) certain resources have been unable to adjust to changing economic conditions

4. Search unemployment
   (a) tends to increase as the costs of search increase
   (b) will tend to be higher with more generous unemployment insurance benefits
   (c) is socially undesirable even if a better job is obtained as a result of additional search
   (d) tends to be reduced as the prevalence of multiworker households increases

5. Inflation occurs when
   (a) prices are high
   (b) the relative price or a necessity such as electricity increases
   (c) there is an increase in the price level as measured by a price index
   (d) living standards decrease

6. Inflation that is *not* correctly anticipated will
   (a) increase the purchasing power of people living on fixed incomes
   (b) hurt borrowers rather than creditors
   (c) not have any significant effect on the distribution of income
   (d) most likely involve some redistribution of income

7. Demand-pull inflation occurs when
   (a) aggregate demand is greater than the value of full-employment GNP
   (b) aggregate demand and employment are rising at equivalent rates
   (c) a rise in the demand for goods is coupled with a decrease in demand for factors of production
   (d) aggregate demand exceeds current GNP but is less than potential GNP

8. If government spending were suddenly reduced, the greatest impact would probably be toward
   (a) reducing price-push inflation
   (b) decreasing the money supply
   (c) reducing demand-pull inflation
   (d) reducing structural inflation

9. A validated inflation
   (a) can go on indefinitely with no necessary fall in output
   (b) will be accompanied by falling rates of output
   (c) will be accompanied by rising unemployment
   (d) is caused by government spending in excess of full-employment aggregate demand

Answers to multiple-choice questions: 1(a)   2(d)   3(d)   4(b)   5(c)   6(d)   7(a)   8(c)   9(a)

# EXERCISES

1. Classify the following situations as frictional unemployment, structural unemployment, search unemployment, or deficient-demand unemployment, and briefly explain your choice:
   (a) An auto assemblyman is laid off, because auto sales decrease with a slowdown in economic activity.

   *deficient demand.*

   (b) A chartered accountant is unable to find a job in her current location at an acceptable pay rate.

   *search unemployment*

   (c) A social worker is laid off, because the government has cancelled the Local Initiatives Program (LIP).

   *frictional in short term ; structural*

   (d) A mechanic in London, Ontario, is laid off when a bus manufacturing firm relocates in Montreal.

   *same as above*

   (e) A business analyst quits one job and has so far been unsuccessful in finding a new job.

   *frictional*

2. What type of government policy would be appropriate for each of the following?
   (a) Demand-pull inflation

(b) Structural unemployment

(c) Cost-push inflation

(d) Structural inflation

(e) Deficient-demand unemployment

(f) Expectational inflation

3. Suppose that there are two labor markets in an economy, each of which is characterized by a rigid money wage which deviates from the equilibrium wage and a completely inelastic supply curve of labor. The total demand for labor in the economy is the sum of the two demand-for-labor curves in the two markets. The demand for labor is equal to unfilled vacancies plus employment. The supply of labor is equal to employment plus unemployment.

The initial situation for the demand for labor in each market is given by the superscript $^0$.

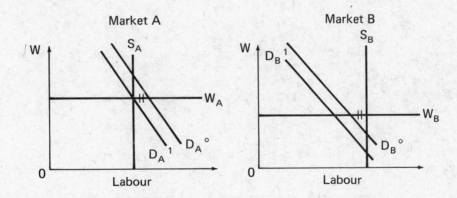

(a) What initial situation exists in market A? In market B?

(b) The authors of the text indicate that a measure of deficient-demand unemployment is unemployment minus unfilled job vacancies. Accordingly, what is the level of deficient-demand unemployment at the initial conditions?

(c) What market adjustments might occur to solve the unemployment and unfilled vacancy problem (two answers)?

(d) Under what conditions might labor be totally immobile as is indicated in the example above?

(e) Suppose aggregate demand for labor decreased and this overall decrease was shared equally in the two markets. The situation is depicted by the curves with superscripts [1]. What would happen to the national unemployment rate? Total unfilled vacancies? Deficient-demand unemployment?

# PROBLEM

## UNEMPLOYMENT IN THE 1970s AND UNEMPLOYMENT INSURANCE CHANGES

In its report of the Canadian labor market, the Economic Council of Canada states:

> In recent years there has been growing concern about Canada's inability to make full use of its labour force potential or to bring levels of unemployment down to those found in most other industrialized western nations, or indeed, in Canada less than a generation ago. Since the beginning of the 1970s, despite a period of pronounced buoyancy with record rates of increase in real output, per capita real incomes, consumer demand, and employment, our seasonally adjusted unemployment rate has remained persistently above 5%. This has occurred even though massive investments were made during the 1960s in education, health, manpower, and regional incentive programs in order to raise the quality of the labour force, meet the demand for new skills, and treat pockets of unemployment selectively and directly. If this has been the situation in times of high economic activity, then in periods of pause and uncertainty such as are being experienced we can expect to face more serious difficulties.*

The following tables provide some information about economic and labor market conditions in the period 1965-1974.

---

*Economic Council of Canada, *People and Jobs, A Study of the Canadian Labour Market* (Ottawa: 1976), p. 3.

| Year | Participation Rate | Annual Changes in Employment | Unemployment Rate | Growth in Labor Force |
|------|------|------|------|------|
| 1965 | 54.4% | 4.8% | 3.9% | 3.0% |
| 1966 | 55.1 | 5.4 | 3.6 | 3.9 |
| 1967 | 55.5 | 3.1 | 4.1 | 3.7 |
| 1968 | 55.5 | 2.5 | 4.8 | 2.9 |
| 1969 | 55.8 | 3.6 | 4.7 | 3.1 |
| 1970 | 55.8 | 1.7 | 5.9 | 2.6 |
| 1971 | 56.1 | 2.7 | 6.4 | 3.1 |
| 1972 | 56.5 | 3.7 | 6.3 | 3.0 |
| 1973 | 57.5 | 5.7 | 5.6 | 4.4 |
| 1974 | 58.3 | 4.5 | 5.4 | 4.1 |

Participation Rates, by Age-Sex Group, Annual Averages, 1965-1974

| Year | 14-19 Years T* | M | F | 20-24 Years T | M | F | 25-54 Years T | M | F | 55-64 Years T | M | F | 65 and Older T | M | F |
|------|------|------|------|------|------|------|------|------|------|------|------|------|------|------|------|
| 1965 | 34.5 | 38.7 | 30.2 | 69.8 | 87.6 | 52.6 | 65.2 | 97.1 | 33.9 | 36.3 | 57.2 | 16.2 | 15.6 | 26.3 | 6.0 |
| 1966 | 35.0 | 38.6 | 31.4 | 71.5 | 87.4 | 55.6 | 65.9 | 97.1 | 35.3 | 36.6 | 57.4 | 16.9 | 15.5 | 26.4 | 5.9 |
| 1967 | 35.5 | 39.4 | 31.6 | 71.3 | 86.0 | 56.6 | 66.7 | 96.9 | 36.9 | 36.3 | 56.8 | 17.0 | 14.7 | 24.7 | 5.9 |
| 1968 | 35.3 | 39.1 | 31.3 | 71.4 | 84.4 | 58.4 | 66.8 | 96.5 | 37.5 | 36.3 | 56.7 | 17.4 | 14.5 | 24.4 | 5.9 |
| 1969 | 34.6 | 37.9 | 31.1 | 71.8 | 84.2 | 59.3 | 67.4 | 96.4 | 38.8 | 36.3 | 56.5 | 17.8 | 13.8 | 23.6 | 5.5 |
| 1970 | 34.6 | 38.6 | 30.4 | 71.0 | 83.2 | 58.5 | 67.9 | 96.3 | 39.9 | 35.6 | 55.7 | 17.3 | 13.1 | 22.7 | 5.0 |
| 1971 | 35.1 | 39.0 | 31.1 | 71.8 | 83.4 | 59.9 | 68.4 | 96.3 | 40.9 | 35.0 | 53.9 | 17.9 | 11.9 | 20.0 | 5.1 |
| 1972 | 36.5 | 40.8 | 32.0 | 72.4 | 84.0 | 60.5 | 69.0 | 96.0 | 42.3 | 33.9 | 52.9 | 17.0 | 10.9 | 18.7 | 4.3 |
| 1973 | 39.1 | 43.7 | 34.2 | 74.0 | 85.3 | 62.5 | 69.9 | 96.1 | 44.0 | 33.7 | 52.1 | 17.5 | 10.6 | 18.3 | 4.4 |
| 1974 | 41.6 | 46.3 | 36.7 | 74.7 | 86.1 | 63.0 | 70.8 | 96.2 | 45.6 | 32.9 | 51.4 | 16.7 | 10.2 | 17.8 | 4.2 |

*Source: People and Jobs*, p. 231.

Refer to the figure on the next page when answering the following questions.

## Questions

1. In the period 1965-1970, what relationship existed between the percentage change in employment and the unemployment rate? Were there any changes in this relationship after 1970?

2. What factor contributed to the major changes in the labor force after 1970? What groups in the economy changed their labor force participation the most? Give some reasons for this change in behavior.

In 1971, with amendments in 1975, the Unemployment Insurance Act was changed substantially. Some of the major changes involved reducing the number of weeks worked to quality for unemployment insurance, extending the entitlement weeks, increasing the benefits per week, and tying benefits into regional unemployment rates. For example, a region with high unemployment qualifies a worker in that region to receive more benefits. Some economists believe that these changes increased the duration and level of unemployment as is shown in the table on the next page.

Labour force growth attributable to increase in the participation rate, 1954–74

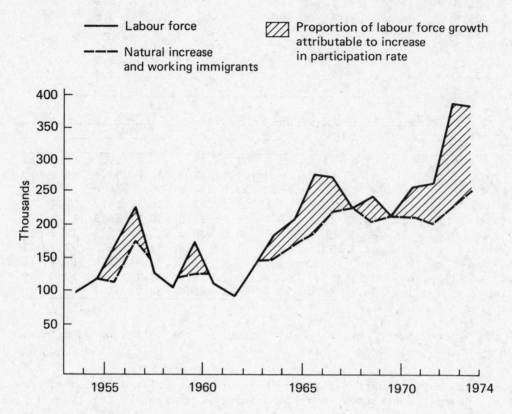

————— Labour force

– – – – Natural increase and working immigrants

[///] Proportion of labour force growth attributable to increase in participation rate

SOURCE People and Jobs, page 71.

Estimated Additional Unemployment Attributable to the
1971 Revisions of the Unemployment Insurance Act, 1972*

|  | Increase in Unemployment Rate | Additional Persons Unemployed[1] |
|---|---|---|
|  | (Percentage points) |  |
| Siedule, Skoulas, and Newton | 0.74 | 66,000 |
| Green and Cousineau | 0.67 | 60,000 |
| Grubel, Maki, and Sax | 0.80 | 71,000 |
| Wallace | 0.6–0.7 | 60,000 |

[1]Determined by applying the estimated increase in the unemployment
rate to the average annual labour force.
*Source:* T. Siedule, N. Skoulas, and K. Newton, "The Impact of
Economywide Changes on the Labour Force," a study prepared for the
Economic Council of Canada, 1974; C. Green and J.-M. Cousineau,
*Unemployment in Canada: The Impact of Unemployment Insurance,* Economic Council of Canada (forthcoming); H. G. Grubel, D. Maki, and
S. Sax, "Real and Insurance-Induced Unemployment in Canada," *Canadian Journal of Economics* (May 1975): 174-91; and Thomas W. Wal-
lace, "The Effects of Unemployment Insurance on the Measured Unemployment Rate," Institute for Economic Research, Queen's University, Discussion Paper No. 155 (Kingston, 1974).
**People and Jobs*, p. 154.

3. Explain why the labor force and search and frictional unemployment might have increased due to the changes in the UI Act.

4. As you saw in Exercise 3, unfilled job vacancies and unemployment tend to be negatively related. As aggregate demand increases, vacancies should rise and unemployment fall, assuming that the composition and the level of the labor force remain constant. Given your answer to parts 1 and 2, what do you predict happened to the job-vacancy—unemployment relationship after 1971?

5. What effects might the changes in the UI Act have had on structural unemployment?

# Conflicts Among Goals: Unemployment Versus Inflation

## KEY CONCEPTS AND DEFINITIONS

1. Demand-pull inflation which occurs when the desired level of aggregate money expenditure exceeds the aggregate supply of goods and services in the economy. In its simplest form, the price level is thus constant up to the full-employment level of GNP and this gives rise to the L-shaped relations between the price level and output.

2. The microeconomic foundations necessary for the existence of the L-shaped relation do not appear to hold true empirically. An alternative is a curve which relates the change in price level to national income in such a manner that as real national income rises to and beyond the full-employment level, the price level increases more rapidly. This relationship is referred to as the Phillips curve.

3. The existence of a Phillips curve relationship between price level movements and aggregate demand implies a conflict between the goals of minimizing unemployment and inflation.

4. Price expectations refer to the possibility that once prices are rising at a particular rate, people come to expect them to continue at that rate and therefore adjust their behavior to incorporate that expectation.

5. The natural rate of unemployment is that rate of unemployment where the level of national income generates no significant demand-pull inflation.

6. Once excess demand appears, the decision to raise money prices will depend on (a) how much of a relative change is desired and (b) what the expected rate of inflation will be over the period in which the price increase is to prevail. Thus actual inflation equals that part due to excess demand plus the expected rate of inflation.

7. As long as national income is sustained at a level above its full-employment level, prices will accelerate as actual inflation rates becoming the basis for expected inflation.

8. At the natural rate of unemployment, any stable rate of inflation is possible provided actual inflation is equal to expected inflation.

9. From a policy perspective, it is crucial to know what the natural rate of unemployment is because any attempt to drive unemployment below this level will create accelerating inflation.

10. Stagflation, or the occurrence of high unemployment and inflation, may result when attempts to reduce inflation, lower the level of aggregate demand while past inflation rates upon which expectations are based, are still feeding into present price decisions.

11. Cost-push inflation can, like demand-pull inflation, produce conflicts between "full" employment and price stability.

12. An <u>incomes policy</u> is direct or indirect intervention by the government in the establishment of wages, prices, and/or profits. The strongest argument in their favor relates to expected inflation. While eliminating excess demand through fiscal and monetary policies, an incomes policy may dampen expectations more rapidly than in the absence of such intervention.

## REVIEW QUESTIONS

1. The "L-shaped" relation discussed in this chapter and the Phillips curve both relate the level of aggregate demand to <u>changes in price level</u>

2. The L-shaped relation assumes that prices (remain stable/~~rise~~) until full employment is reached; at that point, further increases in aggregate demand would cause <u>inflation</u>. This relationship assumes that as unemployment increases, average prices (~~fall~~/remain the same).

3. If the L-shaped relation exists empirically, then there (~~is~~/is not) a conflict between the goals of "full" employment and price stability. The Phillips curve suggests that full employment without inflation is (~~possible~~/impossible).

4. If a Phillips curve exists, policy measures to stop inflation will cause <u>unemployment</u>, whereas measures to achieve full employment will cause <u>inflation</u>.

5. With no expectations that prices will rise in the future, price level changes (will/~~will not~~) be related to the amount of excess demand in the economy. A Phillips curve with zero price expectations is usually thought of as a (short-term/~~long-run~~) Phillips curve.

6. The natural rate of unemployment is shown on the Phillips curve as a point where the curve intersects (full employment/~~less than full employment~~) level of GNP. At this point, the actual rate of unemployment will be (greater than zero/~~equal to zero~~) percent.

7. According to the Phelps-Friedman theory of inflation, actual inflation is equal to inflation due to excess demand (plus/~~times~~) the expected rate of inflation. If expected inflation is 2 percent and excess demand pressures "warrant" a 3 percent price rise, the actual rise in the price level would be (5/~~2~~) percent.

8. The expectations theory of inflation suggests that as long as unemployment is below the natural rate, the rate of inflation will (~~be constant~~/accelerate). If expectations become zero, inflation will eventually equal the rate "warranted" by <u>excess demand</u>.

9. If the economy is operating at the full-employment level of GNP, any inflation is <u>expectation</u> inflation. Thus, the natural rate of unemployment may be consistent with (a given/many) rate(s) of inflation depending on <u>expectation</u>.

10. Given an inflationary situation where both expectations and excess demand factors operate, fiscal and monetary policies must be directed toward reducing <u>excess demand</u> inflation before <u>expectation inflation</u> can be reduced. Some expectations are based on past rates of <u>actual</u> inflation, demand management policies (will/will not) usually result in a swift end of inflation.

11. The major problem in assessing wage and price controls is attempting to measure what would have occurred if they had not been in place. The assessment of the Anti-Inflation Board policies in Canada is clouded by the sudden (rise in unemployment/~~militancy of labor arrears~~).

12. A simultaneous increase in unemployment and inflation suggests that perhaps the <u>natural</u> rate of unemployment has <u>increased</u> or that <u>expectation</u> inflation may have followed <u>excess demand</u> inflation.

13. There is (some/no) empirical proof that the natural rate of unemployment has increased in the past 10 years.

---

If you have not answered all questions correctly, review the text in order to be sure that you have all of the important concepts clearly in mind before going on to the next chapter.

1. changes in the price level  2. remain stable; inflation; remain the same  3. is not; impossible  4. unemployment; inflation  5. will; short-term  6. full employment; greater than zero  7. plus; 5  8. accelerate; excess demand  9. expected; many; expectations  10. excess demand; expectation; actual; will not  11. rise in unemployment  12. natural; increased; expected; excess demand  13. some

---

# MULTIPLE-CHOICE QUESTIONS

1. The Phillips curve shows
   (a) the tradeoff between unemployment and inflation
   (b) that there is little conflict between the two policy goals
   (c) that prices rise before full employment is reached but do not fall even when unemployment becomes quite high
   (d) how much of an increase in aggregate expenditure is needed to achieve full employment

2. The L-shaped supply curve implies
   (a) micro assumptions that seem to contradict observed behavior
   (b) that prices fall as recession gets worse
   (c) that all markets are always in equilibrium
   (d) that changes in aggregate demand do not affect the level of employment

3. The expectational theory of inflation suggests that
   (a) inflation is based entirely on psychological factors
   (b) there is no cure for inflation
   (c) part of all of a given price level change can be explained by what people think inflation will be
   (d) at full employment, there will be inflation because it is expected

4. The short-run Phillips curve is based on the fact that
   (a) inflation will correct itself through changes in real market forces
   (b) expectations about future inflation are zero
   (c) the natural rate of unemployment is changing
   (d) none of the above

5. Prices rise when unemployment is below the natural rate because of all but one of the following:
   (a) producers attempt to increase relative prices
   (b) aggregate demand exceeds aggregate supply
   (c) individual market demand curves shift outward
   (d) aggregate supply becomes horizontal

6. The demand-pull component of inflation
   (a) equals actual inflation minus expected inflation
   (b) can be controlled by incomes policies
   (c) occurs only at the natural rate of unemployment
   (d) equals the expected inflation of the last period

7. Expectations about future inflation are most likely to be based upon
   (a) demand-pull pressures of previous years
   (b) actual inflation rates of the past two or three years
   (c) shifts in the full-employment level of GNP
   (d) future demand pressures in the economy

8. The most important implication of the Phelps-Friedman theory of expected inflation is
    (a) that fiscal and monetary policy is ineffective in combating inflation
    (b) that there is no tradeoff between unemployment and price inflation when unemployment is above the natural rate
    (c) that the Phillips curve is horizontal
    (d) that inflation will accelerate as long as the rate of unemployment is below the natural rate

9. In the long run, given the Phelps-Friedman framework,
    (a) the Phillips curve has a slope of 1.0
    (b) the Phillips curve is vertical at full-employment GNP
    (c) expectations are not important for determining the rate of inflation
    (d) demand management policies are ineffective in reducing unemployment

10. "Wage drift" is a term used to describe
    (a) wage differentials between countries
    (b) wage increases in excess of productivity gains
    (c) interindustry wage differentials
    (d) the widening spread between a wage rate and wage earning

11. Incomes policies which legislate reductions in wage and price inflation
    (a) are designed to reduce the expectations component of inflation
    (b) force markets to adjust to a noninflationary level of output
    (c) allow aggregate supply to expand to match aggregate demand

12. Stagflation may be due to all but one of the following:
    (a) a higher natural rate of unemployment
    (b) cost-push inflation
    (c) excess demand pressures
    (d) lags between demand-induced and expected inflation

13. The present incomes policy in Canada is associated with all but one of the following:
    (a) high administrative costs
    (b) conflict between labor and government
    (c) a redistribution of income in favor of the low income earner
    (d) a rise in unemployment

---

Answers to multiple-choice questions: 1(a)   2(a)   3(c)   4(b)   5(d)   6(a)   7(b)   8(d)   9(b)
10(d)   11(a)   12(c)   13(c)

---

# EXERCISES

1. Below are data on actual inflation, price expectations, and excess demand-generated inflation.

| Time Period | Excess Demand "Generated" Inflation | Expected Inflation = Previous Period Actual Inflation | Actual Inflation = Excess Demand Inflation + Expected Inflation |
|---|---|---|---|
| 0 | 0 | 0 | 0 |
| 1 | 0 | 0 | 0 |
| 2 | 5 | 0 | 5 |
| 3 | 5 | _____ | _____ |
| 4 | 5 | _____ | _____ |
| 5 | 5 | _____ | _____ |
| 6 | 5 | _____ | _____ |

(a) It is assumed that expected inflation in any period is equal to actual inflation in the previous period and that actual inflation in a given period equals the excess demand inflation plus the expected inflation in that same period. Complete the table above.

(b) If the persistent excess demand suggested in the table is consistent with a 4 percent rate of unemployment, what would the "Phillips" curve look like for period 2 through period 6?

(c) If the excess demand were removed by, let us say, restrictive fiscal policy, what would happen to expected inflation and the actual rate of inflation?

2. The data in the table below pertain to the Canadian economy over the postwar period.

| Year | Percentage Change in Consumer Price Index (P) | Average Annual Rate of Unemployment (U) |
|---|---|---|
| 1949 | 3.1 | 2.6 |
| 1950 | 2.8 | 3.2 |
| 1951 | 10.6 | 2.0 |
| 1952 | 2.5 | 2.4 |
| 1953 | -0.9 | 2.5 |
| 1954 | 0.6 | 4.3 |
| 1955 | 0.2 | 4.1 |
| 1956 | 1.4 | 3.1 |
| 1957 | 3.2 | 4.3 |
| 1958 | 2.7 | 6.6 |
| 1959 | 1.1 | 5.6 |
| 1960 | 1.2 | 7.0 |
| 1961 | 0.9 | 7.1 |
| 1962 | 1.2 | 5.9 |
| 1963 | 1.7 | 5.5 |
| 1964 | 1.8 | 4.7 |
| 1965 | 2.5 | 3.9 |
| 1966 | 3.7 | 3.6 |
| 1967 | 3.6 | 4.1 |
| 1968 | 4.1 | 4.8 |
| 1969 | 4.5 | 4.7 |
| 1970 | 3.3 | 5.9 |
| 1971 | 2.9 | 6.4 |
| 1972 | 4.8 | 6.3 |
| 1973 | 7.6 | 5.6 |
| 1974 | 10.9 | 5.4 |
| 1975 | 10.7 | 6.9 |
| 1976 | 7.4 | 7.1 |

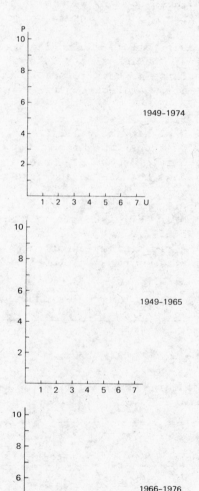

(a) On the three graphs to the right of the table, plot P and U for the three periods indicated.

(b) What can you say about a tradeoff between prices and unemployment in each case? (Try to fit a curve to the data you have plotted.)

(c) Do you think the graphs alone validate or deny the existence of a Phillips curve for Canada?

(d) Is there anything especially different about the two sub-periods, 1949-1965 and 1966-1976?

# PROBLEMS

## 1. POLICIES FOR PRICE STABILITY

Early in 1969, the Government of Canada published its White Paper entitled *Policies for Price Stability,* which led to the establishment of the Prices and Incomes Commission. The White Paper was designed to " . . . examine the problem of rising costs and prices . . . and outline some of the possible causes of this upward price pressure .   . " (p. 3). Canada's price problems stemmed from the possibility of structural unemployment, the impact of the U.S. economy, and "market power" which, when organized by "powerful businessmen, strong trade unions . . . makes it difficult to restore price stability" (p. 7).

The Prices and Incomes Commission was established in late 1969. Its first objective was to plan a conference of business and union leaders to try and reach an agreement on voluntary wage and price guidelines. The conference failed to materialize, and shortly thereafter the steel workers' union settled for a 28-percent wage increase over 3 years with a 13-percent increase the first year. Six days later the Steel Company of Canada raised its product prices by 6 percent. This affair brought a warning from the Prime Minister, who stated that unless these kinds of wage and price increases could be avoided by voluntary agreement, harsh, restrictive monetary and fiscal policies would be imposed upon the economy.

Throughout 1970, there was a lively debate about the role of the Commission and the problem of inflation in general. Some of the views expressed are as follows.

1. Three years (1965-1968) of inflation had led to " . . . strong expectations of continuing inflation." (L. Rasminsky, Governor, Bank of Canada)
2. The idea of voluntary restraints was " . . . the slickest, most sophisticated con job any government had tried to put over the people . . . . " (M. Rygus, International Association of Machinists, Vice President, as reported in *The Globe and Mail)*
3. " . . . it is difficult to maintain that the current inflation is a reflection of excessive demand pressures . . . " (Economic Council of Canada, *Annual Review,* 1970)
4. "I don't accept the trade-off theory—it doesn't apply to Canada anymore." (E. Benson, Minister of Finance)
5. "When the economy starts to cool off, workers will be realistic enough to take that into account in their bargaining." (J. Morris, Canadian Labour Congress, as reported in *The Globe and Mail)*

## Questions

1. Would a Prices and Incomes Commission which had only powers of inquiry, research, and publication be able to deal with the expectation problem noted by Mr. Rasminsky?

2. Mr. Trudeau's threat of harsh monetary and fiscal policies might imply a type of inflation that is not implied by the Economic Council of Canada. Who do you think is correct?

3. Was Mr. Benson's statement correct? Why?

4. Can traditional monetary and fiscal policies deal with inflation caused by market power that is excessive? Explain your answer.

## 2.  TRYING TO WHIP INFLATION

Canada is in the grip of serious inflation. If this inflation continues or gets worse there is a grave danger that economic recovery will be stifled, unemployment increased and the nation subjected to mounting stresses and strains. It has thus become absolutely essential to undertake a concerted national effort to bring inflation under control . . . . *

The above quote introduced the government's plan for an incomes policy and the establishment of an anti-inflation board to regulate wages and profits in order to reduce inflation and permit, at the same time, expansionary policies to reduce the rate of unemployment. Below are data relating to the immediate Anti-Inflation Board period through the end of 1977.

| Quarter | Unemployment Rate | Percentage Change in Consumer Price Index (annual rate) | Percentage Change in Wage Base of Negotiated Settlements (annual) | |
|---|---|---|---|---|
| | | | Private Sector | Public Sector |
| 1975 | | | | |
| III | 7.0 | 10.7 | 19.2 | 20.3 |
| IV | 7.0 | 10.8 | 15.5 | 12.4 |
| 1976 | | | | |
| I | 6.8 | 8.5 | 14.5 | 13.4 |
| II | 7.1 | 7.8 | 11.8 | 10.7 |
| III | 7.2 | 6.5 | 9.8 | 11.0 |
| IV | 7.5 | 5.8 | 8.7 | 9.3 |
| 1977 | | | | |
| I | 8.1 | 7.4 | 8.6 | 8.7 |
| II | 8.0 | 7.7 | 8.3 | 8.5 |
| III | 8.3 | 8.4 | 7.7 | 7.4 |
| IV | 8.5 | 9.4 | | |

*Hon. Donald S. MacDonald, House of Commons, October 14, 1975.

Questions

1. Has the economy responded in the manner hoped for at the time of introducing the policy program in late 1975?

2. Why would labor be especially upset about the impact of the A.I.B. in 1977?

3. What are some reasons for the ineffectiveness of wage and profits controls on prices?

# 40

# Macroeconomic Policy and the Balance of Payments

## KEY CONCEPTS AND DEFINITIONS

1. A commitment to a <u>fixed exchange rate</u> (a fixed value of the exchange rate) forces the policy authorities to be concerned about the balance of payments.

2. A major source of balance-of-payments disequilibrium particularly with respect to the current account is inflation of the domestic price level at a rate different from the rate of inflation in the rest of the world. A country with a higher rate of inflation will experience growing deficits unless it allows its currency to <u>depreciate</u> (fall in price). A country that wishes to maintain a lower rate of inflation (relative to other countries) will have to allow its currency to <u>appreciate</u> (rise in price).

3. Fiscal policy can be used to influence the trade balance by influencing income and hence imports. The effect of fiscal policy on imports depends on the value of the multiplier which is inversely related to the <u>marginal propensity to import</u>. There will be a conflict of objectives if there is a balance-of-payments deficit and a deflationary gap at the same time.

4. The <u>capital account</u> can be influenced by using monetary policy to manipulate domestic interest rates since <u>international capital</u> flows may be sensitive to changes in interest rate differences.

5. An expansionary monetary policy will lower interest rates and, depending on the <u>interest elasticity</u> of international capital, will induce capital outflows. A restrictive monetary policy will have the opposite effect.

6. A conflict of objectives may still exist if monetary policy is used in a situation of unemployment and a balance-of-payments deficit. A lower interest rate will stimulate GNP but also induce more imports and capital outflows.

7. Under a <u>fixed exchange rate</u> there is very little scope for the use of monetary policy for domestic stabilization purposes. An increase in the money supply (to reduce unemployment) causes capital outflows (depending on the interest elasticity) and this tends to reduce the domestic money supply. To counteract this reduction, the central bank must conduct <u>sterilization policies</u> which in this case means purchasing bonds.

8. Under a <u>flexible exchange rate</u>, fiscal policy will be offset by a <u>crowding-out</u> effect unless monetary policy accommodates the fiscal policy change. For example, increases in government expenditures, with a fixed money supply, cause interest rates to rise. Depending on the interest elasticity of investment, domestic investment will fall, thus negating the expansionary effect of the fiscal policy.

9. Under a flexible exchange rate, monetary policy is a powerful tool. If capital flows are highly interest elastic and monetary policy is expansionary, the interest rate decline stimulates domestic spending and also increases in imports and capital outflows, which

in turn cause a depreciation of the exchange rate. This depreciation stimulates exports and decreases imports.
10. A "dirty float" policy refers to government's policy of being officially on a flexible exchange rate but intervening substantially in the foreign-exchange market to influence exchange rate values.

## REVIEW QUESTIONS

1. A country on a fixed exchange-rate system, having a low income elasticity of its exports and a high income elasticity for imports, is likely to experience persistent trade _deficit_.

2. The competitive position of a country to trade internationally should be (increased/decreased/remain the same) if the domestic inflation rate is equal to that of other countries. The equilibrium value of the country's currency should therefore _not change_.

3. If the domestic rate of inflation is higher than the rate of inflation in the rest of the world, the demand for the domestic country's exports should _fall_ and the demand for imports should _increase_. Thus, a persistent and growing trade _deficit_ will result, causing an excess _supply_ of the country's currency in the foreign-exchange market. If the country is operating on a flexible (floating) exchange rate system, it should allow its currency to _depreciate_ continuously to restore a balance-of-payments equilibrium.

4. A country on a fixed exchange rate system and experiencing a persistent trade surplus might consider (devaluing/revaluing) its currency to restore the trade balance.

5. A current account deficit might be eliminated if the government _decrease_ its expenditures or _increase_ taxes. The quantitative effect of this policy will depend on the value of the _multiplier_ and the marginal propensity to _imports_.

6. The capital account of the balance of payments is primarily influenced by (monetary/fiscal) policy.

7. International capital flows, particularly short-term capital, are importantly determined by differentials in _interest rate_ among countries. An increase in the domestic interest rate, *ceteris paribus*, should _increase_ capital inflows to a country. Depending on the elasticity of capital to interest rates, a country should experience a _surplus_ position in its capital account.

8. A country experiencing unemployment and a balance-of-payments deficit should (increase/decrease) its interest rate to solve the balance-of-payments problem but runs the risk of (increasing/decreasing) its unemployment problem.

9. A country operating on a fixed exchange rate system and experiencing a balance-of-payments deficit must (sell/buy) its currency in the foreign-exchange market. This has the effect of _decreasing_ its domestic money supply by a multiple unless the central bank undertakes sterilization policies. _selling bonds_

10. Under a fixed exchange rate system, a country will be forced to keep its domestic interest rate (higher than/lower than/the same as) those existing in the rest of the world.

11. A country on a floating exchange rate is much more able to cope with cyclical variations in economic activity in other countries. If incomes in other countries fall, the country's exports will tend to _decrease_, causing its currency to _depreciate_. As this occurs, its exports should _increase_ and its imports should _decrease_.

12. Suppose a country on a flexible exchange rate which experiences a deflationary gap decides to _____*increase*_____ government expenditures to solve the gap problem. This new (injection/~~withdrawal~~) will (increase/~~decrease~~) income and hence cause its currency to _____*depreciate*_____ in the foreign-exchange market. As this occurs, imports will _____*decrease*_____ and exports will _____*increase*_____ which should help solve the gap problem.

13. However, the efficacy of fiscal policy under a flexible exchange rate is reduced because of the _____*crowding-out*_____ effect. Although an increase in government expenditures increases income it also increases the (demand for/~~supply of~~) money. With a constant supply of money, interest rates will _____*increase*_____, causing investment expenditures to _____*fall*_____ and international capital (inflows/~~outflows~~). These capital flows will tend to (increase/~~decrease~~) the foreign price of the domestic currency, thereby causing imports to _____*increase*_____ and exports to _____*decrease*_____.

14. The efficacy of monetary policy under a floating exchange rate system is (increased/~~deduced~~). An expansion of the money supply to reduce unemployment has the effect of _____*decreased*_____ the interest rate which in turn causes an (~~inflow~~/outflow) of international capital. The equilibrium foreign price of the country's currency should _____*depreciate*_____ in the foreign-exchange market, causing exports to rise and imports to fall.

---

If you have not answered all questions correctly, review the text in order to be sure that you have all of the important concepts clearly in mind before going on to the next chapter.

1. deficit  2. remain the same; not change  3. fall; rise; deficit; supply; depreciate
4. revaluing  5. decreased; increased; multiplier; import  6. monetary  7. interest rates; increase; surplus  8. increase; increasing  9. buy; decreasing  10. the same as  11. fall; depreciate; rise; fall  12. increase; injection; increase; depreciate; fall; rise  13. crowding-out; demand for; rise; fall; inflows; increase; rise; fall  14. increased; decreasing; outflow; depreciate

---

# MULTIPLE-CHOICE QUESTIONS

Questions 1 to 6 assume a fixed exchange rate system and questions 7 to 10 assume a floating exchange rate.)

1. To solve a balance-of-trade surplus, a country should
   (a) devalue its currency
   (b) reduce taxes, increase government expenditures
   (c) increase taxes, increase government expenditures
   (d) increase taxes, decrease government expenditures

2. A country experiencing unemployment and a balance-of-payments deficit may solve both problems by
   (a) increasing the money supply
   (b) decreasing the money supply
   (c) increasing taxes
   (d) decreasing taxes and decreasing the money supply

3. To solve a capital-account deficit, the central bank should
   (a) buy bonds in the open market
   (b) sell bonds in the open market
   (c) decrease the bank rate
   (d) increase taxes

4. A decrease in the domestic interest rate causes
   (a) capital outflows and income contraction
   (b) capital inflows and income expansion
   (c) capital outflows and a decrease in imports
   (d) capital outflows, investment increases, and import increases

5. To sterilize the monetary effects of a balance-of-payments deficit, the central bank should
   (a) revalue its currency in the foreign-exchange market
   (b) sell bonds in the open market
   (c) buy bonds in the open market
   (d) reduce bank reserves

6. If a government seeking to remove a deflationary gap should increase the money supply, it is likely that
   (a) the foreign price of its currency will depreciate
   (b) the foreign price of its currency will appreciate
   (c) interest rates will decline and cause capital outflows
   (d) imports will decline

7. If a country experiences domestic inflation and a balance-of-payments deficit, its central bank might
   (a) buy bonds
   (b) sell bonds
   (c) decrease the bank rate
   (d) revert to a fixed exchange rate and peg the foreign price of its currency below the free-market price

8. Assuming that international capital flows are very sensitive to interest rates and an inflationary gap situation, the government and its central bank should
   (a) increase government expenditures and increase the money supply
   (b) decrease taxes and increase the money supply
   (c) increase taxes and increase the money supply
   (d) increase taxes and decrease the money supply

9. Assuming capital flows are insensitive to interest rates, the domestic money supply is constant, and a deflationary gap, a government policy of decreasing taxes, will cause
   (a) income to rise, interest rates to fall, and a depreciation of its currency
   (b) some increase in income if the crowding-out effect is small and a depreciation of its currency
   (c) some increase in income if the crowding-out effect is small and an appreciation of its currency
   (d) income to rise, interest rates to fall, and an appreciation of its currency

10. Assuming capital flows are sensitive to interest rates, a contractionary fiscal policy which decreases income and the demand for money and thereby reduces the interest rate will
    (a) unambiguously cause an exchange rate appreciation
    (b) unambiguously cause an exchange rate depreciation
    (c) generate an ambiguous effect on the exchange rate
    (d) cause capital inflows and an increase in imports

---

Answers to multiple-choice questions: 1(d)   2(d)   3(b)   4(d)   5(c)   6(c)   7(b)   8(d)   9(b)
10(c)

---

# EXERCISES

1. Assume that Canada experiences a balance-of-payments deficit because of increased foreign oil imports. To pay the oil-producing countries, Canadians must obtain foreign exchange. Suppose that the amount of foreign exchange required in terms of Canadian dollars if $1 million.

Public:

| Assets | Liabilities |
|---|---|
| Foreign currency _____ | |
| Deposits _____ | |

Chartered Banks:

| Assets | Liabilities |
|---|---|
| Reserves with Bank of Canada _____ | Demand deposits _____ |

Bank of Canada:

| Assets | Liabilities |
|---|---|
| Foreign currency _____ | Chartered bank deposits _____ |

(a) Fill in the blanks in each of the three balance sheet.
(b) What do you predict will happen to the level of demand deposits in the banking system if the cash reserve ratio is .1?

2. Assume that a country operates on a fixed exchange rate system and the current foreign price of its currency happens to coincide with the free-market rate. Conditions in the economy change such that the domestic inflation is permanently greater than that in the rest of the world.

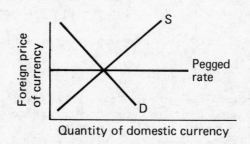

(a) Show the effects of the domestic inflation in the diagram and indicate the extent of the balance-of-payments disequilibrium.
(b) What type of monetary policy might the government pursue to eliminate the balance-of-payments disequilibrium? What implications does this policy have for the domestic inflation rate? The domestic unemployment rate?

(c) Suppose instead that the government allowed its currency to float in international exchange markets. What would happen to the foreign price of its currency? Its domestic inflation rate?

3. You are given the initial conditions existing in an economy which operates on a fixed exchange rate.

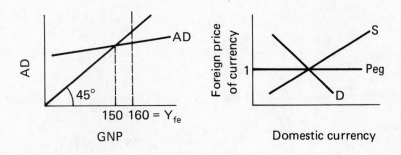

Other information includes:

Domestic inflation and foreign inflation are zero.
Domestic prices are constant for income levels less than full employment.
The tax multiplier is 1.5.
The expenditure multiplier is 2.0.
The marginal propensity to import is .2.
International capital flows are insensitive to interest rates.
Investment is insensitive to the interest rate.
The money supply in the economy is constant.

(a) What type of gap exists and what is its magnitude?

(b) What quantitative change in government expenditures might the government conduct to solve the gap problem? What tax policy might it pursue? *Hint:* These values hinge on the assumption that the interst rate remains constant.

(c) What type of budget policy do both policies in (b) imply?

(d) Suppose that the government financed the expenditure program in part (b) by selling new government bonds to the public. What would happen to the supply of money? The domestic interest rate?

(e) As a result of the expenditure program in part (b), what is the quantitative impact on the current account? The capital account? The balance of payments?

(f) What foreign-exchange transactions are necessitated?

(g) What implications do your answers in part (f) have for the domestic supply of money?

4. Assume the same initial conditions for the economy in question 3 except now assume that international capital flows are sensitive to interest rates. Reanswer parts (d), (e), (f), and (g).

# PROBLEM

## MR. COYNE AND THE EXCHANGE RATE

During the period between 1958 and 1961, a serious conflict of policies existed between the Bank of Canada and the federal government. The Diefenbaker government faced a serious unemployment problem. The unemployment rate was at a postwar high of about 6 to 7 percent during this period. On the other hand, even though the annual rate of increase in prices was less than 2 percent, Mr. Coyne, the Governor of the Bank of Canada, was worried about inflation, or perhaps future inflation. Hence, a basic difference in opinions existed.

Under Mr. Coyne's direction, the bank pursued an extremely tight money policy by allowing exceptionally small increases in the money supply and unusually large increases in the interest rate. The highest increase occurred during 1958 and 1959 as a result of the Conversion Loan, which induced holders of war bonds to hold new bonds at higher rates of interest. As a consequence, the Canadian—United States long-term bond differential increased significantly.

During this period, Canada had a flexible exchange rate with the rest of the world. During most of the period, the price of Canadian dollars rose steadily, selling at a premium relative to the American dollar. In addition, large surpluses on the capital account occurred.

The situation became completely untenable. The government dismissed Mr. Coyne in June 1961. Soon afterward, in his budget speech, the Minister of Finance announced in the Commons that the government felt the exchange rate was too high and intended to use the Exchange Fund to reduce it. The price of the dollar immediately crashed and the government was finally forced to peg the dollar at 92.5 U.S. cents in May 1962. It was not until 1970 that the dollar was freed again.

Questions

1. Why do you think Canada was receiving large amounts of capital inflows during 1958-1961?

2. Why do you think the price of Canadian dollars was rising steadily? Use a diagram in your analysis.

3. What effect would you predict on Canada's exports as a result of the increased price of Canadian dollars? Show this in your diagram in question 2.

4. What would you predict the effect to be on imports into Canada as a result of the increased price of Canadian dollars? Show this in your diagram in question 2.

5. If you had been an exchange-rate speculator in 1961, would you have bought or sold Canadian dollars after hearing the Minister of Finance's speech in the Commons? If all other speculators had acted like you, would this have corresponded with the fact that the Canadian dollar crashed downward between 1961 and 1962?

# Growth in Developed Economies

## KEY CONCEPTS AND DEFINITIONS

1. Investment has been a major cause of long-term <u>economic growth</u> by increasing the capital stock and hence increasing a nation's capacity to produce and its standard of living. Economic growth is often measured by using rates of change in potential real GNP per person or per man-hour.

2. The <u>cumulative effects</u> of a growth rate become large over periods of a generation or more. For example, after 50 years, a growth rate of 3% transforms potential real GNP from 100 to 448.

3. The benefits to growth are (1) to raise the general living standards of the population, (2) to make income redistribution easier, and (3) to increase a nation's national defense and prestige.

4. Growth, while often beneficial, is never costless. There can be substantial social and personal <u>costs of growth</u>. Industrialization, unless carefully managed, causes deterioration of the environment. Furthermore, rapid growth requires rapid adjustments, and these can cause upset and misery to the individuals affected.

5. The <u>opportunity cost of growth</u> is the diversion of resources from current consumption to capital formation. Many sectors of society may not wish to incur this sacrifice if they believe that they will not receive the benefits of growth.

6. The theory of economic growth involves understanding the concepts of the <u>utilization of existing investment opportunities</u> and the <u>creation of new investment opportunities</u>.

7. The nineteenth-century view of the growth process involved the utilization of existing investment opportunities. In formal terms, this is portrayed as a process of accumulating capital, increasing the <u>capital-output ratio</u>, and driving the <u>marginal efficiency of capital</u> down to the limit in which it is zero. The prospects for continual growth were therefore not optimistic.

8. Today most economists recognize that many investment opportunities can be created and attention is therefore given to sources of <u>outward shifts</u> in the <u>MEC</u> schedule.

9. Some of the factors that can cause the <u>MEC</u> schedule to shift outward are (1) innovation; (2) improvements in the quality of human capital (education, health); (3) the size of the population and the labor force; (4) social, religious, and legal institutions which are conducive to change and growth; and (5) international trade.

10. Some opponents of growth predict some future "doomsday" because of the complete exhaustion of natural resources given the growth of the world's population. These <u>doomsday</u> models assume (1) there is no technical progress; (2) no new resources are discovered or rendered usable by new techniques; (3) there is no substitution of more plentiful resources for those that become scarce.

| CHECKLIST | Make certain that you also understand the following concepts: embodied and dis-embodied technical change; "rule of 72." |
|---|---|

## REVIEW QUESTIONS

1. For economic growth to occur there must be an increase in the _____ of a nation. The quantity of total output that a nation can produce at full employment is called its _____ real GNP or national income.

2. For economic growth to result in an increase in the standard of living, total output must increase faster than _____. Thus to measure relative standards of living we divided _____ by _____.

3. The concept of the "growth rate" should be kept separate from the change in the percentage of _____ of capacity.

4. In order to measure changes in real potential income, it is necessary to use (constant/current) dollar figures.

5. To measure labor productivity we use output per _____. With more capital per worker and better trained workers, productivity will _____.

6. By the "rule of 72," a growth rate of 4 percent means that output will double itself in _____ years, if that rate continues.

7. Because investment is necessary for economic growth, an increased rate of economic growth will usually require an increased rate of _____; a reduction of current _____ will therefore be needed.

8. Economic growth is desirable for a developed country such as Canada, because it makes possible an easier _____ of income to the poor. However, growth has costs in using up scarce _____ more rapidly and in causing more damage to the _____.

9. Without any increase in knowledge or technology, the marginal efficiency of capital will _____ as the capital stock increases, and the ratio of capital to output will _____. New profit opportunities from new knowledge or technology will cause the *MEC* schedule to shift to the _____, in which case the ratio of capital to output may _____.

10. Nineteenth-century classical economists thought that investment opportunities would (expand/be used up) and therefore predicted (low/high) rates of return on capital and a (high/low) capital—output ratio.

11. In North America, with enormous growth in the amount of capital, the capital—output ratio over many decades has (risen/fallen/remained about constant). It is clear that not just the quantity but the _____ of productive resources has been important in economic growth.

12. The major threat to future standards of living in the world is from increases in _____ and _____, and from the exhaustion of _____.

13. The model that predicts approxiamte doomsday from these effects in three generations if growth is not sharply limited does not allow for changes in _____, _____, and _____.

If you have not answered all questions correctly, review the text in order to be sure that you have all of the important concepts clearly in mind before going on to the next chapter.

1. productive capacity; potential  2. population; output or income, population  3. utilization  4. constant  5. man-hour; rise  6. 18  7. investment; consumption  8. redistribution; resources, environment  9. fall, rise; right, fall  10. be used up, low, high  11. remained about constant; quality  12. population, pollution, resources  13. technology, supply of resources, prices and substitution

## MULTIPLE-CHOICE QUESTIONS

1. Economic growth can best be defined as
   (a) a rise in the GNP as unemployment is reduced
   (b) an increase in real income
   (c) a rise in potential real GNP per capita
   (d) an increase in investment and the capital stock

2. Economic growth has
   (a) characterized most of mankind's history
   (b) recently been most rapid in countries with the most rapidly increasing populations
   (c) been largely independent of social and legal patterns
   (d) been particularly characteristic of Western countries in the last two centuries

3. Output per man-hour increases as a result of
   (a) a rise in the labor force
   (b) a rise in total output
   (c) better machinery and training supplied to workers
   (d) an increase in the level of wages

4. The most important benefit of economic growth has been its role in
   (a) redistributing income among people
   (b) raising living standards
   (c) helping countries defend themselves
   (d) providing for the employment of scarce resources

5. An increase in the rate of economic growth
   (a) will usually require a reduction in consumption
   (b) will usually be encouraged by an increase in consumption
   (c) seems to be the result of increased investment alone
   (d) will be aided by high interest rates

6. Without technical change or new knowledge,
   (a) diminishing returns to additional investment will cause the capital—output ratio to rise
   (b) the marginal-efficiency-of-capital schedule will become horizontal
   (c) the shortage of investment will cause interest rates to rise
   (d) the marginal-efficiency-of-capital schedule will shift to the left

7. Classical theories of growth
   (a) predicted a declining return on capital
   (b) predicted an increasing return on capital
   (c) predicted a constant return on capital
   (d) had no prediction for the rate of return on capital

8. The major difference between the earlier classical theory of economic growth and the contemporary view is that
   (a) contemporary economists place much more importance on the quantity of labor than classical economists
   (b) classical economists ignored the role of capital accumulation
   (c) contemporary economists emphasize the creation of investment opportunities rather than simply the exploitation of existing opportunities
   (d) classical economists emphasized the role of international trade in economic growth

9. An *embodied* change is one that
   (a) improves the quality of labor
   (b) inheres in the form or nature of capital in use
   (c) is concerned with techniques of managerial control
   (d) is exogenous to the economic system

10. If, for a given state of technology and resource supplies, an increase in population causes a reduction in per capita income,
    (a) investment must have been decreasing
    (b) the optimal population has apparently been exceeded
    (c) labor productivity must have fallen
    (d) inflation is inevitable and will discourage further growth

11. Predictions of future trends based on present rates indicate eventual
    (a) rapidly rising worldwide per capita income
    (b) serious resource shortages from growing population and industrialization
    (c) reversal of damage to the environment with successful and increasing efforts
    (d) leveling off of world population at about 8 billion people

12. The text concludes that the predictions of the doomsday models
    (a) have proved totally incorrect and should be ignored
    (b) were correct until the early 1900s but are now incorrect because of technological change
    (c) place too much weight on a gradual reduction in the rate of population growth to be valid in the present world
    (d) may be avoidable in the future with technological advances, but the problem of timing is crucial

---

Answers to multiple-choice questions: 1(c)   2(d)   3(c)   4(b)   5(a)   6(a)   7(a)   8(c)   9(b)
10(b)   11(b)   12(d)

---

# EXERCISES

1. Assume that the productivity of labor increases by 2.5 percent a year, the labor force increases by 1.75 percent a year, hours worked per member of the work force decline by .25 a year, and population increases by 1 percent a year. Predict:
   (a) The annual increase in real GNP




   (b) The annual increase in output per capita

(c) The number of years to double real GNP

(d) The number of years to double output per capita

2. Explain how each of the following factors would affect per capita GNP, *ceteris paribus*.
   (a) An increase in population

   (b) An increase in current consumption

   (c) A technological innovation

   (d) An increase in current expenditures for education

   (e) An increase in capital stock

   (f) A decrease in the working span of the labor force

# PROBLEM

## POT EQUALS POLLUTION

The title for this problem suggests a simple framework for considering aspects of the growth controversy. P is taken as population, O as output per capita, and T as a technological variable to express how polluting are the methods used to produce or consume output. Pollution can be thought of as that of a particular type (such as sulfur dioxide in air, oxygen-consuming waste in water, solid waste) or more generally as a weighted index of all types of pollution, which of course would constitute a formidable measurement problem.

P, O, and T could all be expressed as having values of 1 in some base year plus a percentage addition to represent the annual growth rate. Thus pollution at the end of $n$ years could be expressed as follows, for an economy in which the annual population growth was 1 percent, output per capita increased annually by 3 percent, and technology in respect to pollution was unchanging:

pollution $= (1.01)^n (1.03)^n (1.00)^n$

This formulation implies that pollution increases proportionally with the increase in total output (P × O) if technology is unchanging. This is not necessarily true. For example, much of the particulate matter in the air comes from volcanic discharges, so that a doubling of man-made output would less than double this form of pollution. On the other hand, because rivers have some natural cleansing powers, a doubling of output could more than double the level of oxygen-consuming discharges into rivers. A simple way out of this problem is to think of T as including the effect of these nonproportionalities.

In the formulation above, pollution would increase 16-fold in 72 years. (You should use the "rule of 72," which states that the doubling time is equal to 72 divided by the annual rate of growth.)

## Questions

1. The annual population increase of 1 percent and per capita output increase of 3 percent are assumptions better suited to developed countries. Assume that 2 percent increases in each are appropriate for the world as a whole. Does this change the projection for pollution over 72 years as made above?

2. What assumption in either of these formulations of the model puts it in the "doomsday" class? What value would the T term have to have to prevent an increase in pollution?

3. Consider how these following interrelationships or developments would influence the variables above and thus the eventual projections for pollution:
   (a) A return to the use of returnable bottles, with significant savings in the energy now used to make nonreturnable bottles, steel cans, and (in particular) aluminum cans

   (b) An increased death rate from respiratory diseases in infants and the elderly, associated with increased air pollution

   (c) The commitment of a $10 billion investment in pollution control facilities to achieve water standards (assume that this also decreases investment funds available for increasing output)

   (d) The reduced death rate following initial increases in output for a very poor country

(e) The reduced birth rate in a country well on its way to development

4. The POT formulation does not incorporate prospective or actual famine. How might economies attempt to adjust to these threats in ways that might reduce the pollution threat? In ways that might increase it?

# 42

# Growth and the Underdeveloped Economies

## Key Concepts and Definitions

1. Economic growth is highly uneven in the world. About two-thirds of the world's population still exist at a level of bare subsistence. The development gap, the discrepancy between the standards of living in countries at the two ends of the world income distribution, is very large.
2. Income per head may serve as a rough index of the level of economic development. The barriers to economic development are (1) a high rate of population increase; (2) resource limitations including financial, social, and human capital; and (3) inefficiency in the use of existing resources.
3. There are two kinds of inefficiency. Using society's resources to make the wrong products is an example of allocative inefficiency. In terms of the production-possibility boundary, allocative inefficiency represents operation at the wrong place on the boundary. X-inefficiency arises whenever resources are used in such a way that even if they are making the right product, they are doing so less productively than is possible. Recent research suggests X-inefficiency may be of major importance in accounting for low incomes and a slow rate of growth.
4. X-inefficiency can be the product of inadequate education, poor health, cultural attitudes, or ignorance. Consequently, adopting techniques used in more-developed countries may prove disappointingly unproductive in less-developed countries.
5. Economic development policy involves identifying the particular barriers to the level and kind of desired development and then devising policies to overcome them. One of the key considerations in the development strategy is how much government control over the economy is necessary and desirable.
6. The active intervention of the government in the economy rests upon the real or alleged failure of market forces to produce satisfactory results. The major appeal of such intervention is that it can accelerate the pace of economic development and change its direction.
7. Educational policy and population control, although important to long-run economic growth, yield benefits only in the future. As a result they frequently are bypassed in search of more immediate results.
8. A country has three sources of funds for investment: (1) from domestic savings, (2) bu loans or investment from abroad, and (3) by contributions from foreigners.
9. A vicious circle of poverty exists in most developing countries, thereby preventing domestic savings as a viable source of funds. A country is poor because it lacks capital and it cannot forgo consumption to accumulate capital because it is poor.

10. Selecting a pattern of development poses difficult choices. A <u>balanced growth policy</u> involves expanding all sectors of the economy. Another choice is <u>unbalanced growth</u> which pushes specialization in only certain areas.
11. The <u>theory of comparative advantage</u> provides the traditional case for unbalanced growth. However, there are important reasons for not pushing specialization too far, including the risks of fluctuations or declines in the demand for a country's principal products and the dependence on foreign trade.
12. Much of the current debate about development involves the importance given to (1) agricultural development versus industrialization, (2) reduction of dependence on foreign trade by development of <u>import substitution</u> industries, and (3) development of an industrial capacity that will create new export industries.

# Review Questions

1. The typical although not completely adequate figure used to compare relative living standards among countries is _____.

2. If a country's national output grows by 2 percent per year and its population grows by 3 percent per year, per capita income (rises/falls/is not affected).

3. The population explosion in the underdeveloped countries, as in developed ones, has been caused by a (rise/fall) in (birth/death) rates.

4. To raise the level of incomes, it is necessary to increase productive capacity, which requires increased _____.

5. In order to raise per capita income by $100, a country with a population of 10 million people and a capital-output ratio of 3:1 will need an investment of $_____.

6. Savings of the public in underdeveloped countries are often not made available for investment because of an inadequate _____ system.

7. Roads and transportation and communications systems are vital to development and are often referred to as _____ capital.

8. Human capital in underdeveloped countries may be inadequate in several ways for successful economic growth. List three: _____
_____.
This can be a source of what the text calls _____-inefficiency in production.

9. Using resources for a high-cost steel plant instead of buying cheaper steel abroad is an example of _____ efficiency.

10. Underdeveloped countries using the same technology as developed countries have been shown to achieve (lower/higher) levels of productivity, due to cultural differences; this effect is called the _____ gap.

11. A country that wants more rapid economic growth and in a certain direction will probably need to use (market forces/centralized planning). The governments of the Soviet Union and China forced their people to consume less and thus achieved increased _____ and _____.

12. In putting greater effort into education for economic development, a country has to choose between two general approaches: _____ and _____.

13. An underdeveloped country is typically short of investment capital because of insufficient domestic _____. Another source of capital is _____. This source requires (less/greater) immediate sacrifice than does accumulation through domestic saving, but costs (more/less) later.

14. A country that imports capital must sooner or later increase its _____ to pay for it.

15. An underdeveloped country with few resources and too much population will have trouble borrowing from private sources abroad because of _____.

16. A country following the principle of comparative advantage in its development will tend to follow a path of (balanced/unbalanced) growth. But too much specialization may be risky for a country if what occurs? _____

17. A developing country has a choice of three alternative strategies, or a combination of them: (a) agricultural development, (b) _____, and (c) industrialization for export.

18. Although the food needs of the rapidly expanding populations of the underdeveloped countries will require them to improve their agricultural output, there are two major difficulties with this approach: (a) if all countries do it, prices will _____, in the short run at least, so that the value of their exports will _____; and (b) mechanized modern farming methods result in (greater/less) unemployment.

19. In countries with much underemployment, production techniques of a (labor-saving/labor-intensive) type are apt to be more economically efficient.

20. The strategy of import substitution usually means (higher/lower) costs of production of goods at home and necessitates keeping out imports by means of _____.

21. The most serious single obstacle in the long run to higher standards of living in the underdeveloped countries is probably _____. Many social scientists feel that programs of _____ are therefore of greatest urgency.

---

If you have not answered all questions correctly, review the text in order to be sure that you have all of the important concepts clearly in mind before going on to the next chapter.

1. GNP per capita  2. falls  3. fall; death  4. investment  5. $3 billion  6. banking  7. social overhead  8. no entrepreneurship, poor health, low educational levels, traditional attitudes; X  9. allocative  10. lower, technology  11. centralized planning; savings; investment, or investment, growth  12. education for the masses, higher education for a few  13. savings; foreign borrowing; less, more  14. exports  15. low profit possibilities, risk  16. unbalanced; changes in tastes or technology, fall in demand  17. import substitution  18. fall, fall, greater  19. labor-intensive  20. higher; tariffs and quotas  21. too rapid population growth; birth control

---

# MULTIPLE-CHOICE QUESTIONS

1. We might define an underdeveloped country as
   (a) one with a per capita national income of less than $500
   (b) one with substantial quantities of undeveloped resources
   (c) one with a low amount of capital per head
   (d) any of the above

2. In choosing between building a steel industry and investing more in education, an under-developed country
   (a) will be better off with the industry so that it can get cheaper steel
   (b) will probably get greater returns in the long run from more education
   (c) will get immediate short-run returns from education
   (d) finds all of the above true

3. When deciding whether growth should be financed by imported capital or domestic savings, an underdeveloped country's leaders
   (a) should realize that finance by savings will yield a greater return later on
   (b) should realize that finance by imported borrowed capital will require less financial sacrifice now but more later
   (c) might want to consider noneconomic consequences of each method
   (d) find all of the above true

4. Medical advances in an underdeveloped country
   (a) increase per capita income
   (b) increase the rate of population growth
   (c) are very expensive to bring about
   (d) have been self-defeating because the death rate from famine has risen equivalently

5. Among the arguments for unbalanced growth are that
   (a) it will insulate the economy from the vagaries of foreign trade
   (b) it will enable the citizens of that country to exercise a wide variety of talents in their work
   (c) it will lead to more rapid growth
   (d) diversification is always more expensive in the long run

6. Developing countries often have balance-of-payments problems because
   (a) as income rises, imports often rise even more rapidly
   (b) most of their exports are primary commodities with low elasticities of demand
   (c) most of their machinery must be imported
   (d) all of the above

7. It is usually important that developing countries improve their agricultural output because
   (a) agricultural surpluses will be needed to feed a growing industrial population
   (b) population is apt to be growing rapidly
   (c) agricultural products may be exported to help pay for needed imports
   (d) all of the above

8. A possible obstacle to scientific agriculture in the underdeveloped countries is likely to be
   (a) too-small peasant plots or large feudal-type estates
   (b) inadequate capital
   (c) a preference for traditional ways
   (d) all of the above

Answers to multiple-choice questions: 1(d)  2(b)  3(d)  4(b)  5(c)  6(d)  7(d)  8(d)

# EXERCISES

1. Why may the gap between the rich and poor countries grow larger, even if both have the same rate of growth? Consider the following example.

|  | Country A | Country B | Difference |
|---|---|---|---|
| Year X, GNP per capita | $2,000 | $100 | _____ |
| Annual rate of per capita growth | 3% | 3% | _____ |
| Year X + 1, real GNP per capita | _____ | _____ | _____ |
| Year X + 23, real GNP per capita | _____ | _____ | _____ |

Use the "rule of 72," recognizing that, for continuous compounding, as in population growth, the doubling time is more nearly the number 69 divided by the annual rate.

2. Use the "rule of 72" for the following (assume annual compounding):
   (a) If real GNP is rising at a steady rate of 4 percent, it will be doubled in how many years? _____ If the population is rising steadily at 3 percent per year, it will double itself in how many years? _____ In how many years, then, will real GNP per capita be doubled in this example? _____
   (b) It is predicted that at current rates of increase the population of the underdeveloped countries (the "third world") will double itself by the year 1996. What must be the approximate annual rate of increase in population in these countries? _____ (The prediction was made in 1971.)

# PROBLEM

## PRODUCTION POSSIBILITIES, EFFICIENCY, AND DEVELOPMENT

Suppose that there are two countries, A and B, both of which are underdeveloped in terms of advanced country standards. Both countries have $x$ units of working labor and $y$ units of land but very little capital. Country A has a population of 8 and country B has a population of 10. Assume that either country produces and consumes only wheat and peanuts. The production possibilities are given in the schedules below and on the next page.

| Country A | | Country B | |
|---|---|---|---|
| Wheat (bushels) | Peanuts (pounds) | Wheat (bushels) | Peanuts (pounds) |
| 100 | 0 | 200 | 0 |
| 90 | 10 | 180 | 18 |
| 80 | 19 | 160 | 35 |
| 70 | 17 | 140 | 51 |
| 60 | 34 | 120 | 66 |
| 50 | 40 | 100 | 80 |
| 40 | 45 | 80 | 93 |
| 30 | 49 | 60 | 105 |
| 20 | 52 | 40 | 116 |
| 10 | 54 | 20 | 126 |
| 0 | 55 | 0 | 135 |

## Questions

1. Plot the schedules on the diagram on the next page. To obtain successive increases in wheat production, what is happening to the rate of loss in peanut production in country A? Country B? What can therefore be said about the change in opportunity costs?

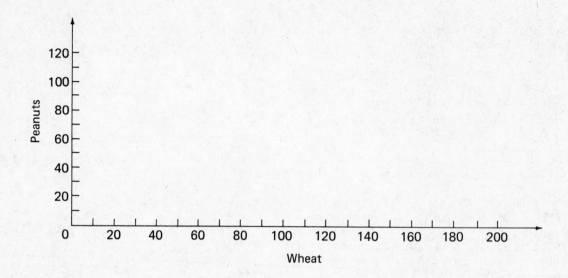

2. Suppose that production and consumption in country A are 16 pounds of peanuts and 80 bushels of wheat and in country B are 160 bushels of wheat and 35 pounds of peanuts. Does production inefficiency exist in either country? What type?

3. If wheat is worth 2 U.S. dollars per bushel and peanuts are worth .5 U.S. dollar per pound, what is the value of GNP in each country in terms of U.S. dollars? What is the per capita level of GNP in each country?

4. Give some reasons why country B is more technically efficient than country A.

5. What type of foreign aid could Canada give to country A to increase its per capita income? How would this affect the production-possibility schedule?

# 43

# Comparative Economic Systems

## KEY CONCEPTS AND DEFINITIONS

1. There are several economic systems in the world today—not just the three that are commonly identified: capitalism, socialism, and communism.

2. Among the important differences among economies are (1) the pattern of ownership of goods and resources; (2) the nature of the decision process used ("market" versus "command" mechanisms); (3) whose values control the economy and how these values are articulated; (4) the nature of the incentive systems used (monetary versus ordered, coercion, or fear); (5) the relative concern about ends (goals) and means (the process of achieving the goals).

3. Central planning plays a major role in the Soviet economy. Long-term goals are given structure by a series of five-year plans, which in turn are implemented by detailed one-year plans. Most of the key decisions are made centrally by the various GOSPLANs (the regional planning agencies), but prices are used both for internal accounting and for the distribution of goods and incomes.

4. Both the nature and the quantity of the goods to be produced are specified by the central planners in the Soviet Union. Consumer goods are sold at government-specified prices that include a turnover tax. Consumers are therefore allowed to buy goods based upon their preferences, a type of market mechanism. However, strong consumer demand for a particular good does not necessarily influence its price and does not call forth an increase in supply from producers.

5. Consumer prices are comprised of two parts: the full cost of resources plus a turnover tax. This is in the form of an excise tax. The size of the turnover tax is determined by planners' ideas of what goods people should be encouraged or discouraged to consume. Goods consumed by low-income groups may have low turnover taxes. Furthermore, the revenue from this tax is used by the state for making new investment.

6. The Yugoslavian economy represents a socialist market-type economy. The state owns the means of production but uses markets to allocate resources. The Yugoslavs sought to avoid three features of the Soviet experience: (1) the inefficiencies in agricultural production, (2) micro inefficiencies in industrial production, and (3) the burden of a large planning operation.

7. As a result, the Yugoslavian economy differs from the Soviet economy by: (1) decollectivity of the agricultural sector (personal ownership of farms if allowed); (2) allowing labor-managed enterprises (workers have authority of the firm's decisions), (3) decentralizing the management of industrial firms. However, the central planners still play the major role in determining investment decisions.

> CHECKLIST  Make certain that you also understand the following concepts: market system; command system; incentive systems; GOSBANK.

## REVIEW QUESTIONS

1. All economic systems face the basic problem of _____ and the questions of how and what to _____.

2. An economic system where the natural resources and means of production are mostly privately owned is known as a _____ system. An economic system where productive assets are predominantly publicly owned is known as a _____ system.

3. We distinguish between an economic system of the market type and one of the _____ type, in which decision making is (centralized/decentralized).

4. For predicting market behavior, not only the question of ownership of means of production but also that of motives behind decisions is important to an economist. Publicly owned firms (may/will not) have profit motives to guide them—they (may/will not) respond to consumer preferences as do private firms.

5. Incentives for work and production are important (only in capitalist/in all types of) systems.

6. The people of underdeveloped countries are apt to be (more/less) concerned about political and economic freedom than about raising their standards of living.

7. Agriculture in the Soviet Union uses about _____ percent of the labor force. State-owned and collective farms produce (all/about two-thirds) of the agricultural output of the Soviet Union; the rest is from private plots. Soviet farm prices and wages have been set at (high/low) levels; compulsion in this sector (has/has not) resulted in high agricultural activity.

8. Managers of firms in the Soviet Union are given (orders/much latitude) about what and how much to produce. In trying to fulfill assigned quotas of output, emphasis is apt to be on (quantity/quality). Wage rates are determined by the (firm/worker/central authorities). Prices are set by the (firm/government/consumer). Centralized direction of output, prices, and wages seems to be economically (more/less) efficient than in a decentralized system; surpluses, shortages, and low quality seem (more/less) common under the former.

9. Russian consumers have (a choice/no choice) of what they buy; however, in the past their demands (determined/did not much affect) prices or what was produced. Soviet planners (are/are not) now becoming more interested in satisfying consumers, partly because it is (now possible/not possible) to produce greater quantities of consumer goods. These subsidized services and the fact that incomes from property are limited contribute to a (more equal/less equal) distribution of income in Russia compared with the United States.

10. Wage and salary differentials in Russia are (not large/much larger than in North America). Medical care and higher education are (free/very expensive) in Russia. Rents for housing are (low/high) and housing is (scarce/plentiful).

11. Successive five-year plans in Russia emphasized (welfare/growth) and therefore concentrated on (consumer/capital) goods. Until recently, scarce capital was used inefficiently because it had (no cost/high cost) in terms of an interest rate.

12. The detailed individual program for production and production requirements of each industry is contained in the (five-year/one-year) plan.

13. The Soviet Union (uses/does not use) a price mechanism to influence consumption. A tax called a _____ tax is imposed on goods; it is frequently (high/low) on luxuries and (high/low) on necessities. Turnover taxes are a way of forcing the people to save and thus provide funds to the state for _____.

14. It is estimated that Soviet real purchasing power per capita is (about equal to/about half of) that of the United States at present. In the postwar period, Soviet rate of growth has been (about equal/about double) that of the United States.

15. Unemployment in the Soviet Union has been caused by (deficient demand/structural changes). The government has (prevented/not been able to prevent) surplus farm labor from moving to the cities.

16. The Soviet central authorities have (total/partial) control over the supply of money through the central bank, called the _____. The commercial banks are (separate from/branches of) the central bank.

17. The Soviet government handled the problem of postwar excess demand by (allowing inflation/confiscating money balances).

18. Two major drawbacks to the Soviet system, as outlined in the text, have been microeconomic _____ and excessive absorption of manpower in the _____ function.

19. The text describes Yugoslavia as a _____ economy. The means of production are owned by _____. The amounts of production and employment in each firm are decided by _____. Marginal cost concepts and certain microeconomic principles are (observed/ignored); resource allocation is probably (more/less) efficient than in the Soviet Union.

20. Management of Yugoslavian firms is (appointed by the state/elected by the workers). Profits go to (the state/the workers) or are reinvested. Incentives for efficient production are thus (high/low).

21. Tendencies toward monopolistic practices by firms in Yugoslavia are (very common/very rare) because of the (ease/difficulty) of organizing new firms.

22. Yugoslavia has been (reducing/increasing) the collectivization of agriculture. Individual farmers produce what they (want/are told).

23. Planning and five-year plans are (sometimes/never/always) used by nonsocialist countries. Implementation of five-year plans is made more effective in Yugoslavia than in nonsocialist countries by the fact that two-thirds of all investment is undertaken by _____.

24. It is (possible/not possible) to claim that one type of economic system is better than all others.

---

If you have not answered all questions correctly, review the text in order to be sure that you have all of the important concepts clearly in mind.

1. scarcity, produce  2. capitalist; socialist  3. command; centralized  4. may, may  5. in all types of  6. less  7. 40; about two-thirds; low, has not  8. orders; quantity; central authorities; government; less, more  9. a choice, did not much affect; are, now possible; more equal  10. much larger than in North America; free; low, scarce  11. growth, capital; no cost  12. one-year  13. uses; turnover, high, low; investment capital  14. about half of; about double; rapidly  14. structural changes; prevented  16. total, GOSBANK, branches of  17. confiscating money balances  18. inefficiencies, planning  19. socialist-market; the state; the state; the firm; observed, more  20. elected by the workers; the workers; high  21. very common, difficulty  22. reducing; want  23. sometimes, the state  24. not possible

# MULTIPLE-CHOICE QUESTIONS

1. All types of economic systems can be said to
   (a) operate for private profit primarily
   (b) operate to favor a wealthy few
   (c) reward only the hard worker
   (d) face the basic problem of scarcity relative to wants

2. All types of economic systems must
   (a) have a mechanism for making choices about production
   (b) have a price system that is flexible and responsive to demand
   (c) do away with large fortunes and inherited wealth if economic growth is desired
   (d) have centralized planning or nothing gets done

3. The ownership and operation by Canada of a major railroad network
   (a) means that Canada is a socialist country
   (b) guarantees better service than if the railroad were privately owned
   (c) is an example of the mixed type of economy so common in the world
   (d) is very unusual among Western capitalist countries

4. The Soviet Union achieved rapid growth since 1928 primarily by
   (a) borrowing capital from other countries
   (b) putting everybody to work efficiently
   (c) investing heavily from tax receipts and suppressing consumption
   (d) centralized, efficient planning that eliminated surpluses and shortages

5. By definition, socialism means
   (a) centralized planning and control of all production
   (b) state ownership of most of the means of production
   (c) no freedom of choice of occupation
   (d) to each according to his need, from each according to his ability

6. It is probably fair to say of the standard of living in the Soviet Union that
   (a) it is much higher than it used to be
   (b) it is as high as that of the United States, but different
   (c) it is about 25 percent of that of the United States
   (d) it has been increased by the large amounts of expenditures on armaments and space exploration

7. The five-year plan is used in the Soviet Union
   (a) to indicate what and how much each firm will produce
   (b) to establish general guidelines for growth and priorities
   (c) to enforce rigid quotas and targets for each industry
   (d) only as window dressing to be ignored in practice

8. Which of the following is *not* true of the price system in the Soviet Union?
   (a) Some prices of agricultural produce from private plots are set by supply and demand.
   (b) Wage rates recognize the need for incentives to induce greater output.
   (c) Prices contain high or low taxes deliberately to influence consumption.
   (d) Prices fluctuate frequently to reflect market conditions.

9. Turnover taxes in the Soviet Union are
   (a) used contracyclically to affect aggregate demand
   (b) used as direct anti-inflationary measures
   (c) the source of much of the investment capital for the economy
   (d) more regressive than a general sales tax

10. It is believed that (at least in the past) capital was used inefficiently in the Soviet
    Union because
    (a) it was so scarce
    (b) their engineers were so poorly trained
    (c) interest rates were set too high
    (d) the cost of capital was not recognized

11. Profits—that is, revenue exceeding cost—in the Soviet Union
    (a) are divided up by the workers
    (b) are partly used for investment
    (c) are forbidden by law
    (d) cannot exist, since production is not for profit

12. The Yugoslav economic system differs from that of the Soviet Union in that
    (a) most workers can choose their occupation
    (b) profits are permitted
    (c) the workers choose their plant management, and the plant determines its own output
    (d) prices are generally determined in free markets

13. The least serious of the following problems for a socialist, command type of system is
    probably
    (a) economic depression
    (b) economic growth
    (c) inflation
    (d) efficient production and distribution

---

Answers to multiple-choice questions: 1(d)   2(a)   3(c)   4(c)   5(b)   6(a)   7(b)   8(d)   9(c)
10(d)   11(b)   12(c)   13(a)

---

# EXERCISE

Compare how the economies of Canada and the Soviet Union would achieve each of the following
results:
   (a) Avoid a shortage of automobiles

   (b) Increase the rate of economic growth

   (c) Produce more beer and less soft drinks

   (d) Redistribute income from rich to poor

# Problem

## COMPARISON OF THE UNITED STATES
## AND THE SOVIET UNION

The Joint Economic Committee of the Congress of the United States had studies prepared on "Economic Indicators in the U.S.S.R." (1964) and "New Directions in the Soviet Economy" (1966). Many of the figures are estimates and may not directly be counterparts of those for the United States, but the quality is good enough for making hypotheses about the differences in the economy they reveal.

You are asked, for each pair of figures below, to hypothesize whether the comparison simply indicates that the United States is more economically advanced than Russia, whether it indicates some difference in the priorities of the two countries, or whether it reflects the differences in operations of a primarily private enterprise versus a centralized economy with most industry nationalized. More than one of these categories may be involved.

| | U.S.S.R. | U.S. | Hypothesis |
|---|---|---|---|
| 1. Consumption of electricity per production worker (kwh, 1962) | 11,492 | 28,771 | |
| 2. Hydro capacity as a percentage of total electric generating capacity | | | |
| 1940 | 14 | 24 | |
| 1962 | 20 | 18 | |
| 3. Percentage of intercity passenger traffic that travels | | | |
| by rail | 79.3 | 2.5 | |
| by air | 8.5 | 4.7 | |
| 4. Number of tractors per 1,000 acres of harvested cropland | | | |
| 1940 | 1.43 | 4.37 | |
| 1962 | 2.49 | 15.90 | |
| 5. GNP per unit of fixed capital stock (index). For United States second figure is for potential GNP. | | | |
| 1940 | 100 | 100 | |
| 1962 | 61 | 137, 125 | |
| 6. Estimated automobile stock (millions—1964) | 1 | 70 | |
| 7. Industrial output per employee (1962) | $3,531 | $10,100 | |
| 8. Per capita figures, 1962 (1961 dollars) | | | |
| Investment | $  486 | $   480 | |
| Defense | 192 | 300 | |
| Consumption | 372 | 1,889 | |
| GNP | 1,158 | 3,004 | |
| 9. Annual growth in GNP per capita (1950-1962) | ≈4.3% | ≈1.7% | |

# solutions to exercises and problems in this study guide

## CHAPTER 1

### EXERCISES

1. (1) What goods and services are being produced and in what quantities?
   (2) By what methods are these goods produced?
   (3) How is the supply of goods allocated among the members of the society?
   (4) Are the country's resources being fully utilized, or are some of them lying idle and thus going to waste?
   (5) Is the purchasing power of people's money and savings constant, or is it being eroded by inflation?
   (6) Is the economy's capacity to produce goods growing or remaining the same over time?
   (a) 1  (b) 2  (c) 4  (d) 3  (e) 6  (f) 5  (g) 1  (h) 2

2. (b) yes  (c) no  (d) approximately 3300 bushels of corn  (e) underutilized  (f) increase in the productivity of land or the reclaim of presently nonarable land

### PROBLEM

1. Opportunity cost.
2. The cost of abatement is being measured specifically in dollar terms and in terms of the forgone or potentially forgone programs of health and education. Thus, to achieve pollution abatement, Canada would have less education and health than would otherwise be the case, assuming taxes are not to increase.

3.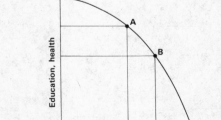

A move from A to B implies more pollution abatement.

4.

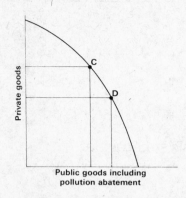

A move from C to D indicates more pollution abatement while not reducing other public goods since the abatement is financed by higher taxes or lower levels of private consumption.

5. The fallacy is simply that pollution abatement is an industry itself. It will create a demand for labor and capital like other industries. The output from the "industry" would be cleaner air and water.

# CHAPTER 2

## EXERCISE

(a) There is an inverse relationship between the percentage change in housing starts and the change in the mortgage rate of interest.
(b) Yes; using the data to plot a scatter diagram, you could examine changes in the two variables to see if they support the hypothesis.

## PROBLEM

1. (a) P  (b) N  (c) N  (d) N  (e) P  (f) P
2. Both parts (a) and (b) could lead to a variety of answers, so only examples of what was intended will be given. For positive statement, data on changes in price indexes and changes in unit labor costs could be correlated to determine the strength and probability of this tendency (see Chapter 3). The normative statement (c) value judgments could include a strong feeling of empathy for those who suffer from inflation the most, a desire for more certainty in the business world and a wish to maintain the real value of savings. Value judgments are sometimes reached by making assumptions about the world that can be tested.

# CHAPTER 3

## EXERCISES

1. (b) 1.5  (c) $Y$ is the variable that *determines* the value of $X$.
2. $S = \$100$; $-50$, $0$; $50$; $100$
3. (a) $S = .07Y$  (b) $C = 1,000 + .95Y$  (c) $c = C/Q$  (d) $R = PQ$  (e) $\Pi = R - C$
4. (a) directly  (b) inversely  (c) directly  (d) directly  (e) directly
5. (a) $TC = 500 + 0.10N$.
   (b) The fixed-cost graph is a horizontal line at 500, whereas the cleanup-cost line would start at the origin and slope upward to the right with a slope of .10.

## PROBLEM 1

3. The slope is roughly 0.90, give or take a little.
4. Since the points on the scatter diagram cluster around the line fitted through these points, the fit is reasonably good.

...n this information, accept the hypothesis with the reservation, perhaps, ...e other variables, similar to disposable income, that also incluence

...t a curved (nonlinear) line would more adequately represent the rela-
...two variables.
...ng.
...ill be to accept the hypothesis.

...b) extreme left blank    (c) third blank from left    (d) same as (c)

| ...loyment |
| --- |
| down |
| up |
| down |
| down |

1. (a) Equilibrium price = $0.60
      Equilibrium quantity = 12 units

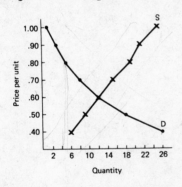

   (b) Column (4): -24, -18, -7, 0, +9, +20
       At equilibrium, excess demand = 0 = excess supply.
   (c) Excess demand: Price will rise because of the competition (demand) for a limited number
       of goods.
       Excess supply: Price will fall as producers attempt to sell accumulated inventories.

2.

| | D | S | P | Q |
| --- | --- | --- | --- | --- |
| 1 | 0 | - | + | - |
| 2 | + | 0 | + | + |
| 3 | + | 0 | + | + |
| 4 | + | + | U | + |
| 5 | - | 0 | - | - |
| 6 | 0 | - | + | - |

## PROBLEM 1

1. (a) The proportion of income spent on such necessities as goods can be predicted to decrease as real income increases.
   (b) During the war and shortly after, food purchases were rationed. As these rations were removed, people could purchase foods denied them during the war years.
2. Constant; eggs and potatoes.
3. As incomes rise, people may be inclined to substitute higher-priced protein goods for the lower-cost fat content goods. Beef would appear to be a good example of this. The decline in pork consumption may reflect that, although incomes have gone up, the very substantial price in pork may have deterred consumption of this product.

## PROBLEM 2

The acceptance of U.S. wines would result in a decline in the demand for French wines and a fall in price. The excellent grape crop in 1973-1974 would cause an increase in the amount (supply) available and so tend to reduce price.

## PROBLEM 3

1. Consumers would quickly switch away from Middle East oil to Canadian oil.
2. As a result of (1), the price of Canadian oil would rise and Middle East oil fall.

# CHAPTER 6

## EXERCISES

1. (a) down  (b) none  (c) 1  (d) down  (e) up
2. (a) (i) 2.0  (ii) 0.26  (iii) 1.00
   (b) Elasticity exceeding unity corresponds to a rise in revenue, less than unity with a fall in revenue, equal to unity with constant revenue.
   (c) The new elasticity is 1.14.
   (d) $Q = 12 - P$
3. $Q = 1,840,000, 4,270,000$; elasticity = 1.52.
4. (a) That it was elastic
   (b) If $TR$ went up with a fall in $P$, it would be elastic.
   (c) They would be cheaper as demand falls.

## PROBLEM 1

1. The expected elasticity was zero; that is, consumption would remain unchanged and the dollar expenditure would therefore double.
2. The formula for elasticity:

$$\frac{\dfrac{Q_2 - Q_1}{(Q_1 + Q_2)/2}}{\dfrac{P_2 - P_1}{(P_1 + P_2)/2}} = e$$

   We do not know the new level of water consumption but we do know that the revenue has gone from $2 × 200,000 gal = $400,000 to $600,000 with the new price of $4 per 100 gallons. Thus the new level of consumption is 150,000 gallons. Substitution in the formula gives an elasticity of .43.
3. Not necessarily. If 150,000 gallons was a minimum amount of water consumption that households would tolerate, then the elasticity would be zero for an additional rate increase.

# PROBLEM 2

1. The price elasticities of demand for education are .35 and .69, respectively, which suggest that they are relatively inelastic.
2. Most likely the taxpayers of the state of Wisconsin.

# CHAPTER 7

## EXERCISES

1. (a) $8,000,000  (b) 2,000,000  (c) 2,000,000; $4,000,000  (d) 3,000,000; $1,50 or
      a little less
2. (a) Revenue would decrease substantially with rightward shift of supply.
   (b) Revenue would increase substantially with rightward shift of demand; this shift, if
       if occurs more rapidly than the supply shift, threatens mass famine.
3. (a) The stock should eventually increase. The higher rent will induce developers and
       builders to construct more units.
   (b) Supplt would have to increase such that the supply schedule intersects the $D_2$ and $r_3$
       intersection.
   (c) Since the physical stock cannot be expanded through the construction of more units
       (the fixed rent would not cover the costs), the number of persons per unit would have
       to increase through, for example, the creation of more apartments out of a single
       building. If square footage is some measure of quality, then such action would consti-
       tute a lowering of the quality of the rental housing stock.

# PROBLEM 1

1.

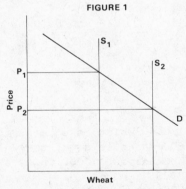

FIGURE 1

At any point in time, the supply of wheat stocks on the market is fixed ($S_1$), and given the market demand ($D$), a price ($P_1$) is determined. Placing wheat stocks on the market will increase supply to $S_2$ and lower the price to $P_2$.

2. This will reduce the output and supply of wheat, thereby raising the price and revenue to farmers if the elasticity of demand for wheat is less than one.
3. (a) If they grow and market other crops, the increased supply will lower the price of these
       commodities.
   (b) If the demand increase is sufficiently large to overcome the supply increase, the price
   will rise (Figure 2). If not, the price will be the same (Figure 3) or decline.

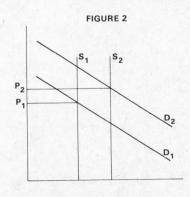

FIGURE 2

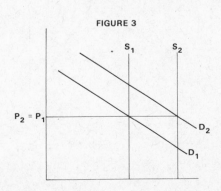

FIGURE 3

## PROBLEM 2

1. It is not very elastic.

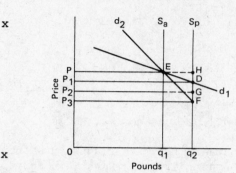

2. This is not easy. Suppose that $d_1$ and $d_2$ are two demand schedules and $S_a$ is the actual amount on the market. The price and output are $p$ and $q$ . If the subsidy encourages the supply to increase to its potential, $S_p$, then the following are possible: If the demand is elastic ($d_1$), price falls to $p_1$. Let us suppose that the distance $p$ to $p_1$ represents the subsidy of $7.00. Total beef producer revenue is $0p$ times $0q_2$, which is greater than before the subsidy, and the consumer gets at a price of $0p_1$. If the demand is inelastic ($d_2$), then the revenue to the producer is $0p_2$ times $0q_2$, where the distance $p_2$ to $p_3$ is the subsidy. It is not clear here that the producer has increased his revenue.

## PROBLEM 3

1. The demand for fluid milk would fall and rise for milk powder.
2. Decline by 9 percent
3. Only if the total demand for milk were to decline

## CHAPTER 8

### EXERCISES

1. Buy; about 250 million
2. (a) Yes; the reciprocal of the dollar price of pounds is 1/2.40 which is equal to .417.
   (b) Yes; the reciprocal of the dollar price of lire is 1/600 which is equal to .00167.
   (c) The pound price of lire is .000833. The lira price of pounds is 1,200. Thus, the reciprocal of the latter is 1/1200 which is equal to .000833.
   (d) No; the cross-rate is .417/600 which is equal to .000695 whereas the pound price of lire is .000833.
   (d) Yes; it could purchase 600,000 lire with $1,000, then purchase 500 pounds with the lire, and then purchase 1,200 dollars. The profit is therefore $200.
3. (a) Since the demand for oil imports is perfectly inelastic, the supply-of-dollars curve will be perfectly inelastic.

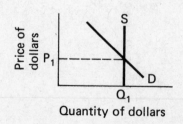

(b) The supply of dollars will shift to the right and the price of the Canadian dollar will depreciate.

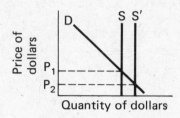

To obtain the same amount of oil, Canadians must supply more dollars and hence the dollar price falls.

4. (a) Demand curve shifts up (Canadian exports increase); price increases.
   (b) Supply curve shifts to the right; price falls.
   (c) Demand curve shifts to the left and supply curve shifts to the right; price falls.
   (d) Supply curve shifts to the left (less imports into Canada); price increases.

## PROBLEM

1. In terms of Canadian dollars per month: October, $777.76; November, $829.12; December, $807.04; January, $814.40; February, $836.56; March, $843.12, for a total cost of $4908.

2. By liquidating his savings of $4670 (Canadian) he would have obtained $4803.54 (U.S.), which is what he needs for his expenses in the United States. However, by cashing-in his savings he loses $186.80 (Canadian) in the form of forgone interest. The total cost is therefore $4856.80 (Canadian).

# CHAPTER 9

## EXERCISES

1. (a)

| Year | Food Intercepts | "Other" Intercepts |
|------|-----------------|--------------------|
| 1920 | 3,150 | 3,150 |
| 1940 | 5,000 | 3,850 |
| 1970 | 7,400 | 7,400 |

   (b) Yes, because in 1940, despite decline in money income, purchasing power for both food and other items has risen. Budget line has shifted outward.
   (c) 1940; with food prices relatively low, family budget could buy more food relative to all other items than 1920 to 1970.

2. (a) Indifference curves should be tangent where price-consumption lines intersect budget lines.

   (b)

| $P$ | $Q_A$ | $Q_B$ | Total Exp. on Beef A | B |
|-----|-------|-------|------|---|
| 1.50 | 400 | 600 | $600 | $ 900 |
| 1.00 | 600 | 1,000 | 600 | 1,000 |
| .75 | 800 | 1,300 | 600 | 975 |
| .60 | 1,000 | 1,500 | 600 | 900 |
| .50 | 1,200 | 600 | | 800 |

    (c) 1. Elasticity = 1
        2. At approximately $1.00, where *TR* is at a maximum

## PROBLEM 1

1. The real consumption of food, clothes, and alcohol/tobacco has fallen, while it has risen for transportation.
2. No. Estimating price elasticity requires the *ceteris paribus* assumption that other prices are constant.

## PROBLEM 2

1. See diagram.
2. Negative income effect.
3. A slight fall in income would result in a reduction of bread consumption, according to this figure, whereas substantial reduction could lead to an increase in bread consumption.

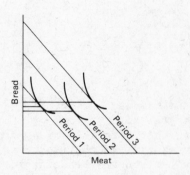

# CHAPTER 10

## EXERCISES

1. (b) If demand was very elastic, then a shortfall in supplies would lead to a decline in total revenue, whereas an elastic demand schedule would suggest a rise in total revenue.
   (c) Builders may try to stockpile at what would appear to be relatively cheaper prices compared with the future. This action would itself drive up prices.
2. (a) Change in income are not considered.
   (b) The income change over a short period of time would be of less concern, in general, than that over 14 years.

## PROBLEM 1

1. (b) Food = .437; alcohol = 1.19; automobiles = 1.70.
   (c) The text states that the more basic the item, the lower its income elasticity and the case of food proves this.
2. (a) Pork: -.68, -.89, -.55; eggs: -.02, -.06, -.12
   (b) It would appear that eggs do not have a close substitute in the consumption pattern or possibly that substitutes have experienced price changes of equal size at the same time.
   (c) They do, although in the case of eggs the demand schedule is not very sensitive to price changes.

# CHAPTER 11

## EXERCISES

1. (a) Approximately 500 square feet
   (b) Yes; the power tool production of food would not be economical until a garden size somewhat in excess of 500 square feet.
1. (a) It is the estimated value of the wear and tear per month
   (b) $250; there is no account taken of a payment for labor to the owner nor a return on his invested savings.

(c) If the excess was all attributable to his labor, that would be roughly $1.56 per hour, leaving no additional money.

(d) $10 a month!

(e) The type of business was one of high risk.

## PROBLEM 1

1. It is a legitimate claim of expenses in the business. One could view it as rent cost if the firm did not own its truck.
2. $250; no payment for the labor given by the owner has been included in the costs.
3. If all the profit went to the owner, that would represent approximately $1.50 per hour—hardly excessive.
4. $10 per month (the excess of revenue over expenditure after the decline in the price of paper)
5. It would suggest that the market views such a business as risky.

## PROBLEM 2

1. Bell Telephone, 7.6%; Bank of Nota Scotia, 3.6%, Steel Co., 4.7%; Koffler, 0.29%.
2. The stable price and high yield suggest a low-risk and low-potential capital-gain stock compared with Koffler. The latter may be reinvesting its profit for future expansion.
3. Government of Alberta, 9.2%; Seagrams, 10.6%; Government of Canada, 5.6%; Ontario Hydro, 10.0%. Government of Canada bonds are deemed to be a very "safe" investment in that they are backed by the resources of the country and the Bank of Canada indirectly. The lack of risk means that they can be sold with a relatively low interest rate.
4. Bonds are fixed at a given amount and their market value does not usually reflect improved profits or growth. People purchase stocks, for several reasons, but one is on the belief that the stock value will rise and the return will be reflected in a capital gain, not the dividend or interest paid.

# CHAPTER 12

## EXERCISES

1. (a)

| Variable Input | Output | Average Product | Marginal Product |
|---|---|---|---|
| 1 | 20 | 20 | — |
| 2 | 60 | 30 | 40 |
| 3 | 120 | 40 | 60 |
| 4 | 200 | 50 | 80 |
| 5 | 270 | 54 | 70 |
| 6 | 324 | 54 | 54 |
| 7 | 364 | 52 | 40 |
| 8 | 384 | 48 | 20 |
| 9 | 396 | 44 | 12 |
| 10 | 404 | 40.4 | 8 |

(c)

| Output | Total Fixed Cost | Total Variable Cost | Total Cost | Average Fixed Cost | Average Variable Cost | Average Total Cost | Marginal Cost |
|---|---|---|---|---|---|---|---|
| 20 | 168 | 80 | 248 | 8.40 | 4.00 | 12.40 | — |
| 60 | 168 | 160 | 328 | 2.80 | 2.66 | 5.46 | 2.00 |
| 210 | 168 | 240 | 408 | 1.40 | 2.00 | 3.40 | 1.33 |
| 200 | 168 | 320 | 488 | .84 | 1.60 | 2.44 | 1.00 |
| 270 | 168 | 400 | 568 | .62 | 1.48 | 2.10 | 1.14 |
| 324 | 168 | 480 | 648 | .52 | 1.48 | 2.00 | 1.48 |
| 364 | 168 | 560 | 728 | .46 | 1.54 | 2.00 | 2.00 |
| 384 | 168 | 640 | 808 | .44 | 1.67 | 2.11 | 4.00 |
| 396 | 168 | 720 | 888 | .424 | 1.82 | 2.24 | 6.67 |
| 404 | 168 | 800 | 968 | .415 | 1.98 | 2.40 | 10.00 |

2. (a)

| Output | Total Cost | Average Total Cost |
|---|---|---|
| 1 | 3.50 | 3.50 |
| 2 | 5.00 | 2.50 |
| 3 | 6.00 | 2.00 |
| 4 | 7.25 | 1.81 |
| 5 | 9.00 | 1.80 |
| 6 | 11.50 | 1.92 |
| 7 | 15.00 | 2.14 |

(c) Minimum average total cost is at 5 units of output.

3. (a) $AFC$ = \$52.78; $AVC$ = \$41.11

(b) \$105.56

(c) Zero

(d) No; even if the airline could fill the remaining 40 seats at the "normal" price, the total cost of the flight would not be covered.

4. (a)

| Q | FC | VC | TC | MC | | AFC | AVC | ATC |
|---|---|---|---|---|---|---|---|---|
| 0 | 50 | 0 | 50 | | | | | |
| 1 | 50 | 4 | 54 | 4 | | 50 | 4 | 54 |
| 2 | 50 | 10 | 60 | 6 | | 25 | 5 | 30 |
| 3 | 50 | 18 | 68 | 8 | | 16.66 | 6 | 22.66 |
| 4 | 50 | 28 | 78 | 10 | | 12.50 | 7 | 19.50 |
| 5 | 50 | 40 | 90 | 12 | | 10 | 8 | 18 |
| 6 | 50 | 54 | 104 | 14 | | 8.30 | 9 | 17.30 |
| 7 | 50 | 70 | 120 | 15 | | 7.14 | 10 | 17.14 |
| 8 | 50 | 88 | 138 | 18 | | 6.25 | 11 | 17.25 |
| 9 | 50 | 108 | 158 | 20 | | 5.55 | 12 | 17.55 |
| 10 | 50 | 130 | 180 | 22 | | 5 | 13 | 18 |
| . | . | . | . | | | . | . | . |
| . | . | . | . | | | . | . | . |
| . | . | . | . | | | . | . | . |
| 20 | 50 | 460 | 510 | | | 2.50 | 23 | 25.50 |

(b) 7

(c) 16

(d) No

(e) Although average fixed costs are declining because of the 50 being spread over more and more units of output, average variable costs are rising and at some point (output level of 8) they offset the falling average fixed costs.

## PROBLEM

1.

| Output in Miles | TVC | TTC | AFC | ATC |
|---|---|---|---|---|
| 5,000 | \$213 | \$1338 | 22.50¢ | 27.00¢ |
| 10,000 | 425 | 1550 | 11.25 | 15.75 |
| 15,000 | 638 | 1763 | 7.50 | 11.75 |

2. Apparently the employee comes out poorly since the 11 cents is less than the *ATC* even at 15,000 miles. But suppose we assume that individual would drive 10,000 miles anyway and receives $550 from the firm for driving an extra 5,000 miles, an excess of $337 over the variable costs of the 5,000 miles. The excess would reduce the fixed costs that he would pay for personal driving.

3. For 10,000 miles per year, roughly 24¢ would be the correct mileage compensation while for 15,000 miles, it would be close to 20¢.

# CHAPTER 13

## EXERCISES

1. (a) At the output levels shown in the first column of the problem, the corresponding average total cost figures are 0.46, 0.39, 0.35, 0.46, and 0.52.
   (b) 60,000
   (c) It increases up to an output level of 80,000, then decreases to an output level of 60,000, and then increases up to the output level of 100,000.
   (d) If the firm could substitute capital for labor in its production processes, a rise in the relative price of labor would lead to more capital being used relative to the amount of labor being used.

2. (a) $2.00, $1.85, $1.80, $1.78, $1.82
   (b) 400,000
   (c) No—proportions of labor and capital are constant.
   (d) Build two plants to produce 400,000 each.

3. (a) One of capital and two of labor
   (b) Two units of each

4. (a)

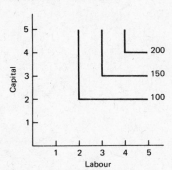

   (b) Very little (likely), because the firm cannot readily substitute one factor for another, according to the isoquant map above.

# CHAPTER 14

## EXERCISES

1. (a) No; *MC* exceeds price.
   (b) It should produce less.

2. (a) 100; 80; 60
   (b) $1,000; $600; $330
   (c) $800; $600; $480
   (d) $200; 0; -$150
   (e) $10; $7.50; $5.50
   (f) $10; $7.50; $5.50
   (g) $8; $7.50; $8
   (h) $2; 0; -$2.50
   (i) At $10, profits will induce entry; at $5.50, losses will induce exist of firms, so industry supply curve shifts.

3. (a) $7.50
   (b) Yes
   (c) No
   (d) Yes, it should increase output to 100.

4. (a) Above-normal profits
   (b) No, not in a perfectly competitive industry, because the abnormal profits will attract firms into the industry and the expanded market size will drive the price back to a level where all firms make only normal profits.
5. (a) Yes. Briefly, there are no excess profits for the firms; they are price takers; any individual firm has a very small share of the total market.
   (b) Price and output will rise and firms will be enjoying above-normal profits, e.g., revenue over and above that sufficient to cover average total costs.
   (c) The market-supply schedule would shift to the right because of the entry of new firms until it intersects the $D'$ schedule at such a point so as to produce a price (equilibrium) the same as the initial price in the market.

## PROBLEM

1.

| AC | MC | AC + tax |
|----|----|----------|
| 0 | | |
| | 4 | |
| 4 | | 4.50 |
| | 2 | |
| 3 | | 3.50 |
| | 1 | |
| 2.33 | | 2.83 |
| | 2 | |
| 2.25 | | 2.75 |
| | 3 | |
| 2.40 | | 2.90 |
| | 6 | |
| 3.00 | | 3.50 |

2. 40,000 units
3. It would raise the selling price above the world price and thus inhibit the firms' ability to compete in foreign markets. The average-cost schedule would be an additional $0.50 per unit of output.

# CHAPTER 15

## EXERCISES

1. (a) 60  (b) $11  (c) $660  (d) $480  (e) $180  (f) output; about 25 to 90 units; price: about $14.75 to $7.50  (g) $7.50
2. (a) The marginal-cost and marginal-revenue schedules

   (b)

   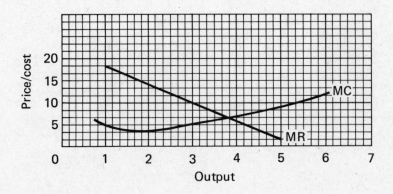

   (c) Four units
   (d) $12.00
   (e) The average-cost schedule
   (f) The average cost of producing an output of four is $9.75 and hence the monopolists' profits are $12.00 - $9.75 times the output.

## PROBLEM 1

The key to working out these answers is the intersection of the *MC* = $1 with the *MR* curve in the diagrams. Since the answers will be obtained graphically, some variations must be expected from the answers below.

1.

|  | *P* | *O* | *TR* | *TVC* | *TC* | *TR - TC* |
|---|---|---|---|---|---|---|
| (a) | $ 8.00 | 2,000 | $16,000 | $2,000 | $22,000 | $-6,000 |
| (b) | 16.75 | 630 | 10,500 | 630 | — | — |
|  | 7.00 | 1,500 | 10,500 | 1,500 | — | — |
|  | — | 2,130 | 21,050 | 2,130 | 21,300 | -250 |
| (c) | 1 to 20+ | 4,500 | ≈45,000 | 4,500 | 24,500 | ≈20,500 |

2. Dr. Lawrence cannot meet his costs under a one-price system and must reject it. The two-price system is predicted to fall slightly short of needed revenues, but clearly the potential revenue is available, as indicated by answer (c). He could use a basic price of about $17.00 for Group I patients and $7.00 for Group II patients and supplement this by more modest charges for those who can't affort $7.00, thus getting additional revenue from the demand below $7.00 sufficient to cover maximum costs of $25,000 if he treats all.

3. (a) By reducing Dr. Lawrence's fixed annual costs, it could make long-run maintenance of medical services available.

   (b) If the government were willing to pay a certain minimum fee, the demand for medical services from the less wealthy would increase and thus raise total revenue. Concessions to these persons in terms of lower fees would then likely not be necessary.

## PROBLEM 2

1. No. At 25¢ per call, total revenue would decline to $75,000 even though more calls were being made. Demand is elastic but not sufficiently so to increase business enough to raise total revenue.

2. Yes. At $1.00 for a call, the number of calls made would fall but revenue would be higher than before. Demand is sufficiently inelastic that calls do not decline so as to offset the rise in cost.

# CHAPTER 16

## EXERCISES

1. (a) Output, $0q_1$; price $0q_4$

   (b) $p_3dfp_4$, or $df \times 0q_1$

   (c) Profits are being made, and firms will enter.

   (d) *ATC* curve will rise; *D* curve will shift to right; *MR* curve will shift according to shift in *D*; *MR* curve will not be affected because in this case advertising is a fixed, not a variable, cost.

   (e) *D* curve should be shifted to left, tangent to *ATC* curve.

2. These answers may be approximate, depending on how students read off the values on the horizontal axis.

   (a) From 5,000 to 7,000, from $10,000 to $10,500

   (b) From 5,000 to 5,500, from $10,000 to $8,250

   (c) From 5,000 to 3,000, from $10,000 to $7,500

   (d) From $10,000 to $11,050

   (e) He would raise his price only if everyone else did; he would not lower it even without retaliation because additional revenue would be less than additional costs. For instance, at 6,000 units *MC* would equal 75 but *MR* would be only 50 cents.

   (f) Yes, no

## PROBLEM 1

1. No, because it is obvious that the firm in question is not a price taker.
2. It does not imply strict marginal-cost-marginal-revenue pricing.
3. If there were no competition for this firm, then taking what they can get from the market could mean exorbitant prices for consumers.
4. They may well be trying to maximize their share of the market or making certain that they maintain their share of the market. Such a pricing policy, which is flexible and not based on any set principle, is compatible with oligopoly—competition among very few firms.

## PROBLEM 2

1. Oligopoly. This form of market structure is suggested because there is obviously some degree of cooperation or implicit agreement within the industry as to what to do when a firm finds itself in a position of excess inventories.
2. No, because there would be no agreement of the kind mentioned in this case. A buildup of inventory would not occur, because, under perfect competition, a firm can sell all it wishes at the market price.
3. Inelastic.

# CHAPTER 17

## EXERCISE

(a) There is a profit incentive for both firms to move away from the present price, because neither firm is producing at the profit-maximizing position where marginal cost equals marginal revenue.
(b) Neither firm knows what the other might do in the case where there is a decision by one firm to alter price. To avoid the possibility of a "price war," they may remain where they are.

## PROBLEM

|  | Milk | Pen | Cigarette | Turbine |
|---|---|---|---|---|
| Number of sellers | Large | One to several plus | Four large | A few |
| Independence of sellers | Great, except for NFO | Apparently independent | Price leadership | Formal conspiracy before price cuts |
| Homogeneity of product | Identical | Differentiated | Brand differentiation | Similar |
| Entry possibilities | Easy | Moderately easy | Difficult for name brand but low-priced niche open | Difficult because of scale (imports available) |
| Ratio of sales to capacity | Seasonally low | High to lower | Low because of depression | Low |
| Ratio of price to costs | Perhaps one to one | High but decreasing | High after price rise | High in relation to variable costs |

1. In all cases sales were low relative to capacity. Circumstances also opened up entry possibilities in each case. In milk, there exist no real barriers to entry and a seasonal surplus of milk; in the pen industry, there are high profits, inducing firms to meet relatively easy production requirements; in cigarettes, small firms had the opportunity to bring out low-priced brands in an industry whose sales suffered from depression; import entry and a slump in demand were decisive in turbines.
2. In both cigarettes and pens, the high ratio of existing price to cost should be added to the combination above. In turbines, variable costs were probably low in relation to total. In milk, large numbers of sellers of a homogeneous product had much to gain by cutting prices.

# CHAPTER 18

## PROBLEM 1

1. "Exclusive ownership (as through command of supply): a commodity controlled by one party" (*source:* Merriam-Webster Dictionary, 1964).
2. Although not an exhaustive list, some of the facts would be:
    (a) discrimination against advertisers
    (b) setting very high advertising rates for those businesses that use newspaper advertising extensively
    (c) fixing the price of the newspaper
    (d) elimination of any competition was by use of "price wars"
    (e) very large profits
3. The simple straightforward definition of the word does not imply that the activities of a firm which fits the definition are detrimental to the public. A monopoly can be *or* may be detrimental to the public.

## PROBLEM 2

1. A sale; giving out coupons with sales slips; a gasoline price war with the same firm charging different prices in different parts of the city.
2. There are a number of factors that could lead to regional price differences in the same product such as sales taxes or transportation costs. What the Court must prove is that if there are different prices, there is no reason for such except to lessen competition.
3. The major problem is to determine that a price policy does lead to less competition. The obvious case would be where one large firm with substantial financial resources lowers its prices below cost and eventually forces all other firms out of business. The remaining firm is then a monopolist and can regain its lost profits by setting a higher than otherwise price. When it comes to the matter of *proving* that a competitor was eliminated because of unfair pricing policies on the part of one firm, the Court would have to show that the "eliminated" firm was managed efficiently and could have remained in operation if it were not for the "unfair" price competition.

# CHAPTER 19

## EXERCISES

1. (a) $p_2$, $q_1$   (b) from $p_3$, $q$ to $p_1$, $q_2$   (c) $p$, $q_3$
2. The answers will depend, in some cases, on the size of the tax changes you specify and the minimum profit level in the case of the sales maximizer. The output tax shifts the $AC$ and $MC$ up while the profits tax only shifts the $AC$ curve. After making the necessary changes, the new output and price levels and thus the changes can be established.

## PROBLEM

1. No. It does not reflect the costs associated with the fact that such a container costs money to dispose of, in terms of adding to the cost of garbage collection, use of land at the disposal site, potential danger if not disposed of properly, and aesthetic costs.
2. It depends partly on where you live. In some localities, or stores, only a limited number of products in refillable containers are available, giving people little opportunity to choose between the two.
3. All products would have to be made available in both types of container. Furthermore, the price of the product in the nonrefillable container would have to reflect the social costs associated with this type of container.
4. The answer here has been implied in the previous questions. Basically, the nonrefillable container may still be used, because the product that the consumer wants is available only in such a container. Furthermore, the price of products in nonrefillable containers probably does not reflect the true social cost of such a container; hence its market price is too low, thereby encouraging demand.

# CHAPTER 20

## EXERCISES

1. *MPP:* 0, 20, 20, 18, 16, 14, 12, 10, 8, 6, 4
   *MRP* (a): 0, \$40, \$40, \$36, \$32, \$28, \$24, \$20, \$16, \$12, \$8
   *MRP* (b): 0, \$38, \$36, \$31.50, \$27.50, \$23.10, \$19.20, \$15.50, \$12.00, \$8.70, \$5.60
   (a) 7; about 5   (b) 5; about 3   (c) 7   (d) because of diminishing returns
   (e) Case (b) is evidently monopolistic with a downward-sloping marginal-revenue curve.
2. (a) The total number of hours supplied will be the sum of the hours from individuals B and C ($h_1 + h_2$).
   (b) Hours offered by individuals B and C increase and now individual A offers hours for the first time. The participation rate has increased from 2 out of 3 to 3 out of 3 adults.
   (c) It appears that only individual B will offer hours (a small amount) to the market. Therefore, the participation rate is .333 (1 out of 3).

## PROBLEM

1.

| | Cumulative Percent of Canada's Income |
|---|---|
| Lowest fifth | 5.5 |
| Second fifth | 18.0 |
| Middle fifth | 35.8 |
| Fourth fifth | 59.6 |
| Highest fifth | 100.0 |

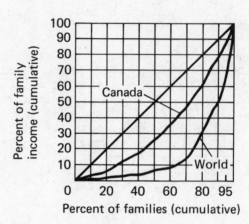

2. Although the world's Lorenz curve is in terms of population, whereas Canada's Lorenz curve is in terms of families, there is no doubt that the Canadian Lorenz curve displays a greater degree of income equality. The world Lorenz curve has a greater displacement from the diagonal. The authors would argue that Canada's Lorenz curve is preferable. Discussion should distinguish between value judgments that consider justice, and economic arguments as to the effect of income distribution on income available.

# CHAPTER 21

## EXERCISES

1. Total cost: 80, 94.50, 110, 126.50, 144, 162.50, 182
   Marginal cost: —, 14.50, 15.50, 16.50, 17.50, 18.50, 19.50
2. (a) $Ow_3$, $Oq_4$
   (b) $Oq$, $Oq_5 - Oq$; horizontal at $w_6$ to $q_5$
   (c) $Ow$, $Ow_2$; $Ow_5$, $Oq_2$, $Ow_1$, $Ow_4$, $Ow_4$. Wage is lower; employment is less than in (a).
   (d) $Oq_4$; wage between $Ow_1$ and $Ow_4$; employment between $Oq_2$ and $Oq_4$
   (e) Supply curve shifts leftward halfway to origin. All wage predictions are raised.

PROBLEM

*A. The Case of the Rural Mill Owner*
1. The supply curve will coincide with the horizontal line at $1.50 to $Q$ of 200.
2. The *MCL* will coincide with horizontal *S* curve at $1.50, up to $Q$ of 200, and then will jump to existing curve.
3. At $Q$ of 200
4. 200
5. Above $2.00

*B. The Case of Ontario's Minimum Wage Increases*
1. The effect on employment will depend on the level of the new minimum wage relative to the equilibrium wage rate for the five industries. For simplicity, assume that all five industries have identical demand and supply curves. If the $1.30 per hour wage is still below or is equal to the equilibrium wage, there should be no effect on employment. Any reduction in employment will depend upon (a) the extent to which the minimum wage is *above* the equilibrium level and (b) the elasticity of the demand for labor.
2. Firms may try to pass on increases in costs to consumers. Their ability to do so will depend on the elasticity of demand for the products that they produce. Second, there may be other ways of reducing costs in the short run by reorganizing production. Third, although no worker is laid off, the firm reduces its demand for labor services by reducing the number of hours worked, including the elimination of overtime.
3. (a) Low-productivity workers because of inexperience, lack of training, or whose job requires low skills
   (b) The report indicates that the incidence of layoffs fell on female workers. The evidence in the table suggests that low-wage jobs were dominated by women.

# CHAPTER 22

EXERCISES

1. (a) $7.47   (b) 1%   (c) 50   (d) 10
2. (a) $42.12   (b) 1%   (c) 50   (d) 10
3. (a) Just barely; it would bring him $13,590 per year.
   (b) Yes, but it just meets the 14% requirement. The annual savings would have a PV of $14,000 × 5.216, which equals $73,024. The $10,000 salvage value has a PV of $2,700. The total is $75,724.
   (c) At 6% the PV of the cost of the medical education is (6.802)($10,000) or $68,000. The worth of the extra medical earnings (15.046 − 6.802)($10,000) or approximately $82,440. The return is over 6%. At 8% the cost is $62,470 and the estimated worth is $56,780. The return is therefore slightly less than 8%, enough for Mr. Schmidt to give his blessing to Hermann's medical career.
   (d) There are 5 years to maturity (assuming the current period is 1974). Take 10% in the tables. Total capitalized value is $99.07 (99.07 = 9.75(3.791) + 100(.621)).
4. (a) 10% since the firm had reached its profit-maximizing capital stock at which *MEC* equals the market rate of interest.
   (b) 8%; solve the equation $1000 = 1080/(1 + MEC)$. The *MEC* of 8% is associated with a capital stock of 11,000.
   (c) Yes, because the *MEC* is at least equal to the new market rate of interest.

PROBLEM

1. The real rate of return on CSBs (defined as the nominal rate minus the inflation rate) was 0 in 1973 and negative in 1974 (approximately −3 percent). Furthermore, investment certificates at the trust companies had higher yields than did the CSBs. Therefore, people, redeemed their savings bonds.
2. He wanted to increase the yield on savings bonds in order to discourage redemptions. More redemptions would have worsened the government's cash position. By giving bonuses at the

date of maturity, he was attempting to encourage people to hold on to their savings bonds until maturity.

# CHAPTER 23

## EXERCISE

The present value of expected income in Nova Scotia is 8000 × 9.427 = $75,416. The present value of expected income in Ontario is ($8500 - $1000) × .909 plus (8500    8.518) = $79,221. Yes, John should move.

## PROBLEM 1

1. b, d, e
2. The proportion of farm population to total population has greatly declined because of relatively low returns to agriculture. Moreover, small retailers have been unable to compete with large corporations that have been able to obtain economies of scale.
3. Yes. The noncorporate entrepreneur furnishes his labor services (management) and capital resources to his enterprise. Whether entrepreneurial income is classified as wages or return to capital has much to do with the overall property-labor split.

## PROBLEM 2

1. Largest investments in formal education are likely to have been made by individuals whose occupations are managerial, professional, and clerical in nature. Craftsmen are likely to have undergone the greatest degree of on-the-job training. All of these occupations are characterized by low probabilities of poverty.
2. Farmers and farm workers, loggers and fishermen, and recreation workers are likely to be subject to large seasonal demands. Services and general laborers are likely to be low-skilled workers. These workers tend to be laid off first if cutbacks in production are necessary. For all of these occupations, the incidence of poverty tends to be high relative to other occupations.

# CHAPTER 24

## EXERCISES

1. (a) rise by $10   (b) rise by $10   (c) shift to left   (d) rise, less than $10   (e) decline
2. (a) be unaffected   (b) rise   (c) be unaffected   (d) be unaffected   (e) be unaffected
   (f) rise
3. (a) Trucking down; railroads up
   (b) Private gasoline consumption down; trucking unaffected; public transportation up
   (c) Airlines down; railroads up
   (d) Foreign publishers down; Canadian publishers up

4. (a)

| APC | MPC | ASC | MSC |
|-----|-----|-----|-----|
| 500 | 500 | 600 | 600 |
| 275 | 50 | 387.59 | 175 |
| 206 | 70 | 327.60 | 210 |
| 177.50 | 90 | 306.25 | 240 |
| 164 | 110 | 290 | 270 |
| 175 | 230 | 315.83 | 460 |
| 192.85 | 300 | 399.28 | 480 |

   (b) $177.50 and $306.25, respectively
   (c) Greater

## PROBLEM 1

A. 1. "Social costs" such as air and water pollution occur through a medium that does not possess private property rights. Consequently, the right to use water and air as part of the overall production process cannot be purchased as other factors of production are purchased.

   2. With no pricing of "free" resources, there is no price signal of their increasing scarcity. This results in there being no attempt to economize on their use or find more technologically efficient ways of using them.

B. 1. Ideally, one would like to charge a rate that reflects the opportunity cost of using the water in its pre-pollution state. On the other hand, the fee could reflect the damage that the pollution is causing to other users, which may be the opportunity cost.

   2. (i) There would be the problem of monitoring the amount and type of pollution.

      (ii) The toxicity of the pollution would have to be determined and monitored.

      (iii) What would be the effect of the effluent fee on the firms' production and employment policies?

## PROBLEM 2

1. One might recommend nothing in the case where there was no measure of the cost of the noise pollution on the residents. If something had to be done, then relocation would be the best because it would be less expensive.

2. By doing so, the factory would be saving $50,000.

# CHAPTER 25

## EXERCISES

1. (a) c, d, f  (b) 3  (c) a, because the supply elasticity is greater with the same demand
   (d) d, because the demand elasticity is less with the same supply

2. A, progressive; B, proportional; C, progressive; D, regressive; E, proportional to $5,000, regressive above $5,000

3. Dimeland would prefer policy (1) as it can spend the money where its preferences dictate. The federal government should follow (2) because it reduces the cost of additional education expenditure to Dimeland by 50 percent, a substantial incentive.

## PROBLEM

The tax is regressive as a smaller share of income is paid in the form of tax as income rises. To answer the second question, simply take 8 percent of the mediun income in each range and observe if the actual tax paid exceeds or falls short of this. The appropriate tax or subsidy can then be calculated. It should be noted that in recent years, this method of measuring whether or not a tax is regressive or progressive has been called into question. For example, a person may have only a limited income but own valuable assets, the latter being excluded in this simple measure of the regressiveness of a tax.

# CHAPTER 26

## EXERCISES

1. (a) Canada: 1 wheat costs 2 beef; 1 beef costs 1/2 wheat.
   Argentina: 1 wheat costs 1/3 beef; 1 beef costs 3 wheat.
   Canada should specialize in beef. Argentina should produce wheat.
   (b) Canada: 1 wheat costs 2 beef; 1 beef costs 1/2 wheat.
   Argentina: 1 wheat costs 3 beef; 1 beef costs 1/3 wheat.
   Canada should specialize in wheat. Argentina should produce beef.

(c) Canada: 1 wheat costs 2 beef; 1 beef costs 1/2 wheat.
(a) Argentina: 1 wheat costs 2 beef; 1 beef costs 1/2 wheat.
Both countries should produce both goods. There would be no gain from trade.
2. (a) A   (b) B   (c) dairy products, watches   (d) 100, 200
3. (a) 99.1; 1970   (b) more; 99.1, 104.1
4. (a) When opportunity cost ratios differ, both partners can have more goods by trade.
   (b) Dollars abroad represent purchasing power for Canadian goods just as dollars at home do.
   (c) Cheaper imports mean more goods for Canadian workers.
   (d) Whether tariffs remain or not, the real costs of production and thus resources required have been reduced as the infant industry developed.
   (e) Imports are the only way in which resources used for exports can be recovered.

## PROBLEM

| Before-Trade Conditions | 1 | 2 (and 2a) | 3 | 4 | 5 |
|---|---|---|---|---|---|
| Opportunity cost: X in A | 1/2 | 1 | 1 | 1 | 25/36 |
| Opportunity cost: X in B | 2 | 1 | 1 | 8/5 | 36/25 |
| $P_X/P_Y$ in A | 1/2 | 1 | 1 | 1 | 25/36 |
| $P_X/P_Y$ in B | 2 | 1 | 1 | 8/5 | 36/25 |

Case 1: (a) X; Y; X; Y
        (b) 100; X; 100; Y; 50; X; 50; Y
        (c) 25; Y; 25; X; A; B
Case 2: (a) Is not; is not
        (b) Absolute; comparative; same; identical; will not
Case 3: (a) Decreasing; specialize; specialize
        (b) 50; 50; production-possibilities frontiers; 20
Case 4. (a) Absolute; comparative
        (b) Y; 40; 40; 40; 15
        (c) Maintain; cheaper
Case 5. (a) More X; Y; X; Y
        (b) High; increasing
        (c) Less; less; increase; 1; 1
        (d) 125; 122; 125; 122
        (e) 22.5X; 22.5Y; tangent; production
After-trade consumption of each product: Case 1, 50; Case 2, —; Case 3, 50; Case 4, 50 in A, 40 in B; Case 5, 62.5

# Chapter 27

## EXERCISE

Current account: (b), (c), (d), (g), (j), (k), (l), (m)
Capital account: (a), (e), (h), (i)
Official reserve: (f)
Balance-of-payments surplus of 777

## PROBLEM

1. A tariff reduction will place some Canadian producers in a more competitive market because of a greater possibility of foreigners selling their products in Canada. If the foreign goods were, for the same level of quality, cheaper, then the production of such goods in Canada would decline and people would be laid off.
2. More exports mean more output and this will be translated into more jobs in the export industry. If there is excess supply in the labor market, part of the increase in the demand for labor can be met from this source. However, it may not always be possible to "match up" jobs in the export industries with the skills of the unemployed. In a regional context, it may be that surplus labor exists in a region where there is no export boom and it may not be easy to encourage labor to transfer from one part of the country to another.

3. A tariff "wall" or protection implies that goods are being kept out of Canada because the foreign producer, upon paying the tariff, could not price his product competitively in Canada. If domestic prices are close to foreign prices plus the tariff, a lower tariff will mean a decline in prices.

# CHAPTER 28

## EXERCISES

1. GNE = (277.1 + 3.6 + 201.5 + 805.0) = 1286.2
   GNP = (785.3 + 84.3 + 117.8 + 109.6 + 126.4 + 75.5 - 10.7) = 1288.2
2. (a) NNP at market prices = 143.5 (161.1 - 17.6)
   NNP at factor cost equals 143.5 - 17.5 (indirect taxes) or 126.0
   (b) Personal income is 126.0 + 25.3 - 18.2 or 133.1
   Personal disposable income is 133.1 - 25.2 or 107.9
   (c) Personal saving is 107.9 - 96.9 or 11.0
3. 1929 GNP in 1961 dollars is 12.23; implicit price deflator 1970 is 85.69 divided by 64.01 or 133.9.
   (a) 116%   (b) 33.9%; 31.5%   (c) 61.4%   (d) 23.7%
4. Real per capita disposable income 1950 was 925.60; 1970 = 1760.55; percentage increase was 90.2%.
5. Inflation rate 1972 was 5.0%; 1973 was 9.2%; 1974 was 14.2%; 1975 was 10.8%.
6. (a) (1) $C$ and $F$                              (7) $S_b$ and $F$
       (2) $I$ (if clippers are considered         (8) (a) $T$
           investment)                                 (b) $F$
       (3) $S_b$ or $S_p$                              (c) $S_b$
       (4) $N$                                     (9) $C$, $M$
       (5) $I$                                    (10) $X$
       (6) $T$                                    (11) $I$
                                                  (12) $G$

    (b) 1, 2, 5, 7, 9, 10, 11, 12

## PROBLEM 1

| | Factor Payment | Expenditure | Reason |
|---|---|---|---|
| 1. | | Business inventory | Part of investment expenditure |
| 2. | | | GM steel purchases are not included since they will be reflected in the sale of final products (cars). Steel in an inter-good to GM |
| 3. | Rent | | Payment to owner of factor |
| 4. | Capital consumption allowances | | Represents a payment of depreciation to owners of capital |
| 5. | Wages of doctors | | Payment to factor of production |
| 6. | | Sales of snowmobiles to foreigners | Expenditure on final goods and services |
| 7. | | School construction | Part of government expenditure on goods and services |

## PROBLEM 2

1. Total value of expenditures in base year is 1646 (weights times prices of each product). The total value next year is 1740. The price index for new year is therefore 1740 divided by 1646 or 1.057.
2. No, because shelter, clothing, and other constitute only 50% of the total weights.
3. Most likely shelter and transportation; weights of shelter and transportation might increase and other components (food, clothing, entertainment, and other) might fall.

# Chapter 29

## EXERCISES

1. (b) 500   (c) .8; yes   (d) It declines.   (e) Savings values are -100, -80, -60, -40, -20, 0, 20, 40, 60.   (f) $C = Y$ at the break-even level of national income. Therefore, $S = 0$.

2.

| Y | Aggregate Expenditure | J | Y - C = W |
|---|---|---|---|
| 0 | 140 | 50 | -90 |
| 50 | 170 | 50 | -70 |
| 100 | 200 | 50 | -50 |
| 150 | 230 | 50 | -30 |
| 200 | 260 | 50 | -10 |
| 250 | 290 | 50 | 10 |
| 300 | 320 | 50 | 30 |
| 350 | 350 | 50 | 50 |
| 400 | 380 | 50 | 70 |
| 450 | 410 | 50 | 90 |
| 500 | 440 | 50 | 110 |

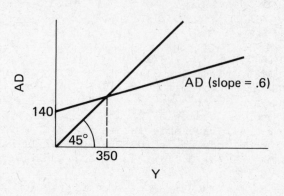

(a) 350; 350; $W = 50$; $J = 50$   (b) $C = 90 + .6Y$; $W = -90 + .4Y$   (c) $C + W = Y$
(d) $MPC = .6$ for all changes in income

3. (a) This is an overproduction situation, because actual output ($Y$) is 100, whereas intended aggregate expenditure is 97. Inventory investment is 3 and is unintended.
   (b) Businessmen would cut production.
   (c) Income would fall, because resource demand has declined. Factor payments are therefore reduced.
   (d) Consumption would fall. This is shown diagrammatically by a movement down the $E$ curve.
   (e) Output or GNP at GNP = 95

4. (a) Disposable income is 0, 100, 200, 300, 400, 500. Comsumption is 350.

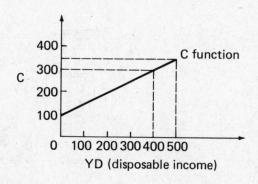

(b) $mpc$ is .5.

(c)

| Disposable Income | Saving |
|---|---|
| 0 | -100 |
| 100 | -50 |
| 200 | 0 |
| 300 | 50 |
| 400 | 100 |
| 500 | 150 |

## PROBLEM

1. The term 100 refers to autonomous consumption, i.e., consumption which does not depend on the level of income. The term .7 refers to the marginal propensity to consume out of disposable income.
2. The slope of the tax function is zero. This implies that taxes do *not* depend on the level of income.
3. The slope of the import function is .1. This implies that for every $1 increase in national income, imports will rise by 10 cents.
4. Disposable income equals total income ($Y$) minus taxes, or $Y - 20$. This is equation 7.
5. $C = 100 + .7(Y - 20)$. This is equation 8.
6. $AD = 100 + .7(Y - 20) + 50 + 50 + (20 - 10 - .1Y)$ or $AD = 196 + .6Y$.
7. $Y = 196 + .6Y$; $Y$ equals 490.
8. $S = (Y - 20) - 100 - .7(Y - 20)$ or $.3Y - 106$.
9. Withdrawals equal $(.3Y - 106) + 20 + (10 + .1Y)$ or $.4Y - 76$.
   Injections equal $50 + 50 + 20$ or 120.
   Therefore, 120 equals $.4Y + 196$ or $Y$ equals 490.

# CHAPTER 30

## EXERCISES

1. (a) .6
   (c) Injections are 40 and withdrawals are 20.
   (d) Declining
   (e) Firms will increase production and employment. As this occurs, factor payments will increase and hence consumption will increase. Withdrawals will increase also because income has incre increased; most likely taxes and savings.
   (f) New equilibrium is 100.
   (g) Yes; 100 equals 1/.4 times 20.

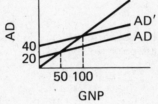

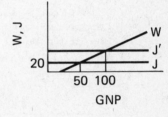

(b)

2.

| | C | ΔC | ΔI | Income | ΔY |
|---|---|---|---|---|---|
| 0 | 80 | 0 | 0 | 100 | 0 |
| 1 | 80 | 0 | 10 | 110 | 10 |
| 2 | 88 | 8 | 0 | 118 | 8 |
| 3 | 94.4 | 6.4 | 0 | 124.4 | 6.4 |
| 4 | 99.5 | 5.1 | 0 | 129.4 | 5.1 |
| 5 | 103.6 | 4.1 | 0 | 133.6 | 4.1 |
| 6 | 106.9 | 3.3 | 0 | 136.9 | 3.3 |
| 7 | 111.6 | 1.9 | 0 | 141.4 | 1.9 |
| Total | 120.0 | 0 | 0 | 150.0 | 0 |

   (a) At each and every round of spending, withdrawals are occurring.
   (b) Yes; a new level of 150. Injections have increased, causing income to rise.
   (c) $1/(1 - MPC) = 5$ or $1/w = 5$.
   (d) The total change in savings will be 10, which is equal to the change in injections. Savings originally were 20, and hence the new level after the multiplier process will be 30.

3.

| | ΔC | ΔW | ΔY |
|---|---|---|---|
| 0 | — | — | -5.0 |
| 1 | -3.0 | -2.0 | -3.0 |
| 2 | -1.8 | -1.2 | -1.8 |
| 3 | -1.1 | - .7 | -1.1 |
| 4 | - .7 | - .3 | - .7 |
| 5 | - .4 | - .3 | - .4 |
| 6 | - .2 | - .2 | - .2 |
| Total | | | |
| | -7.5 | -5.0 | -12.5 |

Multiplier = -12.5/-5.0 = 2.5 or 1/.4 = 2.5

4.

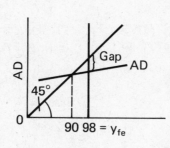
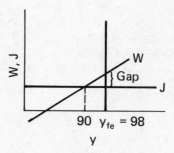

(b) Multiplier = 1/.5 = 2
(c) Deflationary gap = 4
(d) No; an increase in investment of 3.5 generates an increase in national income of only 7.
(e) Yes. (2 times $4 billion = $8 billion.)

5.

| | Injections Curve | | Withdrawals Curve | |
|---|---|---|---|---|
| | Slope Change | Parallel Shift | Slope Change | Parallel Shift |
| (a) Marginal tax rate | no | no | yes (+) | no |
| (b) More *G* | no | yes (+) | no | no |
| (c) *MPS* increase | no | no | yes (+) | no |
| (d) Less imports | no | no | no | yes (-) |

PROBLEM

1. .1; 10
2. .19; 5.26
3. No, because changes of income do not change withdrawals; .46 = (.06 + .3 + .1); 2.17
4. 50; 2.00

# CHAPTER 31

EXERCISES

1.

| Year | Units of Capital Needed | New Machines Required | Replacment Machines | Total Machines to Be Purchased |
|---|---|---|---|---|
| 1 | 10 | 0 | 1 | 1 |
| 2 | 10 | 0 | 1 | 1 |
| 3 | 11 | 1 | 1 | 2 |
| 4 | 12 | 1 | 1 | 2 |
| 5 | 15 | 3 | 1 | 4 |
| 6 | 17 | 2 | 1 | 3 |
| 7 | 18 | 1 | 1 | 2 |
| 8 | 18 | 0 | 1 | 1 |

(a) 50 percent   (b) 300 percent

2.

| Week | End of Week | Inventory/ Sales Ratio | Desired Inventory | Desired Inventory Plus Expected Sales | Weekly Orders for Next Week |
|------|-------------|------------------------|-------------------|---------------------------------------|------------------------------|
| 1 | 200 | 2 | 200 | 300 | 100 |
| 2 | 200 | 2 | 200 | 300 | 100 |
| 3 | 190 | 1.7 | 220 | 330 | 140 |
| 4 | 220 | 2 | 220 | 330 | 110 |
| 5 | 210 | 1.8 | 240 | 360 | 150 |
| 6 | 240 | 2 | 240 | 360 | 120 |
| 7 | 250 | 2.3 | 220 | 330 | 80 |
| 8 | 220 | 2 | 220 | 330 | 110 |
| 9 | 230 | 2.3 | 200 | 300 | 70 |

(a) 100; 120   (b) 70; 150

(c) Orders for inventory fluctuate more widely than sales. This variation in investment spending is a major factor behind economic fluctuations.

3. (a) Capital stock is 300 and since firm has reached its desired level, investment is zero.

   (b) According to schedule A, new desired capital stock is 400. Desired investment is 100. Not necessarily since capital-producing firms may not be able to supply all of the additional capital.

   (c) Somewhere between 300 and 400, perhaps 350. Yes, because desired capital stock at a 14% rate of interest was 300 and not it is 350. The shift in the *MEC* schedule might have been caused by some technological innovation, increased sales, more optimistic forecasts of profits in the future.

4. (a) Disposable income: 0, 80, 160, 240, 320, 400

   (b) 200

   (c) A constant tax rate of 20%

   (d) A constant *mpc* of .5

   (e)

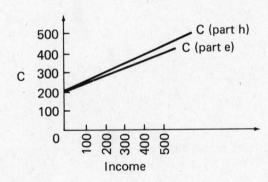

   (f) Tax payments: 0, 10, 20, 30, 40, 50
       Disposable income: 0, 90, 180, 270, 360, 450

   (g)

| Disposable Income | Consumption |
|-------------------|-------------|
| 0 | 200 |
| 90 | 245 |
| 180 | 290 |
| 270 | 335 |
| 360 | 380 |
| 450 | 425 |

## PROBLEM 1

1. The gap widens when real output per employed worker is low (1956-1961 and 1966-1969) and narrows when productivity is high (1961-1966).
2. Association between substantial increases in investment and closing of the gap seems clear. Decreases in investment are associated with increases in the gap. Increased investment represents one component of injections needed to bring aggregate demand to an increasing potential. Furthermore, increased investment has a substantial effect of labor productivity by providing more and better capital equipment per worker.
3. The U.S. gap widens when U.S. investment and labor productivity decrease. If Canada's exports to the U.S. depend on the growth of the U.S. economy, then exports and consequently Canada's GNP will tend to decrease. If U.S. income growth is low, in the absence of other injections, the GNP gap in Canada will widen.

## PROBLEM 2

1.

| Period | $C$ | Auton. $I$ | Accel. | Nat. Income |
|--------|-------|------------|--------|-------------|
| 3 | 225 | 200 | 150 | 575 |
| 4 | 287.5 | 200 | 125 | 612.5 |
| 5 | 306.3 | 200 | 37.5 | 543.8 |
| 6 | 271.9 | 200 | -68.7 | 403.2 |
| 7 | 201.6 | 200 | -140.6 | 261.0 |
| 8 | 130.5 | 200 | -142.2 | 188.3 |
| 9 | 94.15 | 200 | 72.7 | 221.5 |
| 10 | 110.7 | 200 | 33.2 | 343.9 |

2. Trough: period 8; peak: period 4; expansion phase: periods 2 and 3 and period 10; recession phase: periods 5, 6, and 7.
3. During periods 2 and 4, the government should increase the interest rate to dampen investment; during periods 5 to 8, it should reduce the interest rate to increase investment.

# CHAPTER 32

## EXERCISES

1. (a) 400  (b) deficit; 50  (c) surplus; 25  (d) no
   (e) Shift $T_n$ down (to $T_n = .2Y$ or to $T_n = -25 + .25Y$); raise $G$ to 125, or a combination of two. (This implies the assumption that $X = M$ and $S = I$ continually so that equilibrium will require that $G = T_n$).
2. (a) 300  (b) 100  (c) 50
   (d) The injection is multiplied by 2 by subsequent rounds of respending.
   (e) Tax cut or increased government spending, or both
   (f) New $AD = 200 + .5Y$
3. (a) 25  (b) 15  (c) 10
4. (a) $55B  (b) A tax *reduction* of 2½B is required.  (c) A deficit will occur.

## PROBLEM 1

1. The change in the surplus that would result if the economy were at full employment is the indicator we must examine. For this period, it reveals that policy was quite expansionary in 1958, then became increasingly contractionary in 1959 and 1960. It remained generally restrictive with a modest expansionary change in 1961 and 1962.
2. The rising tax revenues, created by improving economic conditions, is known as fiscal drag. It operates to "choke off" some of the expansion and thereby slows the return to higher levels of employment.

## PROBLEM 2

1. It would be expansionary to the extent that people spent the increase in disposable income on Canadian goods and services.
   : Disposable income increase leads to more spending.
   : More spending leads to more production.
   : Increased production leads to increased income and employment.
2. At the time of preparing the budget, it would be difficult to say that the price and wage index movements were pointing to inflation. However, the fairly rapid decline in the unemployment rate and substantial rise in real investment were obvious indicators of an expanding economy. If the goal was to reduce unemployment to 3.5 percent by 1965-1966, the tax cut may well have been necessary to compensate for the fiscal drag that would be occuring at the time.

## PROBLEM 3

1. The reduction in personal income tax was designed to increase the flow of personal disposable income and thereby stimulate spending, production, and jobs. The sales tax reduction, if passed along to consumers through lower-priced goods, would moderate the rate of price inflation. Hopefully, this would moderate wage increases as well.
2. This question cannot be answered by a specific "yes" or "no." The impact on demand, employment, and prices will depend upon the interrelationships and responses that make up the complex nature of the economy. For example, if most of the increase in aggregate demand is spent on Canadian goods and services, there is a good chance that this will not only stimulate production but may also induce businesses to increase their capital spending. Substantial increases in $C$, $I$, and $G$ could therefore do much to reduce the unemployment rate. This could cause bottlenecks and excess demand in some sectors and bring about inflation. To reduce unemployment substantially, this is a chance that the policy makers must take.

# CHAPTER 33

## EXERCISES

1. (1) b  (2) c  (3) a  (4) d  (5) a; the rug serves the function (b).
2. Desired money supply is 20; income velocity is 5. Decision makers have additional money and they try to spend it. This causes prices to rise but real income remains the same since the economy was already at full employment. The price level rises to 1.25 which represents a 25% increase. Notice that the money supply also increased by 25%.
3. (a) At the beginning, cash holdings are $1000; at the end of the first week they are $750; at the end of the third week they are $250; at the end of the month they are $0.
   (b) The average cash holding is $500.
   (c) The average cash holding increases to $600.
   (d) The average cash holding decreases to $250.
4. (a) favorable  (b) unfavorable  (c) unfavorable  (d) neutral  (e) favorable  (f) unfavorable
   (g) unfavorable (favorable or neutral depending on the relationship between the inflation rate on real estate and the general price index)

## PROBLEM 1

1. Yes; by $240 million, because the coins were declared legal tender
2. No; their value is determined by the monetary unit ascribed to them, which exceeds the value of the metal content.
3. No; their nominal value was fixed by the government.
4. If the metal content value exceeds nominal value and/or the collector's price, they would likely be melted down and sold for their metal value. (This is an illegal act!)

PROBLEM 2

| Year | $V_{M_1}$ | $V_{M_2}$ |
|------|-----------|-----------|
| 1968 | 8.2 | 2.7 |
| 1969 | 8.7 | 2.9 |
| 1970 | 8.8 | 2.9 |
| 1971 | 8.2 | 2.6 |
| 1972 | 8.0 | 2.5 |
| 1973 | 8.3 | 2.5 |
| 1974 | 9.1 | 2.5 |
| 1975 | 8.8 | 2.5 |
| 1976 | 9.9 | 2.4 |

1. The broad definition of money gives the most stable value for velocity.
2. One-third
3. Yes, a substantial decline from .17 (1955) to .11 (1975)
4. Both would have caused people to shift to notice deposits, and hence increase $V_{M_1}$. People holding notice deposits would still suffer decreases in purchasing power because of inflation. However, the loss would be less in contrast to that of holding demand deposits or cash.

# CHAPTER 34

## EXERCISES

1. $M_1$ equals 21,538 (7972 plus 13,566); $M_2$ equals $M_1$ plus 44,578 plus 22,541.

2.

| | | | |
|---|---|---|---|
| Currency in vaults | $ 60,000 | Demand deposits | $5,000,000 |
| Deposits in B of C | 1,000,000 | Notice deposite | 1,000,000 |
| Loans to public | 4,000,000 | | |
| Security holdings | 1,500,000 | | |
| Banking building and fixtures | 360,000 | Capital and surplus | 920,000 |
| | $6,920,000 | | $9,920,000 |

3. (a) Reserves +100; deposits +100
   (b) Reserves +10,000; securities -10,000
   (c) Loans +5,000; deposits +5,000
   (d) Reserves +50,000; securities -50,000
   (e) Loans -5,000; deposits -5,000
   (f) Total reserved unchanged; currency +5,000 and reserve deposits with the Bank of Canada, -5,000

4. (a) Required reserves = $10,000. No.
   (b) Deposits -1,000 to 99,000 and reserves -1,000 to 9,000
   (c) Required reserves = 9,900; actual reserves = 9,000; hence reserve deficiency = 900.
   (d) Bank A: reserves +900; loans -900. Bank B: reserves -900; deposits -900.
   (e) No, but bank B has a deficiency of 810.
   (f) Bank B: reserved +810; loans -810. Bank C: reserves -810; deposits -810.
   (g) No, but bank C has a deficiency of 729.
   (h) (-900 + -810 + -729) = -2439. Loans down by 1710.
   (i) 10,000; 9,000

5. Assets: (d), (e), (f)    Liabilities: (a), (b), (c)

6. (a)

| Bank of Canada | | Banks | |
|---|---|---|---|
| Securities: +100 | Bank reserves +100 | Reserves: +100 | Deposits: +100 |

   (b) $500 million
   (c) Interest rate is likely to fall because banks wish to make new loans and hence reduce the loan rate. This feeds through the economy so that other interest rates fall.

7. (a) No; deposits have not been affected.
   (b) Excess reserves are equal to 150 million. Loans can be expanded by this amount.
   (c) Final change in the money supply is 10 times 150 or 1500 millions.

8. Sell bonds at a $93.46 price.

(b) 8%

(c) All interest rates would tend to increase to 8%, because individuals holding securities with yields less than 8% would sell, and hence their yield would increase and the price would fall.

## PROBLEM

1. 
| Bank of Nova Scotia | |
|---|---|
| Currency:  +$100 | Deposits:  +$100 |
|  | (Joe Farmer) |

2. $80. (Reserves must be .2 × $100 = 20)

3. 
|  | New Deposits | Additions to Reserves | New Loans |
|---|---|---|---|
| 2nd gen. | $80.00 | $16.00 | $64.00 |
| 3rd gen. | 64.00 | 12.80 | 51.20 |
| 4th gen. | 51.20 | 10.24 | 40.96 |

4. $500. ($100/c.r.r. = $500). This assumes that all conditions for multiple expansion are met: No cash drain by the public or banks; banks do not hold onto excess reserves; public is willing to borrow.

5. It could have immediately sold $100 of bonds to the Bank of Nova Scotia. Reserves therefore would not have changed.

# CHAPTER 35

## EXERCISES

1. (a) The money supply will fall by $10 millions. This is given by the expression:
   -10 = (1/.1)(-1).

   (b) To maintain equilibrium in the money market, the demand for money must also fall. This can occur from three factors. If real income and/or price levels fall, the demand for money falls. In addition, if the interest rate increases, the demand for money will fall.

   (c) The interest rate is likely to rise for many reasons. First, in order to induce the public to buy bonds, the Bank of Canada will lower the price of bonds. This has the effect of increasing the interest rate. Second, loans will decrease and the interest rate on the loans will tend to rise. As the interest rate on bonds increases, the interest rates on other assets will also tend to rise. Hence the overall interest rate rises.

2. (a) From the transactions motive, a high interest rate means that opportunity costs of holding money are high and hence people will tend to economize as much as possible on cash holdings. According to the speculative demand, since the interest is high, the price of bonds is low. Hence, they speculate that the price of bonds will eventually rise. Hence, they increase their holdings of bonds and reduce their holdings of money.

   (b) People are so convinced that the price of bonds must rise in the future that they hold all bonds and no money from a speculative point of view. However, they still must have some cash to conduct transactions.

   (c) Just reverse the arguments presented in part (a).

   (d) People are so certain that the price of bonds must fall that they hold all money and no bonds in order to avoid future capital losses on bonds.

   (e) None whatsoever. All increases in money are absorbed by the speculative demand.

## PROBLEM

1. Buy bonds from the public. This tends to create excess reserves in the banking system and provides a potential basis for loan expansion and thus an increase in the money supply.

2. Increased; expansion. Banks must be willing to use excess reserves for loans; people must be willing to borrow; there must be no cash drains from the financial system.

   They may have doubts as to the permanency of the policy change.

3. Down, since with a given demand for money and an increased stock of money, the rate should fall. It may also be due to the Bank of Canada's purchase of bonds at increased market prices.

   The change will depend on the elasticity of the demand for money with respect to the interest rate. Given a perfectly elastic demand for money, all money supply increases would be absorbed by holders of cash and as a result there would be no change in the interest rate.

4. (a) (i) A perfectly inelastic *MEC* schedule would produce no increase in desired investment expenditures with a fall in the interest rate.

   (ii) Given sufficient retained earnings, firms may be insensitive to changes in market rates of interest with respect to investment. Hence, they tend to finance investment with internal funds.

   (iii) The *MEC* curve may shift to the left because of general pessimism. This counteracts the movement down the curve.

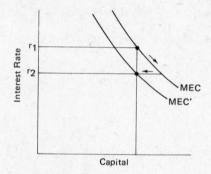

   (iv) There may be insufficient supplies of capital goods though demand has increased.

   (b) Increased production may be possible by greater utilization of the existing capital stock. Therefore, there is no need for investment.

5. (a) The marginal propensity to spend must be positive.

   (b) The longer the income spending lag, the longer it will take for the multiplier effect to have its full impact on the economy.

# Chapter 36

## Exercises

1.

| | Gold Standard | Bretton Woods System | Current Monetary Arrangements |
|---|---|---|---|
| International Monetary Fund | | X | X |
| Effective fixed gold content for U.S. dollar | X | | |
| Fluctuating exchange rate | | | X |
| Special drawing rights | | X | X |
| Dollar convertible to gold domestically | X | | X |
| Adjustable peg | | X | |
| "Dirty" float | | | X |
| Free market for gold | | | X |
| Fixed exchange rates | X | X | |

2. (a) If you anticipated a further decline in the price of the Canadian dollar you might try to negotiate a fixed price of imports in terms of Canadian dollars. Hence, if the price of the Canadian dollar declines even further, you have protected yourself. The importer bears the risk of the exchange rate change. Of course, if you anticipate that the price of the Canadian dollar is going to rise, there is no need to protect yourself. you gain!

(b) You would be selling your Canadian dollars and buying foreign currencies which are either going to appreciate or maintain their value. If you are typical of all speculators, the price of the Canadian dollar would fall in the absence of Bank of Canada policy to maintain the current price.

## PROBLEM

1. Since the demand for oil tends to be fairly inelastic, importers had to pay more for the same amount of oil. *Ceteris paribus,* this will cause greater balance-of-payments deficits and hence the reserve positions of the oil-importing countries fell over the period 1974-1975. Of course, the reserve position of the oil-exporting countries rose substantially.

2. Under the gold standard, the deficits of the oil-importing countries should generate a decrease in their money supplies and hence a reduction in the prices of their products. Exports to the oil-producing countries should rise and exports of oil should fall. The money supply in the oil-producing countries should be increased, generating inflation in those countries.

3. If the OPEC dollars were recycled into investment projects in Canada, (1) employment in Canada should rise by the multiplier process, and (2) Canada's reserves should increase.

4. The price of the Canadian dollar would surely fall, *ceteris paribus.* The Bank of Canada, under a dirty-float system, might attempt to maintain the price of the Canadian dollar by buying Canadian dollars in the world exchange market. This means, however, that the reserve holdings of foreign currencies would fall. Speculators might pick this piece of information up and speculate that the Canadian authorities will be able to protect the price of the Canadian dollar continually. Hence, they will sell Canadian dollars and buy other currencies. The Bank of Canada will have a much more difficult time protecting the price of the Canadian dollar.

# CHAPTER 37

## EXERCISES

1. (a) K  (b) M  (c) M  (d) K  (e) K  (f) M  (g) M  (h) K  (i) M  (j) K
2. (a) Deflationary gap of 500 million
   (b) Yes; the increase in government spending will have an expansionary effect of 1 billion (.5 times 2).
   (c) Since 100 = .8(150) - 2i; i equals 10(%).
   (d) The interest rate would rise to 10.4%. This is shown by the expression: 100 = .8(151) - 2i.
   (e) Investment expenditures would fall by 1 billion (4 times 125 million).
   (f) The crowding-out effect is 100%.

3. (a)
| Period | Tax Payments | Disposable Income |
|--------|--------------|-------------------|
| 1 | 20 | 80 |
| 2 | 24 | 96 |
| 3 | 28 | 112 |
| 4 | 32 | 128 |
| 5 | 36 | 144 |

   (b)
| Period | Disposable Permanent Y | Consumption | Saving |
|--------|------------------------|-------------|--------|
| 1 | 112 | 89.6 | 22.4 |
| 2 | 112 | 89.6 | 22.4 |

   All other periods the same

(c) Disposable income in period 1 increases to 85; consumption would not be .8(85) which equals 68. This is an increase of 4.

(d) The annual permanent disposable income is 113. Consumption per year becomes 90.4 and the total increase over the 5 years is 4.

(e) Permanent income is unaffected even though current disposable income is increased. If the monetarists are correct, consumption expenditures are unaffected and savings increase in order to absorb the increase in current disposable income. Should this occur, fiscal policy has no effect on national income.

## PROBLEM

1. The monetarists argued that notice and term deposits are almost perfect substitutes to demand deposits and hence should be included in the definition of money. Furthermore, the evidence suggests that the income velocity of money using the $M_2$ definition is much more stable than that for $M_1$. Since the income velocity is constant, changes in nominal GNP can be predicted from changes in the money supply.

2. Yes; as increases in the growth rate of $M_2$ occurred, the rate of inflation accelerated. Some economists might, however, argue about the cause of inflation.

3. A positive one except for 1976. The standard model might apply for that year; i.e., a decrease in the growth of $M_2$ caused interest rate to rise.

4. The real rate was about 4.15 in 1971, whereas it was about -1.8 in 1975.

5. Attempt to sell bonds or redeem them and reallocate your funds into assets whose prices increased with the rate of inflation, such as real estate.

6. If the exchange rate had been allowed to appreciate, this would have increased the price of Canadian exports and reduced the price of imports coming into Canada. Decreases in exports would have reduced aggregate expenditures; this might have taken some steam out of the Canadian economy, whereas decreases in the price of imports would have reduced the cost of living for Canadians.

# CHAPTER 38

## EXERCISES

1. (a) Deficient-demand, because of the slowdown in economic activity
   (b) Search, because perhaps of change in location or unwillingness to accept lower pay
   (c) Frictional if short-term; structural if the social worker is unable to find work after a prolonged search
   (d) Frictional if short-term; structural if the mechanic cannot find work in London or refuses to move to Montreal
   (e) Frictional, because prospects are probably quite good that the business analyst will find a suitable job in a short period of time

2. (a) Reduce aggregate demand by increasing taxes or decreasing government expenditures
   (b) Policies geared to retraining and increasing the mobility of resources (labor)
   (c) Wage and price controls might be used. Also, the government could refuse to validate the cost-push inflation and hence not increase the money supply. Furthermore, the government might take a more active role in wage mediation.
   (d) Policies designed to reduce bottlenecks, i.e., increasing factor mobility or policies designed to increase supply in high-demand sectors
   (e) Increase aggregate demand
   (f) Imposition of wage-price controls, restraint in spending, decrease the money supply

3. (a) Market A has excess demand; market B has excess supply
   (b) Since the excess demand in A is equal to the excess supply in B, aggregate excess demand is zero and hence no deficient-demand unemployment exists. Another way of looking at this is to say that unfilled vacancies in A equal unemployed in B.
   (c) First of all, wages should rise in A and fall in B. This will cure the excess demand in A and excess supply in B. Second, labor in B should move to A. This will shift the supply curve of labor to the right in A and shift the supply curve in B to the left. Vacancies are filled in A and unemployment is eliminated in B.

(d) People refuse to leave their current jobs because of nonmonetary considerations; do not know about job availabilities in other markets; are not qualified in terms of skills required by other markets.

(e) The national unemployment rate would increase because unemployment is increased in market B. According to the diagram for market A, unfilled vacancies are eliminated. Since deficient-demand unemployment is defined by the difference between unfilled vacancies and unemployment and given the fact that vacancies are zero and unemployment has risen, hence deficient-demand unemployment exists for the first time.

## PROBLEM

1. Generally speaking, the unemployment rate and the percentage change in employment were inversely related. In 1970 the unemployment rate increased substantially when the percentage change in employment fell. After 1970, employment and unemployment both increased.

2. The major factor affecting the labor force was a rising participation rate, particularly by young adults and females 25-54 years. Young adults may have become disillusioned about the value of higher education and hence joined the labor force. Many theories have been offered to explain the rise in the participation rate of married females. There have been changing attitudes about the role of society both from the demand the supply side. In addition, the wage rate of female workers has been continually rising.

3. The labor force might have increased because people who normally might not have worked may have decided to work for a short period of time and then collect unemployment insurance when they are laid off. The new liberal unemployment insurance regulations might have caused workers to search longer for suitable jobs. This is because increased benefits and longer entitlements reduce the opportunity costs of being unemployed.

4. The unemployment-vacancy relationship shifted to the right. In other words a given number of vacancies is now associated with more unemployment than before.

5. Some economists argue that structural unemployment has increased because of the changes in the act. Remember that the difference between frictional and structural unemployment is duration. Tying the unemployment benefits directly to regional unemployment might have discouraged workers in high-unemployment regions to move to lower-unemployment regions since their benefits would fall. For example, some evidence suggests that structural unemployment increased significantly in the Atlantic Provinces. However, we caution that much more evidence must be forthcoming in order to draw specific conclusions.

# CHAPTER 39

## EXERCISES

1. (a)

| Time Period | Expected Inflation | Actual Inflation |
|---|---|---|
| 3 | 5 | 10 |
| 4 | 10 | 15 |
| 5 | 15 | 20 |
| 6 | 20 | 25 |

(b) Vertical at a 4% rate of unemployment

(c) If, for example, excess demand pressure "disappeared" in period 7, then actual inflation would equal the expected rate and this would remain so. Thus the rate of inflation would become constant (at 25%) and would not decline further unless expectations were altered.

2. (a)

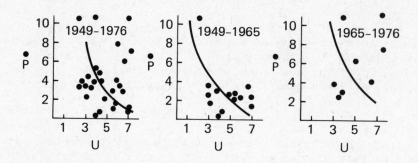

(b) In all three cases, it is impossible to draw a smooth line through all the points. In fact, you will see that whatever reasonable attempt you make, there will be points above and below the line. The one main difference that is visible is that a hand-fitted line for 1965-1976 lies above those drawn for 1949-1976 and below that for 1949-1965.

(c) In simple plotting like this, using annual data can be deceiving. First, price and unemployment relationships may involve lags measured in quarterly year periods. Second, structural changes in the economy and the impact of external forces may change the position of the tradeoff (if it exists) over time. Hence, long-term observations on annual data may not be very reliable in terms of establishing a short-run tradeoff.

(d) The data would suggest that the tradeoff has "shifted" over the postwar period such that a higher rate of inflation has in recent years been associated with a given rate of unemployment.

3. (a) Cause a deficit on current account as higher incomes stimulate imports
   (b) Cause a deficit as the lower interest rate would reduce the inflow of foreign capital
   (c) Reduce investment and employment
   (d) Encourage exports and possibly lead to demand inflation

## PROBLEM 1

1. Only if price makers, unions, etc., felt that the reports of the commission would be the basis for actual antiinflationary legislation.
2. From the available data in Chapter 32 and this chapter, there is little evidence of a traditional demand-pull inflation.
3. Not really. There may still be a tradeoff, but not the one that policy makers had in mind.
4. Yes. But the degree of restrictiveness might be such as to produce a socially and politically unacceptable unemployment rate.
5. Voluntary agreements are likely to be very inequitable. Half the unions and half the corporations might agree and actually hold the line on wages and prices. What about the half that don't? They may well be able to make substantial short-run gains by not agreeing to the restraint.

## PROBLEM 2

1. It is obvious that the rate of change in wages was lower by the end of 1977 but the inflation rate was once again accelerating. Most disappointing, of course, was the rise in the rate of unemployment.
2. By the middle of 1977, the rate of inflation was exceeding the rate of wage increases, indicating that real wages were declining. In addition, there was the rapid rise in the unemployment rate.
3. First and foremost, Canada is an open economy and an incomes policy cannot really control world prices which feed directly into our price index. Second, although wage costs are important to the determination of prices, it may take a long period of time before the impact of lower wage costs "feed through" to lower prices of goods and services. A third reason is food prices which again are very difficult to "control." A good deal of the rising inflation in 1976 and 1977 can be attributed to rapidly rising food prices.

# CHAPTER 40

## EXERCISES

1. (a) Public: Foreign currency +1 million, deposits -1 million. Eventually the public will lose the foreign currency and obtain oil.
    Chartered banks: Reserves -1 million, deposits -1 million
    Bank of Canada: Foreign currency -1 million, bank deposits -1 million
   (b) Demand deposits will fall by 10 million

2. (a) The countries' exports should decline and hence the demand curve for its currency will shift to the left. Furthermore, imports will tend to increase and hence the supply curve for its currency will shift to the right. These two factors will cause a balance-of-payments deficit at the existing pegged rate (the difference between the new demand curve and the new supply curve).
   (b) To eliminate the deficit the government might increase the interest rate by decreasing the money supply. This has two effects on the economy. First, the increased interest rate attracts foreign capital and this should help the balance-of-payments situation. Second, the interest rate increase might reduce investment and hence national income. A lower national income (in real terms) means less importation of goods and this should help the deficit. However, the contraction effect (if it involves real income) might increase unemployment. On the other hand, the contractionary effect of the monetary policy might simply reduce prices.
   (c) The foreign price of its currency should fall. Hence, the price of exports increases and the price of imports falls. If export volume falls, the inflationary pressure in the domestic country should be reduced. Also with the fall in the price of imports, the cost of living should fall.

3. (a) A deflationary gap of 10 divided by 2 or 5
   (b) Increase $G$ by 5 or reduce taxes by 6.67.
   (c) A deficit budget policy
   (d) The money remains the same but the interest rate increases because the demand for money rises to finance more transactions.
   (e) A deficit will be created in the current account since import buying is stimulated by the increase in real income. In fact, imports will rise by $.2 \times 10$ or 2. Nothing should happen to the capital account. A deficit in the balance of payments of 2 is created.
   (f) The central bank, in order to protect the pegged rate, must buy up the excess supply of its currency in the world exchange markets.
   (g) In the process of paying for more imports, the public decrease their deposits in the banks; the banks lose reserves and hence the money supply will decrease.

4. (d) An increase in the domestic interest rate attracts foreign capital, and in the absence of sterilization policies by the central bank, the money supply will increase and hence interest rates should fall.
   (e) The deficit should not be as high as 2 because foreign capital has been attracted.
   (f) The foreign-exchange reserves will not fall as much as before.
   (g) The money supply may not fall at all.

## PROBLEM

1. The Canadian interest rate was above that of the United States, but the widening of the differential attracted U.S. funds because of capital's mobility.

2.

As demand for Canadian dollars shifted out (to *D'*, for example), the price of dollars rose.

3. The increase in the price of Canadian dollars from *P* to *P*$_1$ raises the price of Canadian goods to foreigners. At *P*, the demand for dollars to correspond with capital inflows creates excess demand. To reach equilibrium, the price of the dollar is bid up and some exports will be reduced, shown by the movement up the new demand curve.

4. They would increase as the price of imports declines and this will be represented by a movement up the supply curve.

5. You are likely to have anticipated that the government's actions would decrease the price of the Canadian dollar. If you were holding dollars, you would sell them as soon as possible to avoid a capital loss. If the majority of speculators acted in a similar fashion, the demand curve for dollars would shift inward and the price of dollars would fall.

# CHAPTER 41

## EXERCISES

1. (a) 4%  (b) 3%  (c) 18  (d) 24
2. (a) Decrease
   (b) Increase current; decrease future
   (c) Increase

   (d) Decrease current, increase future
   (e) Decrease current, increase future
   (f) Decrease

## PROBLEM

1. No. With unchanging technology, pollution would be 16 times as great in both cases (4 × 4 instead of 2 × 8 for the second).
2. The assumption of continual growth in both population and output (until a sudden disaster is reached). T would have to have a value of approximately .96.
3. (a) Would reduce T, in respect to air and solid waste pollution particularly
   (b) Would reduce P, especially because of deaths of potentially reproductive infants
   (c) Would reduce T and also O. (While investment in such equipment would count as current GNP, it would not increase future productivities.)
   (d) Would directly increase P.
   (e) Would reduce P; development process implies increase in O.
4. Population controls or actual famine of course could reduce pollution by decreases in P. Intense use of fertilizers and pesticides could increase T.

# CHAPTER 42

## EXERCISES

1.

|              | Country A | Country B | Difference |
| ------------ | --------- | --------- | ---------- |
| Year X       | $2,000    | $100      | $1,900     |
| Year X + 1   | 2,060     | 103       | 1,957      |
| Year X + 23  | 4,000     | 200       | 3,800      |

2. (a) 18; 24; 72  (b) 3 percent

PROBLEM

1. Opportunity costs are increasing in both countries. For example, in country A to obtain an increase in 10 bushels of wheat from 20 to 30, the loss in production in peanuts is 3. However, to increase wheat from 30 to 40, a loss of 4 is required. For country B, an increase of wheat from 20 to 40 requires a loss of 10. An increase of wheat from 40 to 60 requires a loss of 11 pounds of peanuts.

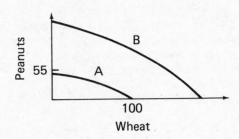

2. A combination of 40 wheat and 32 peanuts represents X-inefficiency or a point inside the production-possibility frontier in country A. It is technically possible for A to produce 40 and 45. However, country B is operating on its productio-possibility frontier.
3. GNP in country A is $2 × 80 plus $.5 × 16 which equals $168. GNP in country B is $2 × 160 plus $.5 × 35 which equals $337.5. Per capita GNP in A is 168 divided by 8 which equals $21. Per capita GNP in B is 337.5 divided by 10 which equals $33.75.
4. Country B has avoided X-inefficiency. Although country A and country B have the same amount of resources, the resources in B are used more efficiently. This may be due to differences in social and cultural attitudes, differences in market organization, or differences in labor skills and productivity. Land quality might also differ.
5. Aid might come in many forms: retraining labor and improving land cultivation by various Canadian experts from agricultural schools in Canada; increasing the capital intensity of production by giving B more tractors and other farm equipment; introducing better peanut and wheat seed. Hopefully, the production-possibility frontier would shift to the right in time.

   Alternatively, living standards in B could be improved by simply giving B more wheat or peanuts as an outright gift. This would allow consumption to be greater than production but it is hard to believe that this is an appropriate long-run solution to B's problems.

# CHAPTER 43

## EXERCISE

(a) An excess demand in Canada would cause prices and profits to rise, thus generating the automobile companies to increase supply. In the Soviet Union, planned quotas are used.
(b) Private investment and public investment might stimulate economic growth in Canada. Government policy might encourage private investment by lowering interest rates. The Soviet Union would simply divert resources from current consumption to capital investment.
(c) More beer and less soft drinks would be produced if there were the appropriate market signals in Canada. For example, if the demand for beer increased as a result of a shift away from soft drinks, the price of beer should rise and the price of soft drinks should fall. (We assume that the government liquor agencies like the Liquor Control Board of Ontario allow this to happen.) Resources will be diverted away from soft drink production and into beer production. In the Soviet Union, planners would devise techniques to shift resources from soft drinks to beer.
(d) Canada uses the tax system and transfer payments. The Soviet Union uses the turnover tax and sets wage rates.

## PROBLEM

1. Increased consumption of electricity simply represents more advanced economy.
2. More underdeveloped hydro resources exist in the USSR and are available to meet growth.
3. The USSR had given low priority to auto transportation and stressed public transportation to meet much lower levels of intercity travel (also reflects stage of development).
4. Agriculture lower priority than industry in the USSR. Organization of large collective farms may permit capital economies.
5. This change in relative capital productivities could represent a difference in stage of development, ability of the Soviet system to raise more capital by compulsion, and failure to allocate capital well because of aversion in the USSR to concept of interest.
6. The Soviet Union had chosen enormous economies of keeping down road, auto, etc., investment. The gap is only partly in the stage of development. (See 2 above.) This policy seems to be changing now.
7. This reflects the stage of development and perhaps the inherent greater efficiency of the U.S. economic system.
8. GNP represents the difference in the stage of development and perhaps economic efficiency. High investment in the USSR represents high priority for growth and the ability of the USSR system to enforce savings. Relatively high defense expenditures were probably deemed necessary by the USSR for near parity to the United States. Attention to consumption in USSR has increased in the last decade.
9. This could reflect greater priority for growth as indicated by investment percentages (see above). U.S. growth of GNP was lowered by three recessions, more a feature of private system. The temporary equality from 1961 to 1966 represented partly a rise to full employment in the United States. The smaller discrepancy in favor of the USSR that has apparently recently prevailed could represent a maturing of the Russian economy.

79  80  81  5  4  3  2  1